THE PSYCHOLOGY OF HUMAN DEVELOPMENT

This book assumes a need for synthesizing into one volume many subjects not usually combined. It provides an opportunity for the teacher to understand the impact of the forces that shape his life and that play a vital part in the development and learning of others, both youths and adults. Topics considered range from pre-natal development, linguistics, cognition, motivation to special chapters which are devoted to adolescence, young adulthood, middle adulthood and aging. This work will make an excellent sourcebook for professional libraries as it contains much information and fact that would be relevant for para-educational, para-medical, and social workers; also physicians will find much use in the materials on psychology and educational application which is pertinent to some areas with which they are constantly involved.

ABOUT THE AUTHORS

KARL C. GARRISON is Emeritus Professor of Education, University of Georgia and Distinguished Professor of Education, Old Dominion University. He received his doctoral degree from George Peabody College. His teaching experience includes: George Peabody College; North Carolina State University at Raleigh where he also served as chairman of the Department of Psychology; Central Connecticut State College; Georgia State College for Women; State Teachers College, Frostburg, where he was Dean of Instruction; and the University of Georgia

(Continued on back flap)

AUTHORS *(Continued)*

where he served as chairman of the Educational Psychology Department. He is the author of many well known texts in the area of psychology of human development and was a Visiting Scholar at Duke University in 1967.

Listed in *American Men of Science, Who's Who in American Education, Who's Who in the South and Southwest,* and *Personalities in the South.* Dr. Garrison is a member of AERA, NEA, Southeastern Psychological Association, Southern Society for Philosophy and Psychology, and is a Fellow in APA. His honor societies include: Phi Delta Kappa, Kappa Delta Pi, Psi Chi, Phi Kappa Phi, Kappa Phi Kappa, and Pi Gamma Mu.

FRANKLIN R. JONES, Professor of Education and Dean, School of Education, Old Dominion University, received his doctorate from Duke University. His teaching experience includes: Duke University, Randolph-Macon College where he served as chairman of the Department of Education; and as Visiting Lecturer in Graduate Education, Richmond University from 1960 to 1964 and the University of Virginia from 1959 to 1964.

Dr. Jones, who has published in education and psychology journals has been listed in *Who's Who in American Education, Virginia Lives, Personalities in the South,* and *Who's Who Among American College and University Administrators.* From 1966 to 1968, he served as president of the South Atlantic Philosophy of Education Society. He has recently been appointed to the Governor's Steering Committee on the 1970 White House Conference on Children and Youth. Some of his professional and honorary memberships include: Pi Gamma Mu, Phi Delta Kappa, Kappa Delta Pi, Alpha Tau Kappa, Virginia Education Association, American Association of University Professors, Associate Fellow in the Philosophy of Education Association, AERA, and the Association of Higher Education. He has served as President of AAUP and on the Virginia State's Executive AAUP Committee. He has lectured at various colleges and made numerous talks to a variety of professional and lay groups. He was a Visiting Scholar at Duke University in 1967.

The Psychology
of Human Development

The Psychology of Human Development

Karl C. Garrison
Distinguished Professor of Educational Psychology
Old Dominion University

Franklin R. Jones
Dean of the School of Education
Old Dominion University

International Textbook Company
Scranton, Pennsylvania

Library of Congress Catalog Card Number: 70-78353

Standard Book Number 7002   2188   3

To our wives,
Linnea and Jane

Preface

Students of developmental psychology recognize that life is not static. The human being from the conception to the time of his death is continuously changing. Research related to the different aspects of development has helped teachers, parents, and others deal more efficiently and more effectively with children, adolescents, adults, and even themselves. The writers are cognizant of the impact of developmental psychology on the home, the schools, and other social and educational institutions. They have chosen materials from the vast amount of research and studies available and brought these to bear upon problems of education and guidance.

Developmental psychology is concerned with changes that occur with increased age, and with factors and conditions that influence changes at different stages of life. The writers have not neglected the later phases of life—adulthood and senescence; however, they recognize that an understanding of any one stage requires an understanding of earlier stages. The developmental sequences are treated with respect to earlier development. Although the writers realize that life cannot be separated into discrete packages, normative data bearing on different ages and stages of life are presented so as to give the students a better understanding of the specific aspects of development as well as the continuity of development from birth to death. The writers are concerned not only with the increase of abilities but also with the decline of abilities, not only with the expanding variety of behavior but also with the restriction of behavior with increased age.

A volume which deals with human development will include useful and recent materials from all areas of behavioral science; it will deal with newer ideas involving communication, cognition, and linguistics, as these relate to development and motivation. Special attention is given in Part III to personal and social development and adjustments during early childhood, late childhood, adolescence, early adulthood, middle adulthood and late adulthood.

One may wonder why one should study all stages of life in order to understand a specific age group. The answer lies in the fact that life cannot be studied as a series of stages or discrete age groups. We speak of a child as "father of the man." We also speak of the adult as a product of his past. There is a basic continuity in the patterns of growth, and any stage of life can best be understood and appreciated when seen in the context of what has gone on before and the pattern of growth that will likely follow. For those working with children, adolescents, or adults it is assumed that a knowledge of the forces that influence development and shape or exert pressure on the individual's life will assist in understanding others. The view and position taken by the authors is that we are concerned with the total individual. We believe that behavior cannot be restricted to "internal" or "external" events, and that no sharp line can be drawn between these; all behavior may be correlated to some degree with internal chemical and physical changes, but it is certainly influenced at all stages in the individual's development by past and present external environmental relationships. Although recent scientific data are not always sufficient to provide conclusive results, there is sufficient information available to furnish a frame of reference for better understanding and guidance.

The writers have collaborated closely in gathering and assimilating data from recent research and in organizing the materials that make up this volume. This has been a cooperative study from beginning to end. Undergraduate and graduate students have been helpful in evaluating the usefulness of the materials through their use in class and their criticisms. The writers are especially indebted to Duke University for a Research Scholar's Grant, to the Duke library, its Librarian, B. E. Powell, and his staff, and to the faculty, especially Professors C. Eisdorfer, A. S. Hulburt, and G. L. Maddox. Grateful acknowledgment is also made to Professor T. L. Thurstone, University of North Carolina, and to Benjamin Clymer, Reference Librarian at Old Dominion University. Several colleagues and graduate students provided assistance by reading certain parts of the manuscript, making suggestions, and helping in editing. Notable are R. T. Harrell, P. Grob, R. D. Strom, A. J. Crandall, J. A. Wise, and C. J. Wheeler. While material and ideas were gathered from many authors and publishers, special recognition is given at the end of each chapter to the sources from which certain materials have been obtained.

Karl C. Garrison
Franklin R. Jones

Norfolk, Virginia
May 1969

Contents

The Psychology
of Human Development

Part **I**

Introduction
and Orientation

Chapter 1

Human Development in a Dynamic Culture

Human behavior differs from animal behavior in that it is more dependent on learning and less dependent on innate behavioral predispositions. In terms of definition, human behavior encompasses all actions of man, most of which are learned. This behavior is largely a product of man's relationship to inner and outer pressures, the demands one makes upon himself, and the environmental demands. The differential circumstances in which he exists account in large part for the fact that man's behavior is more variable and less predictable than that of other species in the animal kingdom.

Man's genetic evolution has favored him in the development of adaptability which enables him to extend his viability by means of creativity. This creativity was accentuated by man's development of the use of language, technology, and socialization patterns. According to White (1949), human behavior originates in the use of symbols. He states: "Human behavior is symbolic; symbolic behavior is human behavior." Anthropologists, educators, and psychologists have emphasized the role of language in education and socialization. Studies in animal life show that communication through sounds is important. This elementary form of communication is important to the survival of animal life. However, only man has developed a system of symbols in the form of words to symbolize objects, feelings, thoughts, and the relationship between them. The child acquires through varied experiences meanings related to various conditions and situations, and uses them to further his understandings. (Special materials bearing on language development are presented in Chapter 6.) Perhaps the crucial differences between animals and man is suggested by Chardin (1955), who states: "The animal knows, of course. But certainly it does not know what it knows."

The Dynamic Culture in Which Man Lives

If the words "Man is the measure of all things," attributed to the Greek philosopher Protagoras (5th century B. C.), can have relevance for existential philosophy today, it has equal relevance for investigators of human behavior as

3

well as for those unaware of the importance of philosophy. Existentialism has at its core the belief that the meaning and purpose of life is to be found in the interpretation of an individual existence. Many writers and philosophers categorized as existentialists would resist such a classification. All would agree to disagree with old philosophical systems as such. Man is indeed the measure of all things—although anyone with a knowledge of logic or philosophy would perceive that the statement proposed by Protagoras is a tautology, a needless repetition. Yet for the philosopher a tautology is a conclusion in a logic exercise where nothing is concluded other than what is already given in the premise—a mere confirmation of the obvious. As man lives, the only certainty is the certainty of innovation, change, and flux. It is *existence* with which this volume is basically involved.

All Cultures Evolve.   An understanding of present-day culture requires us to consider the culture or cultures from which it evolved. The differential circumstances under which men exist, occasioned by variations in his social and physical environment, force a continuous realignment in stimulus and response, making it increasingly difficult to predict development. "The truth is, that man made himself," says Gerard Piel, publisher of *Scientific American,* whose logic comes from the following account of early man and his culture. In an address to the Association for Higher Education in Chicago (1964, pp. 24–25) he states further:

> . . . the plot of history may not be established as far back as 1.7 million years before the present. At a site reliably dated to that distant time, on a buried lake shore in the Rift country of Africa, anthropologists have recently unearthed an assemblage of stone tools. With these tools they found fragments of the bones of the hands that had made them. The hands are not human hands—not our hands. They are the hands of a primate who still used them at times for walking. In the old taxonomy of primates, it was supposed that man had made the first tools; tool-making was the status symbol of membership in our species. Now, it would appear, tools made man. Certainly, toolmaking conferred a competitive advantage on the maker of better tools. But the meaning of this phase of history goes deeper. The truth is man made himself. The record as to bones of hands and skulls is scanty. There is an abundance, however, of the fossils of behavior—the stone tools. In their increasing diversity, specialization and refinement, they give evidence of the evolution of the hand and of the brain, of which the hand is an extension. The tools show, in time, that evolution has quickened because it has entered on a new mode. It has become cultural as well as biological—Lamarckian as well as Darwinian in that acquired characteristics are transmitted from generation to generation by teaching and learning.

Modern man has come to recognize the notion of purpose, for which he searched to validate for centuries and in many areas of the world. Increasing specialization and the use of crude tools prefaced a paralleling elaboration of technology using less enduring materials. The mastery of the environments successively revealed new vistas and new ways of life (and it seems to follow *new goals* and *values*) to the men who progenerated modern men. Witness the parade of circumstances under which men existed only a mere century ago. In a paraphrase of the words of Henry Adams—the living individual in 1850 stood in many respects nearer the first century man than he did to the twentieth.

For two centuries America was predominantly rural, with scattered towns serving primarily as trading centers. As late as the year 1890, 72 percent of the population was classified by the United States Census as rural; whereas by 1960 only 30 percent was listed as rural, with large urban areas growing most rapidly. In 1900 farmers and farm workers made up 36 percent of the working population; in 1960 farmers and farm workers comprised only six percent (Hauser, 1960). During the course of the twentieth century life in the United States has been transformed from a rural existence in which domestic animals did most of the heavy work to an urban existence in which electricity is the prime source of power. In many respects the change has been greater during this century than that of the preceding five hundred to a thousand years.

An Age of Science. We see the results of significant scientific developments in every aspect of life. We are today seeing scientific developments that are destined to change man's way of life. One only needs to recall the theory proposed by Piel, who assumes that the great output and the scientific advances that have been made in geometric proportion are going to release us from our troubles. He states further (*Ibid.,* p. 32):

> The acceleration of history has brought the old regime of scarcity to a sudden end in our time. Industrial technology, fructified by the increase in human understanding, has repealed the iron law that says one man's well-being can be increased only at the expense of his brother's. In its place we are gaining new institutions and values to respond to the new dispensation of abundance. We are learning that, in our day, the well-being of each man can increase only with an increase in the well-being of all men. The ancient habit of truth-seeking has disclosed the noblest and most generous aims to human life and placed in our hands the means to accomplish those ends here on earth.

The total amount of human knowledge has probably doubled from 1950 to 1965. The authors believe this is a certainty. Ralph Wendell Burhoe, Executive Officer of American Academy of Arts and Sciences (1964, p. 35), in a similar vein states, "Largely untapped in the sciences lies a new body of wisdom about human values, values that are at once religious and humane as well as scientific." The need for recognizing the rapid changes taking place is well expressed by Brown (1966, p. 7). He says: "But we must not forget that we are living at a time when science itself is exploding, when old boundaries are falling, and both our dreams and nightmares stand an equal chance to become a reality."

Advances in Health and Medicine. There have been tremendous advancements in health and medicine during the past twenty-five years, and it seems likely that there will be breakthroughs in medicine within the next decade that will dwarf present developments. The life expectancy of the child born today is about twice that of the child born in 1800. According to Davens (1965, p. 47), "Infants born today in the United States have at least four times the chance to celebrate their first birthday as they did in 1915." He adds, "Pregnancy today is only one-seventeenth as risky to the mother's life as it was in 1915." Pneumonia, tuberculosis, poliomyelitis, and other debilitating or fatal diseases can be well-nigh eradicated as a result of modern medical knowledge.

More spectacular is the development of the "mechanical heart." This device, known also as the DeBakey pump, has been hailed as another step toward a workable mechanical heart, now following heart, renal, and liver transplants (*U.S. News and World Report*, 1968, p. 12). The introduction of such new medical adaptations from the physical sciences as the "pacemaker," which is controlled by a transmitter worn outside the body, allows a receiver inside of the membrane sac in the heart to receive pulses or radio signals delivered to the heart through platinum disks and thus control the heart's operation. The use of ultrasonic scanners is now helping medical teams detect blood clots in the lungs (pulmonary emboli). "In very much the same way that the Navy uses sonar to detect the presence of underwater mines three University of Pennsylvania physicians are finding pulmonary emboli before they become fatal. Ultrasound, the Philadelphia researchers declare, can detect clots in the pulmonary circulation faster and with greater accuracy than any conventional technique." (*Medical World News*, 1967, p. 32). The work of the National Institutes of Health, an agency of the U.S. Government, has announced work in eradication of at least twenty hereditary disorders which now can be predicted. This will make it possible for the medical profession to offer a kind of premarital counseling that could ultimately result in sharp reduction of congenital abnormalities.

Advances in medical research are making it possible to save the lives of many children with transmittible birth defects who a decade or so ago would have died before reaching child-bearing age. The medical professions humanitarian interference with the operation of natural selection is saving many lives. It is of some concern to medical investigators as to whether we are weakening our genetic inheritance.

The time is at hand when all can participate in the benefits of medicine as well as other benefits accruing from the results of scientific inquiry. Nevertheless, where science has advanced the frontier of physical life the earthly environment of man is inexorably becoming more difficult.

Increased Knowledge and School Enrollment. When one considers the fantastic growth of scientific knowledge during the past twenty years—knowledge that must be passed on through education to the younger generation—and then looks at our schools and colleges which are expected to accomplish this task, it becomes apparent that we are faced with a formidable task. The growth of knowledge is reflected in the increasing amount of research reported in scientific journals and the vast number of books published each year. Doctoral dissertations and other research studies are being microfilmed so as to make these studies available to a larger number of students and scholars while conserving space in our expanding library facilities. Libraries are providing study rooms, audio and videotape recordings, photocopies and reprints of rare materials, and other media and services to expedite learning and research (Stern, 1965), thus in effect augmenting the educational task of our schools. Today the high school graduate is expected to be as well educated as was the college graduate at the beginning of the century (Tyler, 1965). Add to this the fact that trained teachers are educating students to face problems that haven't yet appeared or are in the formative stage, and the burden placed upon educators becomes somewhat formidable.

This expansion of knowledge is reflected in the vast amount of research in progress, the rise in high school and college enrollment, and the greater number of scholars at work in different fields of study. Spengler (1966, p. 21) points out: "Today more economists are practicing than lived and died in the past four thousand years, and their number is growing even faster than the world's population." Scientific advancements and universal education have resulted in more educational, occupational, and social mobility. In 1919, only 65.2 percent of children in the age group five to nineteen were enrolled in school, by 1965 the enrollment was approximately 80 percent and still growing. As late as 1915 only 5.5 percent of all those of college age were in college. In 1950, the proportion was about 30 percent, while in 1960 this was approximately 40 percent and increasing at a fast rate. This does not include those in business or trade schools. This enlarged holding power of the high schools, shown in Figure 1-1 (Marland, 1965), has caused a rapid build-up in college enrollment, while a better understanding of the needs and learning potentials of preschool children has focused more attention on preschool education, especially for disadvantaged children.

Population Growth. Improved medical care, nutrition, sanitation, and other health measures have done much to alleviate suffering. This has also aggravated problems related to population growth. A 33 percent increase in the birth rate over the death rate is anticipated for the next twenty-five years. This will double the world's population. If the Western world replicates itself at the inverse rate of say, 2 to 1 in favor of death, while the impoverished areas of the world progenerate at a rate of 2 to 1 or more in favor of population growth, what will be the outcome? Can the world find the food? Various opinions have been given on this problem; it is a problem near at hand. However, with the same science man can control birth rates; indeed in the more literate industrialized societies diminished rates of birth have been underway for some time. A total trend toward smaller families started around 1958, following the prolonged post-World War II "baby boom." The total number of births in the United States fell from 3.61 million in 1966 to 3.53 million in 1967. It was estimated in 1968 that the women born during the 1930's will average about 3.3 births per woman when they complete their childhood rearing years between 1975 and 1984 (Population Reference Bureau, 1968). However, the fact remains that among the most illiterate of the "have-not nations" of the world (the most nonindustrial) the population continues to multiply at a rapid rate.

We can see that problems of staggering proportions face the densely populated underdeveloped countries of the world, if food production is to keep pace

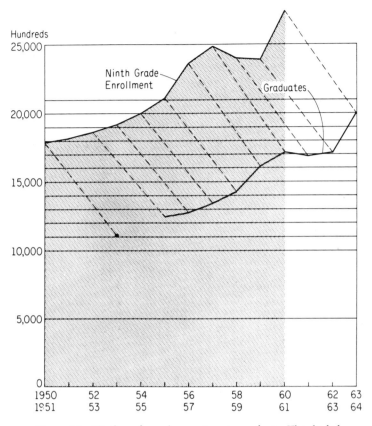

Figure 1-1. Ninth-graders who went on to graduate. The shaded portions show ninth-grade enrollment as of the school year indicated at the bottom. The diagonal line shows how many students graduated four years later. Figures for graduates who were ninth-graders in 1951–52 are not available.

with population growth. The supply of readily cultivable land is almost exhausted in many countries; new land can be brought under cultivation only at a high cost, although there is a vast storehouse of food in the oceans and seas. According to data presented in Figure 1-2, the world population will outstrip food per person at an early date, if immediate steps are not taken to control the birth rate in certain areas of the world. Concerning the problems related to population growth and increased urbanization, Spengler (1966 p. 17) states:

> . . . As matters stand, two demographic processes are bound to bedevil man increasingly and, if they are not soon resolved, will greatly diminish whatever prospect he has of establishing a society both peaceful and great, both moral and aesthetic. These two processes are continuing growth in a finite world and increasing concentration of people in progressively large megalopolitan centers. Progeny and space will have to be rationed much more effectively in the future than in the past.

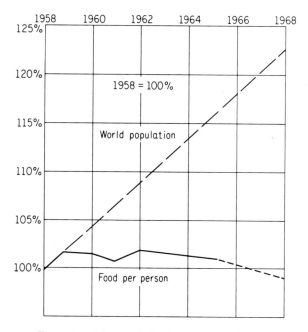

Figure 1-2. The graph indicates that under the present trend, world population will outstrip food per person by an additional 25 percent over 1958's rate. (Advertisement for the Hugh Moore Fund.)

The Impact of Technology. While the world's population is expanding rapidly, the needs for manpower in the highly industrialized area of the world are fast decreasing as a result of automation. Although automation as such is not new, its effects are becoming more pronounced. What is new is the number and variety of jobs being done by automatic operations, and the implications of this for the future of man. More extensive automatization in our economy is reflected in the widespread use of computers as well as in the use of machines to do the jobs formerly done by skilled workers. The effects of these on human values will surely be felt in the near future. Their impact on the nature of education will indeed be far-reaching.

It appears that we are swiftly approaching a new robotized culture in which we will have a large surplus of workers, 20-hour work week, youth programs designed in part to keep youth off the labor market, and early retirement. The impact of these changes will be most keenly felt by youth and older workers forced into retirement. The adult worker will also need to adjust to this enforced leisure, which is already creating problems in the United States, Russia, and wherever the short work week exists. However, the unskilled youth without a high school education are the most vulnerable, although unemployment among high school graduates without a skill or without work experiences is high

(Freedman, 1965). The question arises: What skills should young people develop that will insure them against elimination from the labor market by automation?

Changes in Family Structure and Life Activities.   Every year since 1948 an average of one in five Americans changed residence. A profile of Americans on the move shows that families in the low-income category and professions move more often than the remainder of the population. However, moves of lower-income families are usually local, while about 30 percent of upper-income family moves are from one state to another. Young families do the most moving, as do families with young children. The continuous moving by families of all income and age brackets has been associated with an increase in apartment living. Gone are the ancestral homes quartering three generations, the support of the communal family, a haven for spinster aunts, and the help of the grandmother in raising the children. Goode (1963, p. 7) to the contrary states:

> Like most stereotypes, that of the classical family of Western nostaglia leads us astray. When we penetrate the confusing mists of recent history, we find few examples of this "classical" family. Grandma's farm was not economically self-sufficient. Few families stayed together as large aggregations of kinfolk. Most houses were small, not large. We now see more large old houses than small ones; they survived longer because they were likely to have been better constructed. The one-room cabins rotted away. True enough, divorce was rare, but we have no evidence that families were generally happy. Indeed, we find, as in so many other pictures of the glowing past, that in each past generation people write of a period still more remote, their grandparents' generation, when things really were much better.

It may well be true about the nature of construction of homes in past generations, but Goode offers no evidence that the larger kinship family didn't reside in small homes or even hovels. If the kinship or communal family pattern was the typical family organization of fifty to one hundred years ago—which would seem reasonable to assume within this setting—one could expect considerable emotional and economic support to a degree not attained in the conjugal arrangement of the 1960's. Ogburn (1955, pp. 99-100) studied the process of social change, emphasizing the impact of technology on the family and daily life. He found in his research that the average household dropped from 5.5 persons in 1850 to 3.5 in 1950, suggesting that the large household was not typical even a century ago.

Urbanization invariably follows industrialization. A United Nations conference on the mental health aspects of urbanization sponsored by World Federation for Mental Hygiene in 1957 noted the following sequence: industrialization—urbanization—mental health problems. Mental health problems are closely related to the family and its functioning in a new social situation (Dybwad, 1959, p. 3). The psychology of the city dweller must be one that cannot be involved in the affairs of strangers or even the need of recognition of people met in the daily rounds. It must follow generalizations developed in the studies of people like George Simmel about urban life (1950, 1955).

1. The psychological basis of the metropolitan type of individual consists in the intensification of nervous stimulation which results from the swift and uninterrupted change of outer and inner stimuli. The blasé attitude and indifference stems basically from the need of psychic protection by the city dweller.
2. Metropolitan life underlies a heightened awareness and a predominance of intelligence in metropolitan man. Reaction to metropolitan phenomena is shifted to that organ which is least sensitive and quite remote from the depth of the personality. Intellectuality is seen to preserve subjective life against the overwhelming power of metropolitan life.
3. Punctuality, calculability, and exactness are forced upon life by the complexity and extension of metropolitan existence and are most intimately connected with its more economic and intellectualistic character.
4. Money is the common denominator of all values; it hollows out the core of things, their individuality, their specific value, and their incomparability.
5. Cities are seats of the highest economic division of labor; this has made the individual a small wheel in the enormous organization of things and powers and tears from his hands all progress, spirituality, and value, in order to transform them from their subjective form into the form of a purely objective life.

Indeed one does not seem able to bear to speak to all of those within several blocks of where he lives in a large city. The chance of knowing people and being secure prohibits the usual freedom for children and the pleasantries among adults. In the urban society where peoples have to be selective, it is not just a matter of choosing friends from a particular class group that we identify with. Thus the city dweller has a strong need for emotional support from family or friends and for financial security. In our time we witness a change from the ideology of scarcity to an ideology of plenty. A series of publications that are sociological in nature have within the past decade or more emphasized this great change. These publications include the works of David Riesman in *The Lonely Crowd,* the works of Vance Packard in *The Hidden Persuaders, The Organization Man* by W. H. Whyte, Jr., and *The Affluent Society* by John Galbraith.

Promises, Problems, and Threats

When men lived in narrow valleys and mountain passages, problems related to mass populations in large urban centers were nonexistent. The problems of urban man with his urban culture are of recent origin. Closely related to industrialization and automation is increased leisure time. What shall man do with this time? Will the 20-hour week actually benefit man and mankind? It has been suggested that retirement may occur as early as age 40. Will this open great vistas for man to study the aesthetic, to embark on cultural advantages? Will it lead to self-improvement? The need for ever-increasing, faster, and more accurate information has thrust a technology upon man which is rapidly changing his life activities and values—which may completely dehumanize him, if we are to believe the warnings of Mumford (1964) who has been concerned with the automation of knowledge. Referring to the stultification of knowledge, he says (pp. 11-12):

I detected a peculiar factor that had no parallel in the Pyramid Age: the automation of knowledge. The institutions that have promoted this special kind of automation are now the man power plants and the control centers of the grand system of mechanized production, and depersonalized consumption, and machine-fed leisure that characterizes our Western way of life. Nowhere has this become more evident than in our recent educational programs. Those who have been instrumental in the automation of knowledge, from Francis Bacon onward, have from the beginning coupled this method with the economy of abundance that mankind for so many ages had vainly dreamed of achieving: an economy under which, as Aristotle said, the "shuttle would weave by itself, the lyre play by itself," and loaves of bread would spring out of the oven untouched by human hands. The dreams of such an economy, with its promise of wealth and freedom for all, date back to the earliest urban civilizations; and it was then that other dreams that have now been realized—the dream of human flight, of instantaneous communication, of total control over the physical environment—were first expressed in art and fable. Our age has seen those dreams come true. Powers that only the gods of the Bronze Age possessed are now our daily commonplaces. So, perhaps, it is no wonder that the leading exponents of automation, inflamed by their success and still prompted by ancient fantasies of god-like omnipotence and omniscience, now seek to extend automation to every other human activity.

Effects on Man's Values.   Age-old customs are being questioned; age-old beliefs are being challenged. Fleming (1968) states: "Today, chaos, acrimony, and confusion are apparently the order of the day. Church attendance has declined for several years, and leveled off in 1966 at 44 percent of the population." The values that one chooses, the attitudes that he forms, what his existence means to himself are important to an understanding of the self. The ideological concept that man has about himself and about his fellow man is an important factor in how his life develops. The historical underpinnings provided by a religious faith which not only stablized one's self-concept but also provided a projection of a future life have been questioned, threatened, and in some cases demolished. It has been charged that loss of faith has been brought about by scientism and philosophy—philosophy, more so perhaps because it has raised questions about the extent and validity of man's knowledge.

The vigorous attack on the projection of certainty which was thought by many philosophers to be simply anthropomorphic, particularly during the Age of Enlightenment and the Age of Reason, raised the question as to whether a relationship of cause and effect really could be determined. It was David Hume who suggested it was invalid to use an assumption such as Descartes had employed to prove his own existence. Man's essential importance in a universe has lessened under his inventiveness, his deductive logic and syllogism.

Some Effects on Man's Philosophy.   The ideology of religion and philosophy affects man's attitudes, values, and philosophy of life. We are witnessing important changes in man's concept of himself, God, and his relationship to God. The three-dimensional universe of Heaven above, Hell below, and the earth between is completely out of harmony with advancements in geography, physics, and astronomy. In recent years the concept of the Bible as the Divine

Word has been seriously and widely questioned, and a new concept of God has arisen. This has led to a changed concept of God, which for many scientists bridges the gap between religion and science. The dictum that "God is dead" is part of this and needs careful defining. Today we are born in a world where not only vast material changes but important moral changes are taking place as well. The child of tomorrow will be called upon to reevaluate religion, morals, democracy, and human relations. He will need an anchor to guide him in his efforts to find answers to problems and questions that perplex him.

The climate today is such that, rightly or wrongly, man is less willing to abide by authority as to what moral direction he should take on many issues. The critics of organized religion and the churches point to the institutionalization of charities and group humanitarianism in indicating fallacies and failures of these agencies. The weakness of the groups who project moral principles is obvious to many, even to those that are the greatest adherents of church membership and of religious organization. Our present culture is characterized by a society where sanctions no longer have the same power and where a latent and even obvious fearsomeness exists among the generations. Those who are forty or fifty years of age did not grow up in a period in which there was constant concern for the peace of the world and for one's own individual comfort in the Western civilization. Certainly prior to World War I there was considerable opportunity for laissez faire, for uninterrupted periods of time. For the American nations the period between World Wars I and II was tranquil, and if one discounts troubles which are not in any sense relegated to an incidental situation, the depression of the 1930's did not wreak the kind of havoc threatened by the advent of the atomic age and the hydrogen bomb in terms of pervasive insecurity and general foreboding.

Augmented Mental Health Problems. It has already been suggested that the accumulation of scientific knowledge has led to considerable controversy about the role of religion as it affects mental health. When psychoanalytical needs of individuals were examined—primarily by Sigmund Freud and his followers—and release of inhibitions became essential to general health, there was a willingness in the twentieth century to assume a relativism which makes man accountable only to himself. Reduction of tension provided the necessary therapy. Most investiagtors feel that this is a type of prostitution of what was really intended by Freud. However, Freud was hardly advocating libertinism in stating that a guilt complex frequently caused people to become maladjusted and psychoneurotic. The Viennese "father of psychoanalysis" has been attacked specifically for weakening moral principles. One hardly knows at what point in history the eroding process began, if it did in fact begin. One might hypothesize that it took place when it became secularized to the extent that knowledge was allowed to have its freedom or be disseminated without duress, at least in some areas. The prevailing moral code, some contend, is largely a tyranny tempered by hypocrisy.

All of this is said in order to point up the present general agreement that there is justifiable reason for misconduct or misalliance in terms of codes of morality and sanctions. It has been pointed out that the psychoanalytical movement itself has not condemned religious belief as such, but only where such belief is used as a substitute for psychotherapy. (Kaplan, 1961, p. 147) says:

> The peace of mind or soul recurrently promised is not the peace which passes understanding but one which can well be understood in psycho-analytic terms. It is the rootless security found in an external source of morality and personal integrity. Such a sense of security is without ground, either in a real self or external reality. It is the outlook of a child for whom the world is still a nursery.

Man's Search for Identity.   The other problem of man has been one in which he constantly seems to have some difficulty deciding *what he is*. Copernicus struck a blow to human pride when he asserted that the earth was not the center of our solar system; so did Darwin when he implied that man was not made in God's image and was perhaps a little lower than the angels. Changes in absolutes, social upheaval, and religious and social decay have produced significant alterations in man's relationship to his fellow man and his relationship to God. Today there is a strong reaction especially among young people, against the Church as an institution. When the Jesuit magazine *America* asked young readers to comment on an editorial, "The Rebellious Generation," the replies they obtained were more intense than expected. The youngsters were critical of priests who they claimed had immured themselves in walls of protocol, reverence, and propriety; of the church for its attitude toward birth control; and of church practices that failed to give them a personal relationship with God.

Today's religious unrest in both the Protestant and Catholic churches is focused primarily on the Church as an institution. Thus many people accuse the Church of clinging to outworn attitudes and habits that have little relevancy to life problems of today. This ferment does not mean that there is an abandonment of spiritual values, but rather that they cannot be found in the discipline and loyalty expected or demanded by the Church. In a survey reported by Fleming (1968) among day students at one large city college, some 67 percent of the young people said they had discussed religion within the past week, 70 percent of the discussions were at informal gathering places; another 26 percent were held at home; only 2 percent took place at a church or other religious center. Although one should be careful about extrapolating these results to other colleges or to all religious groups, there is considerable evidence, both direct and indirect, that young people as well as older adults are searching for a religious philosophy that has direct meaning in their lives. In many cases the Church leaders have responded by actively participating in what have hereto been regarded as secular problems.

The need for identity is perhaps stronger today than at any time in our recent history. Technology has stripped man of his feelings of importance in the factory or office. The institutionalizing of our lives deprives us of a feeling of

"How do I know what I will do when I finish high school? Maybe automation will do away with all the jobs I want."

close identity to lifelong institutions. Young people in particular turn to various ideological groups, clubs, and other social organizations in their search for identity. This need is discussed further in Chapter 5, which deals with motivational patterns.

Problems Related to Industrialization and Urbanization. Industrialization and abundance have multiplied man's wants at a time when population is rapidly using up major resources and filling the land areas of the world. Man's habitat is continuously becoming more problematic due to air pollution, water pollution, industrial wastes, fallout, and other conditions that threaten his health and well-being. Already, closely related to the growth in the rates of lung cancer and deaths attributed to respiratory difficulties is the amount of air pollution so closely associated with Western culture. A 1968 UNESCO Conference gave the earth about 20 years before it would start to become uninhabitable. A very serious aspect of water pollution is the continual dumping into the sea of an estimated one half million different biologically active molecules, one of the most abundant of which is DDT (Ehrlich, 1968). Man has been slow in making the necessary adjustment, although movements are underway to alleviate the conditions. For example, it will be mandatory by 1968 in certain states such as California to have converters installed in automobiles, in order to convert the carbon monoxide of the exhaust to carbon dioxide.

Urbanization, with its noise, heavy traffic, red tape, rules and regulations, and multiplication of agencies that separate people from direct contact with basic services and goods, brings with it disassociation and disorder. The beauty of our countryside, forests, and parks needs to be protected from destructive forces.

The increase of leisure time has been accompanied by psychological and social problems. Advanced technology and the removal of man many times away from the initial production of things most basic to life is a by-product of industrialization. And, although there is a threat in expanding technology, Labor Secretary Wirtz suggested (Arnstein, 1964, p. 312): "There is no reason to be afraid of machines. . . . There is great reason, however, to be concerned about how hard it is to get people who are educated and trained to see what machines are doing to people who are not educated and trained."

Another problem related to the urban setting involves the sex mores. This is a social problem of long duration, especially in Western culture where it has been the concern of the Judaeo-Christian religion throughout the centuries. Kinsey and his associates (1948, 1953) noted that public protestation and private practice in sexual matters are at variance. The continuous emphasis on sex in our movies, the widespread use of sex in advertisements, and the taboo placed on sex education until recently have frequently aggravated and misdirected the sex drive of adolescents and youth. At the same time, there is little or no opportunity of satisfying these aroused desires in the socially acceptable ways that have been handed down to us through the Judaeo-Christian culture. As Luchins (1964, pp. 47-63) points out,

> . . . the boy or girl who is expected to abstain from sexual activity is at the same time exposed to stimuli which play up sex. The result may be that these over-stimulated desires become central in the youth's view of the situation, and that obstacles to these needs loom very large. Consequently, the youth may feel that he is blocked and hemmed in on all sides.

Automation and Its Relation to Violence.   The transition into a robotized culture in which a surplus of workers will appear will require changes in our concept of the individual's place in society. This is clearly implied by Berg (1965, p. 205): "The pattern seems to be shaping toward an abrogation of law with resort to physical violence by some people who are directly affected by the current social and technological changes." Churches, homes, and railway trains have been bombed. Human beings have been stoned, shot, and mobbed by those who rebelled at the portents of cultural change. Psychologically, we see evidence of generalization in such events. That is, if anything is disliked, the response seems to center more and more frequently in violence. Yet such violence is commonplace at a time when we have only just entered the period of rapid cultural change and affluence. What will it be like when the shock wave of change is fully upon us? Obviously, society cannot be dedicated to the rule of law and at the same time permit violence in defiance of law to continue indefinitely. This will surely be at once the critical test of our society and the first signpost of the road we shall follow. If violence is met with violence, we shall probably be on our way to Orwell's *1984* and a society of iron regimentation.

A central problem during the period of cultural transition now upon us is the handling of violence. That is the emerging task of psychology and other behavioral sciences. If our society fails in this task, the traditional patterns of violence as a tool will prevail, and our world is well schooled in these techniques.

It seems highly probable that we shall be faced with problems of delinquency and crime which will dwarf our present problems in these areas. The crimes of violence on the streets in many cities during the summer of 1967 are likely to be repeated on a larger scale where conditions produce violent reactions by idle youths without goals, without controls, and without religious convictions. We are being forced to ask ourselves such questions as: What happens to self-respecting young people whose rosy dreams of childhood and adolescence are blasted by idleness or a make-work program? What happens to workers laid off or retired at age 50, no matter what the size of the pension check? What happens to a man who works but 20 hours a week, year after year, on a job that has little meaning to him, save that of providing just enough money to take care of his basic needs? The problem of making a successful and mature social and emotional response to the challenge of vacant time or a meaningless job is one that must be faced in an age of automatization.

Problems Related to the Space Age and Atomic Power. In the areas of communication and transportation, the world has changed dramatically. Today the streamliner of recent years is a slow and cumbersome way of transportation. The earth with its 25,000-mile circumference can be circled in less than a day. Propinquity is not alone a matter of shrinkage in earth span but is felt through rapid and easy communication. The "One World" idea proclaimed by Wendell Willkie a quarter of a century ago has become a reality. This has brought forth promises, perils, and threats. The space age will enlarge the possibilities and problems of man, thus bringing forth additional perils to man's safety and actual survival.

A problem that is destined to affect man's existence involves the uses that will be made of atomic energy. Without assessing blame, the aftermath and knowledge of the devastating results of Hiroshima remain a blot upon mankind. There is the constant threat of increased possibility of misuse of atomic energy with the jockeying for power. The amount of fall-out and the effects of strontium 90 on life are not yet fathomed. The United States, Russia, and certain other countries continue to develop more destructive atomic weapons. The tremendous quandary placed upon the shoulders of the administration officials of the United States and its armed forces when they recently, by accident, dropped a several megaton atomic bomb in the Mediterranean, indicates the seriousness of problems of defense and of the use or misuse of atomic power.

Studying Human Development

The purpose of studying and understanding human development is based upon several broad assumptions.

1. Western culture is significant and worth studying, hence a knowledge of human psychology enhances individual adjustment to its environment.

2. A knowledge of differential behavioral patterns provides a basis for assisting the young to reach the objectives and goals chosen by our society. In other words, man is not just passively cooperating with nature in the education of youth, but is also a catalyst in the process.

3. Man can improve his condition by increasing his information on human development and alleviate many existing inequities in Western societies.

4. Because Modern man has assumed an existentialist concern for identification, he must seek the basic etiology of human behavior.

5. Finally, a knowledge of the principles of behavior is a basic requirement for efficiently achieving any humanly desirable end.

Problems in Studying Human Development. The problems involved in studying human behavior and development are complex, due in a large part to the difficulties encountered in securing samplings of subjects and in controlling the different factors affecting them. One of the oldest and simplest method of studying development is to trace the physical development of individuals over a period of years. This method provides considerable data relative to growth in height and weight. With the advent of the testing movement many studies were conducted around problems related to educational, mental, and psychological growth during childhood and adolescence. These studies were followed by studies dealing with physiological growth and with behavior changes during the growing years.

Although the authors recognize the value of studying various aspects of growth and development, they hold it essential to consider the different forces and conditions that affect development at all stages of life. Development in a changing environment is not simply a biological phenomenon, but involves the socioeconomic, politico-cultural, and scientific-philosophical settings. Thus it is essential that we study human development in a setting with multitudinous influences consonant with the raw facts of a technological and hydrogen-bomb age. Such a study demands a presentation of human development in a dynamic culture—a culture that includes a variety of recognizable forces which impinge upon man, together with other influences, subtle but nonetheless inextricably related to the change and shaping of man. When one considers that man has an ever larger part in determining his state of being, it is easily seen that the old metaphysical formulas will have diminishing effect on behavior. Rather than the philosophical cliché of exploring the abyss of causation, man questions what is implicit in the inquiry, Who and what is he?

If the foregoing is valid, then what is the setting in Western culture in which man develops? This chapter introduces the broad effects of differing kinds of setting, all of which affect man in varying degrees. Chapter 1 deals in kaleidoscopic fashion with the problems of human development in a scientific age, especially characterized as an age of rapidly changing conditions. Special attention will be given to the problems man faces in growing up in a scientific age, a technological age, an age when the established ideologies are being seriously challenged.

Research on Human Development. Arnold J. Toynbee has pointed out that man is astonishingly good at dealing with the physical world, but just as astonishingly bad at dealing with human nature; therefore, an inch gained in the understanding of and command over human nature is worth a mile gained in the understanding of and command over physical nature.

Since human behavior is so enormously varied, so delicately complex, so obscurely motivated, most people despair of finding valid generalizations to explain and predict the actions, thoughts, and feelings of human beings—that is, of constructing a science of human behavior. The literature of the behavioral sciences has grown so fast in recent years that the job of distilling the pertinent essentials is at best difficult and at worst foolhardy. Berelson and Steiner in *The Inventory of Scientific Findings on Human Behavior* list 1,045 findings from scientific study, not all absolutely true, not all final or definitive, but among the best established generalizations of this scope. This suggests that the problems of studying human development are vast and complex.

Research into human development has involved many fields comprising behavioral science, such as psychology, sociology, anthropology, education, and to a lesser extent biology and genetics. The authors have attempted to draw together from these different sources recent materials, bearing on human development in some eclectic fashion. It is admittedly superficial to a degree. But to serve the needs of teachers, social workers, and nurses, and para-educational or medical workers who need educational and psychological information primarily, we believe an overall attempt should be made to pull together relevant materials which will aid in understanding the forces exerting pressure on the individual and society in a dynamic culture. This work covers the life span from prenatal life to old age.

The Uniqueness of Individual Development. Understanding human development would be much easier if people developed and behaved according to a common pattern. However, this is not the case, as is pointed out in Chapter 2. Individuality in development is commonly observed by parents as they describe the development and behavior of their different children. Susie, for example, was always active and apparently "keyed up." She learned to walk at eleven months of age; displayed unusual motor coordination at age 20 months; and continuously demanded the attention of her parents during the preschool years.

Susie's younger brother, Harold, was a more deliberate type from early infancy. He would examine objects carefully before placing them in his mouth, did not walk until around fourteen months, and was considerably behind his older sister in arriving at verbalization. In fact, Harold didn't seem to go through the usual process of learning to talk; he seemed to skip the word stage, and began talking soon after age two by using sentences. Norms would have furnished little help in predicting the language development of either Harold or Susie. Each moved at an individual pace along individual lines.

In a comprehensive longitudinal study of development (the California Growth Study), the same subjects were followed for a period of twenty-five years. Bayley noted considerable variation in these subjects (1955). In a particular feature such as height or vocabulary, a child may, over a period of years, shift from high to average, or the reverse, as compared to his age-mates. Such shifts are of sufficient frequency that we should assume, in general, they are normal patterns of growth.

The Life Span Approach.   Since this volume is to follow the life-span approach, an overview of the materials that will be included is here presented. This has to do with the different periods or stages of life. Bayley (1963, p. 125) has pointed out that "any behavior that is being studied, if it is to be adequately interpreted must be seen in reference to the age or ages of the individual under study, and to their probable status in the developmental cycle."

The developmental process is described in Chapter 2. This should furnish the reader with the orientation and understanding of development needed for studying the subsequent chapters. The chapters comprising Part II are organized so as to present a life-span approach to the major topics studies: physical growth, the development of motivational patterns, the development of language abilities, intellectual development, the development of cognition, and the development of attitudes, ideals, and values. Part III deals with the social development and problems of adjustment at the different stages of life. In this Part, life is divided into six stages: early childhood, late childhood, adolescence, early adulthood, middle adulthood, and late adulthood. It should be pointed out, however, that these are not distinct stages; one stage moves into another with no clear line of demarcation. There are developmental tasks and problems somewhat characteristic of each of the six stages. Special consideration will be given to these in Part III.

The developmental aspects of the beginning years (from birth through the fifth year) are well known to those knowledgeable of child development. From babyhood to first-grade entrance the dramatic changes in body and socialization are such that this phenomenon will never again be repeated. The average child from age 6 to 12 or 13 not only grows physically at an enormous rate but actually doubles his size in growth and weight, reaching two-thirds of his adult height during this time; in addition, he exhibits certain characteristic behavior patterns. In short, success in school work, play with peers, and coexistence at home are fundamental. Investigators Kagan and Moss (1962) found that such behavior as passive withdrawal from stressful situations, dependency on the family, ease of arousing anger, involvement in intellectual mastery, social interaction anxiety, and sexual behavior patterns evident during ages 6-10 or 11 appear to relate to behavior in adulthood.

Adolescence, which is sometimes used synonymously with puberty, is a period of transition from childhood to adulthood—an in-between period. The transition is age-related but only in terms of average, for the early maturing youngster of twelve may be increasingly characterized by adolescent behavior rather than child behavior. On the other hand, a few 17-year-olds may be struggling with entrance to puberty. This transition is evident in the developmental tasks unique to this group. These are presented later in the present chapter.

The early adult years are characterized by the establishment of independence, which for most young adults means economic self-sufficiency, responsibility for heterosexual activity, career, and home establishment. With growth into adulthood commitments to social convention and community betterment are often seen in involvement in fraternal and civic club activities. For most women, marriage comes between 18 and 21, for men between 20 and 23. In 1967 the surplus of women over men in America in the age brackets was nearly 600,000. By 1970 it is anticipated that a dramatic shift will take place with the surplus of almost 200,000 men (*U.S. News and World Report,* 1967, p. 68.) Middle and late adulthood are periods characterized by an extension of many problems of early adulthood along with some new problems. These years comprise the materials of Chapters 14 and 15.

Somehow the child must be taught the heritage of his culture. Many institutions are either directly or indirectly concerned with this. A basic assumption of developmental theory is that adult behaviors are frequently established in early childhood. This assumption is supported by retrospective reports obtained from the verbal statements of adults. However, it has been difficult to produce objective results based upon data showing the stability of childhood behavior patterns. Kagan and Moss (1960) analyzed data available on a group of "normal" adults from the Fels longitudinal research population. The findings dealt specifically with the long-term stability of passive and dependent behavior manifested in situations which are frustrating and/or demanded problem-solving activity.

The subjects consisted of 27 male and 27 female adults born between 1930 and 1939, who had been through a comprehensive assessment program which included an average of five hours of tape-recorded interviews and a variety of test procedures. The correlations revealed "that passive and dependent behaviors are quite stable for women but minimally stable for men" (p. 243). The greater social acceptance of passive and dependent behavior in females would seem to account for the greater stability of dependency among women than among men.

The results of this study reveal the role of early cultural setting on adult behavior patterns. The more complicated our world becomes the more essential it becomes that institutions concerned with human development be (a) founded on scientific information about human development, and (b) be organized in harmony with the social, physical, and philosophical setting in which the child develops—although it must be recognized at all times that the cultural setting is continuously undergoing rapid changes. It is to be hoped that the study of the cultural setting in which the child, adolescent, and adult live will take into consideration the fact that our culture is in a state of transition, and that individuals must be trained to meet problems that exist in a changing rather than static culture.

Developmental Tasks

According to Havighurst (1952) a pattern of expectations for development appears as a result of biological changes and cultural influences. Socializing agencies, such as the home and school reward the child for attainments and punish him in some manner for failures to achieve developmental tasks in harmony with expectations. These developmental tasks are closely related to social expectations of the individual at different age levels in a particular culture.

Some Developmental Tasks in American Society.   According to Havighurst and others, there is a time sequence in the arrangement of developmental tasks in a particular culture. Also, they do not occur at random; rather, one accomplishment sets the stage for the next. Lists of these tasks have been developed based upon inferences and observations from educational, psychological, and sociological investigations. A list adapted from Havighurst's studies and arranged in order of the six periods of life adjustments discussed in Part III is presented in Table 1-1.

TABLE 1-1
List of Developmental Tasks for Different Life Periods
(Adapted from Havighurst)

Age Span	Developmental Tasks
Infancy and early childhood	Learning to walk Learning to talk Learning to take solid foods Learning to control body wastes Learning sex differences and modesty Forming simple concepts of physical and social reality Learning to relate oneself emotionally to parents, siblings, and others with whom he is closely identified Learning to distinguish "right" and "wrong"; acquiring a conscience Developing good motor coordination, such as learning skills used in games Acquiring a self-concept by building wholesome attitudes toward one's self
Middle and late childhood	Learning to get along with age-mates Learning an appropriate masculine or feminine social role Developing skills in reading, writing and calculating Developing concepts necessary for daily living Developing conscience, morality, and a scale of values Achieving personal independence Developing attitudes toward groups and institutions
Adolescence	Achieving new and more mature relations with age mates Achieving masculine or feminine sex role Accepting one's physical self and using the body effectively Achieving emotional independence of parents and other adults Selecting and preparing for an occupation Courtship and preparing for marriage Developing intellectual skills and concepts necessary for civic competence Desiring and achieving socially responsible behavior Acquiring a set of values and ethical standards as a guide to behavior

TABLE 1-1 (Continued)

Age Span	Developmental Tasks
Early adulthood	Preparing for family life; selecting a mate Learning to live with a marriage partner Starting a family; rearing children Preparing for and getting started in an occupation Assuming civic responsibility Managing a home Finding a congenial social group Achieving adult civic and social responsibility
Middle adulthood	Establishing and maintaining an economic standard of living Assisting teen-age children to become responsible and well-adjusted children Developing adult leisure-time pursuits Accepting and adjusting to the psychological changes of middle age Adjusting to the emancipation of children from close family ties Adjusting to aging of parents, kinspeople, and other older people
Late adulthood	Adjusting to decreased strength and health problems related to aging Adjusting to retirement and reduced income Adjusting to death of spouse Adjusting to changed living conditions Meeting civic and social responsibilities Adjusting to increased leisure-time Establishing an explicit affiliation with one's age group

Characteristics of Developmental Tasks. There are special characteristics of developmental tasks. An understanding of these is most useful to the student of human development. The following factors should be carefully studied and applied to the developmental tasks at different stages in human development:

1. Some developmental tasks are common to all cultures and appear at approximately the same time in different cultures. Such tasks are closely interwoven with man's physiological characteristics and physical structure. For example, children in all cultures learn to walk during the first two years of their life.

2. The nature of some tasks is closely interwoven with specific cultures. The age for choosing an occupation and entering the working world varies from culture to culture. The longer period of schooling required in present-day Western culture has resulted in a delay of the date when individuals enter different vocational pursuits.

3. Some of the tasks need to be learned only once in a life time. Learning to walk, once mastered during early childhood, is sufficient for a life time, provided that some handicapping condition doesn't appear.

4. Some tasks are learned gradually over a long period of time. Learning one's sex role begins at an early age and extends through the period of early adulthood when husband and wife learn their marital roles as father and mother.

5. Some tasks occur at different ages in different cultures. This is especially true for marriages and homemaking. Even in Western culture these tasks appear earlier among individuals from the lower classes than among individuals from the middle classes.

6. Some tasks occur in different forms in different cultures. Occupational and sexual roles vary with different cultures. Sexual mores also vary with cultures, and with social class in a specific culture.

Implications of the Theory of Developmental Tasks.   The theory of developmental tasks, according to Havighurst (1952, p. 5) has important educational implications.

First, it helps in discovering and stating the purpose of education in the schools. Education may be conceived as the effort of society, through the schools, to help the individual achieve certain of his developmental tasks.

The second use of the concept is in the timing of educational efforts. When the body is ripe, and society requires, and the self is ready to achieve a certain task, the *teachable moment* has come. Efforts at teaching, which would have been largely wasted if they had come earlier, give gratifying results when they come at the teachable moment, when the task should be learned.

This point of view assumes that the curriculum should be organized to a marked degree around objectives set forth in developmental tasks for different age groups. Such a point of view has merit, but doesn't give sufficient attention to the maturation level of the individual and to individual differences in readiness for the different learnings.

The theory of developmental tasks has important and significant implications to the personal and social adjustments of individuals during early, middle, and late adulthood. These implications must be appraised in terms of cultural expectations of individuals of each sex at the different stages of life; although the mental, physical, physiological states of individuals at different stages of life will have an important bearing. Such states will vary considerably with different people. Late adulthood today does not seem to have the same meaning and significance to a large percentage of middle-class adults that it had during the early part of the present century.

Summary

Man's genetic evolution has favored him in the development of adaptability and creativity. These were accentuated by man's development of the use of language, science, technology, and socialization patterns. An understanding of human development must take into consideration the cultural forces that impinge upon man. Culture in the United States today is characterized by rapid and significant changes. This may be noted in scientific developments that have altered man's ways of life and are destined to produce even more profound transformations. Advances in health and medicine have more than doubled life expectancy since the middle of the eighteenth century. Our greatly expanded knowledge is reflected in the vast amount of research in progress, the sharp rise in high school and college enrollment, and the increased number of scholars engaged in scientific and other types of scholarly research.

There has been enormous growth in the world's population with more and more of it concentrated in large urban areas. And, while the world's population continues to multiply, the needs of manpower in the industrialized areas are rapidly decreasing as a result of automation. This has brought forth important vocational changes as well as social changes involving the family structure and life activities. Thus cities, governments, and families alike are beset with difficult problems.

Our affluent society faces promises, problems, and threats. Age-old customs are being questioned, age-old beliefs being challenged. The age of certainty seems to be largely in the past, while the certainty of today is that changes will continue to take place in every avenue of life. This condition has brought forth a challenge to man's philosophy and religion; we are called upon to reexamine many old ideas and beliefs that were accepted earlier without question.

A widening of urbanization followed industrialization, and increased mental-hygiene problems seem to have followed urbanization. Man is today having difficulty deciding *what he is.* This may be observed among the youth in particular. Changed sex mores, growing violence in our cities, and more complex individual and family problems are some of the threats we can observe. What to do with our greater leisure and wealth is largely an unsolved problem.

Perhaps an understanding of human development will help in understanding, predicting, and directing behavior. The fact that man is able to learn provides educational forces with the basis for preparing citizens for a changing world, which is moving toward a one-world concept. And, although principles of development are set forth in Chapter 2, uniqueness of individual development prevents the mass approach to the production of efficient and effective citizens in a changing world. The developmental tasks set forth for the different life periods furnish a broad guide and should serve as objectives for an educational program in the home, community, school, and church.

References

Arnstein, G. E. "The Mixed Blessing of Automation," *School and Society* (Oct. 31, 1964), p. 312.

Bayley, Nancy. "On the Growth of Intelligence," *American Psychologist*, Vol. 10 (1955), pp. 805–818.

Bayley, Nancy. "The Life Span as a Frame of Reference in Psychological Research," *Vita Humanus,* Vol. 6 (1963), pp. 125-139.

Berg, I. A. "Cultural Trends and the Task of Psychology," *American Psychologist,* Vol. 20 (1965), pp. 203-207.

Brown, C. C. "Psychophysiology at an Interface," *Psychophysiology*, Vol. 13 (1966), pp. 1-7.

Burhoe, R. W. "Human Values in an Age of Science and Technology," *Current Issues in Higher Education.* Association for Higher Education, National Education Association, Washington, D.C., 1964, p. 35.

Davens, E. "A View of Health Services for Mothers and Children," *Children,* Vol. 12 (March-April 1965), pp. 47-54.

De Chardin, Teilhard. *The Future of Man.* New York: Harper, 1955.

Dybwad, G. "Family Life in a Changing World," *Children,* Vol. 6 (Jan.-Feb. 1959), pp. 3-9.

Enrlich, P. R. "Population Control Earth's Last Chance," *The Wall Street Journal,* December 3, 1968.

Fleming, T. J. "What's Happening to Religion," *Virginia Pilot, This Week Magazine* (Feb. 25, 1968), pp. 6-9.

Freedman, Marcia K. "Perspectives in Youth Employment," *Children,* Vol. 12 (March-April 1965), pp. 75-80.

Goode, W. J. *World Revolution and Family Patterns.* New York: Free Press, 1963.

Hauser, P. M. "More from the Census of 1960," *Scientific American,* Vol. 207 (1962), pp. 35-37.

Havighurst, R. J. *Human Development and Education.* New York: McKay, 1953.

Kagan, J., and H. A. Moss. *Birth to Maturity.* New York: Wiley, 1962, pp. 154, 174, 266.

————. "The Stability of Passive and Dependent Behavior from Childhood and through Manhood," *Child Development,* Vol. 31 (1960), pp. 577-591.

Kaplan, A. *The New World of Philosophy,* Lectures Three and Four. New York: Random, 1961.

Kinsey, A. C., et al. *Sexual Behavior in the Human Female.* Philadelphia: Saunders, 1953.

————. *Sexual Behavior in the Human Male.* Philadelphia: Saunders, 1948.

Luchins, A. S. "On the Theories and Problems of Adolescence," *Journal of Genetic Psychology,* Vol. 85 (1954), pp. 47-62.

Marchand, S. P. "Ferment in the Schools," *Children* (March-April 1965), pp. 47-63.

Medical World News, Vol. 8 (Sept. 1967), p. 32.

Mumford, L. "The Automation of Knowledge," *Current Issues in Higher Education,* Association for Higher Education, National Education Association, Washington, D.C., 1964, pp. 11–12.

Ogburn, W. F. *Technology and the Changing Family.* Houghton, 1955, pp. 99–100.

Piel, Gerard. "The Acceleration of History," *Current Issues in Higher Education,* Association for Higher Education, National Education Association, Washington, D.C., 1964, pp. 22-32.

Population Reference Bureau, Inc., 1968.

Simmel, G. *Conflict* (trans. Kurt H. Wolff). New York: Free Press, 1955.

————. *The Sociology of George Simmel* (trans. Kurt H. Wolff). New York: Free Press, 1950, pp. 409-424.

Spengler, J. J. "The Economist and the Population Question," *American Economic Review,* Vol. 56 (1966), pp. 1-24.

Stern, B. H. "Automation and Adult Education," *Educational Forum,* Vol. 29 (1965), pp. 307-311.

Tyler, R. "The Knowledge Explosion: Implications for Secondary Education," *Educational Forum,* Vol. 29 (1965), pp. 145-153.

United States Bureau of the Census, *Statistical Abstract of the United States,* 1960, 81st ed. Washington, D.C.: Government Printing Office, 1960.

U. S. News and World Report, "Husband Hunting: the Choices" (Oct. 2, 1967), p. 68.

————, "New Heart for Old—Another transplant" (Jan. 15, 1968), p. 12.

White L. "The Concept of Culture," *American Anthropologist,* Vol. 61 (1949) pp. 227-251.

Chapter 2

The Development Process

The words "growth" and "development" are frequently used interchangeably, and although they are different, they are also inseparable; neither takes place alone. Growth has at times been described as quantitative changes involving size and structure. Growth may be observed in the increase in size of the child's body, or it may refer to an increase in the size and structure of the internal organs and of the brain. There is the functional aspect of growth as well as the structural. This may be noted in increased capacity of the brain to function in learning activities, and increased understanding reflected in mental growth.

Development, on the other hand, has been described as qualitative in nature. In this case development is conceived of "as a progressive series of orderly changes leading toward the goal of maturity" (Hurlock, 1964, p. 1). Development implies a progressive change leading toward maturity. Thus maturation is closely associated with development. Maturation implies the fact that the individual's functional abilities emerge and progressively change toward a full realization.

Genetic Factors in Development

Ontogenetic development may be thought of as beginning with the fertilization of the germ cell from a female (an egg) by a germ cell from a male (a sperm). However, we should realize at all times that "All life comes from previous life." The new individual can best be thought of "as beginning from the processes which are initiated at fertilization" (Carmichael, 1954, p. 62). In the process of development the fertilized cell divides and redivides until thousands of cells are formed. It is estimated that from the time of conception until birth there is an increase in weight two billion times. Where do the materials of the cell from which the individual is formed originate? Where does enough matter come from to cause the fertilized cell to grow, divide, and redivide, and increase in weight two billion times? We perceive at the outset that the materials making up the fertilized cell are most important. We also note the importance of environmental forces and conditions during the nine-month period before birth.

The Chromosomes and the Genes. Each cell contains a nucleus rich in a highly complex nucleoprotein called deoxyribonucleic acid (DNA). DNA ap-

27

pears to be a basic living substance capable of duplicating itself so as to form more DNA. In the nucleus of every cell there lie a number of rodlike, darkly stained bodies which are called *chromosomes*. These may be observed in Figure 2-1. "The DNA of a chromosome is a linear array of many genes. Each gene, in turn, is a chain of about 1000 nucleotides in a precisely defined sequence which, when translated into amino acid, spells out a particular protein or enzyme" (Kornberg, 1968, pp. 68-69). According to findings reported by Tjio and Levan (1956) and substantiated by later students of genetics, the normal human somatic cell contains 46 chromosomes, 23 in the germ cell, the egg or the sperm. When the egg and the sperm unite, each contributes 23 chromosomes, so that the fertilized egg from which all the body cells are derived contains 46 chromosomes.

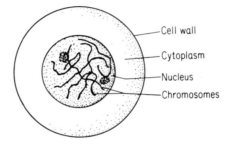

Figure 2-1. A typical cell.

The chief importance of the chromosomes is that they provide the means by which potentialities are transmitted, for it is in the chromosomes that the genes are found and these furnish the basic hereditary materials. A gene is a small region in a chromosome composed of a giant nucleic acid molecule or part of a molecule, which according to Strauss (1960) consists mainly of a chemical, deoxyribonucleic acid (DNA), which contains nucleotides or four bases (thymine, cytosine, adenine, and quanine). These, in various combinations, seem to be capable of encoding all the characteristics that an organism transmits from one generation to another.

In some cases the organism has more or less than 46 chromosomes because of abnormal chromosome behavior in the ovaries of the mother, or in the eggs produced by her ovaries, or in the sperm of the father. Studies in genetics indicate that abnormalities of chromosomes are the basis of many disorders and anomalies in children. The chromosomes have been studied by characterizing the location of the centromere (a characteristic constriction in the chromosome), the overall length of the chromosomes, and the length of the arms on either side of the centromere. The ratio between the lengths of the two arms separated by the centromere is constant for any one chromosome pair (Kang, 1966, p. 60).

Present technical means enable students of genetics to detect abnormalities in the number of chromosomes as well as some relatively massive structural abnormalities in individual chromosomes. This is shown in the case of the mongoloid presented in Figure 2-2. The mongoloid normally has 47 chromosomes and is characterized by specific abnormalities in physical structure and mental retardation (Smith *et al.*, 1960). Cases of mongolism have been reported where the normal complement of 46 chromosomes appeared in the somatic cells. However, the structure of these chromosomes was abnormal with an extra chromosome in one group and a deficiency in another (Polani et al., 1960).

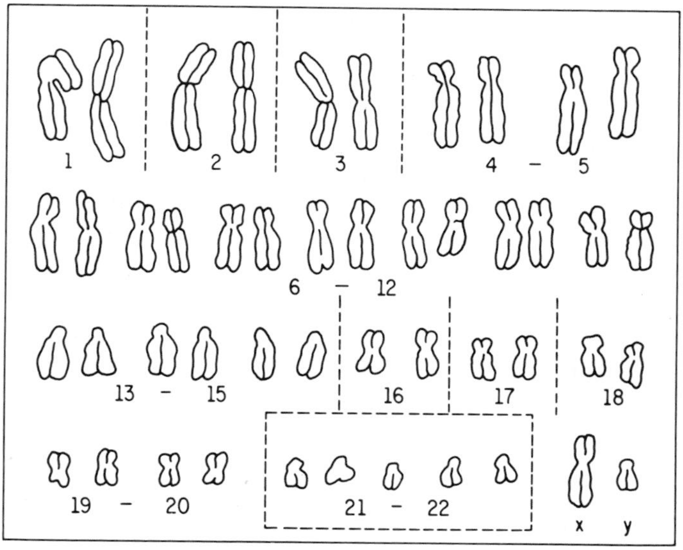

Figure 2-2. The chromosome karyotype of a male afflicted with Mongolism. Note the extra chromosome between position 21 and 22, where there are normally only two chromosomes in each position. The X and Y chromosomes in the lower right corner are the sex chromosomes. (Kang, 1966.)

The genes of a special pair of chromosomes determine the sex of the child. In the female the pair of chromosomes are alike and are referred to as XX chromosomes, while in the male the sperm cells carry a single Y chromosome; the other half carry a single X chromosome. A fertilized egg that receives a Y chromosome from the sperm will produce a male baby; a fertilized egg from an X chromosome from the sperm will yield a female baby.

Many types of abnormality of the sex chromosome have been described as a result of investigations of disturbed physical sex development. According to Kang (1966):

.... Abnormalities of the sex chromosomes have been demonstrated in four conditions: Klinefelter's syndrome, Turner's syndrome, the triple-X female, and in some hermaphroditism and pseudohermaphroditism. Patients with Klinefelter's syndrome have a general male appearence with male external sex organs but are sterile, frequently mentally retarded, and have nuclear chromatin bodies characteristic of females. The sex chromosomal pattern of XXY is found in the majority of individuals with this syndrome.

Turner's syndrome usually occurs in persons who appear to be females but who are sterile, fail to show breast development, are retarded in growth, and have webbing of the neck. Most of them also have a congenital heart defect and are mentally retarded. In most cases, the sex-chromatin pattern is negative and the karyotype analysis reveals 45 chromosomes, only one sex chromosome being present. However, sexchromatin positive cases of Turner's syndrome have been reported.

Several cases of females with an XXX pattern have been reported. Such women are usually fertile and their offspring normal.

Abnormalities of sex chromosomal patterns have also been found in a few patients with a confusion of sexual organs.

The chromosome is handed down generation after generation. If this were an immutable structure, there would be no change from generation to generation. However, Morgan in 1910 recorded the results of nearly a year of study of many generations of *Drosophila* (vinegar fly) in which a male appeared with white eyes, although previous generations had brilliant red eyes. This was the beginning of a new concept in genetics referred to as gene mutation. This discovery led to much additional research so that further mutations were observed.

In 1927 Mulker demonstrated through the use of X-rays that genes could be made to mutate at a vastly increased rate. This discovery was most important and has helped us in understanding genetic damage and change resulting from mothers exposed to X-rays or other damaging conditions. Materials bearing on this are presented in Chapter 3, dealing with prenatal development.

The Operation of Heredity. The particular combination of genes received by a child is a matter of chance, although each gene from the mother's chromosome is paired with a corresponding gene from the father's. Perhaps the most important difference between modern genetic concepts and earlier viewpoints of heredity is that today we conceive of the transmission of individual particles of hereditary material from parents to offspring; earlier viewpoints postulated a blending of the hereditary elements of the pairs of chromosomes. The unit factor of heredity is the *gene*.

The first law of heredity points out that the paired genes derived from the two parents, which influence the development of traits, retain their individuality and segregate unaffected by each other to pass into different gametes, and are able to enter into new combinations when they unite to form a new pair. This law is known as the *law of segregation* and was discovered by the Austrian monk Gregor Mendel (1822-84), experimenting during his spare time in the Augustinian monastery garden at Brunn.

Mendel discovered from his experiments with peas that when the round-yellow pea was crossed with the wrinkled-green pea, the first generation yielded round-yellow peas, but when these hybrids were crossed in another generation different combinations appeared. Out of this and related discoveries arose the law of *dominance* and *recessiveness,* indicating that when the two genes (one from each parent) are different, one may dominate over the other. A striking illustration of this in human beings is the characteristic of red hair. If a red-headed woman married a man with dark hair, the children resulting from this marriage would all have dark hair. Such children would, however, carry a recessive trait for red hair. The results from a marriage of two homozygous types (children resulting from the marriage of the redheaded woman and the dark-haired man) would be as follows:

> ¼ dark hair
> ½ dark hair (red hair recessive)
> ¼ red hair

Since the pure dark hair and the homozygous types are indistinguishable, three-fourths of the children should have dark hair and one fourth red hair.

Important modifications of the law of segregation discovered since Mendel's time, include the law of linkage. When a trait is affected by a gene lying within the X chromosome, it is said to be *sex-linked.* This means that the X chromosome carries genes for characteristics other than those that determine sex. Such characteristics will be linked with sex in heredity; they are not linked to a particular sex, but such characteristics follow the distribution of the X chromosome in both sexes. It has been estimated that as many as 60 traits are sex-linked while 20 others are thought to be sex-linked (Montagu, 1963). Perhaps the best known sex-linked trait is color blindness. "Among whites, 2 men out of every 25 suffer from some lack of ability to recognize red and green. Less than 1 woman out of 200 women suffers from a similar defect." (Montagu, p. 187.)

Mendel's laws of inheritance apply to both plants and animals and have been most useful to geneticists. The result is a vast and complex body of knowledge, important to students of genetics but beyond the scope of our discussion here. The theory of the individuality of the gene was considered to be largely unalterable until the National Science Foundation reported the findings of Professor Alexander Brink of the University of Wisconsin in 1959.

"Brink found," Montagu states (p. 65), "that the gene that produces color in the kernel of the purple variety of Indian corn can be permanently modified by bringing it into combination in a hybrid with the color gene from the stippled variety of Indian corn. The stippled gene produces the same pigment, but not as much, as the purple-corn gene." Additional evidence has been produced since Brink's discovery to corroborate his findings. Genetics have come to realize that a complete and accurate separation of the influences of heredity and environment is not possible within the framework of our present knowledge and may not be clear even after the exact nature of gene operation is determined. As Snyder (1965, p. 70) has stated:

> . . . As the zygote divides and forms a ball of cells, some cells are on the outside, some on the inside. Already different conditions exist for different cells. Slightly different chemical reactions are set up by the same genes under these

differing conditions, and these lead in turn to still differing reactions; or, in some cases, certain genes act strongly under certain conditions of the surrounding cytoplasm, less strongly under other conditions.

Genetics and the Operation of Heredity.   The postulation of the Watson-Crick structure for DNA (deoxyribonucleic acid) which established that the nucleotide bases in DNA do replicate by finding their complement, has important ramifications. DNA is like a plant manager. Enzymes (furnished by the genes) are its section foreman. The cytoplasm of the cell is a stockroom full of necessary raw materials, including the high-energy phosphates which supply the "push" required to join groups of atoms into molecules. They discovered further that DNA carries the blueprint for proteins and RNA (ribose nucleic acid) does the work of making them. What happened as a result of this revelation was from 1958 to 1965, twenty-four persons in chemistry or joint categories medicine and physiology won Nobel prizes, fourteen worked directly on genetics, proteins or nucleic acids. This research has stripped the cell of its secrets, made possible an understanding of organisms via genetics, and has brought together the geneticists, the biochemists and others to work on the common problems of applied genetics. The increased use and establishment of genetic evaluation clinics has been generated. These are already producing far-reaching findings.

Recent studies have linked RNA closely with learning and memory. Studies of the flatworm, called the planarian, reveal that it has the ability to grow a new head if its head is severed from the tail. The flatworm was taught to respond in a certain way prior to having his head separated from the tail. After growing new heads, the old tails seemed to remember what they had learned. However, if the trained planarian was given a shot of a chemical that destroys RNA, the old tail after the head was severed no longer remembered what he had been taught. Evidence has been presented from studies by McConnel and others (*Science News Letter*, 1966) that if uneducated Planaria worms are fed a diet consisting of educated worms the results will be improved learning, memory, and transfer of materials learned. Such studies offer much promise to man in his studies of the relation of memory to the complicated molecules in the cells of the brain.

Much has been said about the operation of heredity and equality. It should be noted that equality means that all humans are entitled to equal opportunity to develop their potentials to the fullest, not that these potentials are equal. Yet Adler (1957, p. 31), one of the founders with Freud of the psychoanalytic movement, wrote:

> Investigators who believe one of the characteristics of an adult are noticeable in his infancy are not far wrong; this accounts for the fact that characteristics are often considered hereditary. But the concept that character and personality are inherited from one's parents is universally harmful because it hinders the educator in his task and cramps his confidence. The real reason for assuming that character is inherited lies elsewhere. This invasion enables anyone who has the task of education to escape his responsibilities with the simple gesture of blaming heredity for the pupil's failures.

Hereditary Factors.   The characteristics usually closely associated with inheritance are color of the eyes and hair, pigmentation of the skin, blood types, body build, and other physical features. The rapidly accumulating knowledge in cytogenetics reveals the wide diversity of ways in which heredity operates. The question of chromosome abnormality in spontaneous abortions and stillbirths has been explored by Carr (1963). He reports a high incidence of chromosome abnormalities.

Hereditary disorders of metabolism such as phenylketonuria (PKU) have been detected through modern biochemical techniques. This is a disorder resulting from an inborn error of metabolism. Prior to comparatively recent use of the low phenylalanine diet most PKU cases were severely retarded inmates in institutions. With the development of treatment procedures, increased efforts have been made to identify PKU cases as early as possible. Early treatment tends to prevent irreversible brain damage.

Genetic loadings causing metabolic diseases such as PKU (excess phenyl-pyruvic acid) galatosemia, albinism, or sickle-cell anemia, and other nutritional and infection diseases are largely under control. One might wonder if our knowledge of genetics helped. In a world where an estimated 150,000,000 persons are genetically importuned, we have developed use of insulin to protect the diabetics, hemophiliacs have blood-clotting drugs, babies unable to tolerate galactose have been provided with a modus vivendi. Evidence thus far of harmful mutations due to radiation in the children born in Hiroshima and Nagasaki since 1945 reveals no monsters, nor does it show marked increase in genetic disease (Beadle and Beadle, 1966, p. 221). It should be pointed out that recessive mutations are hidden in the phenotype in the first generation, so that evidence will have to be taken from the second generation for a fuller evaluation. Investigation through successive generations on rats introduced to equivalent amounts of radiation from atomic explosions does show noticeable effects. Cataracts, sterility, and shortened life are in considerable evidence. Rats are not men, it is true, but an investigation shows incidence of cancer in radiologists over nonradiologists in a 12 to 4 ratio (Lewis, 1963, p. 1493).

The Interaction of Heredity and Environment.   The difficulty of ascribing all behavior tendencies to either heredity or environment is well illustrated by a series of experiments on audiogenetic seizures in mice. The fact that susceptibility to fatal seizures is high in some strains and low in others supports the conclusion that seizure incidence is genetically determined. However, there is scientific evidence that the incidence of seizures can be significantly altered without changing the genetic constitution.

Studies have been conducted in which fertilized eggs recovered from the tubes or uterus of females of one strain were implanted into the uterus of a different strain. This has been accomplished by using seizure-susceptible females as donors and seizure-resistant females as hosts. In this way the genetic characteristics of the fetal rats are unaltered; however, their susceptibility to fatal seizures was found to be lower than that of those of their own genetic strain produced in a normal manner, but higher than that of the "foster" mothers in whose uteri they developed (Ginsberg and Hovda, 1947).

A somewhat different situation is found in the case of inherited visual difficulties. Such a condition will affect the individual adversely in proportion to opportunities provided for the individual to develop.

Menninger (1961) suggests the possibility that we inherit "peculiar neural arrangements which facilitate certain types of reaction" (p. 27). This theory is supported by results from a study by Jost and Sontag (1944), who became interested in the wide differences found in the excitability and intensity of emotional reactions observable among children even during the first year of life. Using pairs of identical twins, siblings, and unrelated children six to twelve years of age as subjects, the investigators obtained measurements of skin resistance, pulse rate, salivation, respiration, vasomotor persistence, autonomic balance, "heart period," and volar conductance. The results furnished evidence for a pattern of relationship between the different physiological measurements obtained and heredity. This is indicated by the following correlations:

Identical twins	.43 to .49
Brothers and sisters	.26 to .40
Unrelated pairs	.02 to .16

The results from this study indicate that the child does inherit a structure that predisposes him to react emotionally according to a pattern set forth by environmental circumstances and conditions. Through learning he develops certain emotional responses within limits set forth by his heredity. It thus seems that favorable environmental forces are essential for the hereditary determiners of the genes to operate effectively.

Differentiation and Integration. In the process of fertilization the egg abandons its structure and function as an unfertilized egg and emerges as a new structure different from that of the male or female from which it emerged. The newly formed organism that develops from the fertilized egg is thus different in structure and function from anything else that has existed before. It is in this way that each individual is biologically unique. Differentiation is a central problem in biology that poses important problems for students of genetics. Most evidence supports the conclusion that "each cell of multicellular plants and probably of animals carries the full amount of genetic information; yet the cells follow a regulated and coordinated program to become different in structure and function during the development of an individual." (Smith 1965, p. 1847.)

The physiological growth of the individual tends to achieve increased differentiation. There is, however, a continued trend toward an integration of differences. The organism functions as an integrated whole, with each part responsive either directly or indirectly to every other part. The Andersons have pointed out that the criteria for physiological growth are *differentiation* and *integration*. This is true not only for a harmonious self but also for a harmonious society.

Through integration there is a participation of the different parts of the body toward goals and the full realization of the *self*. This may be observed in the two-year-old child's manner of eating. Preferred handedness may be noted as food is picked from his plate with one hand while the other hand is used to steady himself or the plate. The fingers function in a specific way. The entire act of getting the food to the mouth is further coordinated with the opening of the mouth as the hand gets closer to it. With increased maturity acts of greater complexity are performed involving increased differentiation and integration of the different parts of the body in service of the self.

Modifications of the Rate and Pattern of Growth.   Although the dynamic force for the rate and pattern of growth is set forth by the genes the child inherits, these can be altered at all stages of life. These alterations or modifications may result from (a) the interacting of the genes, (b) chemical imbalance in the mother during the prenatal stage, (c) interference with fetal development, (d) brain damage, (e) prenatal accidents, (f) accidents at birth, and (g) an environment unfavorable to optimum growth and development.

If, as it now appears, all inheritance, memory and learning are ordained in the codon sequences of DNA and its derivatives, then manipulation of all human behavior is possible by chemical means. This concept sheds new light on growth, development, and education. Anthropological discussions of improvement by controlled breeding may become less important as more is learned about DNA and its derivatives. If man is really to control his own heredity and development, past progress in breeding becomes simply historical. Science now envisions human development by way of three new approaches: by a change in the genetic code before birth, by evolving superhumans, with superbrains and physiques; by drugs, hormones, or enzyme therapy to alleviate imperfections; and finally, the ultimate "triumph," reproduction of man in the laboratory, *in vitro*.

The new microbiological knowledge will be an immense power, far greater than man has ever had. The ability to manipulate life at its source, is power at its ultimate. The ethical, moral, legal, religious, and social issues that will be raised, will set forth new concepts of divinity and the power of the state. For good or evil these discoveries may be the most fateful development in the history of man. McConnel (1966) has attempted to tie the newer research on DNA and its derivatives into a neat package, correlating heredity, learning and memory; in effect all have been a matter of evolutionary phenomena. The bulk of evidence suggests that complex associative learning can be found as far down the phyletic scale as the flatworm (planarian), and that simple forms of learning, such as reactive inhibition and habituation can be found even in the protozoans. He also noted that the centers of speech, sight, balance, and probably emotion are intimately related to the DNA-RNA complex. Not only are these chemicals concerned with genetic coding and replication, but they appear to be the central facets of memory, learning, and thought. As Sontag (1950) has pointed out, this is true for human beings as well as for lower forms of life.

As far as science is concerned, all that we can be sure of is that genetically a child brings into the world a physical and psychological potential for develop-ment. The psychological and cultural influences of the home, school, and society become very important with birth. These will have a profound and lasting effect upon his physical, psychological, mental, and emotional development and upon his total behavior patterns at all stages of his development. The effects of en-vironmental forces and conditions are inescapable. The influence of any environ-mental factor will depend upon the nature of the hereditary materials upon which it operates; conversely, any single hereditary factor may operate differ-ently between individuals as a result of environmental conditions (Kallman, 1956-57). The adverse effects upon the child of growing up in an impoverished environment have been well stated by Bruner (1959, p. 91):

> In general an impoverished environment, one with diminished heterogeneity and a reduced set of opportunities for manipulation and discrimination, produces an adult organism with reduced abilities to discriminate, with stunted strategies for coping with roundabout solutions, with less taste for exploratory behavior, and with a notably reduced tendency to draw inferences that serve to cement the disparate events of its environment such as between the light of a candle flame and the likelihood of its burning when you put your nose to it.

Character and personality develop gradually through interaction of heredity and environment. The educator will be helped in his task if he realizes that the success of the educational process depends upon the right environment being provided for the optimal development of the heredity endowment of each child. This will require diverse environments if the best results are to be obtained. Human welfare, both with individuals and with societies, is predicated upon a desirable genetic endowment of human populations. Health and disease, physical and mental, depend upon the interaction of heredity and environment. That an appalling amount of human misery may be largely due to defective heredity cannot be gainsaid. Measures on both the genetic and environmental sides must be taken if this misery is to be alleviated rather than enhanced.

Maturation and Learning

Attempts to define maturation have met with considerable difficulty. Early scientific usage of the term by geneticists emphasized development occurring within the germ cell prior to the process of fertilization. Gesell (1933) was one of the first students of child development to broaden the definition to include those developmental phenomena that seem to occur in an orderly manner with-out the influence of external stimulation. Hall-Quest (1957, p. 612) calls it "a process toward an integrated self," and states further:

> . . . . At any moment of organic maturation new traits and powers appear which are not only the sum of separate gains of development but wholly new manifestations of realized organic potentiality. Thus, ability to conceptualize is more than a sum of particular sense perceptions; it is a new, integrated, emergent power of the maturer organism. This emergent characteristic is well illustrated in

the individual's power to reproduce or procreate. Not until certain anatomical and glandular maturation has been attained is parenthood possible. Similar emergence of powers is true of the individual's mental life.

Olson (1959) uses the term to cover the anatomic, physiologic and chemical changes of the body, involving a period of time and not appreciably influenced by experiences.

Maturation is more than physiological changes; it also incorporates functional changes. As the individual's life equipment reaches its ultimate growth, it is used for more complex actions. That is, units which were at one time independent or self-contained, subordinate themselves in the service of higher-level functions. This may be observed in the young child who has learned to walk; then he learns to run, to hop, and skip. All these activities are later combined into a larger or more complex form of behavior when he learns to ride a bicycle.

The Significance of Maturation. Learning and maturation are closely interwoven in all aspects of the child's development. This may be noted in the development of the infant child. It is a matter of common observation that three- and four-month-old infants, regardless of the opportunity for practice usually cannot sit alone and that most normal eight-month-olds can sit alone. However, Spitz (1945) has shown that the eight-month-old child does not sit by himself if he has been completely denied the opportunity of practice.

In several early experiments twins were used as subjects in studying the effects of maturation as distinguished from learning (Gesell and Thompson, 1929; Hilgard, 1932). This is known as the method of co-twin control. This method involves giving one of a selected pair of identical twins a certain type of experience, while the training is delayed for the other member of the pair. In the study by Gesell and Thompson, beginning at the age of 46 weeks, Twin T was given training in stair climbing, while Twin C was given no such training. After six weeks of training, Twin T climbed the case in 26 seconds. At the beginning of the fifty-third week, Twin C was given training in stair climbing. At this time she climbed the staircase in 45 seconds, but after two weeks of training she was able to climb the stairs in ten seconds. Thus Twin C rapidly reached an achievement level as high as that attained by Twin T, primarily because of her advanced maturation when she began practice in stair climbing. Similar results have been obtained with infants in studies involving manipulating cubes, cutting with scissors, language development, memorization, and the like.

In phylogenetic functions such as crawling, standing, and walking training may be useful in establishing neurological balance. In some aspects, however, it may be a detriment, especially when such training is begun at too early a stage and is carried on with considerable persistence. The studies involving twins show that progress in learning activities such as stair climbing depends to a marked degree upon maturation with opportunities to practice after the individual has reached the desired maturational level. Readiness for learning such activities as roller skating and tricycle riding depends upon maturation and experience. One should not interpret the results of studies bearing on the role of maturation as implying that early opportunities for children's learning simple motor skills or for language acquisition are unimportant, and that maturation tends to take care of development so that learning takes place readily when practice is given at the desired time. Such an interpretation fails to take into consideration more subtle results of early and late training. How, for example were interpersonal relations affected? How did the practice or delay of practice affect the self concepts of these children? How did these experiences affect the creativeness, initiative, or desire to learn?

The Role of Learning.   Learning is usually defined in terms of changes that have taken place as a result of experience. Hurlock (1964) states: *"Learning* is development that comes from exercise and effort on the part of the individual" (p. 15). The sound of the fire truck going down the street has meaning to the child because of past experiences in seeing and hearing the fire truck moving down the street. Learning involves responses to stimuli or situations in one's environment. Children living in environments where opportunities are limited

Child development is enhanced by varying experiences.   (Courtesy Eliot
Pearson, Tufts University.)

will not develop their hereditary potentialities to the degree that those living in environments where there are better educational opportunities.

Growth and learning are not separate entities. They represent a unity which operates throughout the entire period of development. Millard (1958) illustrates this with a reading growth curve and a growth curve for weight. These curves, shown in Figure 2-3, show a striking similarity when placed together.

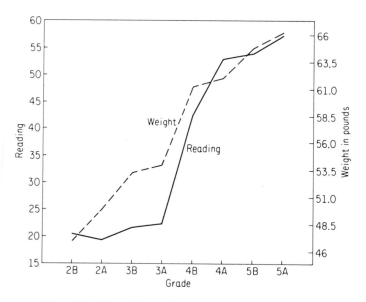

Figure 2-3. Illustrating similarity in design of curves in reading and weight (Millard).

Learning may take the form of training, in which the responses of the individual are directed in harmony with a purpose. In the home, parents begin special types of training at an early age so that the child will behave in the manner that society expects him to behave. However, much of the learning of the child takes the form of imitation; the child imitates through his speech and overt behavior older children and adults in his environment. Many individuals and institutions contribute to teaching the child the cultural patterns of his group. The term *enculturation* is used to describe the process whereby the child learns the cultural ways his groups expect him to follow. The process of enculturation requires the child to adjust his innate biological characteristics to the prevailing cultural practices in his society (Herskovits, 1948, p. 401). Homo sapiens is the only biological group that developed a culture requiring each newborn member to modify his biological characteristics according to the cultural expectations of the different groups making up his cultural environment.

Behavioral Changes Resulting from Learning.   Some specific kinds of learning will be treated more fully in subsequent chapters dealing with different aspects of growth and development. The main kinds of behavioral changes resulting from learning will be presented here. First of all we note significant changes in behavior involving motor skills. The child learns to ride a tricycle, followed by learning to ride a bicycle, and later learning to drive an automobile. He learns to swim, jump rope, climb, dance and to perform many sensorimotor skills involving the use of tools.

The famous Russian physiologist Ivan Pavlov (1849-1936) studied the process of salivary conditioning by introducing an irrelevant stimulus, the sound of a bell, just prior to the presentation of food. He noted that after a number of such presentations the flow of saliva would occur in response to the sound of the bell when no food was presented. While this experiment in itself may seem to offer us little about the role of learning, we note that much learned behavior can be explained by this process, known as *conditioning*.

Another kind of learning that occurs relatively early in life is a progressive discrimination between stimuli and a progressive differentiation of responses to different stimuli. The infant child is soon able to differentiate the mother who feeds and cares for his needs from other members of the family. At a later stage he responds differently to the father, who plays with him when he arrives at home. This progressive differentiation occurs involving older sisters and brothers as well as others with whom he comes into contact. When he goes to school he acquires reading skills through a process of progressive differentiation. Throughout all stages of learning, he is continuously growing intellectually through progressive discrimination of things and conditions in his environment.

Another variety of behavioral change that occurs through learning can best be described as *organization*. The process of concept formation, described in Chapter 6, involves classifying materials encountered in different experiences into categories. The orange, apple, peach, and pear are referred to as *fruit*. The chair, bed, and table together form the single category *furniture*. The process of organization enables the individual to code large amounts of materials for effective use at a later date when it is needed. It is important in perceptual learning, since it enables us to grasp meanings readily.

Reasoning and creative achievements involve a superior sort of organization. In reasoning or problem-solving behavior, different combinations of experiences are brought together into an alignment with one another so as to arrive at a particular goal or solution; while in creative behavior materials from various experiences are brought together so as to produce new or novel results. In the creative experiences we can also see the individual portraying his psychological world, which is a most important aspect of learning. This is implied in the following statement from Goodenough and Tyler (1959, p. 124): "Probably the most basic and important task each human being faces is to organize his own particular psychological world."

Some Principles of Growth

Every species, whether human or animal, follows a pattern of development peculiar to that species. This pattern may be noted from the beginning of a new life with the fertilized egg throughout various stages and ending with senescence and death. Since human development during the fetal period is orderly, it is possible to give a "timetable" of the development of structures and functions. This timetable may be altered by unusual or abnormal conditions within the uterus. The study of mice by Ginsberg and Hovda, presented earlier in this chapter, shows that the same genes under different environmental conditions will produce different results. Thus we note that developmental irregularities may result from either faulty genes or unfavorable environmental conditions in the uterus. The interaction of heredity and environment must be taken into consideration in an attempt to set forth principles of growth.

The Direction of Development. The general direction of growth moves in a progressive manner from the head region downward. Note the size of the head of the organism during the early stages of prenatal development shown in Figure 2-4. The head of the newborn child comprises approximately one-third of his total weight. This developmental direction is referred to as the cephalocaudal (head-to-tail) sequence. A correlated type of developmental direction is the proximodistal (near-to-far) pattern, which means that development proceeds progressively from the axis outward. The extremities are the last to mature. In terms of morphological changes, the later years of life are marked by the same order of deterioration.

Figure 2-4. In the early stages of parental development, the head develops first. (Adapted from *Heredity and Prenatal Development*, a McGraw-Hill Text-Film.)

These developmental directions are characteristics of both structural and functional changes. At a given time in the infant's development, the head, shoulders, and arms are more developed than the legs and feet. At a functional level one may expect the infant to display at a given time better control of his arms than his legs, and he will coordinate the gross movements of the arms before he can make good use of his fingers.

Development is Continuous. It was pointed out earlier that growth and development begin with the fertilization of the egg and significant changes take place throughout life until senescence or death, although this development is not constant with the different structures and functions. For example, in vocabulary growth the first year seems unimportant. Actually the child is experimenting with making sounds and is gradually acquiring a comprehensible vocabulary through associating words with objects and certain kinds of experiences in his everyday environment. The normal child growing in a stimulating environment in which a variety of words are used will develop a considerable vocabulary by the time he is six years of age. There is a continuous rapid development of the vocabulary throughout the elementary school years. This growth proceeds at a decelerated pace through high school and college and may persist throughout the adult years unless the individual remains mentally alert and keeps encountering new words in his experiences.

The appearance of baby teeth seems to occur quite suddenly. This, however, is not the case. Teeth may be observed in the jaw of the fifth fetal month, but do not mature to the point that they are ready to cut through the gums until around the fifth month after birth. The apparent growth spurts are not as irregular in nature as they appear, especially when we take into consideration the more subtle aspects of different growth features. The fact that development is continuous is most important to those confronted with child training and guidance. By understanding growth sequences, one is able to better predict growth at different stages. Also, it is well to realize that what happens at one stage in the child's development has an important influence on the following stage.

The Rate of Growth Is Not Even. Although growth is described as continuous, specific aspects of growth do not occur at the same rate at different times. This was pointed out in the case of the development of the teeth. It may also be observed in the growth in height and weight. The educational and psychological aspects of growth are also uneven. The individual's maturational level at a particular time will vary with the different characteristics or abilities being tested. This uneven development is illustrated in Figure 2-5 for specific growth factors. The pupil shown in Figure 2-5 is superior in his emotional and social development. Earlier studies of mental growth led to the conclusion that the IQ was constant, indicating that the increase from year to year in intelligence followed a constant or stable course. Later studies showed that this was not the case, rather considerable variability was manifested in test scores, especially during the preschool years. Bayley (1955) concludes from retests of the same children over a period of years that "intelligence is a dynamic succession of delaying functions, with

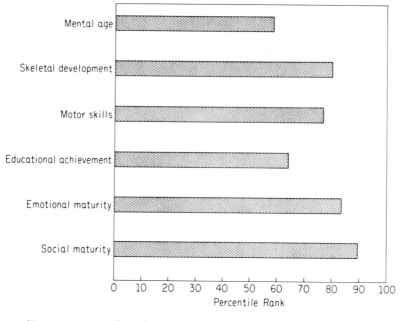

Figure 2-5. A profile of the maturity of one pupil in several areas of growth.

the more advanced and complex functions in the hierarchy depending on the prior maturing of earlier simpler ones (given of course, normal conditions of care)."

Children Differ in Rate of Growth. Although children tend to follow a somewhat similar pattern in their development, each child grows at his own unique rate; each child is continuously changing in his own way. Bayley's study (1956) of individual pattern of development in height and weight presents evidence for differences in rate of maturation. Many children who enter school at the age of six are too immature to begin reading or to deal successfully with other educational tasks that confront first grade children. Various growth curves show that some children develop faster than others. This has been illustrated by Olson (1947) in growth curves for reading. As Figure 2-6 indicates, James, John, and Billy show approximately the same reading ability at the age of six years. However, significant differences appear with further educational growth.

It is important for teachers to understand individual differences in growth rate. Parents frequently overlook this basic principle when they make comparisons of the development of their own children. They should realize that Sammy, who is a late maturer and thus develops physically slower than his older brother developed, may actually end up taller than his older brother. The timing of the growth spurt, which takes place just prior to the beginning of adolescence, will vary considerably with individuals of the same sex. The failure of teachers and

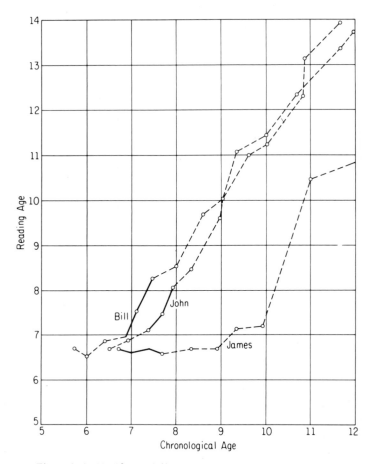

Figure 2-6. Significant differences in growth in reading ability
appear among children similar in reading ability at age six.
(After Olson.)

parents to recognize these differences in rate of growth and timing of certain
growth features is often a source of misinterpretation and faulty guidance.

All Growth Is Interrelated. Although we speak and write of physical
growth, mental growth, emotional growth, and other aspects of growth, we
should realize at all times that it is the total individual who is growing. Bijou
and Baer (1961, pp. 14-15) state: "The developing child may be adequately
regarded, in conceptual terms, as a cluster of interrelated responses interacting
with stimuli." Some of the stimuli emanate from the child's external environment, some from the child's own responses, and some from his biological structure and functioning. Thus the individual is not only a living creature responding
to forces and conditions in his own body, he is also the source of many of his
responses. From this point of view he is a part of his own environment. His
behavior at home and his achievement at school are functions of the total self.

The growth of the child as a unified whole may be observed in his growth in the ability to creep, crawl, and walk. In the average child this growth will be accompanied by wider contacts with his physical environment, enlarged interests, increased attention span, and changed social behavior. These changes are furthermore accompanied by changes in the personal self, observable in increased independence. This interrelation may be observed at all stages of life and may be noted in a reverse order in late life when the individual's environment becomes more limited along with increased dependence. The interrelation may be observed in the educational achievement of the child at school. The results of a study by Tilton (1947) indicate that the total growth of the child must be considered if remedial activities in the elementary school are to be effective.

The Significance of Age

There is general agreement among psychologists that development occurs as a result of maturation and learning. It is further recognized that maturation and learning involve a time element and that important changes take place with age. Development can be described as a rhythmic flow of quantitative and qualitative changes proceeding in specific directions in a predictable sequence.

Quantitative and Qualitative Changes. Six classifications of change in human anatomic growth are described by Meredith (1965). The first of these is *complexity*. The individual develops from a single cell to a multicellular embryo to a fetus with partially developed appendages, to the neonate with appendages but lacking visible teeth and different bones. This complexity and completeness of development continues after birth through childhood, adolescence, and various stages of maturity.

A third and fourth classification of change referred to by Meredith include *size* and *shape*. Significant changes take place during childhood in height, weight, length, size and number of bones, and volume of organs and glands. Some parts of the body undergo important changes in shape. The heart, for example, passes through its stages as a tube, a helix, and finally a pyramid. The face is short and round, then long, and then proportionally short again. There is an elongation of the larynx as it develops and assumes its permanently elliptical shape.

There are important changes involving *position* in which body organs and segments pass through periods of migration (nerves extended outward, kidneys move upward, testes downward). There are also changes in the position of the heart, stomach, and ovaries. The feet, toes, fingers, and teeth undergo significant changes during the growing period. Most of the organs change by way of all three movements—migrating, tilting, and rotating.

The fifth and sixth changes listed by Meredith involve *pigmentation* and *texture*. The iris of the eyes, hair, skin, and some fibers (as in the heart) follow varying cycles from lightness to darkness. As the organism grows older there is a decrease in tissue water content. The bones of the child are more porous than that of the adult and contain more water content but less mineral. There is a change in water content in the kidney organic materials and in the skin, making the skin less elastic with age.

Measurable Levels of Growth.   Levels of growth are frequently used in comparative approaches to development over some specific period of time. These different levels are based upon age units, which have been determined from measurements taken on large numbers of children representing different chronological ages. For example, dental-age scales have been constructed based upon the number of permanent teeth boys and girls have at different age levels. A boy who has the same number of permanent teeth that the average ten-year-old boy has will have a dental age of ten years, regardless of his chronological age. Growth curves have been constructed to show mental ages (MA), vital ages (VA), height ages (HA), weight ages (WA), dental ages (DA), anatomical ages (AA), emotional ages (EA), social ages (SA), and educational ages (EdA).

These measurable levels of development are useful to those concerned with growth and development at all age levels. However, there are developments at all age levels. However, there are developmental changes involving quality which should be given more attention than is usually given. These qualitative changes are especially important in evaluating developmental changes during the years following maturity and are used in the medical clinic in the evaluation of health and vitality of the different organs of the body during the different stages of maturity.

Identity and the Life Cycle.   Erikson (1959) has developed a useful chart for depicting identity at different stages in the life cycle. This is presented in Figure 2-7. The first year of the child's life is identified with the mother or mother substitute. It is during this time that he establishes a sense of trust, provided he receives the love and attention characteristic of most mother-child situations. From age 1 to 3 he establishes a sense of autonomy through associations with the different members of his family, including close kin and friends. It is essential for him to identify himself as a person and to develop a favorable concept of himself if he is to be successful in developing initiative and responsibility.

The second stage of childhood, beginning around age three, is characterized by the beginnings of role behavior. The child's learning at this stage is eminently intrusive and vigorous. He continues to explore his world and learns more about himself and his role in the family structure. The third stage is in reality an extension of the second, with the child more clearly defining his role or roles and directing his activities toward the satisfaction of goals. He assumes increased initiative and more responsibility. Close identification with members of the family continues, although almost complete autonomy is attained. He is at this time interested in individuals outside his immediate home, although he may display fear or distrust of strangers. A fourth stage in the child's growth is the school age and task identification period. "Children now also attach themselves to teachers and the parents of other children, and they want to watch and imitate people representing occupations which they can grasp—firemen, policemen, gardeners, plumbers, and garbage men." (Erikson, 1968, p. 122.)

Growth Period	1	2	3	4	5	6	7	8
VIII Maturity								INTEGRITY vs. DESPAIR
VII Adulthood							GENERATIVITY vs. STAGNATION	
VI Later Adolescence						INTIMACY vs. ISOLATION		
V Early Adolescence	Temporal Perspective vs. Time Confusion	Self-Certainty vs. Self-Consciousness	Role Experimentation vs. Role Fixation	Apprenticeship vs. Work Paralysis	IDENTITY vs. IDENTITY CONFUSION	Sexual Polarization vs. Bisexual Confusion	Leader and Followership vs. Authority Confusion	Ideological Commitment vs. Confusion of Values
IV 6–11 Years				INDUSTRY vs. INFERIORITY	Task Identification vs. Sense of Futility			
III 4–5 Years			INITIATIVE vs. GUILT		Anticipation of Roles vs. Role Inhibition			
II 1–3 Years		AUTONOMY vs. SHAME, DOUBT			Will to Be Oneself vs. Self-Doubt			
I Infancy – 1st Year	TRUST vs. MISTRUST				Mutual Recognition vs. Autistic Isolation			
Widening Radius of Significant People	1	2	3	4	5	6	7	8

Figure 2-7. Growth period showing identity and the life cycle. (After Erikson, 1968.)

During the early school years the child develops a sense of accomplishment, and for some children a sense of failure which tends to stifle creativeness and a sense of initiative. The sense of identity is developed during the preadolescent and early adolescent years through associations with peers, most frequently like-sexed peers in Western culture. During late adolescence a sense of intimacy is established, normally with an individual of the opposite sex. This may be observed in Western culture through the courtship practices referred to in Chapter One. In a recent study of ninth-grade pupils by Garrison (1966) it was found that getting married, home, family, and children were their greatest concerns about the future (see Table 2-1). All of the girls responding to the question about marriage indicated that they expected to marry, although several girls did not respond to this question. Over 90 percent of the boys indicated that they expected to get married.

TABLE 2-1
Response to Questions About "My Greatest Concerns About the Future"
(After Garrison)

Concerns	Boys, percent	Girls, percent	Average percent
Getting married, home, family, children	18.8	22.7	20.75
Country, nation, world conditions	12.4	12.7	12.55
Atomic war	10.8	14.0	12.4
Career, job	10.8	6.0	8.4
Russia, communism	6.4	9.7	8.05
Integration	3.6	12.0	7.8
Happiness, security, health	10.4	4.7	7.55
Religion	4.4	5.2	4.8
Education	5.2	3.0	4.1
Space travel, reach moon	4.0	4.0	4.0
Miscellaneous	13.2	6.0	9.6

Adulthood is characterized by parental sense and a vocational career, while maturity brings with it a sense of responsibility and integrity. These are important in Western culture. Advanced maturity brings with it a sense of detachment for many individuals, especially when they are forced to withdraw from the world that they have been an integral part of for many years. Special materials dealing with this are presented in Chapter 14.

Summary

The development of the individual begins with the fertilized egg which consists of 46 chromosomes, 23 from the male and 23 from the female. The chromosomes are most important in that they furnish the means by which potentialities are transmitted. Abnormalities of the chromosomes are the basis of many disorders and anomalies. The genes of a special pair of chromosomes determine the sex of the individual; a fertilized egg that receives a Y chromosome from the sperm produces a male baby, while a fertilized egg from an X chromosome from the sperm produces a female baby.

The first law of heredity is that of *segregation,* which points out that the paired genes derived from the two parents do not blend but retain their individuality and segregate unaffected by each other to pass into different gametes. Mendel's discovery of dominant and recessive traits led to further discoveries, including the law of linkage. More recent studies have shown that genes are not unalterable, indicating the environmental factors may operate from the time of the fertilization of the egg cell. The rate and pattern of growth can be altered at all stages of life. These alterations may result from (a) the interaction of the genes, (b) chemical imbalance in the mother during pregnancy, (c) interference with fetal development, (d) brain damage, (e) prenatal accidents, (f) accidents at birth, and (g) an environment unfavorable to optimum growth and development.

Learning and maturation are interwoven in all aspects of the child's development. Studies using the method of co-twin control have shown that there is a close relation between learning and maturation, especially during the early years. Learning depends upon opportunity and stimulation as well as maturation. Where opportunities are limited the child will not develop his full hereditary potentialities. The acquisition of a culture depends upon learning with many institutions and individuals making contributions.

The interaction of heredity and environment may be observed in principles of growth set forth. Some of these are (a) growth tends to follow a cephalocaudal pattern and a proximodistal pattern; (b) development is continuous, beginning with the fertilization of the egg; (c) the rate of growth is not even; (d) children differ in rate of growth; and (e) all growth is interrelated.

Important developmental changes take place with age. Six classifications of change in human anatomic growth are described. These are changes in complexity, size and shape, position, pigmentation, and texture. Levels of growth are used in comparative approaches to development over a period of time. These are usually expressed quantitatively, although there are important qualitative changes that occur at different stages in the life span.

A chart, developed by Erikson, is useful for depicting identity at different stages in the life cycle. This chart shows a widening radius of significant people influencing the individual with an increase in age. This begins with the mother and extends to the larger community. There are also significant feelings and attitudes shown, beginning with a sense of trust in the parents and leading to parental sense and a sense of integrity in adulthood and maturity.

The chief importance of the chromosomes is that they provide the means by which potentialities are transmitted, for it is in the chromosomes that the genes are found and these furnish the basic hereditary materials. A gene is a small region in a chromosome composed of a giant nucleic acid molecule or part of a molecule, which according to Strauss (1960) consists mainly of a chemical, deoxyribonucleic acid, or DNA, which contains nucleotides or four bases (thymine, cytosine, adenine, and quanine) which, in various combinations seem to be capable of encoding all the characteristics that an organism transmits from one generation to another.

In some cases the organism has more or less than 46 chromosomes because of abnormal chromosome behavior in the ovaries or in the sperm of the father. Studies in genetics indicate that abnormalities of chromosomes are the basis of many disorders and anomalies in children. The chromosomes have been studied by characterizing the location of the centromere (a characteristic constriction in the chromosome), the overall length of the chromosomes, and the length of the arms on either side of the centromere. The ratio between the lengths of the two arms separated by the centromere is constant for any one chromosome pair (Kang, 1966, p. 60).

"Silly, eh son? After a few years you won't think so. Then when you get old you'll think it foolish."

References

Adler, A. *Understanding Human Nature.* New York: Premier Books, Fawcett, 1957.

Bayley, Nancy. "Individual Patterns of Development," *Child Development,* Vol. 27 (1956), pp. 45-74.

———. "On the Growth of Intelligence," *American Psychologist,* Vol. 10 (1955), pp. 805-818.

Beadle, G., and Muriel Beadle. *The Language of Life.* New York: Doubleday, 1966.

Bijou, S. W., and D. M. Baer. *Child Development, a Systematic and Empirical Theory.* New York: Appleton, 1961.

Bruner, J. S. "The Cognitive Consequences of Early Sensory Deprivation," *Psychosomatic Medicine,* Vol. 21 (1959), pp. 89-95.

Carmichael, L. "The Onset of Early Development of Behavior," L. Carmichael, ed., in *Manual of Child Psychology,* 2nd ed. New York: Wiley, 1954, pp. 60-185.

Carr, D. H. "Chromosome Studies in Abortuses and Stillborn Infants," *Lancet,* Vol. 2 (1963), pp. 603-606.

Erikson, H. *Identity, Youth and Crisis.* New York: Norton, 1968, p. 94.

Garrison, K. C. "A Study of the Aspirations and Concerns of Ninth-Grade Pupils from the Public Schools of Georgia," *Journal of Social Psychology,* Vol. 69 (1966), pp. 245-252.

Gesell, A., and Helen Thompson. "Learning and Growth in Identical Twins: An Experimental Study on the Method of Co-Twin Control," *Genetic Psychology Monographs,* Vol. 6 (1929), pp. 1-124.

Ginsberg, B. E., and R. B. Hovda. "On the Physiology of Gene-Controlled Audiogenic Seizures in Mice," *Anatomical Record,* Vol. 99 (1947), pp. 65-66.

Goodenough, Florence L., and Leona E. Tyler. *Developmental Psychology,* 3rd ed. New York: Appleton, 1959.

Hall-Quest, A. L. "Genetic Psychology," *Collier's Encyclopedia,* Vol. 8 (1957), pp. 611-613.

Herskovits, M. J. *Man and His Works: The Science of Cultural Anthropology.* New York: Knopf, 1948.

Hurlock, Elizabeth. *Child Development,* 4th ed. New York: McGraw-Hill, 1964.

Jost, H., and L. W. Sontag. "The Genetic Factor in Autonomous Nervous System Function," *Psychosomatic Medicine,* Vol. 6 (1944), pp. 308-310.

Kallman, F. J. "The Genetics of Human Behavior," *American Journal of Psychiatry,* Vol. 113 (1956-57), pp. 496-501.

Kang, Ellen S. "The Genetic Basis of Some Abnormalities in Children," *Children,* Vol. 13, No. 2 (1966), pp. 6-62.

Kornberg, A. "The Synthesis of DNA," *Scientific American,* Vol. 219 (1968), pp. 64-78.

Lewis, E. B. *Science* (Dec. 13, 1963), p. 1493.

McConnell, J. V. "Learning in Invertebrates: Comparative Psychology," *Annual Review of Psychology,* Vol. 28 (1966), pp. 107-133.

Menninger, K. A. *The Human Mind,* 3rd ed. New York: Knopf, 1961.

Meredith, H. V. "Physical Growth," *Collier's Encyclopedia,* Vol. 11 (1965), p. 475.

Millard, C. V. *Child Growth and Development in the Elementary School Years,* rev. ed. Boston: Heath, 1958.

Montagu, A. *Human Heredity,* 2nd ed. Cleveland: World, 1963.

Olson, W. C. *Child Development,* 2nd ed. Boston: Heath, 1959.

Polani, P. E., J. H. Briggs, C. E. Ford, C. N. Clark, and J. M. Berg. "A Mongol Girl with 46 Chromosomes," *Lancet,* Vol. 1 (April 1960), pp. 1721-1722.

Science News Letter, Vol. 89 (Jan. 1966), p. 6.

Smith, H. H. "Meetings," *Science,* Vol. 150 (1965), pp. 1847-1849.

Smith, D. W., K. Patan, E. Therman, and S. L. Inhorn. "A New Autosomal Trisoly Syndrome Multiple Congenital Anomalies," *Journal of Pediatrics,* Vol. 57 (1960), pp. 338-345.

Sontag, L. W. "The Genetics of Differences in Psychosomatic Patterns in Childhood," *American Journal of Orthopsychiatry,* Vol. 20 (1950), pp. 479-489.

Spitz, R. A. "Hospitalism: An Inquiry into the Genesis of Psychiatric Conditions in Early Life," in O. Fenichel (ed.), *The Psychoanalytic Study of The Child.* New York: International Universities Press, 1954, pp. 53-74.

Snyder, L. H. "Heredity, *Collier's Encyclopedia,* Vol. 12 (1965), p. 70.

Strauss, B. S. *An Outline of Chemical Genetics.* Philadelphia: Saunders, 1960.

Tjio, J. H., and A. Levan. "The Chromosome Number of Man," *Hereditas,* Vol. 42 (1956), pp. 1-2

Tilton, J. W. "An Experimental Effort to Change the Achievement Test Profile," *Journal of Experimental Education,* Vol. 15 (1947), pp. 318-323.

Part **II**

The Course
of Development

Chapter 3

Prenatal Period and Infancy

At different stages in development certain traits stand out more conspicuously than others. This makes it possible to mark off major periods, each of which is characterized by a certain form of development distinguishing it from other periods. Because of individual variations in rate of growth and other characteristics, the age limits for these periods cannot be accurately stated. The point that separates one age limit from another is arbitrary and could readily and accurately be shifted forward or backward (English, 1957).

This chapter deals with the first two major development periods with their characteristic forms and significant elements related to them. These provide the foundation and background for the different aspects of growth and development presented in subsequent chapters. Physical and motor development, the development of motivational patterns, language development, the development of intellectual patterns, and the development of cognition have their beginning in infancy. These can be better understood when the student has a better understanding of the influences of prenatal life, and the importance and significance of infancy.

The Prenatal Period

Embryologists usually divided prenatal life into three periods. The first period, referred to as the *germinal period*, consists of the first week or two after fertilization—the time of fusion of the nuclei of the two parent cells. During most of this period the ovum remains a free organism. It is not attached to the mother and does not seem to get any sustenance from her. It does not increase in size, although important internal changes are taking place. The fertilized cell divides and redivides so as to form a globular mass of cells. The development of a small cavity in the interior of the mass is the first indication of a change of form leading toward the embryonic period.

The embryonic period is the time from the attachment of the ovum to the mother to the time when the general form and structure of the body parts are formed. This period lasts from around the end of the second week to the end of the sixth week. A baby's brain begins to form about the second week after conception; the most critical period lasts until about the eleventh week. Factors which cause birth defects during the critical first few months of pregnancy frequently cause mental retardation. During this period there is a very rapid growth in size, and differention of the bodily parts is produced to about 95 percent completion. By the end of this period a truly human being is formed that can be differentiated by the trained observer from the monkey and the other forms of mammals that may resemble man. However, the new life is very different in body proportions from the adult, child, or even the newborn baby.

The fetal period is the third and last stage of prenatal development. It includes about the last 32 weeks of the prenatal life of the normal individual. This period is characterized by the rapid growth in "absolute" size; with the individual showing a greater increase in percentage of growth than at any other similar period of time. During the early part of the fetal period, growth is characterized mainly by an increase in the number of cells through cell division; during the latter part of this period the rate of cell division diminishes and increase in size is accomplished through an increase in the size of the individual cells.

Prenatal Influences.   Many factors and conditions present during the mother's pregnancy, as well as conditions at birth can have an adverse effect on the developing offspring. These factors have frequently been confused with hereditary factors; although it is not possible to draw a clear line of demarcation between the operation of heredity and environment, especially during the prenatal life of the organism. Detecting the cause of birth defects and of prenatal and natal birth injuries has become one of the most promising fields of medical research. Discoveries thus far have shown that there is much the expectant mother can do to improve her chances of having a healthy, normal baby, with an undamaged brain. The obstetrician has within his power the prevention of many crippling conditions if he can care for the expectant mother during this period.

Emotional states of mother.   That the emotional state of the mother may have significant influences on the child during the prenatal period is borne out by a number of studies. Sontag (1950) bearing on this indicates that babies born to mothers suffering from emotional disturbances tended to have more than the usual difficulties in the weeks following birth, including gastrointestinal upsets and other illnesses. The infants of mothers who were emotionally disturbed during pregnancy frequently exhibit behavior characteristics of an irritable and hyperactive autonomic nervous system. Sontag early pointed out that the presence of feeding difficulties of a motor or secretory nature from birth must presume their etiology and basic disturbances during intrauterine life. In cases of prenatal development of such a condition, prolonged nervous and emotional disturbances of the mother during the later months of pregnancy seem to be important (p. 1001).

Malnutrition.   Malnutrition of the mother deprives the fetal organism of necessary food from the maternal blood stream. The effects of this were clearly shown in an early study by Ebbs and his co-workers (1942). They compared the offspring of 120 pregnant women on a poor diet with 90 pregnant women of the same socioeconomic status on a good diet. In every comparison the mothers and their babies who were on a good diet did better than the mothers and their babies who were on a poor diet. The results set forth in Table 3-1 showed that an inadequate diet seriously interfered with the efficiency of the pregnant mother as well as the welfare and development of the fetus. These findings have been confirmed by many more recent studies.

One major purpose of prenatal care is to check for the likelihood of toxemia and other complications and to prevent them if possible. The maternity and infant legislation enacted in 1963 and revised in 1965 has done much to reduce crippling conditions that have their beginning during the prenatal period among the poverty-stricken families. Malformations including congenital blindness and other visual abnormalities frequently appear where the mother's diet is deficient in carotene and vitamins.

Infections and viruses. Growth in recognition that maternal virus infection can damage the fetus is one of the dramatic developments of the mid-century. The fetus does not develop antibodies, and immunization does not become active until sometime after birth. Interest in maternal viral infection has been

TABLE 3-1
Comparison of the Effects for Expectant Mothers with a Poor and Good Diet

		Diet	
		Poor	Good
Prenatal maternal record	Poor-Bad	36.0 %	9.0 %
Condition during labor	Poor-Bad	24.0 %	3.0 %
Duration of the first stage of labor	Primapara	20.3 hours	11.1 hours
	Multipara	15.2 hours	9.5 hours
Convalescence	Poor-Bad	11.5 %	3.5 %
Record of babies during first			
two weeks	Poor-Bad	14.0 %	0.0 %
Illness of Babies during First			
Six Months			
Frequent colds		21.0 %	4.7 %
Bronchitis		4.2 %	1.5 %
Pneumonia		5.5 %	1.5 %
Rickets		5.5 %	0.0 %
Tetany		4.2 %	0.0 %
Dystrophy		7.0 %	1.5 %
Anemia		25.0 %	9.4 %
Deaths		3.0 %	0.0 %
Miscarriages and Infant Deaths			
Miscarriages		7.0 %	0.0 %
Stillbirths		4.0 %	0.0 %
Deaths:			
Pneumonia		2.0 %	0.0 %
Prematurity		1.0 %	0.0 %
Prematures		9.0 %	2.0 %

SOURCE: *Milbank Memorial Fund Quarterly*, Vol. 20 (January 1962), pp. 35–36.

acute since it was first demonstrated that German measles in the mother during the early months of pregnancy can result in malformation and mental defect in the fetus. Data presented by Swan (1948) showed that if the mother contracts rubella (German measles) during the first four months of pregnancy the chances are three to one that she will give birth to a congenitally defective child. Also, smallpox, chicken pox, mumps, scarlet fever, erysipelas, and recurrent fever in the pregnant mother can have a deleterious effect upon the developing fetus (Goodpasture, 1942).

Infection from the parent—especially syphilis in its active phase—affects the fetal nervous system; although the results of such an infectious condition may not become apparent until some time after birth. A wasting disease in the mother such as cancer or tuberculosis may deny the fetus necessary food. Maternal toxemia and eclampsia may cause insufficient oxygen in the blood (anoxia) of the modern infant. There is no known cause in at least half the cases of all of the children born each year with birth defects and with brain damage. Dr. Gordon Brown of the University of Michigan, School of Public Health, suggests that viruses are the most logical suspect (Beck, 1968, p. 76).

Drugs. In addition to diseases which are closely related to birth defects, there are many drugs that may be harmful to the fetus. At one time it was thought that the placenta, the organ which forms inside the uterus to nourish the unborn infant, filtered out infections agents, drugs, and other substances that could harm the unborn child. It is now known that injurious, as well as nourishing substances, can pass through the placenta into the developing child. Some of these materials, especially certain viruses and drugs, have far greater effect on the immature tissues of the unborn baby than they do on the mother (Beck, 1968, p. 40). The ill effects of thalidomide in 1961 and 1962 gave a loud alarm to the medical profession of the possible dangers of other drugs and medicines. Pregnant mothers are today warned of the dangers of drugs as simple as aspirin, especially during the first three months of pregnancy.

Radiation and Rh influences. Radiation has been found to be an important influence on the offspring (Yamazaki, 1954). This was observed in the effects of the Hiroshima and Nagasaki areas following the atomic bombings during World War II.

The Rh factors, so named because they were first discovered in the blood of a rhesus monkey, may produce an incompatibility in the blood of the mother and child. When a mother has no Rh factors (Rh-negative) has a baby who has Rh factors (Rh-positive), a substance from the baby stimulates the development and substance in the mother which, in time, may act upon the blood cells of the baby and prevent them from distributing sufficient oxygen. This deprivation of oxygen leads to an alteration of the infant's development. The Rh disease has been found in about one in every 150 to 200 full-term deliveries. However, medical advancements have virtually eliminated this as a factor producing brain damage or other damaging conditions when adequate services and safeguards are provided.

Smoking. According to the report of the Surgeon General's Committee on Smoking and Health (1962), women who smoke cigarettes tend to have babies of lower birth weight and a greater number of premature deliveries than non-smoking women. Over two decades ago Hesse (1946) pointed out that nicotine absorbed by the smoker acts upon the ganglia of the autonomic nervous system and upon the respiratory center; it increases the acidity of the gastrointestinal tract; it constricts the arteries, thereby increasing blood pressure; it causes the heart to beat faster; and it produces irritation and congestion of all organ membranes. The maximum effect according to Sontag and Richards (1938) seems to appear between the eighth and twelfth minute after the cigarette has been smoked, and cardiovascular response is more marked after the eighth month of pregnancy.

Position before birth. The position of the embryo and fetus before birth may under certain conditions adversely affect the development of the fetus. A relatively common defect is a bone malformation in the legs or feet, probably resulting in some cases at least from lack of movement of the fetus during the later stages of pregnancy. The birth process itself can endanger the normalcy of the organism. It is during the months just preceding birth and the period of birth where good medical care can prevent many crippling conditions.

Lack of good medical care. One of the dangers of the lack of good medical care of expectant mothers is PKU (defined above), a body-chemistry error that frequently leads to severe mental retardation. Prior to the comparatively recent development of the low phenylalanine diet, most known PKU patients were severely retarded inmates of institutions. And, although much remains to be learned about the control of PKU, infants who show a rise in phenylalanine in the blood shortly after birth should be placed on a special diet that includes a powdered formula that contains a minimum of phenylalanine and foods such as citrus foods that contain no amino acid.

Glandular factors. Based on a two-year study at the Royal Victoria Infirmary, Newcastle-on-Tyne Vallace-Owen and Wilson concluded that more than four out of five women who give birth to deformed babies are apparently latent diabetics (Silcock, 1967). A latent diabetic mother is one with excess anti-insulin in her blood but without the normal symptoms of the disease. Starting in 1965, the investigators found that 28 of 32 mothers of deformed children had an excess of anti-insulin substance, while only 14 of 50 mothers of normal children had an excess of the substance.

The studies cited indicate that the mental and physical health of the mother is important to the well-being of the infant. In a study by Rosen and others (1968) the characteristics of mothers of low-birth-weight infants as compared to mothers of normal full-term infants were as follows:

1. The mothers were more careless about their health.
2. The mothers were more apt to have a history of previous low-weight births.
3. There was a more frequent history of psychiatric illness.

4. The age of mothers is usually under 20 years or over 35 years.
5. Mothers frequently weighed under 120 pounds before pregnancy.
6. Mothers were more prone to toxemia.
7. There was a higher risk of untreated syphillis.
8. Mothers more likely to be febrile with premature rupture of membranes.

The Premature Infant. As of 1966 it was estimated that 30 percent of all expectant mothers in the United States receive no prenatal care. The most obvious effect of lack of prenatal care is the likelihood of the offspring being born prematurely. There is some relatively recent evidence that prescribed amounts of alcohol consumed by the mother is helpful in the prevention of premature births, (*Time,* 1968). Premature contractions were eliminated by having the patient drink a prescribed amount of whiskey daily. Later refinements led to intravenous doses of alcohol. No affect on the infant was noted.

An infant is considered premature if he is born between 28 and 38 weeks. Additional evidence of prematurity is birth weight of less than 5½ pounds or head circumference of less than 33 centimeters. In general, the smaller the infant at birth, the less chance he has of survival. Eichenlaub (1956) noted that an infant weighing 3 pounds and 5 ounces has four times as good a chance of surviving an infant weighing less than this.

One of the dangers associated with the child born prematurely is PKU, which as we have seen is an inborn disease of protein metabolism. The disease is transmitted by a single recessive autosomal gene. It is considered a rare disease, since it occurs only in about four persons in 100,000 and causes only about 15 percent of the cases of mental retardation (Lyght, 1966). In the normal person phenylalanine is converted into tryosine. In an individual with PKU this conversion fails to take place or is greatly reduced causing excessive quantities of phenylalanine to accumulate in body fluids. The central nervous damage which results in mental retardation, due to this accumulation of phenylalanine is not completely understood. It is now felt that if dietary control is begun within the first three months of life the probability is good that mentality will develop normally, barring other problems. Once mental deficiency has become established, however, the outlook for improvement is poor. The treatment consists of a diet very low in phenylalanine found in proteins.

Differences have been found in the health status of premature and full-term babies. Premature babies have more illnesses, especially nasopharyngeal disturbances. According to Hurlock (1964, p. 103),

> As they grow older, they suffer slightly more from such physical defects as malnutrition, dwarfism, and obesity. The most serious defect associated with prematurity is poor vision. Because of the difficulty in establishing respiration at birth, many prematurely born infants must be given oxygen. . . . Developmental retardation is especially apparent in *motor control* . Prematurely born babies are retarded in the use of the index finger for pointing, in the pincer grasp, in particular and motor control and in locomotion.

The effect of paranatal complications on the 30-month development of a group of 249 Negro, single-birth, premature children was studied by Cutler and others (1965). These children were compared with 32 full-term Negro children selected on the basis of an uneventful paranatal course and because of similarity in socioeconomic background. The investigators found at the end of a 30-month period "a significantly higher incidence of neurological abnormalities among the males with a consequent depression in psychological scores" (p. 275). The premature children, even those without neurological abnormalities, had depressed IQ's and gross-motor scores in comparison with those of full-term children.

Prognosis of Prematurely Born Infants. The intellectual development of prematurely born children has been widely studied. Alm's conclusion from a careful review of the literature and from his own studies were that the prematurely born child had retarded physical and mental development during the first two or three years, but if one excludes those suffering from brain injury the average level of intelligence approximates that of the full-term infant.

More recent reviews dealing with premature infants furnish a less favorable prognosis. (Knobloch, 1959.) It seems that the smaller the premature baby at birth, the greater is the likelihood of an abnormality of development. (Knobloch, 1959.) This is borne out by Knobloch and others (1956) in a comparison of 500 prematurely born children at the corrected age of 40 weeks with that of 492 full-term children. A direct relation was found between birth weight and the incidence of abnormalities; 50.9 percent of those with a birth weight of less than 1501 grams had defects ranging from minor neurological damage to severe intellectual deficiency.

A follow-up study by Dann, Levine, and New (1958) is important, since it included 73 babies weighing 1,000 grams or less at birth or in the immediate postnatal period. Less than half had normal vision, and two had cerebral palsy. The average IQ score was 94. In a follow-up study (1964) of 65 of the original 73 babies plus 27 additional ones, an average IQ of 94.8 was obtained for the prematurely born children compared with an average of 106.9 for the siblings, with 59 percent of the prematurely born having eye defects.

It is difficult to ascribe causal relations because of the possibility of other factors that may be involved. There is a lower incidence of adequate medical care and thus a higher incidence of premature babies in the lower social classes; in these classes there is also a lower average IQ than in the middle and upper classes. In a study of 363 primiparae in Aberdeen, Baird (1959) noted an excess of low intelligence-test scores among women who gave birth to premature babies. There seems to be many variables which make it difficult to draw specific conclusions about the relation of prematurity and later development; although there is considerable evidence for the conclusion that the smaller the premature baby at birth, the greater the likelihood of brain injury and the associated conditions. This was noted in an early study by Asher and Fraser Roberts (1949) in which an excess of low birth weights was observed among a sample of backward children.

Early Responses

As a result of homeostatic adjustments, the infant maintains a relatively calm, balanced state. Involuntary actions of bodily mechanisms help the child realize a remarkably stable internal temperature, and supply certain elements essential for meeting internal and external emergencies. The reflexes are part of the homeostatic system that protect the child from harm and overstimulation, and stimulate him to activity.

Crying and Smiling.   Crying and smiling appear as innate responses. The crying at birth is considered the first response to distress and violent stimulation. According to Koehler (1954) smiling first appears after the baby has drunk to satiation. Later it occurs as a response to someone bending over the infant; finally it appears as a friendly response to known persons (Ahrens, 1953). As evidence that it is an innate response, Freedman (1965) noted that children who are born blind still show the smiling response. The cries of the newborn infant gradually become differentiated so that by the time he is three or four weeks old the alert mother can tell from the tone and intensity of the cry and from bodily movements accompanying it what the crying signifies. Hunger cries are loud and interrupted by sucking movements. Cries of pain, such as colic, are characterized by a peculiar, high-pitched scream, alternated with a forceful flexion and extension of the legs.

The most common causes of crying during the early weeks after birth are hunger and over-heating, while noise, light, clothing, and vomiting are the least causes (Aldrich et al., 1945). A greater variety of causes of crying appear as he grows older. By the time he is three months old he will likely have learned that crying serves a useful purpose of gaining attention. Normally the baby cries less and less as he grows older. Although marked individual differences in the amount of crying will be observed at each age. By the age of six weeks babies whose needs have been met promptly cry very little, while children whose parents do not respond promptly to his cries are *conditioned* to cry and this becomes a generalized response which the body uses (Stewart et al., 1954). The baby has learned to use noncrying methods of communication (Rosenzweig, 1954).

Nursing and Sucking.   The child's tongue, cheeks, hard and soft palate, gums, and lips are sufficiently developed at birth to participate in the important life function of sucking and nursing at birth. However, the act of sucking, like other functions, is developmental; the premature infant is considerably less efficient than that of the full-term baby.

Sucking has important implications other than that involving the taking of food. It seems that the infant uses his bodily responses in relating himself to others, and also as a substitute for such contacts when others are absent. This, according to Fleischal (1957), constitutes for the infant a communicative bridge between the inner self and the outer environment. Greene (1958) hypothesized that the intrauterine fetus experiences a primitive sort of object relationship with the recurring rhythm of the mother's body, and that this relationship was continued into his postnatal life until such responses as breathing and sucking come to provide a medium by which he can develop his own object world.

The question of breast versus bottle-feeding has been considered by both pediatricians and child psychologists, and different speculations presented. In an investigation by Adams (1959) mothers who bottle-fed their babies were to be more independent, to be more rejecting of the baby, and more inclined to experience sexual difficulties than mothers of breast-fed babies. These mothers also seemed to have more conflicts in other areas of home life. However, there was sufficient overlapping in the personality characteristics and problems of the two groups of mothers to make it unsafe to generalize from these results. Certainly it is possible for the breast-feeding mother to reject her child and for the bottle-feeding mother to experience warm acceptance of the child. The infant's need to be fed and the mother's preparedness to feed, make up the interacting variables. In this connection we must distinguish between the physiologic process which enabled the mother to bear the infant and provide nourishment for him and the emotional attitudes which appear in her nursing behavior.

Sensory Responses. Sufficient data are available to warrant our conclusion that normal newborn infants are capable of responding to auditory stimuli (Peiper, 1963). A study by Steinschneider and others (1966) was designed to determine whether normal infants differ in their sensory capacities, i.e., their ability to discriminate varying intensities of auditory stimulation. Cardiac and motor responses were also studies to ascertain the interrelation between response systems.

Nine full-term neonates (3 males and 6 females) took part in the study. The findings were in harmony with earlier findings that infants do respond to auditory stimulation. There was also evidence that infants differ considerably in auditory sensitivity. They noted that

> In general, there is much agreement between the cardiac and motor-response systems. In both systems, increased intensity of stimulation is associated with a greater magnitude of response systems. In both systems, increased intensity of stimulation is associated with a greater magnitude of response as well as a shorter latency.

The results of Fantz's studies (1963) have shown conclusively that the infant's visual equipment is much better developed in the early months of life than had previously been believed. Fantz noted that infants made visual discrimination between patterned stimuli within 48 hours after birth.

Taste is relatively well developed at birth. The infant's reactions to sweet are positive, while his reactions to salt, sour, and better are negative. Children react to changes in their food formula by two to three months (Breckenridge and Murphy, 1961).

In the past, some students of child development claimed the sense of smell was well developed at birth. However, studies by Lipsitt and others (1963) show that the intensity of the olfactory stimulus needed to produce a reaction from the infant increased rapidly during the days immediately following birth. More research is needed before one can differentiate the different elements involved in the response at this stage and the interrelation of these elements.

The Startle Response.   Sudden, violent auditory and visual stimuli, loss of support, and restraint precipatates physiological activity—an "emergency reaction" (Cannon, 1929). Watson and Raynor (1920) interpreted these responses as inborn fear responses appearing during infancy. The infant involuntarily responds with generalized mass activity and gross motor movements, including a characteristic muscular flexion of the fingers, kicking, squirming, and crying. This is a state of excitement that involves the total organism; emotional responses subsequently develop through the process of differentiation as suggested later in this chapter.

Individuality in Infants

Just as infants differ at birth in size and body type, so they differ in tempo, rhythm, and sensitivity to different kinds of stimulation. The extent to which these differences are a result of heredity, prenatal life, birth conditions, or by the emotional states of their parents, has not been determined. Results of studies of infants have provided considerable information about their characteristics, indicating a wide range of variability on different traits.

Differences in Activity.   Individuality may be observed in the motor activity of the newborn. Some infants show poorly developed reflex responses as well as hand-mouth contacts. Also marked differences appear in mass activity, with some infants in constant motion, even during the sleep period. Sontag (1946) suggests that these variations result partly from the general physical conditions of the infants, partly on the maturity of the infant at birth, and partly on the activity level of the infant during fetal life.

An important observation of infants is that they are different from one another, even prior to birth. Thus we are able to label infants as active or quiet in the early days after birth. Investigators have attempted to determine the conditions and factors in the environment that influence infants so as to produce increased individual differences in other ways.

Studies by Ainsworth (1964) and Ambrose (1961) show that somewhere in the middle of the first year, the infant seems to shift his attachment from human beings in general to an attachment to one, two, or three human beings—perhaps members of his immediate family. Ambrose's observations of smiling show that at 17-25 weeks general social smiling begins to decay, while there is increased smiling at his mother or persons who care for him.

Differences in Sensitivity.   Infants also differ in sensitivity to varying kinds of stimuli. In a study by Birns (1965) thirty healthy full-term babies were tested and observed during four sessions. The first session always occurred on the first day of life and the last session on the fourth or fifth day. The stimulation applied to each baby consisted of a soft tone, a loud tone, a cold disk applied to the baby's thigh, and a pacifier inserted in the baby's mouth. The major finding was that babies could be differentiated within the first five days of life in terms of a consistency of their reactivity to external stimuli. Some neonates consistently responded moderately and others were characterized by mild-intensity responses. In general babies who responded to one stimulus responded vigorously to all stimuli and stability from day 2 to day 5 was established (pp. 252-253).

Differences in Needs for Food, Activity, and Rest. Infant individuality in activity was referred to earlier. There are also significant differences in their needs for food and rest. Research has supported ideas early expressed by Cannon concerning the wisdom of the body, in which the baby will at times reject certain foods and at other times accept heartily particular foods. Such ideas have forced pediatricians and others to modify feeding schedules in harmony with the individuality of each child. By carefully observing the time after a feeding when an infant becomes restless and displays a keen interest in food, one is able to develop a feeding schedule based on the needs of the particular child.

Differences in the sleep and activity of infants may be observed during the first month or six weeks of the baby's life. Again, through observing the sleep needs or demands of a particular infant, it is possible to develop a sleep schedule based on the individual needs of the child.

Development During Infancy

After birth the behavior of the infant child becomes more complex and frequently more difficult. During the first year the stimulation for mental, motor, and emotional development seems to come largely from within. One normal healthy child may walk as early as 12 months of age, whereas another normal healthy child does not walk until he is 15 months old, is attributed largely to genetic differences. For example, Dennis and Dennis (1940) noted in an early study that Hopi children bound to cradle boards throughout infancy began walking at about the same time as children who are not so restrained.

Physical Development. The rate of growth during the first year of life is rapid in comparison to later years. Weight at birth for normal nine-month babies will vary from 5 to 12 pounds; the weight at six months will be approximately twice that of birth. Body length at birth will usually vary from 17½ to 23 inches. There is a gain of about an inch a month during the first six months. The gain in sitting height is most pronounced during the months immediately following birth so that by nine months both boys and girls will have reached half of the sitting height they attain by the age of 17.

The growth principle set forth in Chapter 2 that different parts of the body grow at different rates is quite noticeable during infancy.

The contention that basic maturational changes in autonomic control occur within early months is supported in a study by Lipton and others (1966) show-

The infant is likely to find walking a difficult task involving the whole body.

ing a decreasing variability of heart-rate response with age. Each of 14 infants
was studied during two or more experimental sessions on the second to the fifth
days after birth and again at approximately age 2½ and 5 months. The data
presented in this study indicated that stability of certain aspects of the responses
occur after age 2½ months. This indicated that it may be possible to predict
subsequent autonomic functions from data obtained at age 2½ months.

Neuromuscular Development. In a study by Aldrich and Norval (1946)
twelve developmental steps of neuromuscular growth were chosen for study in
an unselected group of 215 infants. These infants were studied from birth to the
early part of their second year. Observations of the age of attainment of each of
the twelve achievements were made and a graph showing the average curve and
the variation was developed. Then achievements are shown in Figure 3-1.

Motor test scores of 1,409 infants ages 1-15 months from a relatively hetero-
geneous population were used by Bayley (1965) in evaluating motor development during infancy. Of the infants tested 680 were boys and 729 were girls. An
effort was made to test equal numbers of boys and girls at each age from each
source. Approximately 55 percent of the babies were white, 42 percent were
Negro, and 2.3 percent of other races.

The average scores for the Negro infants were found to be consistently
superior to those for the white infants throughout the age range. This may
indicate a genetic difference in which the Negroes were more precocious than

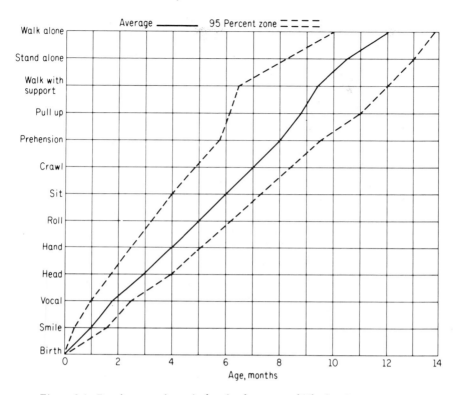

Figure 3-1. Developmental graph for the first year of life showing average age for the achievements selected and zone in which 95 percent of the infants' developmental graphs fell. (Aldrich and Norval, 1946, p. 306.)

the whites in their motor coordination. Another explanation that has been offered is that the Negro infants came from a predominantly lower socioeconomic class and were consequently left to move about more freely with fewer restrictions of such things as clothes and play pens. Gerber (1962) noted this difference between African babies whose families had become Europeanized and those who had maintained their native customs. Bayley (p. 409) noted that "the first year of life in the human infant is predominantly characterized by rapid development, given at least a minimally adequate environment." The small individual differences in rates of development may be attributed both to inherent differences in such rates, and to environmental conditions.

According to Solomons and Solomons (1964), one factor that exerts considerable influence on motor scores of four-month-old infants is birth order. Comparisons between the birth weight and motor scores of his sample of 22 first-born infants and 46 subsequent born showed that first-born infants made higher motor scores at four months of age than later-born infants. This can best be accounted for by the greater amount of attention given to the motor activities by parents of first-born children. No sex differences were noted in either group of infants. There was a slight difference in the scores of infants weighing less than five pounds and eight ounces and infants with a greater birth weight, with the lighter infants having lower motor scores. No consistent differences were found in motor scores among the infants in the higher weight categories.

There is evidence, however, from various studies that, within normal limits, developmental status in the first year of life is a poor indicator of later motor functioning.

Prehension.   At birth the infant is unable to use his fingers as separate units since they are controlled by the cortical regions of the brain, which are at that time poorly developed. However, the hand is a useful conductor of sensations and is an effective medium for the child to explore the world about him. In the early stages of his development he examines his fingers and toes and reaches into space, touching objects within the reach of his poorly coordinated arm and hand movements. He explores the unique properties of the objects about him, and thus begins to differentiate between himself and the things about him in this environment.

The development of prehension is most important to the child's early intellectual and motor development. An early study by Halverson (1931) dealt with the prehension of infants ranging in age from 16 to 52 weeks. Through photographic records the investigator reached the following conclusions about the infants' behavior responses to a one-inch red cube:

1. At 16 weeks, no infants are likely to touch the cube. Accuracy in reaching improves gradually and steadily from 16 to 52 weeks. The distinguishing differences between the younger and older infants concerned the time actually required to grasp the cube, amount of cube displacement, number of adjustments necessary for a firm grasp, and the type of grasp.

2. The critical age in infant prehension in 28 weeks. At this age they have the longest single regard and the greatest total duration of regard for the cube. At this time the hand begins to free itself from forearm control in reaching for objects. Instead of directing the whole hand toward the cube, the infant passes only the index and medius fingers over it. Finger manipulation begins to replace the pawlike behavior of the hand, and active thumb opposition begins to replace the palm grip.

3. Prior to the age of 28 weeks, the aid of the second hand is required in grasping. The most common forms of lifting the cube from the table are (a) a purely elbow flexion, and (b) a hand-elbow action, in which the hand, after grasping the cube, rotates on the edge of the little finger before elbow flexion begins.

4. The development of reaching and grasping follows the principle maturation from the larger to the finer muscles. The early approach patterns consist largely of shoulder and elbow movements, illustrating the principle of development from the general to the specific.

5. The increase in the number of higher types of grasp and in the amount and variety of finger manipulations of the cube by infants from age 16 to 52 weeks are due in part to the skeletal development of the fingertips.

Development of Vision. Certain color discriminations may be observed as early as the third or fourth month. However accurate perceptions of color depends upon maturation and learning. Illingworth (1962) presents the following schedule of visual development in infants.

4 weeks:	Watches mother intensely when she speaks to him. Opens and closes mouth. Follows dangling object when brought to midline less than $90°$.
6 weeks:	When supine, follows many objects from side to midline ($90°$).
8 weeks:	Fixation of eyes. Convergence. Focusing.
12 weeks:	When supine, watches movements of hands (until 24 weeks). Follows dangling objects from side to side.
20 weeks:	Smiles at mirror image.
24 weeks:	No more hand regard.
28 weeks:	Pats image of self in mirror.
40 weeks:	Looks around corner for object in mirror.

Memory and Learning. The development of the cortex at birth is not sufficiently advanced to assume that the newborn remembers the birth experiences or the experiences during the early period after birth. We should not discount the significance of birth and experiences during the weeks and months following birth on the life of the infant. However, there is little if any scientific evidence to support the viewpoint of some psychoanalysts that birth is a normal traumatic experience for the baby; it does mark an important change in his way of life. At this stage he relinquishes his parasitic existence within the mother and assumes an active existence, responding to a wider range of stimuli.

Questions have been raised about the learning of infants during the first months of life. Learning of a simple rudimentary form in the form of adaptation to a feeding schedule appears at this stage. This is observed in marked restlessness whenever the scheduled feeding time arrives and he is not fed. However, this is a form of adaptability that does not imply consciousness on the part of the baby.

Emotional Behavior in Infancy. In an early study by Bridges (1932) the emotional behavior of 62 infants in the Montreal Foundling and Baby Hospital was observed and recorded daily over a period of three or four months. The emotions during the early days after birth are best characterized by the term "excitement." There is little differentiation of emotional reactions at this stage. The presentation of certain strong stimuli produced a form of agitation in which the arm and hand muscles tensed, breathing quickened, and the legs made jerky, kicking movements. Lowering the babies suddenly into their cribs, or lifting them quickly frequently produced startled and excited reactions.

The three-month-old baby will cry and display other signs of distress when placed in an unusual position. Also, at this age the emotion of delight is becoming more clearly differentiated from excitement on the one hand and non-emotional quiescence on the other. Delight may be expressed upon the sight of his mother or bottle when he is hungry. The child kicks, opens his mouth, breathes faster, and tries to raise his head upon seeing his bottle. He smiles when an adult talks softly to him and he gives crooning sounds when being fed, nursed, or rocked. With increased age distress and delight come to be expressed more in specific vocalizations.

A diagram showing the approximate ages of the appearance of the different emotions was prepared by Bridges and is presented in Figure 3-2. The diagram showing the ages for the emergence of various emotions are designed to show how emotions become differentiated during the first two years; it is not presented as a scale for emotional development during infancy.

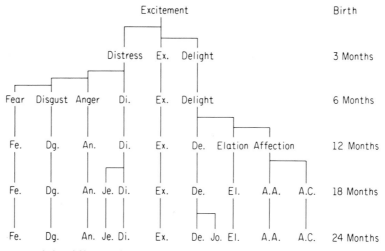

Key: A.A. = Affection for adults, A.C. = Affection for children, An. = Anger
De. = Delight, Dg. = Disgust, Di. = Distress, El. = Elation, Ex. = Excitement,
Fe. = Fear, Je. = Jealousy, Jo. = Joy.

Figure 3-2. Showing the approximate ages of differentiation of the various emotions during the first two years of life.

Development of Social Behavior. Although smiling is frequently regarded as the beginning of social development, it seems likely that social behavior begins with the first responses made by the infant to any social situation. According to Ainsworth (1964) the same principles of infant social development appears in all infants regardless of cultural influences. However, she found African babies somewhat more accelerated in their social development on the Gesell Developmental Schedules than other babies she studies. She hypothesized that this may be associated with the fact that the African babies studied were breast-fed and experienced more interaction with adult figures than many infants in our culture.

The development of social behavior of the infant has been summarized by Illingworth (1962) as follows:

4 weeks:	Watches mother intently when she speaks to him. Opens and closes mouth.
8 weeks:	Vocalizes and smiles. Shows interest in surroundings.
12 weeks:	Excited when presented a toy. "Talks" a great deal when spoken to.
20 weeks:	Smiles at mirror image. Discovers his own body.
24 weeks:	Annoyed when toy is removed. Holds arms out to be picked up. Looks to see where dropped cube has fallen. Shows likes and dislikes for food.
28 weeks:	Imitates. Tries to attract attention by cough.
32 weeks:	Tries persistently to get hold of toys out of reach. Responds to "NO."
36 weeks:	Compares two cubes by bringing them together.
40 weeks:	Pulls mother's clothes to draw attention. Waves "bye-bye", Pat-a-cakes. Repeats performances when laughed at.
44 weeks:	Drops toys deliberately to be picked up.
48 weeks:	Anticipates body movement in nursery rhyme. Interest in pictures in book.

Influences Affecting the Individual Child

It was pointed out earlier in this chapter that unfavorable influences during the prenatal period will have a detrimental effect upon the offspring. Masland and others (1958) summarized the major studies of the diet in pregnancy and its relation to the intelligence of the offspring. There is considerable evidence that diets deficient in calories and essential foods are associated with a decreased intelligence of offspring. It is logical then to theorize that certain diets will result in an improved IQ in the offspring. Considerable theoretical presentations and some experimental studies have furnished evidence that the child's intelligence may be altered during the early stages of life. Much remains to be done in this field, and we may expect significant developments affecting growth and development during the prenatal years of infancy.

Cultural Expectations. Although the biology of the infant largely determines the expectations set forth for him, each culture has its own ways of inducting the child into the particular society. Concerning this Whiting and Child (1953, pp. 63-64) state:

In all societies the helpless infant, getting his food by nursing at his mother's breast and having digested it, freely evacuating the waste products, exploring his genitals, biting and kicking at will, must be changed into a responsible adult obeying the rules of society... Child training everywhere seems to be in considerable part concerned with problems which arise from universal characteristics of the human infant and from universal characteristics of adult culture which are incompatible with the continuation of infantile behavior.

Psychological Needs. Years ago it was learned that if babies admitted to pediatric hospitals were not returned to their mothers immediately upon recovery, they developed marasmus, a condition characterized by loss of muscle tone, low-grade fever, hemoglobin, and lethargy. The cure for this condition was to return these children to their homes as quickly as possible so that they would receive the stimulation and attention normal in most families but lacking in the typical hospital ward. In these infants the whole child was responding to the lack of stimulation essential for the health and well being of the child (Lemkan, 1961).

Many institutions that care for babies have instituted practices of giving the babies personal attention, with the results of a noticeable decline in death rate. Studies reveal a close relationship between affectionate, acceptant behavior by the parent and general well-being of the infant child (Pease and Gardner, 1958).

The results of the study by Sontag (1950) of the effects of the mother's emotional states during pregnancy, cited earlier in the chapter, are supported by a more recent study by Davids and others (1963) in which a battery of psychological tests was administered to fifty pregnant mothers. The mothers were classified into a "high anxiety" and a "low anxiety" group on the basis of scores on a manifest anxiety scale. Eight months following child birth, a psychological evaluation of the mother and child was made. This assessment revealed that the "high anxious" mothers evidenced significantly more negative child-rearing attitudes than the "low anxious" mothers. Also, the children from the "low anxious" mothers tended to receive a score indicative of a more favorable general emotional tone than did the offspring of the "high anxious" mothers (p. 1001). However, we should be careful about generalizing causation from association. The emotionally disturbed mothers may have a genetic constitution different from that of nondisturbed mothers. Thus the infants born to these mothers may have inherited emotional potentialities so as to make early adjustments difficult, or the mother's emotional characteristics may have affected their care and relations with their infants. Regardless of the exact causal relationship, it seems likely that an emotionally stable mother is more likely to have an undisturbed baby than one whose life is characterized by confusion.

Love and Affection.   The development of love and affection is "intimately tied up with satisfaction of body needs, appetites . . ." (Schlosberg, 1954). Affection first appears as an outgoing, striving, approaching kind of behavior. Söderling (1959) observed the age of the first smile in 400 normal ful-term infants, and noted the following:

First Smile	Percentage
Before 2 weeks	0
2–3 weeks	11
3–4 weeks	49
4–5 weeks	21
5–6 weeks	19

Jersild (1952) noted that babies under five months of age fix their gaze on a person's face, kick, hold out and wave their arms, smile, and try to raise their bodies. By the sixth month the baby has sufficient control over his arm movements to reach the loved ones.

During the early months there is a close relation between love, food, and relief from discomfort. Food brings the child and mother, or mother substitute, into close contact. Also, the mother continuously provides the baby with relief from discomfort, at later stages. The attitudes and manners of the mother feeding her infant and caring for him when he is uncomfortable, determine the quality of his later affections. As pointed out in Chapter 2, this is the period when the child develops a sense of trust. A happy, loving, understanding mother provides a climate in which the baby feels secure, comfortable, and friendly; an impatient, hostile mother provides a climate of fear, suspicion, and distrust.

This is shown in the results of a series of studies of infant monkeys by Harlow and Harlow (1962). The investigators examined the infant-mother affectional bond, using in many experiments mother surrogates made of cloth. The infants became attached to the cloth mother surrogates, showing a distinct preference for them over a wire mother substitute, especially in fright-producing situations. Since, both the wire-mesh mother and the terry-cloth mother supplied adequate food to the infant monkeys, it would appear that food alone was not the only source of gratification of the mother-infant relationship. Although the terry-cloth mother provided the infant monkey with food and tactile comfort, it did not provide certain other important experiences that a real mother provides, and which seem to be essential for normal development. The monkey raised with the terry-cloth mothers developed abnormal behavior patterns in later years. The investigators describe their later behavior as follows (p. 42):

> ... They are without question socially and sexually aberrant. ... The entire group of animals separated from their mothers at birth ... must be written off as potential breeding stock. Apparently their early social deprivation impairs their ability to form effective relations with other monkeys, whether the opportunity was offered to them in the second six months of life or in the second to fifth year of life.

The findings by Harlow support earlier speculations about human infants by Ribble (1943). Intimate mothering is fundamental to fulfillment of basic infant needs. Infants who experience consistent, normal mother love, develop better physically; they also tend to develop attitudes of trust and confidence, as well as a personality responsive to the attention and affection of others. There is evidence too that trauma or deprivation of mothering during infancy is significantly related to later ability to learn (Denenberg and Bell, 1960). Developmentally speaking infancy is a period when the child develops the basis for normal healthy social relations in adulthood.

Summary

The prenatal period and infancy provide the foundation and background for subsequent development. Embryologists usually divide prenatal life into three periods: germinal period, embryonic period, and fetal period.

Many expectant mothers in the United States receive no prenatal care; the most obvious effect of this is the likelihood the offspring will be born prematurely. The premature infant is more vulnerable to difficulties than the full-term baby.

Many factors and conditions present during the mother's pregnancy can have an adverse effect on the developing offspring. Some of these conditions presented in this chapter are: (1) emotional states of the mother, (2) malnutrition, (3) infection, (4) drugs, (5) radiation and Rh influences, (6) smoking, (7) position, (8) lack of medical care, and (9) glandular factors.

As a result of homeostatic adjustments, the infant maintains a relatively calm, balanced state. The reflexes are part of the homeostatic system that protects the infant from harm and overstimulation, and stimulate him to activity. The first response of the infant to distress is the birth cry. After birth the cries gradually become more differentiated. The full-term infant's tongue, cheeks, hard and soft palate, gums and lips are sufficiently developed at birth to participate in the important life function of sucking.

Individuality may be noted in the sensory and motor responses of the infant. Differences in activity level may be noted prior to birth. Infants also differ significantly in their needs for food and rest.

The rate of growth during the first year of life is rapid in comparison to later years. Sex differences in motor development are insignificant during infancy, although the first-born are significantly advanced over later-born children. This seems to result from the greater attention to the motor development during infancy given to the first-born child. Pronounced changes in physical development, emotional development, and social development occur during the first year.

The following influences affecting the individual child during infancy were described in this chapter (1) cultural expectations, (2) psychological needs, (3) love and affection. The importance of the mother figure was emphasized.

References

Adams, A. B. "Choice of Infant Feeding Technique as a Function of Maternal Personality," *Journal of Consulting Psychology*, Vol. 23 (1959), pp. 143-146.

Ahrens, R. "Beitrag zur Entwicklung des Physiogenie-und Minikennens," *Zeitcher Exper. Angen. Psychol.*, Vol. II (1953), pp. 413-454.

Ainsworth, M. D. "Patterns of Attachment Behavior Shown by the Infant in Interaction with his Mother," *Merrill-Palmer Quarterly*, Vol. 10 (1964), pp. 51-58.

Aldrich, C. A., and M. Norval. "A Developmental Graph for the First Year of Life," *Journal of Pediatrics*, Vol. 29 (1946), pp. 304-308.

Aldrich, C. A., C. Sung, and C. Knop. "The Crying of Newly Born Babies," *Journal of Pediatrics*, (1945), Vol. 26, pp. 313-326; Vol. 27, pp. 428-435.

Ambrose, J. A. "The Development of Smiling Response in Early Infancy," in B. M. Foss (ed.), *Determinants of Infant Behavior*. New York: Wiley, 1961.

Asher, C., and J. A. Fraser Roberts." A Study of Birth Weight and Intelligence," *British Journal of Social Medicine,* Vol. 3 (1949), p. 56.

Baird, D. "The Contribution of Obstetrical Factors to Serious Physical and Mental Handicap in Children," *Journal of Obstetrics and Gynecology,* Vol. 66 (1959), p. 743.

Bayley, N. ' Comparison of Mental and Motor Test Scores for Ages 1-15 Months by Sex, Birth Order, Race, Geographical Section, and Education, and Education of Parents," *Child Development,* Vol. 36 (1965), pp. 379-411.

Beck, Joan. "Guarding the Unborn," *Today's Health,* Vol. 46 (January 1968), pp. 39-41, 76.

Birns, B. "Individual Differences in Human Neonates' Responses to Stimulation," *Child Development,* Vol. 36 (1965), pp. 249-256.

Breckenridge, M. E., and M. N. Murphy. *Growth and Development of the Young Child.* Philadelphia: Saunders, 1961.

Bridges, K. M. B. "Emotional Development in Early Infancy," *Child Development,* Vol. 3 (1932), pp. 324-341.

Cannon, W. B. *Bodily Changes in Pain, Hunger, Fear, and Rage,* 2nd ed. New York: Appleton, 1929.

Cutler, R., C. B. Heimer, H. Wortis, and A. M. Freedman. "The Effects of Prenatal and Neonatal Complications on the Development of Premature Children at Two and One-Half Years of Age," *Journal of Genetic Psychology,* Vol. 107 (1965), pp. 261-276.

Dann, M., S. Z. Levine, and S. V. New. "The Development of Prematurely Born Children with Birth Weights and Minimal Postnatal Weights of 1,000 g. or Less," *Pediatrics,* Vol. 22 (1958), p. 1037.

Davids, A., R. H. Holden, and G. B. Gray. "Maternal Anxiety During Pregnancy and Adequacy of Mother and Child Adjustment Eight Months Following Childbirth," *Child Development,* Vol. 34 (1963), pp. 993-1002.

Denenberg, V. H., and R. W. Bell. "Critical Periods for the Effects of Infantile Experience on Adult Learning," *Science,* Vol. 131 (1960), pp. 227-228.

Dennis, W., and M. G. Dennis. "The Effect of Cradling Practices upon the Onset of Walking in Hopi Children," Journal of *Genetic Psychology,* Vol. 56 (1940), pp. 77-87.

Ebbs, J. H., A. Brown, F. F. Tisdall and W. A. Scott. *The Milbank Memorial Fund Quarterly,* Vol. 20 (1942), pp. 35-36.

Eichenlaub, J. E. "The Premature," *Today's Health* (December 1956), pp. 38-39, 46.

English, H. B. "Chronological Divisions of the Life Span," *Journal of Educational Psychology,* Vol. 48 (1957), pp. 437-439.

Fantz, R. L "Pattern Vision in Newborn Infants," *Science,* Vol. 140 (1963), pp. 296-297.

Fleischal, M. M. "The Problems of Sucking," *American Journal of Psychotherapy,* Vol. 11 (1957), pp. 86-97.

Freedman, D. G. "Hereditary Control of Early Social Behavior, in B. M. Foss, (ed.), *Determinants of Infant Behavior,* III. London: Methuen, 1965.

Gerber, M. "Test de Gesell et Terman-Merill appliques en Uganda," in *The Growth of the Normal Child During the First Three Years of Life: Modern Problems in Pediatrics,* Vol. 7. Basel, Switzerland: S. Karger, 1962.

Goodpasture, E. W. "Virus Infection of the Mammalian Fetus," *Science,* Vol. 99 (1942), pp. 391-396.

Greene, W. A. "Early Object Relations: Somatic Affective, and Personal," *Journal of Nervous and Mental Diseases,* Vol. 126 (1958), 225-243.

Halverson, H. M. "An Experimental Study of Prehension in Infants by Means of Systematic Cinema Records," *Genetic Psychology Monograph,* Vol. 10 (1931), pp. 107-286.

Harlow, H. F., and M. K. Harlow. "Social Deprivation in Monkeys," *Scientific American,* Vol. 207 (November 1962), pp. 136-146.

Hesse, E. *Narcotics and Drug Addiction.* New York: Philosophical Library, 1946.

Hurlock, E. B. *Child Development,* 4th ed. New York: McGraw-Hill, 1964.

Illingworth, R. S. *The Development of the Infant and Young Child Normal and Abnormal.* Edinburgh: Livingston, 1967.

_____. *An Introduction to Developmental Assessment in the First Year.* London: National Spastic Society, 1962.

Jersild, A. T. *In Search of Self.* New York: Teachers College Press, 1952.

Knobloch, H. "Syndrome of Minimal Cerebral Damage in Infancy," *Journal of American Medical Association,* Vol. 120 (1959), p. 1384.

Knobloch, H., R. Rider, P. Harper, and B. Pasamanick. "Neuropsychiatric Sequelae of Prematurity," *Journal of the American Medical Association,* Vol. 161 (1956), p. 581.

Koehler, O. "Das lachelm al angeborene ausdrucksbenegung," *Z. Meuschel Verevn. Konst. Lehre.,* Vol. 32 (1954), pp. 330-334.

Lemkan, P. V. "The Influence of Handicapping Conditions on Child Development," *Children,* Vol. 2 (March-April 1961), pp. 43-47.

Lipsitt, L. P., T. Engen, and H. Kaye. "Developmental Changes in the Olfactory Threshold of the Neonate," *Child Development,* Vol. 32 (1961), pp. 337-347.

Lipton, E. L., A. Steinschneider, and J. B. Richmond. "Autonomic Function in the Neonate: VII. Maturational Changes in Cardiac Control," *Child Development,* Vol. 37, (1966), pp. 1-16.

Lyght, C. E. (ed.). *The Merck Manual of Diagnosis and Therapy,* 11th ed. Mercke, Sharpe and Dohme Laboratories, 1966.

Masland, R. L., S. B. Sarason, and T. Gladwin. *Mental Subnormality.* New York: Basic, 1958.

Pease, D., and D. B. Gardner. "Research on the Effects of Noncontinuous Mothering," *Child Development,* Vol. 29 (1958), pp. 142-148.

Peiper, A. *Cerebral Function in Infancy and Childhood.* New York: Consultant's Bureau, 1963.

Ribble, M. "Infantile Experience in Relation to Personality Development," in J. McHunt, (ed.), *Personality and Behavior Disorders.* New York: Ronald, 1944, pp. 621-659.

Rosen, M., et al. "Differences Between Mothers of Low-Weight and Term-Size Infants," *Obstetrics and Gynecology,* February 1968.

Rosenzweig, S. "Babies Are Taught to Cry: A Hypothesis," *Mental Hygiene,* Vol. 38 (1954), pp. 81-84.

Schlosberg, H. "Emotion," *Collier's Encyclopedia,* Vol. 7 (1954), p. 261.

Silcock, B. "Diabetes, Deformities Related," *The Charlotte Observer,* January 26, 1967.

Söderling, B. "The First Smiles," *Acta Paediat.,* Vol. 48 (1959), Supplement 117.

Solomons, G., and H. C. Solomons. "Factors Affecting Motor Performance in Four-Month-Old Infants," *Child Development,* Vol. 35 (1964), pp. 1283-1296.

Sontag, L. W. "The Genetics of Differences in Psychosomatic Patterns in Childhood," *American Journal of Orthopsychiatry,* Vol. 20 (1950), pp. 477-48.

_____. "Some Psychosomatic Aspects of Childhood," *Nervous Child,* Vol. 5 (1946), pp. 296-304.

Sontag, L. W., and T. W. Richards. "Studies in Fetal Behavior," *Monographs of the Society for Research in Child Development,* Vol. 3, No. 4, (1938).

Steinschneider, A. E. L. Lipton, and J. B. Richmond. "Auditory Sensitivity in the Infant: Effect of Intensity on Cardiac and Motor Sensitivity," *Child Development,* Vol. 37 (1966), pp. 223-252.

Stewart, A. H., et al. "Excessive Infant Crying (Colic) in Relation to Parent Behavior," *American Journal of Psychiatry,* Vol. 110 (1954), pp. 687-694.

Surgeon General's Committee on Smoking and Health: Report. United States Public Health Services, 1962.

Swan, C. "Rubella in Pregnancy as Aetological Factor in Stillbirth," *Lancet,* Vol. I (1948), pp. 744-746.

Time Magazine, February 9, 1968, pp. 76-78.

Watson, J. B., and R. R. Raynor. "Conditioned Emotional Reactions," *Journal of Experimental Psychology,* Vol. 3 (1920), pp. 1-4.

Whiting, J. W. W., and I. L. Child, *Child Training and Personality: A Cross-Cultural Study.* New Haven: Yale University Press, 1953.

Yamazaki, I. N., et. al. "Outcome of Pregnancy in Women Exposed to the Atomic Bomb in Nagasaki," *American Journal of Diseases in Children,* Vol. 87 (1954), pp. 448-463.

Chapter 4

Physical and
Motor Development

The growth of an individual from birth to complete physical maturity constitutes a considerable amount of time—almost one third of the normal life span. Growth involves changes in the physical and development. It was set forth in Chapter 2 that these changes result from the interaction of heredity and environment. The physical and motor self at all stages of life may be thought of as a result of conditions set forth in the germ plasm, prenatal and birth conditions, past experiences following birth, and present environmental stimulation.

Growth in Body Size

Growth in body size is controlled by the growth hormones, secreted by the anterior lobe of the pituitary gland. The manner in which these hormones affect growth in body size will be discussed later in this chapter. Although growth in height and weight are the most obvious changes in body size, the development of the bones furnishes us with a good basis for evaluating physical development. Growth of the bones is affected by the thyroid glands and hormones produced by the gonads—androgens in the male and estrogens in the female. These hormones act as retarding forces or influences on the growth hormones by stimulating the deposition of calcium, which causes the bones to ossify and produce the closure of the epiphyses (ends) of the bones.

Growth in Height and Weight. Although growth in height and weight is the most conspicuous feature of growth during childhood, they constitute only two closely related aspects of growth. And, while there is considerable variation in growth in height and weight of children, there is a pattern of growth that is similar. This may be observed in Figure 4-1, showing average and individual growth curves for height (Meredith, 1935). While there is considerable variation in the height and weight of children, there is a pattern of growth that is similar. The first several years after birth are characterized by rapid growth in height. At birth the average baby measures between 19 and 20 inches in length and weighs

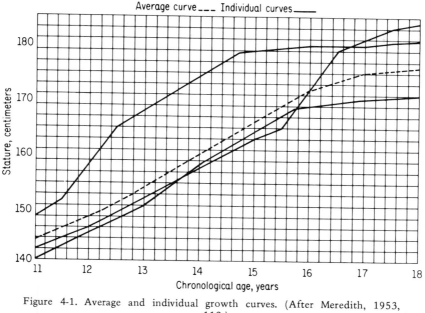

Figure 4-1. Average and individual growth curves. (After Meredith, 1953, p. 112.)

between 6 to 8 pounds, although weight variation occurs from around 3 pounds to 16 pounds. At the end of the fourth month his height has increased about 4 inches and his weight has doubled that existing at birth.

Growth in height and weight during the preschool years is considerable; the average child's height will double during this period while his weight increases fivefold. After this time there is a continuous deceleration of the rate of growth in body size until near the onset of puberty, when there is a spurt of growth in height followed closely by a similar spurt in weight.

Tables of averages for children's growth are likely to be misleading, since children of the same age vary enormously in their rate of development. Such tables do furnish useful information about growth trends. The materials presented in tables provide information about the average height and weight at different ages. They do not reveal the wide range of differences in growth rates even for children of the same sex. Actually differences in rate and pattern growth in height and weight may be observed among brothers or sisters. This is shown in Figure 4-2, where individual growth curves have been plotted for five sisters (Ford, 1958).

There are rapid increases in height during the first years. This is followed by a gradual decelerating rate of growth until the prepubertal spurt. At age 11, when the average American girl begins her prepubertal growth spurt, she is 58 inches tall. By age 13 she is 63 inches tall, while the average boy at 13 measures about 62 inches. From then on boys increase in height at a more rapid rate than

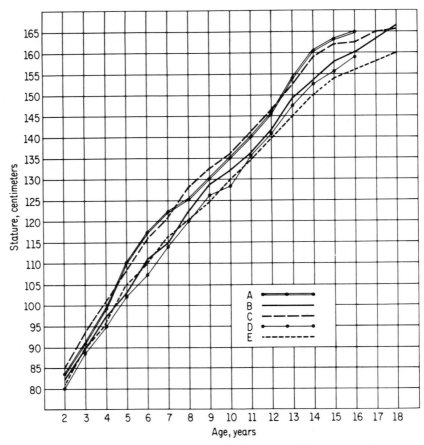

Figure 4-2. Individual growth curves for five sisters. (After Ford, 1958.)

girls and continue the increase approximately a year longer, so that at 18 he measures approximately 69.5 inches while the 18-year-old girl measures about 68 inches (Hurlock, 1964, p. 120). The widest disparity in deviation is at 12 years for girls and 14 years for boys. Since there is a close correlation between the skeletal age of a child as determined by X-rays of the bones of the hand and wrist and the proportion of adult height obtained, adult height can be predicted with a relative high degree of accuracy (Bayley, 1956).

The weight growth curve is quite similar to that for height. During the second and third year, the average gain in weight is from three to five pounds annually. Therefore, gains in weight are at a slower pace until near the onset of puberty. The average American girl of 11 weighs approximately 88.5 pounds, while the average boy weighs 85.5 pounds (Hurlock, 1964, p. 120). The boy surpasses the girl in weight during the subsequent years. The greatest deviation (S.D.) in weight occurs around age 13 for girls and 15 for boys.

There is pronounced growth in weight during the early teen years followed by a falling off in weight on the part of many girls. The emphasis is upon slenderness as the ideal physique for teen-age girls. After the teen years there is in general a period of weight stability, although many adults gradually add weight. This becomes a serious health problem for many adults, especially during the middle adult years, a period characterized by an excess of eating accompanied by very little physical activity.

The determination of the optimum weight at different ages is difficult, since there are a number of factors to be considered, including height, body build, family characteristics, and the ratio of muscular weight to fat weight. One cannot use tables of averages based on height and body build, since most likely the average adult in the United States is overweight. More and more attention is being given to the overweight problem among adults and many diet fads have appeared. In general the best way to lose weight is to reduce caloric intake, and the best means for maintaining a desirable weight is to consume the number of calories needed by the body for maintaining a certain weight. This seems to be a matter of arithmetic and self-control or "will power," with advice or help from the physician when needed.

Skeletal Development. Skeletal development is associated with the development of the bones. Bone development consists of growth in size of the bones, and changes in number and composition of the bones. This follows the same general pattern as that described for growth in height—that is, rapid changes occur during early childhood, followed by a decelerated rate of growth, only to be followed later by the preadolescent or early adolescent spurt.

Growth of bones. The child's bones differ from those of the adult in proportion, shape, composition, position, and even in number. The infant at birth has about 270 bones. The number gradually increases, so that there are about 350 bones at puberty. Children's bones contain more water and less mineral matter than those of adults and are more vascular in nature, allowing larger quantities of blood to flow through them. The larger quantity of blood causes the child to be more susceptible to bone diseases resulting from infection, although it does enable the nutritive need to be more adequately met.

The bones of the young child are not firmly knit together. They grow in length by becoming longer at the ends; therefore, young joints are longer and the ligaments are loosely attached. X-ray pictures taken at frequent intervals during the developmental period show a strip of cartilage which serves to separate the bone shaft (diaphysis) from the other bony masses at the ends. Children's bones continue to grow as long as this cartilage exists. There is an inverse correlation between the distance of hand bones and the maturational age. However, one should not equate bone size with maturity. A child may be relatively small yet relatively mature in his skeletal or bone structure. It is the differentiation and integration of the bony tissue that reveal the relative stage of maturity. When the bones fuse, skeletal growth stops.

Ossification. The ossification of the bones was early used by Baldwin and others (1928) in measuring the anatomical development of children at different age levels. The bones of the face and cranium develop directly within the corrective tissue, while the skeletal bones generally develop in the cartilage. X-ray pictures of the hand and wrist bones show the development at the ends of the bones (the epiphyses), and reveal the stage of ossification or hardening of the bones (Greulich and Pyle, 1959). At birth there is an absence of the carpal (wrist) bones; a gradual change in the shape of the bones occurs during childhood; and a complete union of the epiphyses and diaphyses may be observed in the 18-year-old girl.

Ossification is dependent upon the secretion of a hormone from the thyroid gland and upon the nutrition of the child. If there is an inadequate mineralization as a result of dietary or thyroid deficiency, bone deformities are likely to result. One of the more obvious results is bowed legs. (One should keep in mind that we are referring to a condition resulting from diet deficiency and occurring several years later than the common result of early walking, which tends to be self-correcting as the leg muscles develop and tighten.)

There is evidence from many studies that on the average children from the middle and high socioeconomic groups mature physically earlier than those from the low group. Studies of Chinese children by Low and others (1964) show that skeletal maturation is advanced in high socioeconomic groups over that of low groups. Bone development also furnishes a basis for predicting puberty (sexual development) as well as certain other aspects of development (Harding, 1952). The studies by Low and others of Chinese children support the findings by Harding. The investigators conclude that intercorrelations between skeletal age and height and skeletal age and weight are sufficiently high for group prediction of one measure from another within certain age ranges, and that skeletal age is most closely correlated with height during the adolescent growth period (p. 1335).

Dentition.   Decidious teeth are formed early in life. The age of their eruption varies from child to child, with the first tooth generally appearing around 6 months. Other decidious teeth appear during the first 2 to 3 years. This is followed by a quiescent period until around 6 years, when the first permanent teeth has been used as a basis to indicate the stage of skeletal development. Dental-age scales are available for both boys and girls. Although there are wide individual differences in the timing of the eruption of the permanent teeth, each child tends to be consistent in timing for the different teeth, being slow, average or accelerated (Stuart and Stevenson, 1959). The "wisdom teeth" erupt last, usually between age 17 and 25. The acquisition of the permanent teeth closely follows the growth patterns for height and weight—with girls ahead of boys at all stages. Somewhat related to this sex difference, Greulich (1951) noted from studying the effect on growth of wartime hardships in Guam and of the atomic bombing in Hiroshima and Nagasaki that girls are less easily thrown off their growth curves than boys.

Changes in Body Proportions.   The rapidity of growth during infancy makes that period a very important one. When infant growth is studied in detail, modifications in relative growth rates may be observed. In comparison to growth in size, change in body proportions are slight. However, longitudinal data reveal significant changes occurring continuously throughout the growing years. The proportional growth of the head steadily diminishes; the legs grow relatively longer until puberty begins, after which the stem length increases proportionally more, and the trunk of the body develops more rapidly during the years of pubescence (Bayley, 1956).

Changes in body proportions, especially the growth of legs, causes the child to appear less apelike. There is a 40 percent increase in the length of the legs during the first two years; at eight years they are 50 percent longer than at two years. The length of the arms increases even more during these periods, there being an increase of over 60 percent from infancy to age 2, and an increase of almost 50 percent from age 2 to age 8. There is also a close relationship between body build and the onset of puberty. The child with an endomorphic build— (broad hips and relatively short legs)—is likely to mature earlier than the average, while the child with an ectomorphic build—(slender body, broad shoulder, and long legs)—usually matures later than the average. Like the endomorphic child, the one whose build is muscular and compact—the mesomorphic—is slightly earlier than the average in reaching maturity. Obese children as a group reach puberty about a year earlier than their age-mates whose weight is more nearly average (Kralj-Cereck, 1956). Girls who mature earlier than the average are more endomorphic in body build during adolescence than girls who mature at an average age or slightly later than the average (Acheson and Dupertius, 1959; Zuk, 1958).

Physiological Changes with Age

Longitudinal studies are the best means for determining the rate, characteristics, and periodicity of physiological growth at different stages of life. However, since reliable and interpretable data on changes in body composition are difficult to obtain, information about physiological changes in many areas is incomplete. Mental hygiene problems, behavior problems and disorders, and health problems can be better understood when interpreted in light of physiological changes that occur at different stages from infancy until the advanced years of life.

Endocrines and Development. The endocrines (ductless) are glands distributed throughout the body. The endocrines differ from each other in structure, function, and nature of their secretions. They secrete directly into the blood stream rather than through ducts and are referred to as ductless glands. Scientific studies show a close relationship between developmental changes and hormones from the endocrines. The hormones from the pituitary glands are particularly important.

One of these is the growth hormones, which enables a normal healthy well-nourished child to attain his normal body size. If there is a deficiency of this hormone, the normal growth will be retarded, and a form of pituitary dwarfism will result. On the other hand, if an excess of growth hormone is produced during this growing period, pituitary gigantism will follow. The other pituitary hormone of special importance in maturation is the gonad-stimulating hormone. The action of these hormones in the normal healthy child will cause the immature gonads to grow and develop over a period of time into mature ovaries or testes. These hormones also help to sustain the normal function of the ovaries or testes of the individual during adulthood. A deficiency of these hormones during late childhood would retard the normal growth and development of the ovaries or testes; an oversupply would tend to produce precocious sexual development.

The gonad-stimulating hormones act upon the pituitary gland so as to reduce the effect of the growth hormones and reduce the rate of growth. The importance of properly timed action of the growth and gonad-stimulating hormones has been pointed out by Greulich (1944) as follows:

> If the testes or ovaries begin to function at the requisite level too early in life, growth is arrested prematurely and the child ends up abnormally short. If, on the other hand, the adequate production of the ovarian and testicular hormones is unduly delayed, growth, particularly that of the limbs, continues for too long a period and the characteristic bodily proportions of the eunuch are attained. It appears, therefore, that normal growth and development is contingent upon the reciprocal and properly timed action of pituitary (growth) and gonadal hormones.

The notion that children are sexless is not borne out by studies related to gonadotrophic hormone secretion in children. Nathanson and others (1941) reported that the excretion of gonadotrophic hormone in early childhood in both sexes is slight. Average curves for boys and girls show that during the early years the amount of androgens secreted into the urine is only slightly less for girls than for boys. The difference becomes more pronounced after age 11. It has been found that before ages 10 or 11 both boys and girls excrete measurable amounts of male and female hormones, although not an excess of either.

Thyroxin from the thyroid gland also influences growth. It regulates the rate of oxidation in the body and thus influences cellular activity. It also influences the development of the bones, the nervous system, circulatory system, muscular development, and has an important bearing on the functioning of the reproductive organs. A deficiency of thyroxin before birth results in *cretinism,* a condition characterized by retardation in growth, delay in dentition, delayed if not complete arrest of sexual maturation; maladjustments of the neuromuscular system, defective speech, low basal metabolic rate, and lowered body temperature. In most cases there is a serious retardation in mental development. However, treatment may result in near-normal or normal mental development, depending upon the degree, the time of onset of the deficiency, and the age at which treatment was begun. A follow-up study of 128 cases reported by Smith and others (1957) showed that 45 percent of severe cretins treated during the first six months after birth attained an IQ of over 90; of those who developed a hypothyroid condition between age 2 and age 12, 77 percent had an IQ of over 90.

Age Changes in Metabolism. There is little change in basal metabolism during childhood until the time of puberty. There is a continuous decrease in basal metabolism throughout the teen years for both boys and girls. Individual curves show a marked increase just before, or at puberty for girls, followed by a significant decrease. There are, however, cases which do not conform to this pattern. The individual slump in metabolic rate of boys is above that of the girls relative to surface area (Garn, Clark and Portray, 1953). This may be due to the greater resting oxygen consumption than fat, and muscular children a greater consumption than fat ones. Differences in body size and muscle mass do not account for all the sex differences, nor for the increase in sex difference which occurs at puberty. Garn and Clark (1953) have shown that boys have a higher oxygen consumption per body weight even when compared with girls of the same muscular bulk at least from puberty or slightly before. It seems likely then that the male acquires a specific metabolic stimulus, most likely from androgenic steroids.

The pre-schooler is developing greater control in large muscular coordination activities. (Courtesy Eliot Pearson—Tufts University)

Blood Pressure, Heart and Pulse Rate. The growth of the heart, like that of other organs of the body, follows a course of its own. There is a gradual and continuous growth of the blood vessels during childhood.

The heart grows rapidly until the fourth year, followed by a period of relatively slow growth. The rate of growth increases during preadolescence and reaches its peak about the time of the peak of growth in weight. With puberty there is an increased rate of growth of the heart; its weight almost doubles during the adolescent years, and its transverse diameter increases by almost 50 percent (Marsh, 1953). Boys' hearts are slightly larger than girls' during most of childhood; whereas from approximately nine to fourteen years those of girls' are larger. After age thirteen boys' hearts continue to grow at a rapid rate. Those who work with children in physical activities should recognize the small size of the heart relative to the total weight and provide regular rest intervals for quick recovery from fatigue.

The basal heart rate falls gradually through the growing years, with perhaps a check to this decrease around the time of peak stature growth, and a stabilization of its rate throughout adulthood. There is also a sex difference established during early adolescence, with the heart rate for girls being faster than that for boys (Illiff and Lee, 1952). This difference persists during early adulthood. The mouth temperature of girls and boys shows a gradual decrease during childhood. This decrease for girls seems to stop around ages 10 or 11 (Illiff and Lee). The heart rate is fairly closely related to body temperature in healthy individuals. The difference of about 0.7 degrees between boys' and girls' temperature at age 17 may account for the difference of about five beats per minute in their heart rate at the same age, with the average for girls being higher than that for boys.

A marked change in both blood pressure and pulse rate occurs with physiological maturity. The relation of these changes to sexual development may be observed in girls at the time of the onset of puberty. Shock (1944) presented data on 50 girls tested periodically for both blood pressure and pulse rate. The data revealed a sharp rise in blood pressure the three years prior to puberty and for six months following puberty, then settling to a new level of about 106. It appears that sexual maturity operates to stabilize the increase in blood pressure and to reverse that of pulse rate. There is a gradual decline of pulse rate following menstruation.

Largely because of the red-cell increase, the blood volume increases more in boys than in girls at puberty. In childhood there is no sex difference when the blood volume is considered in relation to height or weight. After puberty the male volume is higher (Sjostrand, 1953).

Respiratory Changes. There is a steady and continuous growth of the lungs during childhood, followed by an increased rate of growth during adolescence, especially among boys. Vital capacity is frequently used as a measure of lung growth. This consists of the amount of air that can be exhaled from the lungs following a deep breath. Ferris and others (1952) presented data on liters of air exhaled by boys and girls from ages 5½ to 17½. The boys were found to excel girls during the early years of life; at age 11 little sex differences were found. Beginning around age 11½, the vital capacity of boys excelled that of girls, and the difference increased during the growing years. The average vital capacity of adult males is greater than that of females throughout the adult years. This difference is affected both by the larger lungs of males as well as the greater amount of physical activity of males.

Fat Thickness and Developmental Status. In view of the "supernutrition" and growth status of American children, it is important to consider the relation between fatness and developmental status in childhood and adolescence. Since calories are growth-promoting, one would expect fatter children to be both taller and developmentally more advanced than leaner children.

A study reported by Garn and Haskell (1960) furnishes evidence that fatness during childhood is related to height and maturity status. The study consisted of data from serial radiographs, anthropometric measurements, and maturational information on 259 clinically healthy children. A consistent positive relationship was found between fat thickness, size, and skeletal age, especially between ages 1.5 and 12.5. Thereafter the relationship regresses toward zero in both sexes.

Since the data collected were longitudinal in nature, it was possible to study the long-term effects of fat. The fat thickness in prepubertal girls (8.5 years and prepubertal boys 9.5 years) was correlated with the age of menarche and tibial union* for girls and with age of tibial union for boys. These correlations show that fatness has long-term effects. The writers conclude: "Thus, fatness results in accelerated growth and advanced maturation in both sexes" (p. 748). The investigators suggest that fatter children are neither taller nor shorter as adults, since fat-size correlations tended to regress toward zero after the twelfth year.

Nutritional Needs

Food needs have been classified into two fundamentally different kinds: (1) those concerned with energy requirements and (2) those concerned with structural requirements. Energy is required for maintaining such activities as beating of the heart, digestion of foods, glandular secretions, and muscular activities. There is also an energy requirement involved in growth. These requirements are obtained mainly through carbohydrates and fats. The structural requirements include the needs for materials that go to make up tissues and to regulate their functions (Breckenridge and Vincent, 1965).

Energy Requirements. The amount of energy needed in terms of calories will vary considerably from individual to individual, since it is dependent upon a number of variables. It differs with the size of the individual as is indicated from the calorie requirements set forth for different age groups in Table 4-1. The 12-15-year-old boy with a weight of 98 pounds needs 600 more calories than his brother in the 9-12-year-old category who weighs only 72 pounds.

The calorie requirement will also depend upon the rate of activity of the body processes while at rest—the basal metabolic rate. The faster the metabolic

*Tibial union refers to the year during which the proximal epiphysis of the tibia fused with the diaphysis.

TABLE 4-1

Recommended Daily Dietary Allowances (Calories)[*]

	Age (years)	Weight (lb)	Height (in.)	Calories
Children	1–3	27	34	1300
	3–6	40	42	1600
	6–9	53	49	2100
Boys	9–12	72	55	2400
	12–15	98	61	3000
	15–18	134	68	3400
Girls	9–12	72	55	2200
	12–15	103	62	2500
	15–18	117	64	2300

*Recommended Dietary Allowances, revised, 1963, Food and Nutrition Board, National Academy of Sciences, National Research Council, Washington, D.C., 1964.

rate—heart beat, respiration—the greater will be the number of calories used in a given period of time. Energy requirements will also differ in accordance with the efficiency of the body in using food. In some individuals food is digested and turned into energy more efficiently than in others. The caloric needs of an individual will also depend on his rate of growth. During the early years after birth when growth is rapid there will be an added need for food to take care of the rapid rate of growth.

Structural Requirements.   Structural requirements include the needs for materials that go to make up tissues. The body does not require all the chemical substances in a ready-made form; it can provide some of these if the necessary materials are provided. What is most needed is a balanced diet of "protective" foods—foods rich in the essential ingredients.

The vitamins, as regulators of body processes, are essential for physical health and development during childhood and adolescence, Vitamins A, D, C, K, thiamine, riboflavin, niacin, folic acid, B_6, and B_{12} are recognized as contributing to the health and growth of children and adolescents. The food needs are not as great after age 3½, since there is a decelerated rate of growth. However, this increases with increased activity and with accelerated growth during the preadolescent period. According to Johnston (1957), the calorie requirements of the preadolescent and the adolescent girl parallels her rate of growth.

Minerals serve as constituents of tissues; for example, calcium and phosphorous are responsible for the strength or rigidity of the bones. An inadequate amount of these minerals during childhood and adolescence would produce among other things poor teeth and rickets. Calorie restrictions or deficiencies of single nutrients, brought on by infections, emotional episodes, or other stress that may impair the appetite at a time when the needs of the body are high, are reflected in bones as striations or arrested growth lines.

Obesity.   Much attention is given to obesity today, since a relationship has been established between obesity and certain heart conditions, and vascular diseases. Also, our present-day culture emphasizes slenderness rather than fatness as an attractive feature of one's personal appearance. Obesity is also a handicap in physical activities and thus a deterrent to physical fitness.

Phosphorus and iron are essential components of all living cells. The importance of phosphorus for muscle, glandular, and nerve tissue is well known. Iron and copper are essential for the function of the lungs and for life activities of all the tissue.

In recent years scientists have been much concerned with the causes of obesity, and considerable attention is being given to the control of body weight so that in many circles diet is a common occurrence. At one time most cases of obesity was attributed to glands. In a study bearing on this, Mayer (1955) describes three types of obesity: (1) metabolic, with lesions involving biochemical factors, (2) regulatory, resulting from a dysfunction in the central nervous system, and (3) inactivity, characterized by a low-energy output. The results of experiments with rats showed that high-fat diets caused extreme obesity only in certain strains of rats. These results suggest that diet for the obese child does not always prove as successful as is sometimes claimed.

Stefanik and associates (1959) have emphasized the importance of exercise in weight control; although there are those who minimize this since it takes considerable exercise to reduce weight. Obese children are, however, far less active physically than children of average weight. The obese child and adult are in a vicious circle insofar as activity and weight control are involved. They are in general inactive largely because of their excessive weight; they remain fat unless they go on a reducing diet because they are inactive.

Glandular malfunctioning has proved to be extremely rare as a cause of obesity, and is seldom given as the major cause. It has been observed that obesity appears among members of some families more frequently than members of other families, as was suggested in the case of different strains of rats. In addition to heredity, diet, and lack of exercise, obesity seems to thrive in certain settings in which eating satisfies needs other than those earlier referred to as energy and structural. Bruch and Touraine (1940) observed that the obese children of their study typically lived in an overprotected environment frequently characterized by a dominating mother and a submissive father. The overprotection of the mother was frequently a means of hiding an indifferent or hostile attitude toward the child. The child's eating was a substitute for affection denied him. The early observations of Bruch and Touraine have been verified by later case studies of obese children (Osmundsen, 1965). The findings and observations of Haslim and Van Itallie at St. Luke's Hospital in New York are quoted by Osmundsen indicated that obese people actually lack hunger, and lose weight rapidly when placed in certain feeding situations.

Motor Development

The development of strength, coordination, speed, and precision in the use of the arms, legs, and all the body muscles follows the principles of growth set forth in Chapter 2. The preschool years are thought of as the manipulative years. During this period the child explores his environment and satisfies many of his needs through motor activities. With maturation and learning, new skills are acquired which have an important bearing on other aspects of development including the child's self-concept.

Growth in Body Control. Every motor skill the child acquires is a result of two major developmental processes—the sequence of events leading to locomotion and the one leading to prehension or manipulation with the fingers. Both sets of motor activities are dependent upon the coordination of different parts of the body with the eyes, ears, and other sensory processes. This may be observed as eye-hand coordination involved in prehension as eye-ear-cerebellum coordination (balance) involved in self-feeding (Bayley, 1965).

In harmony with the principles of development set forth in Chapter 2, growth in motor abilities begins with control of the head and neck and works downward and proceeds from the central part of the body outward. Motor development during infancy—the first year—was described in Chapter 3. Important individual differences appear among infants in various aspects of development. There is evidence, however, from various studies that within normal limits developmental status in the first years of life is a poor indicator of later motor functioning.

By the end of the first year a child is able to use his finger and thumb in pincer movements, and within a few months he will manage to propel himself from place to place with amazing rapidity. At this point in his development of motor control he has a strong motivation to practice his newly acquired abilities to move and to manipulate, along with an intense curiosity about his environment. He runs from one room to another, from his yard into streets and other yards; he pokes, prods, pulls, twists whatever he encounters; and because his attention span is very short he searches persistently for new items and new areas to analyze. Danger has little meaning for him, and he comes into repeated conflict with danger-conscious parents who frustrate his curiosity. The parents themselves find it increasingly discouraging to protect the small child from harm and yet continue to provide him with opportunities to improve his motor skills and his intelligence. As the young child grows older, he is able to occupy himself at different tasks for longer periods of time, and usually to everyone's benefit, especially his own. Ashton (1963), who has taught for more than two decades among the Maori and white children in New Zealand, contends that all children have only two sides to their nature—the constructive and the destructive; she insists that to the extent a teacher encourages the one she diverts energy from the other.

Growth in Motor Ability. Beyond the early years, most of the differences found among children when learning complex motor skills—especially the differences in higher beginning success—result from variations in experiences and motivation (Millard, 1958). Where gross motor skills involving the large muscles are involved, the older children have a significant advantage, partially because they have a greater ability to sustain attention and follow directions.

As the child develops, new motor learnings are needed. The changed physical self brings on added demands. Furthermore, our culture makes certain motor demands on individuals at different age levels. These demands become less with advanced age, so that the older person is not expected to perform as well as the person during the earlier and middle years of adulthood.

Strength normally increases at a rapid pace during the first twenty years of life, but at different rates from year to year. According to Jones (1949) the development of strength during late childhood and adolescence is more conspicuous than any other aspect of physical development. He notes that boys are twice as strong at age 11 as they were at age 6, and their manual strength doubles from age 11 to age 16. The physically immature child of nine or ten is at a great disadvantage in physical competition with others of his age.

Learning Motor Skills.   Physical fitness, motor coordination, and the acquisition of motor skills are closely associated with an individual's physical development, although the acquisition of complex motor skills requires training and practice.

There is evidence from many sources that children who receive training in the acquisition of motor skills such as jumping rope, hopping, throwing, and catching will be superior to those who receive no training (Seils, 1951). Frequently children will concentrate for a time on learning a simple level. At different stages they will combine the new skills with others that were formerly performed independently. When the new and more complex skill is acquired, the lesser skills included in the performance become subordinate to the more complex skill.

Many motor tasks require not only coordinations involving such activities requires attention to certain details that are only indirectly involved in the skill but necessary for correct performance. The skill involved in the act of bowling requires certain finger movements for holding the ball, a controlled twist of the wrist, shoulder movements, body movements, leg movements, and accurate eye-hand coordination. Complete concentration in the performance of the act along with the total body movements is necessary for a successful performance. Related to the performance of a skill Metcalf (1954, p. 33) suggests that "the greater the variety of basic natural skills employed in a single game, the greater the resulting satisfaction and educational value of that game or sport."

The acquisition of motor skills during early childhood is limited by the maturational level. Although about half of three-year-olds are capable of climbing stairs, low inclined planks, packing boxes, jungle gyms, and the like, very few are able to hop and skip. Gutteridge (1939) noted in an early study of motor skills during early childhood that the ability to hop on one foot was mastered by the majority of children prior to age 6. Skill in skipping developed more slowly. Although children frequently practice ball throwing from age 2 or 3, it is not until after age 4 that a sizable percentage attain a fair degree of proficiency. By age 6 the majority of children are able to throw a ball.

Between ages 6 and 12 there is a pronounced growth in children's ability to run, jump rope, climb, play hopscotch, skate, ride bicycles, swim, and slide. Also, during this period more complex motor skills are acquired through special training. Growth in the ability to perform motor acts reaches its maximum around age 13.5 or 14 for girls and around 17 for boys. Tests of agility, control, strength, and static balance show the greatest increase for boys after age four-teen. Speed of voluntary movement increases continually from early childhood at a progressively slower rate (Espenschade et al., 1953).

Age and Motor Performances.   Motor performances usually reach their peak during the teen years, except perhaps for complex performances requiring years of practice and strength. Glassow and Kruse (1960) studied the develop-ment of physical fitness among children from age 6 to 14. Both boys and girls improved in endurance as measured by the 600-yard run and skill as measured by a 100-yard run until about 11 years. After age 11, boys continued to improve on the 100-yard run, although their improvement was slower. Girls on the other hand ceased to show any improvement in the skill after age 11 and actually regressed in their performance on the 600-yard run, so that by age 17-20 they were no better in performance than the 6- to 8-year-olds. This decline in effi-ciency on the part of girls was earlier noted by Jokl and Cluver (1941) in their pulse rate, respiration, and level of fatigue. It seems likely that the early decline in motor ability among girls is a result of their way of life after age 13 when they develop an increased interest in social activities and a fall off of interest in athletics and other forms of muscular activities after this age.

In a study by Bachman (1966) 192 subjects were tested on two large-muscle motor tasks in order to determine the relation between age and sex on the amount and rate of learning. The subjects were confronted with two learning tasks, the first of which was to maintain the body upright while standing on a pivoted platform (stabilimotor) with the objective of preventing any movement of the board, whereas the second task required the subject to maintain balance while attempting to climb an unsupported vertical ladder.

Both sexes reached their peak in the amount of learning in the 30-34 years age bracket; although the increase from the lower age group was not significant. "The stabilimotor learned scores showed no systematic tendency to rise or fall throughout the entire age range 26-50" (p. 184). There was a slight decline of learning rate for the ladder-climb task after the 38-42 age group. Bachman concludes: "The rate of learning in large muscle skills is independent of sex over the range 26-50 years. The rate of learning is probably also independent of age over this range" (p. 186).

Different measures of reaction time show a decline with age. Growth curves for three measures of reaction time are presented in Figure 4-3 (Miles, 1931). The reaction measures of the subjects were elicited by an auditory stimulus. The hands were used in the pursuit reaction, the forefingers in the digital reactions

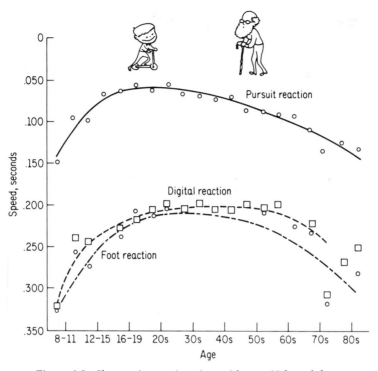

Figure 4-3. Changes in reaction time with age. (Adapted from
W. R. Miles. "Measures of Certain Human Abilities Throughout
the Life Span," *Proc. Nat. Acad. Sci.*, 1931, Vol. 17, p. 631.)

and the foot in the foot reactions. The speed of pursuit reactions in which the
hands were used increased regularly until around age 30, when a decline sets in
which becomes quite rapid around age 70. The general patterns of the forefingers and foot reactions are somewhat similar with both showing a continuous
rise until the 20's, and then a tendency to level off followed by a deceleration
until age 60, when deceleration is very rapid. How much of this decline is related
to lack of continued physical activity involving speed of reaction and how much
to physical and physiological changes accompanying age is unknown. Studies of
individuals who have continued physical activities involving speed of reaction,
such as playing tennis, indicate that much of the deceleration immediately following the twenties is a result of lack of practice.

Reaction time was segmented by Botwinick and Thompson (1966) into
premotor and motor components. Comparisons were then made between 17
men (median age 20.0), and 15 women (median age 20). The time between
stimulus presentation and occurrence of increased muscle firing was the premotor time, while the motor time was the total reaction time minus the premotor
time. The reaction times were slower for the advanced age groups. However, no
significant sex differences were found.

Maximum muscular strength depends not only upon structural maturity but upon physical activity to bring it to maximum function. The decline in physical strength is closely associated with the decline in physical activity, which usually occurs in the mid-20's and continues throughout the adult years. The decline is most pronounced in the flexor muscles of the forearm and in the muscles which

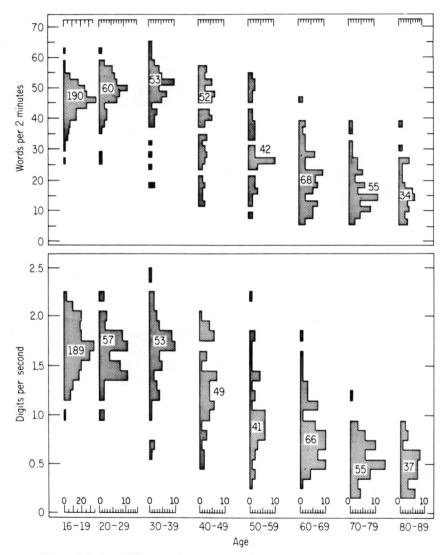

Figure 4-4. Age differences in writing speed. Frequency polygons are shown for each age group. The number of subjects in each age group is indicated on the individual distributions; the number of individuals in a single interval may be estimated from the frequency scales on the abscissa.

raise the body. There are wide differences in the decline of strength with age. A decline in average grip strength of 17 percent from the maximum has been noted at age 60. This decline continues so that by age 75 the maximum grip strength is about equal to that of 12-15-year-olds (Britton and Britton, 1954).

Cratty (1964) summarized the most recent studies of motor learning and concluded that the capacity to learn physical skills becomes fairly well established during adulthood and remains fairly stable until the fifties. After age 50 there is a gradual and continuous decline in motor learning ability.

Handwriting is a complex skill, learned through practice over a relatively long period of time. Birren and Botwinick (1951) found that speed of handwriting seems to slow down with advancing age, although measurements presented in Figure 4-4, show individual differences covering a wide range at different age levels. These differences may be noted at different age levels, indicating a personal adaptation in the speed of performance by each individual.

Summary

Physical development is the most obvious aspect of development and has an important bearing on the child's total development. There is a pattern of growth in height and weight of children. The most rapid period of growth is the early years following birth. This is followed by a continuous deceleration of the rate of growth until near the onset of puberty. At this time there is a spurt of growth in height followed by a spurt of growth in weight. The curves of growth for girls is about one and a half to two years ahead of that for boys. There are both qualitative as well as quantitative changes in the bones during the period of growth. The ossification of the bones furnishes a good basis for estimating anatomical development. This is dependent upon the secretion of a hormone from the thyroid gland and upon the nutrition of the child. Important changes appear in body proportion during the period of growth.

Significant physiological changes appear during childhood; the most important of these are those related to the endocrines. There is a continuous decrease in basal metabolism throughout the teen years, with that of the boys being higher than that for the girls. There is a gradual and continuous growth of the blood vessels during childhood; with puberty there is a rapid rate of growth for the heart. Also, a marked change in both blood pressure and pulse rate occurs with physiological maturity. Vital capacity is used as a measure of lung growth. Boys excel girls in lung capacity during the early years of life; at age 11 there is little difference. After about age 11½ the vital capacity of boys excels that of girls.

Nutritional needs increase as the child nears adolescence. However, a number of factors account for differences in nutritional needs. Most cases of obesity can be traced to consuming more calories than the body needs for growth, energy, and the metabolic processes.

The development of strength, coordination, speed, and precision in the use of body muscles follows the principles of growth set forth earlier. Body control begins with control of the head and neck and works downward and proceeds from the central part of the body outward. Beyond the early years, most of the differences found among children when learning complex skills result from variations in experiences and motivation. Children who receive training in the acquisition of motor skills such as hopping, throwing, and catching will be superior to those who receive no training. However, the acquisition of motor skills during early childhood is limited by the maturational level.

Motor performances reach their peak during the teen years, except for complex performances requiring years of practice. There is a decline in motor performances for girls after age 11 or 12, depending upon cultural norms. Different measures of reaction time show a decline with age. How much decline in motor performances during adulthood is a result of age and how much to lack of continued physical activity is unknown. Certainly, the decline in physical strength is closely associated with the decline in physical activity, which frequently begins in the 20's. It seems that the capacity to learn physical skills becomes fairly well established during adulthood and remains fairly stable until the 50's; after age 50 there is a gradual and continuous decline.

References

Acheson, R. M., and C. W. Dupertius. "The Relationship between Physique and Rate of Skeletal Maturation in Boys," *Human Biology*, Vol. 29 (1959), pp. 167-193.

Ashton. W. S. *Teacher.* New York: Simon and Schuster, 1963, pp. 99-100.

Bachman, J. C. "The Influence of Age on the Amount and Rate of Learning Two Motor Tasks," *Research Quarterly, AAHPER,* Vol. 37 (1966), pp. 176-186.

Baldwin, B. T., L. M. Bresby, and H. V. Garside. "Atomic Growth of Children, a Study of Some Bones of the Hand, Wrist, and Lower Forearm by Means of Roentgenograms," *University of Iowa Studies in Child Welfare,* Vol. 4, No. 1 (1928).

Bayley, Nancy. "Comparisons of Mental and Motor Test Scores for Ages 1-15 Months by Sex, Birth Order, Race, Geographical Location, and Education of Parents," *Child Development,* Vol. 36 (1965), pp. 38-411.

———. "Individual Patterns of Development," *Child Development,* Vol. 27 (1956), pp. 64-65.

Birren, J. E., and J. Botwinick. "The Relation of Writing Speed to Age and to the Senile Psychoses," *Journal of Consulting Psychology*, Vol. 15 (1951), pp. 243-249.

Botwinick, J., and L. W. Thompson. "Components of Reaction Time in Relation to Age and Sex," *Journal of Genetic Psychology,* Vol. 108 (1966), pp. 175-183.

Breckenridge, Marian E., and E. Lee Vincent. *Child Development.* Philadelphia: Saunders, 1965, pp. 114-115.

Britton, J. H. and J. O. Britton. "Work and Retirement for Older University Alumni," *Journal of Gerontology,* Vol. 9 (1954), pp. 468-474.

Bruch, H., and G. Touraine. "Obesity in Childhood: V. The Family Frame of Obese Children," *Psychosomatic Medicine,* Vol. 2 (1940), pp. 141-206.

Cratty, B. J. *Movement Behavior and Motor Learning.* Philadelphia: Lea and Febiger, 1964.

Espenschade, Anne R., R. Dable, and R. Schoendube. "Dynamic Balance in Adolescent Boys," *Research Quarterly, AAHPER,* Vol. 24 (1953), pp. 270-275.

Ferris, B. G., Whittenberger, and J. R. Gallagher. "Maximum Breathing Capacity and Vital Capacity of Male Children and Adolescents," *Pediatrics,* Vol. 9 (1952), pp. 559-570.

Ford, E. H. R. "Growth in Height of Ten Siblings," *Human Biology,* Vol. 30 (1958), pp. 107-119.

Garn, S. M., and L. C. Clark. "The Sex Difference in the Basal Metabolic Rate," *Child Development,* Vol. 24 (1953), pp. 215-224.

Garn, S. M., L. C. Clark, and R. Portray. "Relationship between Body Composition and Basal Metabolic Rate in Children," *Journal of Applied Physiology,* Vol. 6 (1953), pp. 163-167.

Garn, S. M. and J. A. Haskell. "Fat Thickness and Developmental Status in Childhood and Adolescence," *American Journal of Diseases of Children,* Vol. 99 (1960), pp. 746-751.

Glassow, R. B., and P. Kruse. "Motor Performance of Girls Age 6 to 14 Years," *Research Quarterly, AAHPER,* Vol. 31 (1960), pp. 426-433.

Greulich, W. W. "The Growth and Developmental Status of Guamanian School Children in 1947," *American Journal of Physical Anthropology,* S.S., Vol. 9 (1951), pp. 55-70.

———. "Physical Changes in Adolescence." *Forty-third Yearbook of the National Society for the Study of Education,* Part 1. Chicago: Department of Education, University of Chicago, 1944, Chap. 2.

Greulich, W. W. and S. I. Pyle. *Radiographic Atlas of Skeletal Development of the Hand and Wrist,* 2nd ed. Stanford, Calif.: Stanford U. P., 1959.

Gutteridge, M. V. "A Study of Motor Achievements of Young Children," *Archives of Psychology, N.Y.,* No. 244 (1939).

Harding, V. S. V. "A Method of Evaluating Osseous Development from Birth to 14 Years," *Child Development,* Vol. 23 (1952), pp. 247-271.

Hurlock, Elizabeth B. *Child Development,* 4th Ed. New York: McGraw-Hill, 1964

Iliff, A., and V. A. Lee. "Pulse Rate, Respiratory Rate, and Body Temperature of Children Between Two Months and Eighteen Years of Age," *Child Development,* Vol. 23 (1952), pp. 237-245.

Johnston, J. A. "Adolescence." *Brenneman's Practice of Pediatrics* (I. McQuarrie, ed.), Vol. 1. Hagerstown, Md.: Prior, 1957.

Jokl, E., and E. H. Cluver. "Physical Fitness," *Journal of the American Medical Association,* Vol. 116 (1941), pp. 2382-2389.

Jones, H. E. *Motor Performance and Growth.* Berkeley, Calif.: U. of California Press, 1949.

Kralj-Cereck, Lea. "The Influence of Food, Body Build, and Social Origin on the Age of Menarche," *Human Biology,* Vol. 28 (1958), pp. 393-406.

Low, W. D., S. T. Chang, K. S. F. Chang, and M. M. C. Lee. "Skeletal Maturation of Southern Chinese Children," *Child Development,* Vol. 35 (1964), pp. 1313-1336.

Marsh, M. M. "Growth of the Heart Related to Bodily Growth during Childhood and Adolescence," *Journal of Pediatrics,* Vol. 2 (1953), pp. 382-404.

Mayer, J. "Regulation of Food Intake and the Multiple Etiology of Obesity in Weight Control," in E. S. Eppright, P. Swanson, and C. A. Iverson (eds), *A Collection of Papers Presented at the Weight Control Colloquim.* Ames, Iowa: Iowa State College Press, 1955.

Meredith, H. V. "The Rhythm of Physical Growth," *University of Iowa Studies in Child Welfare,* Vol. 11, No. 3 (1935), p. 112.

Metcalf, H. G. "Physical Education," *Colliers Encyclopedia,* Vol. 16 (1954), pp. 33-34.

Miles, W. R. "Measures of Certain Human Abilities Throughout the Life Span," *Proceedings of the National Academy of Science,* Vol. 17 (1931), p. 631.

Millard, C. V. *Child Growth and Development in the Elementary School Years,* rev. ed. Boston: Heath, 1958.

Nathanson, I. T., L. E. Towne, and J. C. Aub. "Normal Excretion of Sex Hormones in Childhood," *Endocrinology,* Vol. 28 (1941), pp. 851-865.

Osmundsen, J. A. "Tests in Obesity," *The New York Times* (Jan. 17, 1965), p. 10E.

Peckas, P. S., and R. P. Heald, "Nutrition of Adolescence," in *Forty-third Yearbook of the National Society for the Study of Education,* Part 1. Chicago: Department of Education, University of Chicago, 1944, Chap. 4.

Seils, L. G. "The Relationship between Measures of Physical Growth and Gross Motor Performance of Primary-Grade School Children," *Research Quarterly of the American Physical Education Association,* Vol. 22 (1951), pp. 244-260.

Shock, N. W. "Physiological Changes in Adolescence," *Forty-third Yearbook of the National Society for the Study of Education,* Part 1. Chicago: Department of Education, University of Chicago, 1944, Chap. 4.

Sjostrand, T. "Volume and Distribution of Blood and Their Significance in Regulating the Circulation," *Physiological Review,* Vol. 33 (1953), pp. 202-228.

Smith, D. W., et. al. "The Mental Prognosis in Hypothyroidism of Infancy and Childhood," *Pediatrics,* Vol. 19 (1957), pp. 1011-1022.

Stefanik, P. A., F. P. Heald, and J. Mayer. "Caloric Intake in Relation to Energy Output of Obese and Non-Obese Adolescent Boys," *American Journal of Clinical Nutrition,* Vol. 7 (1959), pp. 55-62.

Stuart, H. C., and S. S. Stevenson. "Physical Growth and Development," in W. E. Nelson (ed.), *Textbook of Pediatrics,* 7th ed. Philadelphia: Saunders, 1959.

Zuk, G. H. "The Plasticity of the Physique from Early Adolescence through Adulthood," *Journal of Genetic Psychology,* Vol. 92 (1958), pp. 205-214.

Chapter 5

The Development of
Motivational Patterns

Few topics in psychology have been treated in so many different ways as motivation. Some terms that have been or are presently used with reference to motivation are instincts, interests, drives, goals, needs, wants, conscious and unconscious motives, and wishes or desires. When statements are made involving these terms, we note that frequently the reference is to reinforced stimuli or to descriptions of behavior. Although philosophers, psychologists, and biologists have reflected on the nature of motivation their studies and reflections have not led to an acceptable conception of its nature. A vast amount of experimental data is available as a result of studies within the past decade or more.*

Basic Concepts and Theories

Motivation as an activation force or condition affects every area of human behavior. Its influence ranges from the directing of a single act to that of some activity pattern, e.g., choosing a vocational career.

As to the source and origin of the "mainspring" of human behavior, there is currently widespread disagreement. No attempt will be made to present a description of the various theories, since the writers are primarily concerned with the operation of driving forces and the development of motivational pattern among different groups and individuals. One cannot separate a segment of human behavior from the component parts which have made man as he is—his close relationship to other animals, his physiological and psychic origins, his innate demands, and the environmental circumstances and conditions in which he lives. A general working model to understand behavior and motivation in the broadest sense would be to subsume a knowledge of these components. The subsequent presentation of motivational components and patterns include self-actualization

---

*The reader is referred to a comprehensive review based on nearly three thousand references by C. N. Cofer and M. H. Appley, *Motivation: Theory and Research,* Wiley, New York, 1964.

theories as the basic framework for studying the behavior of man in his dynamic culture.

Instincts and Motivation.   The explanation of behavior by statements such as "Blood will tell" or "After all, he came from good stock" represents a tendency found in early students to attempt to account for a person's behavior in terms of his inheritance. Other theories have attempted to explain behavior in terms of man's inherited physical constitution and include the term "instincts." The issue of what behaviors are instinctive and what are learned was the subject of considerable discussion and study *prior to* the early part of the twentieth century. Many lists of instincts were compiled by different students of psychology.

In recent years psychologists have made little use of instincts, especially as they apply to man. It is generally recognized that the complex pattern of behavior is quite variable and depends to a large degree upon learning, although the goal or end state to which it is directed may be quite specific.

Categories of Classification. The bulk of research on motives has to do with the conditions that activate them. A laboratory experimenter, for example, motivates his subjects by issuing instructions or by manipulating incentives. However, for a personality psychologist, motivation is not only a transient state produced by external conditions, but an intrinsic characteristic of a person, a characteristic that he carries with him and may be observed from time to time or from circumstance to circumstance. It appears, therefore, that when the component parts of personality are consistent, the kind or pattern of motives in a person, their strength, and the likelihood of their being aroused in any given situation constitute a stable quality of personality. To speak of one person as socially minded in his behavior and another as self-centered is to describe them in terms of intrinsic motivational characteristics. A full description of personality usually includes the assessment of intrinsic personality.

Researchers in motivation utilizing behavioristic methodology can be identified through three categories (1) Need-reduction, (2) Pleasure-pain, and (3) Self-actualizing theories. The *need-reduction* theory holds behavior is based upon the individuals seeking to satisfy primary needs and that secondary needs grow out of the basic ones through a process of conditioning. S-R theories (Hull, 1951) and homeostatic models are important to this approach of explaining motivation. *Pleasure-pain* theory, sometimes called hedonism, assumes that motivation is broadly the pursuit of pleasure and the avoidance of displeasure by the human organism. The reverse responses, other than what is generally expected, are accounted for through the law of effect. In the *self-actualizing* theories broadly based and influenced by the psychoanalytic literature, major emphasis is placed upon efforts of the individual to reach his ultimate potentialities.

Theories of motivation may be further classified into drive theory and personality theory. The first of these theories has largely dealt with animal behavior below man whereas studies into the latter theory have been subjective and existential. Drive theory is predominantly physiologically oriented as it involves homeostatic adjustment, physiological pressures and tension reduction. This theory is usually related to learning based on reinforcement. Independent variables here are usually deprivation and stimulation. The dependent variable is usually seen as motor response of locomotion (Mowrer, 1960).

There are many personality theories, such as the classical psycholanalytical theory, based upon Freud, Jung, and Adler, the neo-Freudian based upon the work of Fromm and Sullivan, the dynamic theory of Lewin, and the self-actualizing theories of Maslow and Rogers.

Freud's Contribution to Motivational Theory.   The structural approach of Freud's theory says that the *id, ego,* and *superego* are central features of personality structure. According to Freud's theory, behavior is determined by unconscious drives which affect behavior in devious ways. These drives result from an accumulation of psychic referred to as *libido.* The infant has libidinal impulses that are unrelated to reality. Freud contends that the libido represents the total psychic energy possessed by the individual, and arises from the sexual and aggressive needs of the individual. Although psychic energy is thought to be objectless at birth, the growing child gradually becomes involved with other people and with objects in his environment. The libido is basic to Freud's theory of psychosexual development described more fully in the forthcoming discussions of the id, ego, and superego.

The term *id* was introduced by Freud to describe complex mental processes. This involves primitive and basic biological impulses and is, as Fenichel (1945, p. 16) states: "A dynamic driving chaos of forces which strives for discharge and nothing else but which constantly receives new stimulation from external as well as internal perceptions." The id is also the container of the libido which has already been described as psychic energy. The primary stage of the id is known as the oral stage of psychosexual development which is further subdivided into the oral sucking stage and the oral biting stage. Until around age 18 months, the child's chief source of pleasure and contact is with its mouth.

Through the process of identification, the *ego* develops. The processes in the id are entirely unconscious, while consciousness is the function of the ego. The infantile ego develops in relation to the external world and reflects the helpless and dependent infant's efforts at altering and alleviating painfully intense stimuli. In the beginning, perception and mobility are closely tied. Immediately on stimulation, there is motor discharge. To delay action, while withstanding consequent tension, is the basis of all more advanced ego functions. Infantile perception is closely related to the state of the biological drives. The separation of stimulation and response allows the interposition of more complex intellectual activities such as are involved in thinking, imagining, and planning. The ego develops the capacity to test reality vicariously, to imagine the consequences of one or another course of action, and to decide upon future directions to achieve its end. The ego can briefly be summed up as psychological workings. The ego is a secondary process in which realistic thinking takes place and which distinguishes between things in the mind and things in the environment. The experience of ego identity depends on the acquisition of memories and the development of language.

As the ego develops, the child passes through this second stage of psychosexual development. The second stage is the anal period from about six months to three years of age. During this period the child identifies with his parents. The child also learns how to use his toilet training as a power device.

The superego has been explained to some degree in this chapter as internalized attitudes and values, and whose development depends upon the development of those aspects of the ego that furnish the individual values and guides as personal standards. The superego is the social side of the personality which emphasizes internal organization of personality and deemphasizes the environment. The superego can be summed up as the conscience, moral judge, ideals, values, etc.

As the superego develops, the child passes through the third and fourth stages of psychosexual development. The third stage is the phallic period. Some psychologists place this period between the third and fifth years while other psychologists place it between the third and seventh years. During the phallic period, the child begins identifying with biological functions and sex. The "oedipal conflict" is repressed at this time.

The fifth stage in the genital period is the mature and responsible stage of psychosexual relationships that emerges from the earlier stages of sexual activity.

Freud's emphasis is upon emotional experiences as determiners of behavior, and the "unconscious mind" as the seat of maladjustments, rooted in early forgotten or repressed experiences damaging to the individual's ego. And, although there has been considerable controversy over some aspects of Freud's theories of psychoanalysis, many of his basic ideas are widely accepted today. The following ideas are utilized in our analysis of child behavior today and will be given careful attention in later chapters.

1. Early childhood experiences are crucial to later development.
2. Human behavior is influenced by unconscious as well as conscious motives.
3. There are different levels or degrees of conscious awareness.
4. Most behavior is an outcome of a multiplicity of determinants.
5. Individuals employ certain protective devices, known as defense mechanisms, to protect and enhance the ego.

The Drive Concept of Motivation

Much of the research that has been undertaken on motivation has involved studies with animals as subjects and with deprivation involving food or water. In recent years studies have included mating behavior. The pattern of research has been influenced by the observation that animals deprived of food or water are in a state of heightened activity. There has been much controversy about the underlying cause of this heightened activity and many theories have been projected. The most generally accepted explanation is that deprivation produces an imbalance in the body chemistry which leads to an energizing condition referred to as *drive*. Such a viewpoint assumes that the drive only energizes behavior.

At birth the energizing function of drive is entirely or almost entirely unlearned. This may be observed in the behavior of the two- or three-week-old infant. After the infant has been fed and made comfortable, his entire body tends to be relaxed. However, after about three hours following the feeding, he begins making movements with his hands and arms; he turns his head, and he moves his legs and feet. At a later stage the entire body is in motion, and restlessness appears. He makes sounds, whimpers, cries—at first not so loud, then louder, with total body action and deeply flushed features accompanying the crying. Almost every parent has observed these expressions and recognizes them as symptoms of hunger. The drive in its energizing function has put the baby's whole self in motion.

Homeostatic Theory of Drives.   The drive theory that assumes that the drive only energizes behavior involves the concept of homeostasis, which is simply the idea that the organism acts in such a way as to maintain internal stability or normal physiological balance. This may be observed in the adaptation of the infant to extreme changes in temperature. The importance of homeostasis has been stated by Young (1961) as follows:

> . . . . In order to maintain homeostasis an organism *needs* (must find) certain nutritive substances in its environment: Oxygen, water, protein, fat, carbohydrates, minerals, and vitamins. Moreover, an organism *needs* to maintain itself within a limited range of external temperatures as an aid to keeping a stable temperature. Further, an organism *needs* to protect itself from attacks of enemies in order to survive. The requirements for survival are also requirements for maintaining homeostasis. *Needs* can thus be defined objectively in terms of the requirements for existence.

Richter (1942) cites evidence of the "wisdom of the body" being such that homeostasis plays a therapeutic role. Children, suffering from rickets, and given freedom to select their food, choose those rich in calcium. Homeostatic adjustments served to cure the rickets. Animals with deficiencies or defects are known to profit from the same processes.

More commonly known homeostatic adjustments include changes of heart beat in response to temperature, activity, or emotional stress. The endocrine glands function to correct deficiencies or excesses in blood chemistry. Man, despite living in frigid or torrid zones, maintains a constant body temperature. Thus we can infer that homeostasis plays an important role in needs and motivation.

Activity is intrinsic in living tissues. In the awakened state the infant or child is in a state of continuous activity. This activity is periodically interrupted by rest or sleep. Although the activity of the child is periodically interrupted by sleep he is never completely inactive. It was pointed out in Chapter 3 that infants spend the major portion of their lives in sleep, although wide differences appear in the amount of sleep needed. It is difficult to judge just how much sleep a particular child needs, although it is important to recognize individual differences in such needs. Homeostasis operates in maintaining the child in a normal manner. The difficulties of self-regulation of sleep are aggravated by happenings in the child's world that disturb his equilibrium. Such disturbances as malnutrition, illness, anxiety states, and intense stimulation may make a child wakeful when he actually needs rest and sleep.

Not so commonly known is the idea that some authorities think of homeostasis in terms other than strictly physiological processes. Dobzhansky (1959), a geneticist, asserts that education may be regarded as a singularly efficient homeostasic mechanism. Although it is known that the heart and liver do carry on processes of self-repair, not so much is known about adjustment to chronic emotional stress and physical deprivation. In future years we will most likely discover how homeostasis includes the functions of self-recovery and maintenance of mental and emotional equilibrium.

The Sensitizing Function of Drive. When a drive energizes the organism, it is in a state of increased activity and thus more likely to encounter drive-reducing stimuli. Accordingly, some students of motivation conceive of motivation as tension-reducing. This is the sensitizing function of drive and depends more upon learning than the energizing function; in some cases it has been affected by classical conditioning, in others by instrumental learning. *Generalization* now operates to make behavior which earlier satisfied the hunger drive worth exploring when the stimulation from hunger appears.

Social or learned drives or motives may operate in a similar manner. The young child deprived of attention or love frequently reacts intensely to the slightest attention of the teacher or some other adult figure. This is closely related to the sensitizing function of drive. Hartup (1958) noted that preschool children who have been deprived of adult attention for a short period of time, strive harder and achieve more in an apparent effort to gain attention than preschoolers not so deprived.

The Selective Function of Drive. The two-week-old baby, discussed earlier, who becomes progressively more restless with the passage of time following his last feeding and cleaning, exhibits in his highly active state a number of different behaviors involving the entire self. All these movements diminish or cease when the bottle is between his lips, except for increased sucking. At a later stage the mere sight of the mother with the bottle ends the excessive random movements, and he prepares for receiving the bottle by holding out his hands to grasp the bottle while his lips and salivary glands get in a state of readiness for the feeding act.

Studies of more complex motivations of behavior show that the individual is frequently unable to identify the factors that are energizing his behavior. The factors involved in the raised level of activity that accompanies food deprivation are complex, and become more complex with increased maturity and learning. It was early pointed out by Hull (1951) and later by Spencer (1956) that a goal object, such as food, acquires motivational value through learning or conditioning in which the organism comes to anticipate it in a particular situation. In the case of the growing child that has learned that food is provided after he has been appropriately dressed and placed in a familiar place where he has previously been given food, the various features of his external environment are capable of arousing responses relating to eating, such as salivation, licking the lips, and smiling. The stimuli associated with eating acquire the property of energizing these responses relating to eating.

It may be stated that learning involves selecting and fixing responses, through the process of reinforcement. Although man, in common with other organisms, has a biological structure which determines that some stimuli will be reinforced such as food, sex stimulation, water, and air, his reinforcement system seems to be largely learned. Many potent reinforcing stimuli have become important to man because of experiences that made them reinforcers. Skinner (1938) has furnished us with provocative ideas about the role of reinforcement, both reward and punishment. According to Skinner an organism arrives at a given type of behavior through a series of progressive approximations that enables the organism to satisfy his wants or reach a goal. The behavior activities that enable the organism to reach his goal is progressively integrated into his behavior repertoire. Reaching a desired goal on the part of the organism is rewarding to him. Rewarding the organism when the goal is reached is a means of reinforcing certain behaviors. Continuously rewarding the child immediately after he reaches a particular goal strengthens such behavior patterns. The aspects of reward most important in learning are its amount, consistency, and immediacy.

Primary and Secondary Drives.   Students of motivation who emphasized the homeostatic concept recognized that human motivation could not be explained in terms of basic drives alone. In studying animal behavior it was noted that motivational concepts other than those of the basic physiological drives had to be used. The basic physiological drives have been referred to as primary drives; the additional elements that were introduced to describe more complex forms of motivation were referred to as "secondary drives." The secondary drives are learned, much in the same ways as skills and concepts are acquired.

According to the drive-reduction theory of motivation, the basic source of motivation is internal stimulation associated with deprivation. When food is obtained, the stimulation is reduced and the activity of the organism comes to function as a substitute for the internal stimulation resulting from deprivation. According to this theory, the stimulus closely associated with the stimulus operating simultaneously with the primary drive acquires the property of functioning as a drive. However, such drives will disappear in time if they are not associated with the primary drive.

The theory of the operation of secondary drives presumes that there is frequent reinforcement of the secondary drives. The secondary drives alone do not appear sufficient to explain all behavior, especially the more complex forms noted among different cultural groups and individuals. Learned differences in motivational stimuli appear in the variations that occur in individuals within and between particular cultural groups. Furthermore, differences in motivational stimuli appear between different age groups. Various terms are used in describing these differences such as values, needs, wants, feelings, interests, attitudes, goals, aspirations. All of these terms suggest that people find different stimuli reinforcing.

Operation of Motives

Understandings regarding motives and the motivation of behavior are perhaps the most important contributions of twentieth-century psychologists. Piaget (1926) and other students of early child behavior emphasized that during childhood motivated behavior tends to be self-centered. At a later stage, notably during adolescence, the individual is motivated by influences that lie outside the physical self. These influences expand as a result of education and broader experiences to include intimate groups, organizations, and institutions. Some of the important motives that operate effectively among adult groups that will be presented here are aspiration levels, cognitive motives, and interests. One could also include here attitudes, ideals, and values. These are discussed in Chapter 9, and are closely related to motivation and motivational pattern.

Motives are based on inherent characteristics of the individual, although they are modified by experience. Satisfaction in school achievement contributes to goal-directed behavior. An infant's motives lack direction and specific associations with conditions or objects in his environment; but upon experiencing the consequences of satisfying behavior, his behavior becomes more goal-directed. Motives acquire direction and attachment to goals, through reinforcement from satisfying experiences; they also become motive-incentive conditions. Frandsen (1967, p. 278) states: "Incentives are the rewarding objects, situations, and events which the child has learned will satisfy his internal motives." It appears that motives initiate goal seeking; discovered goals give direction to behavior; and incentives satisfy motives and selectively reinforce goal-achieving behavior.

Level of Aspiration.   Level of aspiration relates to an immediate goal; it is the level of performance in a task which an individual thinks he can accomplish on a subsequent performance. Studies involving children and adults show wide individual differences in their statements about goals and aspirations. The influence of success or failure in past experiences with the task has a bearing on the level of aspiration pattern for the task. This was noted in an early study by Sears (1940) of the aspiration level of children in the fourth, fifth, and sixth grades. The children were arranged in three experimental groups, based on their previous school performances. Children in the success group had shown evidence of success in all academic school subjects; those in the failure group had experienced failure; and the differential group had experienced success in reading and failure in arithmetic. The three groups were given familiar reading and arithmetic tasks and, following the first goal-setting sequence, feelings of success or failure were experimentally induced in them by telling them they had either done well or not done well, regardless of how they had actually performed. The level of aspiration was determined for each child by asking him how many seconds he thought it would take him to complete the reading or to solve the arithmetic problem.

A comparison of the discrepancy norms for the three groups is presented in Figure 5-1. This represents the difference between actual performance on the

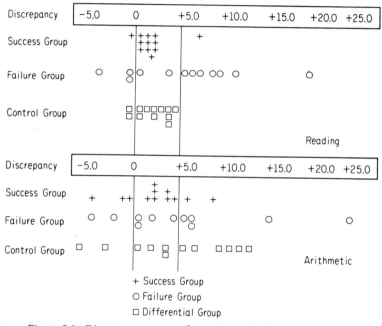

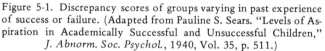

Figure 5-1. Discrepancy scores of groups varying in past experience of success or failure. (Adapted from Pauline S. Sears. "Levels of Aspiration in Academically Successful and Unsuccessful Children," *J. Abnorm. Soc. Psychol.*, 1940, Vol. 35, p. 511.)

first trial and the level of aspiration set for the next trial. Most children of the success group set levels of aspiration in the reading task slightly above their past performances; most members of the failure group set them erratically. On both tasks the success group was the most realistic. Induced feelings of success led all to more realistic goal setting; in all three groups, induced feelings of failure produced increased variability in subsequent goal setting. In a later study by Byers (1958), involving three eleventh-grade classes in United States history, comparisons were made between the level of aspiration of students who had experienced previous academic success and those who had experienced lack of success as indicated by grade-point average. These two groups of students set six consecutive goals throughout the academic year. Students with a record of previous academic success achieved higher grades and set goals more realistically than those with a record of previous academic failure. Related studies indicate that the effects of failure on the level of aspiration are more varied than the effects of success; failure also frequently leads to withdrawal from goal setting.

The level of achievement motivation seems to be established during the early years and remains fairly stable. In a study reported by Moss and Kagan (1961) ratings on achievement obtained at age 6 were found to be positively correlated with ratings obtained at ages 20-29. Evidently the achievement motive or need exhibited during the first four years of school is a good index of achievement during adolescence and adulthood.

Cognitive Motives.   Cognitive motives refer to the intrinsic satisfactions one receives from mental activities involving knowing and understanding cognition. Cognitive motives include curiosity, desire to know, and interests. Curiosity and exploratory behavior appear during infancy and are characteristics which human beings share with many animals. Montgomery (1954) noted that opportunities for exploratory behavior, without extrinsic rewards, is sufficient to motivate learning in rats.

With cognitive motives present, children do not require candy or other extrinsic rewards to enlist their participation in learning. This may be observed in two groups of junior high school youngsters visiting a "science fair," one with an understanding and interest in developments in science and the other with little understanding and interest in developments in science. The results of a study by Maw and Maw (1961) with two groups of 31 children in each, matched for intelligence revealed that the group in the upper third of a clan of 145 fifth-grade children, ranked for curiosity, was significantly superior in learning and remembering facts from free choice learning situations than children drawn from the lower third of the class, ranked for curiosity. The mean scores on the retention test was 17.36 and 9.24 for the high- and low-curiosity groups respectively.

An individual's interest in science, music, history, or art refer to activities he has come to enjoy and to approach with pleasure. As in the case for curiosity, the satisfaction is in the cognitive activity, which may be highly individualized for different students. Interests develop on a wider scale and become more differentiated with increased maturity.

Interests as Motives.   Although demonstrations of the advantages of interest-motivated learning are complicated by the presence of many variables, studies show positive correlations between interest and achievement at school. A classroom study by Edwards and Wilson (1959) dealt with the preference of college students for reading and understanding materials in natural science or materials in humanities. In an elective course in chemistry, the 93 students who preferred natural science materials showed a larger gain, corrected for differences in intelligence, than the 83 students who preferred the humanities. In a subsequent study of success, as measured by scoring at or above the 85th percentile on the *Background of Natural Science* test, Barrilleaux (1961) found that excellence in science depends upon both superior IQ and high interest. This and other related studies suggest that superiority in a field of study seems to be a product both of relatively high aptitude and interest in it (Wesley et al, 1950).

Early studies by E. K. Strong showed that different patterns of interests appear among people working in different vocations. One person becomes highly active when given the opportunity to actively participate in a social activity. In general, those who are energized by special conditions or events seek out those conditions or events when his work or other aspects of his environment fails to provide them. The person who is energized by social activities will seek out clubs, organizations, or special groups when the occasion arises.

Motives: The Concept of Needs

A number of students of human development have made use of *needs* in explaining behavior. Whenever a person acts he is presumably attempting to attain a goal. The goals of the pupil or teacher in a learning situation may have a common element such as achieving. We can better understand this consistency by referring to the need for achievement. A need in such a case is a broad motive that makes certain behavioral responses and goals desirable and important. When behavior is aroused by a condition or situation, it is customary to say that a certain need exists which relates to some aspect of the situation. A person aroused by situations that require a high degree of knowledge or skill is described as one with a strong need for achievement. Such a person will seek out conditions or situations that will furnish him an opportunity to achieve or succeed. Individuals differ widely in the conditions or situations that arouse them—that is, they differ in their needs. Many different classifications of needs have been presented, but none meet the criteria of scientific accuracy; they are more a matter of convenience than a result of scientific inquiry and theory.

A classification of needs can be justified by its usefulness for research and for explaining more complex behavior patterns. The classification presented by Murray (1938) resulted from considerable research, and seems to have brought forth a better understanding of the role of needs in human motivation. Murray postulated that the individual is motivated by psychogenic needs, which he regarded as a learned-reaction system built in some way on the foundation laid by viscerogenic needs—needs derived from simple deprivations such as hunger and thirst. Some of the most generally recognized needs listed by Murray are as follows: acquisition, achievement, recognition, dominance, deference, autonomy, aggression, affiliation, nurturance, succorance, and cognizance. Maslow (1943, 1948) suggested an organizational principle for a system of needs involving an integrated set of needs, arranged in hierarchial order based on the relative importance of the satisfaction of needs.

The term *basic* is frequently used in classifications of man's needs. The significance of this term is evident when one attempts to evaluate the importance of different needs listed in the various classifications. If we attempted to enumerate all the motives that may be found among the different subcultures of our society we would find the task too complex. Investigators of human motives have accordingly set forth a limited classification of needs, such as Maslow's sixfold classification. The writers have made use of a twofold classification: (1) essentially physiological, and (2) essentially social-psychological in nature. The first of these is closely related to primary drives, discussed earlier.

Needs Essentially Physiological. *Needs for food, water, oxygen, sleep, and activity.* These are the needs of the organism for food, water, oxygen, sleep, activity, and sensory satisfaction. Such requirements are easily satisfied in America, where many people are well fed and adequately housed. Satisfaction of these may best be indicated in the statistics on infant and child mortality, which since the turn of the century has been so low that average life expectancy has been extended considerably. Actually, these needs in American society amount to emergency needs and explain the behavior of very few individuals. The consequence is that motivational needs of a higher level tend to dominate young children and adults in our culture.

A crying, fretful, restless baby may be indicating that he is hungry, thirsty, or in need of rest. But with feeding, sleeping, bathing, and activities so carefully scheduled by mothers it is doubtful that the physiological motives ever become dominant. In short, the crying, restless baby probably will be as readily comforted by being picked up, cuddled, kissed, and talked to as he will be by being given the breast or bottle. His restlessness then may be indicating other needs than the physiological. He wants attention. Nonetheless the avenue to satisfying need for nurturance is through the sensory equipment (touch), and therefore this sense can be considered physiological. This observation illustrates an important principle of behavior: motives are usually multiple and complex rather than being singular and simple. No claim is made here that physiological needs are unimportant—they are simply so readily satisfied that they quickly become fused with higher order needs. The social-psychological needs become more pronounced from babyhood onward.

The sex drive. The drive to sexual behavior arises from tension in the body derived primarily from the functions of the sex glands. However, the incidence of sex is not the exclusive function of the glands; external stimulation and conditioning are also important. This fact may be noted early in life. The role of learning has been studied in rats as well as other animals. McGill (1965, p. 76) concludes from his studies:

> There is a basic similarity in the mating pattern of the four most common laboratory rodents—rat, hamster, guinea pig, and mouse. The male's response to a receptive female usually involves a series of mounts and intromissions which normally result in ejaculation. Beyond the basic similarity a great deal of variation is found in the temporal pattern of the behavior.

Based on a review of theories of sexual behavior Young (1961) proposed two mechanisms which may be roughly classified as *appetitive* and *consummatory*. The sex drive is derived from internal glandular secretions, which may be regarded as appetitive; sexual behavior grows out of affective reactions between individuals, and is rooted in a background of social responses. In light of this it is not surprising to find that individuals exposed to an early background in which sexual behavior was looked upon as vulgar would develop distorted ideas about sexual behavior and deviant sex patterns.

The emerging interests of adolescents toward members of the opposite sex receives its impetus from the biological changes in which the sex glands have become more active. This has been verified in studies of some species of animals, notably primates, where a limited amount of sex play appears just before the pubertal stage of development is reached. The sexual drive is greatly enhanced near the time of puberty. A study by Stone and Barker (1939), comparing the attitudes and interests of premenarcheal and postmenarcheal girls of the same age gives us a better understanding of the effects of the operation of the sex drive in middle-class culture in California.

The subjects of the study by Stone and Barker consisted of 1,000 girls of two large junior high schools of Berkeley, California. Significantly greater heterosexual interests and attitudes were indicated on an inventory by the postmenarcheal girls than by the premenarcheal girls. The data also supported the hypothesis that postmenarcheal girls would have a stronger interest in adornment and display of person. The results also showed the interests of the postmenarcheal girls to be more mature than those of the premenarcheal girls.

Although the drive to sexual behavior is physiological, the direction and pattern of an individual's sex behavior is to a marked degree culturally determined. Baller and Charles (1961, p. 130) state:

> The selection of the sex *object*—the kind of person to whom one is attracted—is largely a matter of environmental influence. Cultural values and norms, the restrictiveness or permissiveness of the individual's guidance into sex knowledge and experience, the accessibility of a sex partner at a particular time and place; these and other environmental factors have much to do with the individual's expression of his sex urge.

By the time the boy or girl arrives at pubescence in our society, he has acquired much information about sex and has been bombarded by television and stories with sex presented in seductive manner. The results of puritanical teachings combined with the mass communication materials highly tinged with sex are such that the individual reaches puberty frequently confused.

Social-Psychological Needs. The use of the term *basic* when applied to physiological needs is quite apparent. It is less apparent when applied to the social-psychological needs. However, an examination of data available on such needs as safety and love suggests that these could logically be dealt with as physiological needs, indicating the difficulty encountered in classifying needs.

Complexity of social-psychological motives or needs. In the course of one's development and adjustment to internal and external pressures, many habits are acquired which are frequently peculiar to particular situations and to the individual concerned. People who are accustomed to watching their favorite television program after dinner, for example, are frequently frustrated by developments which interfere with their televiewing that particular program. Thus any list of social-psychological needs must take into account the diversity of habits acquired by different individuals. These habits are forms of behavior acquired that satisfy certain needs and are sometimes regarded as drives to behavior. The writers prefer to think of social-psychological drives as acquired internal manifestations or urges, although such motives do not operate separately; rather, individual behavior is an expression of a complex of interrelated urges, motives, or needs. A variety of motives prompted the college student to go to college, to choose a particular area of study, and to engage in certain out-of-school activities. Such choices may involve long-term goals, and the individual is propelled to action involving these goals by needs which are satisfied along the way.

The identification and study of needs are made more difficult by the fact that many of our social-psychological needs are "unconscious" in the sense that the individual himself is unable to recognize the true motives back of a particular act. This may be observed in the case of a parent's reaction to an unwanted or rejected child. Feelings of guilt may result in the parent being overattentive to the child—just the opposite of what might be expected from such feelings about the child. Since motives are frequently "unconscious," attempts to evaluate the motives or needs of an individual requires the drawing of inference and conclusions from case studies and subtle responses in unstructured situations. Attempts by an individual to make an objective self-appraisal of his motives are useful but fraught with difficulties because of the nature of man's needs.

Safety needs. Sensory organs, muscular activity, and the intellect are safety-seeking equipment. They warn the individual of danger and carry him away from it. The safety needs appear among infants in diverse ways. An indication of the child's need for safety is his preference for some degree of routine. Maslow (1943) states:

> Young children seem to thrive better under a system which has at least a skeletal outline of rigidity, in which there is a schedule of a kind, some sort of routine, something that can be counted upon, not only for the present but also far into the future. Perhaps one could express this more accurately by saying that the child needs an organized world rather than an unorganized or unstructured one.

However, these needs are well met in much of childrearing practice—provision of space for play, attractive and suitable toys, and family interest and pride in the baby's development. Medical care and innoculations, which are routines of postnatal care, are provided by the great majority of parents. Some schools require certificates of health and innoculations as a stimulus to those who might otherwise neglect them. Again, the health records of American children attest to the adequacy with which safety needs are approached. The result is a current crop of children who can progress toward satisfaction of higher-level needs.

It seems that safety needs related to the psychological are somewhat less likely to be met adequately. Strife in world affairs, rapid technological change, unprecedented mobility and continually closer contacts with people lead many to assert that this is a period of extraordinary strife; but this has been said in previous generations since the time of Plato. At any rate, children do see reflected in their parents, considerable anxiety, and the result is that a perennial need is succorance—aid and comfort in times of stress. Shirley (1938, p. 345), in an analysis of the needs of preschool children, concluded:

> The need most commonly expressed was for succorance or security, and that second in importance was the need for autonomy or independence; the needs for affiliation and for recognition tie for third place, and those for nurturance, blame-avoidance, and achievement tie for fourth.

Belongingness and love needs. When physiological and safety needs are adequately met, the need to give and receive love emerges as the next priority. Menninger (1950) calls attention to the fact that this is a difficult lesson—giving and receiving love—and many adults have not learned it. Babies and children can exist, but they cannot live a mentally healthy life without love. Antonovsky (1959) found that children who are given love show less evidence of dependency (they need not seek what they have), they show less aggressive behavior, and initiative is higher. Again we see a lower level need (love) replaced by a higher one (self-actualization).

Much debate on breast feeding versus bottle feeding and early versus late toilet training has been resolved by the discovery that the method or timing is much less important than the emotional atmosphere in which the child is fed and trained—and we can continue to say, the atmosphere in which he learns in school is more important than the particular methods employed.

The importance of the satisfaction of the need for affection during infancy was emphasized in Chapter three in the life of infant monkeys. Studies by the Harlows (1962) showed that monkeys deprived of love during the early years failed to develop normal social relationships in their adulthood. The investigators described them as follows:

> They are without question socially and sexually aberrant. . . . The entire group of animals separated from their mothers at birth . . must be written off as potential breeding stock. Apparently their early social deprivation permanently impairs their abilty to form effective relations with other monkeys, whether the opportunity was offered to them in the second six months of life or in the second to fifth year of life. (p. 142)

In our society the thwarting of love, affection and belongingness is perhaps most commonly found in cases of maladjustment and more severe psychopathology. However, in our culture love and affection, as well as their possible expression in sexuality, are usually looked upon with ambivalence and are most likely hedged about with many restrictions and inhibitions (Maslow, 1943).

Achievement need. McClelland and others (1963) present data from a study by Winterbottom (1953) supporting the hypothesis that differences in achievement motivation result from different experiences in early life. In her study, achievement scores were obtained from stories told by 29 normal boys. The mother's attitude toward independence training was obtained from a questionnaire given the mothers in an interview.

The main results from Winterbottom's study are summarized in Table 5-1, which shows that mothers of achievers make more restrictions during the early

TABLE 5–1

Average Number of Demands and Restrictions
Below and Above Age 8 by Mothers of Children
With High and Low *n* Achievement
(After McClelland et al.)

	Mother's Demands		Mothers Restrictions	
	Age 7 and Below	Age 8 and Above	Age 7 and Below	Age 8 and Above
Sons with high *n* achievement (*n* = 14)				
Mean	11.71	7.43	8.79	4.50
S.D.	4.68	4.62	3.56	3.42
Sons with low *n* achievement (*n* = 15)				
Mean	6.07	12.13	5.80	9.60
S.D.	4.05	3.94	3.92	5.02
Difference between means	5.64	−4.70	2.99	−5.10

stages of a learning process such as learning to read, to perform arithmetic computations, and to acquire other tool subjects. The restrictions on the part of the mother were largely withdrawn after the initial learning, around age 8, leaving the child on his own. The picture is that of controlling and supervising the child during the early stages of learning while he internalizes certain desires and wants, and then leaving him alone. In this way increased self-control is established through internalized behavior in which there were initially consistent, outer controls from the parents—especially the mother.

Status or esteem needs. Behavior at this need-seeking level begins to approach independence and self-reliance. Whereas at the receiving love level one's mere existence or presence is the excuse for love, at the status level it is one's performance, unusualness, or superiority that counts. Status needs are being sought when the child shifts from a "Here I am," orientation to a "See, I can do this." He is, in short, seeking to merit the acceptance and respect that he gets or hopes to get.

Whether it is acceptable or unacceptable behavior (from an adult viewpoint) the child only repeats those actions that are successful. If a temper tantrum gets him the attention he wants, that behavior is reinforced. If being a "little man" or "fine young lady" earns words of praise, then that is the action that tends to be repeated. If reinforcement is received for accomplishments of good conduct at home or accomplishments of satisfactory grades in school, or good citizenship in peer groups, then the child has reasons to congratulate himself for earning esteem.

Satisfaction of the self-esteem need leads to feelings of self-confidence, worth, and adequacy—or a positive self-concept. Continuous thwarting of this need through failure and disapproval produces feelings of inferiority, worthlessness, and inadequacy—or a negative self-concept.

Kvaraceus and associates (1959) found many factors contributing to the occurrence of delinquency but high among them was a lack of self-esteem. Stable children had parents who cared for and respected them and gave firm but not repressive discipline. Norm-violating children came from homes where there was conflict between spouses and children and where family values conflicted with school values. The contrasting milieu of the types of children clearly illustrates the fact that fulfillment of status needs derives from tangible sources, and these sources can be manipulated.

Self-actualization needs. When persons have had their physiological, safety, love, achievement, and status needs fairly well satisfied, they are in the fortunate position of enjoying good mental health. This is a situation wherein life can be enjoyed to its utmost because of the opportunity to satisfy the need for self-fulfillment. In children such a state permits them to be creative, adventuresome, independent, curious, and free. In adults, such a state is reached by people who have become so much "one with the world" that achieving their goals is an end in itself—not a means of further need reduction.

Tentative speculations regarding the climate for stimulating self-actualization can be drawn from the research on fostering creative talent in school. Although there is considerable diversity in descriptions, there is also some helpful consensus. Teachers who foster creativeness are willing to "get off the beaten track." They are sensitive and flexible and are able to form close relationships with the adventuresome student. They are willing to undertake difficult tasks, ready to work hard, admit their mistakes. They are not particularly concerned about conformity and are sometimes regarded as "odd" by their colleagues. They find fault with things as they are but have constructive suggestions for improvement. It should be obvious that such teachers might have no great appeal to the pupil who is seeking safety and acceptance or belonging needs, nor sometimes to an unenlightened administration.

Motivation and Patterns of Behavior

The basic principle in our discussion of motives, needs, and goals has emphasized neither the incitement nor the behavior. The classification of needs that were presented were considered in relation to our culture. However, anthropologists have suggested that people in different societies are more alike than we would think from our first impressions. The differences we first observe seem startling, but are actually superficial rather than basic, e.g., differences in dress, make-up, style of hair, food tastes, and preferred drinks.

These needs are not to be considered exclusive or single motives that propel individuals toward certain determined goals. Examples may be found in physiologically motivated behavior such as certain activities related to self-esteem. Clinical psychologists have long since noted that any behavior may be a channel through which flow various determinants. This implies that most behavior is multimotivated; it tends to be determined by multiple needs operating simultaneously rather than by only one of them.

One of the primary values of the needs concept is that it furnishes a basis for understanding the perceptions and motives of groups and individuals from different social class groups and cultures. According to Lipset (1959) two basic values, equalitarianism and achievement have remained dominant in American culture. Although they may appear contradictory at times, they remain dominant values. Lipset (1959, p. 219) states:

> The value equalitarianism still largely determines the nature of our status system; and in spite of dire predictions that the growth of large corporations has meant a decline of upward mobility and a consequent fall in achievement motivation, American society is still characterized by a high level of actual achievement in the population as a whole.

Sex Differences. Sex differences in interests, problems, and motives may be observed during the preschool years. Important sex differences appear in motivational patterns involving marriages, vocational, and other aspects of life. Crutchfield (1962) noted in his study that females consistently earned higher conformity scores than did male. Evidence was further offered that high-conforming females tend to be generally characterized by easier acceptance of the "conventional" female's role. With increased age both men and women develop strong needs for acceptance and security, this need being higher for women than for men.

Needs have an important bearing on one's perception of things in his world. Bruner and Goodman (1947) noted that poor children tend to overestimate the size of coins more than children from economically privileged homes. The materials presented subsequently will deal with the role of the needs concept in some rather typical patterns of behavior at different stages of life.

The Self Concept. A basic fact that may be observed in the early life of a child is that the person whom the individual refers to as "I" is most significant to him. His physical body may be crippled; his physical skills may be very limited; and his efforts at social participation may be at times thwarted. Yet he must attain a satisfying self-concept. The development of a favorable self concept is related to the satisfaction of the need for love, achievement, and self-fulfillment.

It was pointed out in Chapter 3 that during infancy the child engages in finding himself and important things or persons in the world about him. One's self concept goes through a succession of stages beginning with the close attachments to the mother substitute during infancy and proceeding through to adulthood while attempting to satisfy such needs as love, belongingness, achievement, and self-fulfillment. The self-concept gradually extends beyond the self and one's role in the family to one's role at school, with his peers, with older adults, and with things and conditions in one's expanding world. Highly motivated students tend to have a positive concept, while poorly motivated students tend to have a negative concept. The latter group of students lack self-confidence and feel insecure in their school activities.

Problem Behavior. At all stages of development psychologists are interested in the why of behavior. We should realize in this connection that patterns of problem behavior such as enuresis (bedwetting) during childhood or vandalism during adolescence are motivated. Although these are undesirable habits formed during the growing period, the resultant behavior was motivated at each stage of development. Hunger and breaks in routine during infancy produced upsets in the baby's system of balances, and the homeostatic adjustments brought into play are sufficiently strong to produce behavior described as "problem behavior."

The need for security may sometimes be observed when the child enters school for the first time. The five- or six year-old may revert to earlier behavior such as thumb-sucking, which seems to provide some relief from his feelings of insecurity. The child from a minority group, if rejected by other children through prejudice carried over from their home experiences, may display a great deal of hostility and aggression, or withdraw from the group. It is at this point that competent and understanding teachers frequently help by seeing that the child's needs for acceptance and belongingness are met, so as to prevent problem behavior.

Motivational Patterns and Social Interactions.   Frequently social interactions within a group are impeded by motivational patterns of certain individuals of the group. This may be observed in the case of Tom, a high school sophomore.

Tom has two younger sisters. He received more than his share of attention from his parents. Thus he developed a strong need for dominance in a group where he was involved. His IQ was approximately 115, and he got along especially well in classes where he could display his abilities and skills. He came from a middle-class home and developed good verbal skill at an early age. He seemed to get along with his teachers, especially female teachers, better than with his classmates. Through his superior verbal ability and help from some of his teachers, he was elected president of the freshman class. He had many ideas of

Development of Motivation Patterns. "Operation Male," Arlington, Massachusetts, Public Schools, brings men teaching aides into primary grades to enhance boy's self-image.

his own for freshman activities, but gave little consideration to the ideas of others. Although Tom made a bid for presidency of the sophomore class, he received very little support because of his dogmatism as president of the freshman class. Thereafter, he withdrew from activities of the sophomore class and formed a clique with a small group of students who were quite different from most students and didn't challenge Tom's ideas, although they were erratic or illogical.

Tom's strong need for being dogmatic makes it hard for him to get along with others who have their own ideas, even though they are less dogmatic than Tom. The extent to which personality conflicts based on the satisfaction of needs arise is brought out in a recent study reported by Haythorne and Altman (1967).

Four personality dimensions were used in a study involving the problem: "Can the strains of isolation be reduced by careful psychological pairing?" The problem involved the pairing of individuals in isolation, where interpersonal conflict becomes exaggerated, since there is little chance for blowing off steam outside. The four personality dimensions or needs studied were:

1. Need for *achievement:* defined as the desire or need to accomplish some overall goal—a task-orientation, or work-orientation.
2. Need for *dominance:* the need or desire for control over others, for individual prominence—a self-orientation.
3. Need for *affiliation:* the need and desire for affection, and association with others.
4. Need for *dogmatism:* the need to believe that one's own opinions and ideas are the only important ones; an inability to tolerate dissent; ethnocentric personality.

Eighteen pairs of men—young sailors in boot training—were selected for studying the effect of isolation. They were tested and rated on the four traits: achievement, dominance, affiliation, and dogmatism. They were matched so that in one-third of the pairs both were high in each of these dimensions, in one-third both were low, and in the final third one was high and one low.

Each pair was confined to a small room (12 feet by 12 feet) and isolated from outside contacts for 10 days. They were given a certain amount of work to do on a fixed schedule but were free to talk, read, play cards and checkers for several hours each day. They were not free to communicate in any way with the outside. They had no mail, radios, watches, or calendars.

Records were kept of the activities, stresses, and conflicts of the different combination of pairs. Of the four groups that had the most trouble, including severe arguments and fighting, three pairs were both high in dominance, and two were strongly contrasting in their need for achievement—indicating that putting together in isolation two domineering men, or one who was a driving "go-getter" and one who was not, would most likely lead to trouble. The dogmatic pairs of isolates had a lot of active social interchange, including arguments. The pairs with contrasting needs for affiliation were the most consistently passive and withdrawn of any pairs. Their method of adjusting to incompatibility was withdrawal, in contrast to that of the dominance incompatibility, which led to a volatile aggressive relationship.

The investigators present a good description of what we may expect of individuals in a personal and social way when they have vastly different needs. They state:

> Dominance and dogmatism are egocentric qualities—they reflect primary concern for the self—whether in relation to other persons (dominance) or to ideas and/or things (dogmatism). Need for affiliation and need for achievement are sociocentric qualities—they reflect concern for joint relationships between the self and others (affiliation) and as members of a group striving for a common goal outside the self (achievement). (p. 22).

Personal Needs and Vocational Choice. There is evidence from many studies that personality characteristics and personal needs are related to vocational choices. A comparison by Sternberg (1955) of the personality patterns of college students majoring in different fields revealed significant differences. The sharpest differences found were between students majoring in the fine arts and those majoring in science and mathematics. Zuckerman (1958) analyzed the scores of 68 student nurses on the Edwards Personal Preference Scale. He noted that the student nurses scored significantly higher than female college students on the abasement and nurturance scales and lower on the autonomy, dominance, and aggression scales.

An investigation by Parker (1966) was designed to determine the role of career orientation and marriage orientation in the vocational development of college girls. Based on results from 180 subjects who completed the Career and Marriage Attitude Inventory Parker concluded:

1. In their vocational development, career-oriented, marriage oriented, and mixed-oriented college girls do not differ significantly in respect to grade-point average, key-figure influence, emergence and persistence of occupational preferences, and work experience.
2. Girls primarily interested in marriage, or in mixing marriage with a career, had interests in more occupations that serve as interim jobs than did the girls primarily interested in a career.

It seems that the girl with a strong achievement need may be more career-oriented. Also, according to the findings of Parker girls who are marriage-oriented regard their job as secondary to their marriage and are not interested in preparing for a job where there are good opportunities for advancement to a better position. With women entering into more different areas of work in ever increasing numbers, it is likely that more women in the future will be occupation- or career-oriented. How this will affect marriage stability, one can only conjecture. Frequently the two play different but supporting roles in their work activities. Furthermore, men and women may have different motivational patterns in connection with their work as a career.

The results of these studies are supported by those of a study by Astin and Nichols (1964). Astin and Nichols secured responses from 5,495 college students of recognized ability to a 55-item questionnaire. They suggest from the responses obtained that students who are planning careers as military officers, business executives, and lawyers are similar in that they have a relatively strong desire for prestige and for status and power. Similarly, women who choose the career of homemaker, in medicine, technician, nurse, and secretary or clerk are similar in that they express a great desire for personal comfort and have a relatively high interest in goals concerned with family or marriage.

Personal Needs of Teachers. The personal needs of teachers will vary with sex and field of teaching. The needs of teachers, most frequently male, aspiring to administrative positions will generally be different from those aspiring to achieve. Administrative positions tend to satisfy the needs for dominance and money to a greater degree than do teaching positions; teaching more nearly satisfied the needs for nurturance, succorance, and academic achievement.

Garrison and Scott (1961) compared the scores on the Edwards Personal Preference Scale of 530 female college students preparing to teach in different areas. Some findings from this study may be summarized as follows:

1. Women students preparing to teach in academic subjects in high school manifested a greater need for achievement than those preparing to teach in nonacademic areas and in elementary schools.

2. Women students preparing to teach in the lower elementary grades showed a greater need for nurturance than those preparing to teach in most other areas.

3. Women students, except for those preparing to teach in special education, showed a greater need for succorance than the female population in general.

4. Prospective teachers of lower elementary education manifested a significantly smaller need for heterosexuality than did the students in most other areas.

5. No significant differences were shown by the prospective teachers in any areas of teaching relative to the following needs: endurance, deference, aggression, and dominance.

Motivational Needs of Executives.   According to Maslow's theory of hierarchy of needs, one would not expect an increase in salary to an executive, whose basic needs for survival and comfort are already satisfied, to be important. If increased salary satisfied only lower level needs, then this assumption is obviously correct.

However, there is both empirical and scientific evidence that increased pay for individuals with a high salary satisfies other needs. This is brought out in a study by Lawler (1967) involving the salary of executives. He contends that *"Pay is a unique incentive—unique because it is able to satisfy both the lower order physiological and security needs, and also higher needs such as esteem and recognition"* (p. 24). Individuals in responsible positions, such as administrators and managers, frequently think of their pay as a form of recognition for a job well done and as a mark of achievement. Pay is a form of recognition that is visible. It is in America, an important indicator of the value of a person to an institution or an organization. It is because pay satisfies higher-order needs as well as lower-order needs that it continues to be important to managers regardless of their income. This is indicated by the executive when he stated. "I want my salary to be six figures when it appears in the next annual report." It appears that pay may be important to lower level and middle level managers while the needs for security, esteem, autonomy, and self-realization are more important for upper-level executives. However, autonomy and self-realization needs are usually rated high by all three levels of managers.

Motivators and Job Satisfaction.   It is generally believed that job satisfaction results from a combination of motivators along with favorable working relations and conditions. Those job aspects that form the content of the job have been labeled motivators; while those job aspects that related to the job context are labeled hygiene factors.

In a study reported by Halpern (1966), data were obtained on 93 subjects from the files of a university counseling service. The subjects were males with an average age of 32.5 years; they had worked on an average of 3.9 jobs. Part of a questionnaire they completed asked them to rate different aspects of their best job, using a 7-point graphic rating scale. In addition each subject rated his overall satisfaction with the job.

Correlations between ratings on the different factors and job satisfaction ratings are presented in Table 5-2. Two findings are apparent in the results. First,

TABLE 5-2

Correlations between Motivator and Hygienic Factors and
Overall Satisfaction (After Halpern)

Factor	Correlations with Job Satisfaction	Average Ratings
Motivator		
Achievement	.76	5.8
Work itself	.76	6.5
Responsibility	.57	6.4
Advancement	.46	5.3
Hygiene		
Company policy	.46	5.2
Supervision	.47	6.1
Interpersonal relations	.35	6.0
Working conditions	.29	5.0

the subjects were equally well satisfied with both the motivator and the hygiene aspect of their job. Second, the motivator factors contributed significantly more to overall satisfaction than did the hygiene factors. These findings reveal the importance of such factors as achievement, work itself, and responsibility in relation to job satisfaction.

There is a difference, however, between workers in different areas and from different cultural backgrounds. Based upon studies of intrinsic and extrinsic job motivations Centers and Bugental (1966) conclude: "White-collar workers consistently placed a greater value on intrinsic sources of job satisfaction than did blue-collar workers. Correspondingly, blue-collar workers consistently placed a greater value on extrinsic sources of job satisfaction." In general, blue-collar workers probably are more preoccupied with satisfying their basic needs than are workers in higher occupational levels. The same generalization may be made about many white-collar workers at the lower salary schedule. In harmony with the theory of the hierarchy of motives it is only after these basic needs are satisfied that they become interested in the personal growth aspects in the work

environment (Malinovsky and Barry, 1965, p. 450). The job motivators of
workers at higher occupational levels stem from the work itself—the skill required, the interest value of the work, and conditions of work.

Changing Time Perspective.   It seems that the immediate problem faced by
many people is that of finding enough time to do the things they want to do.
This, despite the fact that children and adolescents have been almost completely
relieved of work and the hours of labor for adults has been continuously reduced. More important, perhaps, is the time limitation upon the achievement of
long-term goals measured in terms of years. The relation of time perspective to
age is a major variable in developmental psychology (Frank, 1939; Lewin, 1939).
Lewin has pointed out that in early childhood the psychological future is vague,
undifferentiated, and extends only slightly into the future—but with adolescence
a rosy future looms for many youth. However, at this age, the future is somewhat indefinite and frequently made up of dreams, some of which are realistic
and others are not so realistic. There is evidence that present-day adolescents are
more realistic than youth of thirty or more years ago. This may be attributed in
part to improved educational and guidance programs.

A study by Jones (1968) involving college students in different age groups
has a direct bearing on worries, problems, and satisfactions at different age-
levels. A comparison was made of the responses of college students in different
age groups on the following: biggest worry now, future goal now, and most
satisfying aspects of life now. The results for four age groups are presented in
Table 5-3. The greatest worries for college students in the lower age brackets
were school completion and financial problems; the greatest for those in the
upper age brackets were school completion and children. Future goals, especially
important among the 21-30 age group were marriage, having children, vocational
success, and having a good family life; although vocational success was listed by
a sizeable group of students at all age levels studied. The most satisfying aspects
of life now centered around family life and occupation for all groups, except the
19-21 age group; love, college work, and general friendships were the most
satisfying aspects of life now for the 19-21 and 21-30 age groups.

In the 1930's the typical adult seems to have felt that there is still time, so
he willingly invested in the future in terms of furthering his education in some
cases, buying a home, and obtaining a job that provides for his security. For the
forty- and fifty-year-old person, time is *now;* frequently individuals feel as this
stage that they have reached the "top of the hill" and must get the most out of
life now or never. After fifty, most individuals think more and more of the
present, leaving plans for drastic changes to younger minds. Time is now and the
"good old days" are past, and the future is progressively viewed more dimly.
These are broad generalizations not applicable to all individuals. Such factors as
financial status, occupation, health, size of family, and interests will be reflected
in time perspectives at different age levels. Some of these will be discussed in
subsequent chapters.

TABLE 5-3

Responses Of 538 Graduate and Upper-Level Undergraduate Students by
Individual Statement of Biggest Worry Now, Predominant Future
Goal Now, and Most Satisfying Aspect of Life Now by
Sex & Age Groups (After Jones)

Major Category	N = 186 19–21		N = 252 21–30		N = 82 31–40		N = 38 41–50	
	Male	Female	Male	Female	Male	Female	Male	Female
Biggest Worry Now								
School completion	14	48	40	46	14	10	2	4
Financial	10	28	36	24	6	8	1	1
War	8	6	8	2	0	4	1	1
Marriage	2	6	2	8	0	1	0	0
Occupation choice	4	2	9	5	4	0	0	0
Children	0	2	2	6	4	8	8	8
All others (or no response)	14	42	38	26	13	9	4	8
Future Goal Now								
School completion	14	12	17	16	17	16	4	3
Marriage	2	14	10	22	1	1	0	1
Have children	0	10	5	15	0	2	0	0
Vocational success	4	38	60	60	11	15	8	2
Have good family life	2	18	4	22	2	2	1	1
Marriage compatibility	0	8	1	1	1	1	0	0
All others (or no response)	29	31	34	16	7	2	2	14
Most Satisfying Aspect of Life Now								
Family life	0	8	29	38	14	16	10	9
Occupation	0	8	16	22	16	7	4	4
Marriage	0	16	2	5	0	2	2	5
Love	2	14	14	9	0	0	0	0
College work	10	16	21	23	0	0	5	2
Friendships (general)	2	6	6	14	2	4	0	0
All others (or no response)	35	43	28	4	6	9	19	25

SOURCE: F. R. Jones, unpublished data, January 1968.

Summary

Motivation is an activating force or condition and effects every area of
human behavior; it has received the attention of philosophers, psychologists, and
biologists for many decades, and many theories have emerged. One basis for
classifying theories is that of the drive theory and personality theories. Drive
theory is predominantly physiologically oriented and has depended to a marked
degree on experimental work with animals. Freud has given us one of the most
complete description of a personality theory of motivation, with the emphasis

upon emotional experiences as determiners of behavior and the "unconscious mind" as the seat of maladjustments.

Drives have been described as energizers. Homeostasis is an important drive; it involves the maintenance of internal stability or normal physiological balance. There are also the sensitizing and selective functions of drive; these depend largely upon learning. Reinforcement is important in the acquisition of drives. Drives have been classed as primary and secondary drives. The basic physiological drives have been classed as primary drives; more complex forms of motivation make up the secondary drives.

The operation of motives may be observed in goal setting, level of aspiration, cognitive motives, interests, and values. A need may be thought of as a broad motive that makes certain behavioral responses and goals desirable and important. When behavior is aroused by a particular condition or situation, we may say that a certain need exists related to some aspect of the situation.

Needs or drives are classified as (1) essentially physiological, and (2) essentially social-psychological needs are frequently complex, involving immediate and remote goals. Many of these are unconscious. Some of the most important social-psychological needs are safety, belongingness and love, achievement, status or esteem, and self-actualization.

Important sex differences appear in motivational patterns, with females consistently earning higher conformity scores. The need for belongingness and security operates in subtle ways and is frequently found in deviant behavior. Differences in motivational patterns affect social interactions with groups and vocational choices. The motivational pattern of teachers does not follow a single pattern, although most teachers display a motivational pattern involving achievement, interactions, ethical, and material values. Girls in general with a strong achievement need are more career-oriented and less oriented toward marriage and a family than girls with a weak achievement need. Pay satisfies higher-order needs as well as lower-order needs, as may be noted in the needs of executives. Background factors affect the motivation of workers. Blue-collar workers place a greater value on extrinsic sources of job satisfaction and less on intrinsic sources than do white-collar workers.

The intensity of certain motivators change with age in harmony with changing attitudes and needs of individuals at different stages of life.

References

Antonovskky, H. F. "A Contribution to Research in the Area of Mother-Child Relationships," *Child Development,* Vol. 20 (1959), pp. 37-51.

Astin, A. W., and R. C. Nichols. "Life Goals and Vocational Choices," *Journal of Applied Psychology,* Vol. 48 (1964), pp. 50-58.

Baller, W. R., and D. B. Charles. *Psychology of Human Growth and Development.* New York: Holt, 1961.

Barrilleaux, L. E. "High School Science Achievement as Related to Interest and IQ," *Educational and Psychological Measurements,* Vol. 21 (1961), pp. 929-936.

Bruner, J. S., and C. C. Goodman. "Value and Need as Organizing Factors in Perception," *Journal of Abnormal and Social Psychology,* Vol. 42 (1947), pp. 33-34.

Byers, J. L. "An Investigation of the Goal Patterns of Academically Successful and Unsuccessful Children in a United States History Class," unpublished master's thesis, University of Wisconsin, 1958.

Centers, R., and D. B. Bugental. "Intrinsic and Extrinsic Job Motivations among Different Segments of the Working Population," *Journal of Applied Psychology,* Vol. 50 (1966), pp. 193-197.

Crutchfield, R. S. "Conforming and Character," *American Psychologist,* Vol. 10 (1955), pp. 191-198.

Dobzhansky, T. "Human Nature as a Product of Evolution," *Knowledge in Human Values.* New York: Harper, 1959, p. 82.

Edwards, T. B., and A. B. Wilson. "The Association between Interest and Achievement in High School Chemistry," *Educational and Psychological Measurements,* Vol. 19 (1959), pp. 601-610.

Fenichel, O. *The Psychoanalytic Theory of Neurosis.* New York: Norton, 1945.

Frandsen, A.. N. *Educational Psychology,* 2nd ed. New York: McGraw-Hill, 1967.

Frank, L. K. "Time Perspectives," *Journal of Social Psychology,* Vol. 4 (1939), pp. 293-321.

Garrison, K. C., and Mary H. Scott. "A Comparison of the Personal Needs of College Students Preparing to Teach in Different Teaching Areas," *Educational and Psychological Measurements,* Vol. 21 (1961), pp. 955-964.

Halpern, G. "Relative Contributions of Motivator and Hygiene Factors to Overall Job Satisfaction," *Journal of Applied Psychology,* Vol. 50 (1966), pp. 198-200.

Harlow, H. F., and Margaret K. Harlow. "Social Deprivation in Monkeys," *Scientific American,* Vol. 207 (Nov. 1962), pp. 136-146.

Hartup, W. W. "Nurturance and Nurturance—Withdrawal in Relation to the Dependency Behavior of Preschool Children," *Child Development,* Vol. 29 (1958), pp. 190-201.

Haythorn, H., and I. Altman. "Together in Isolation," *Transaction,* Vol. 4 (1967), pp. 18-22.

Hull, C. *Essentials of Behavior.* New Haven: Yale U. P., 1951.

Hunt, J. M. "How Children Develop Intellectually," *Children,* Vol. 11 (1964), pp. 83-91.

Jones, F. R. Unpublished study on file, School of Education. Old Dominion College, Norfolk, Va., 1968.

Kvaraceus, W. C., et al., *Delinquent Behavior: I. Culture and the Individual.* National Education Association Project, Washington, D.C., 1959, pp. 87-90.

Lawler, E. E. "How Much Money Do Executives Want?" *Transaction,* Vol. 4 (1967), pp. 21-29.

Lewin, K. "Field Theory and Experiment in Social Psychology: Concept and Methods," *American Journal of Sociology,* Vol. 44 (1939), pp. 868-896.

Lipset, S. M. "Constant Values in American Society," *Children* (Nov.-Dec. 1959), pp. 219-224.

McClelland, D. C., J. W. Atkinson, R. A. Clark, and E. L. Lowell. "Origins of Achievement Motivation," in R. G. Kuhlen and G. G. Thompson (eds.), *Psychological Studies of Human Development,* 2nd ed. New York: Appleton, 1963.

McGill, T. E. "Studies of Sexual Behavior of Male Laboratory Mice: Effects of Genotype Recovery of Sex Drive and Theory," in F. A. Beach, (ed.), *Sex and Behavior.* New York: Wiley, 1965, pp. 76-88.

Malinovsky, M. R., and J. R. Barry. "Determinants of Work Attitudes," *Journal of Applied Psychology,* Vol. 49 (1965), pp. 446-451.

Maslow, A. H. "A Theory of Human Motivation," *Psychological Review,* Vol. 50 (1943), pp. 370-396.

————. "Some Theoretical Consequences of Basic Need Gratifications," *Journal of Personality*, Vol. 16 (1948), pp. 402-416.

Maw, W. H., and Ethel W. Maw. "Information Recognition by Children with High and Low Curiosity," *Educational Research Bulletin*, Vol. 40 (1961), pp. 197-201, 223-224.

Menninger, W. C. "Mental Health in Our Schools," *Educational Leadership*, Vol. 7 (1950), pp. 510-523.

Montgomery, K. C. "The Role of the Exploratory Drive in Learning," *Journal of Comparative Philosophical Psychology*, Vol. 47 (1954), pp. 60-64.

Moss, H. A., and J. Kagan. "Stability of Achievement and Recognition-Seeking Behaviors from Early Childhood through Adulthood," *Journal of Abnormal and Social Psychology*, Vol. 62 (1961), pp. 504-513.

Mowrer, O. H. *Learning Theory and Behavior*. New York: Wiley, 1960.

Murray, H. A. *Explorations in Personality*. New York: Oxford U. P., 1938.

Parker, A. W. "Career and Marriage Orientation in the Vocational Development of College Women," *Journal of Applied Psychology*, Vol. 50 (1966), pp. 232-235.

Piaget, Jean. *The Language and Thought of the Child*. New York: Harcourt, Brace, and World, 1926.

Richter, C. P. "Total Self-Regulatory Functions in Animals and Human Beings, *Harvard Lecture Series*, Vol. 38 (1942), pp. 63-103.

Sears, Pauline S. "Level of Aspiration in Academically Unsuccessful Children," *Journal of Abnormal and Social Psychology*, Vol. 35 (1940), pp. 489-536.

Shirley, Mary M. "Common Content in the Speech of Preschool Children," *Child Development* (1938), pp. 333-346.

Skinner, B. F. *The Behavior of Organisms: An Experimental Analysis*. New York: Appleton-Century-Crofts, 1938.

Spencer, K. W. *Behavior Theory and Conditioning*. New Haven: Yale University Press, 1956.

Sternberg, C. "Personality Trait Patterns of College Students Majoring in Different Fields," *Psychological Monographs*, Vol. 50, No. 403 (1955).

Stone, C. P., and R. G. Barker. "The Attitudes and Interests of Pre-Menarcheal and Post-Menarcheal Girls," *Journal of Genetic Psychology*, Vol. 54 (1938), pp. 27-71.

Wesley, S. M., D. Q. Corey, and Barbara M. Stewart. "The Intra-Individual Relationship between Interest and Ability," *Journal of Applied Psychology*, Vol. 34 (1950), pp. 193-197.

Winterbottom, M. R. "The Relation of Childhood Training in Independence to Achievement Motivation," University of Michigan, microfilm, 1953.

Young, P. T. *Motivation and Emotion*. New York: Wiley, 1961, p. 139.

Young, W. C. "The Hormones and Mating Behavior," in W. C. Young, (ed.), *Sex and Internal Secretions*. Baltimore: Williams and Wilkins, Vol. II, pp. 1173-1239.

Zuckerman, M. "The Validity of the Edwards Preference Schedule in the Measurement of Dependency Rebelliousness," *Journal of Clinical Psychology*, Vol. 14 (1958), pp. 379-382.

Chapter **6**

The Development of Linguistic Skills

The development of language is perhaps man's most important means for acquiring an understanding of his culture and for broadening his knowledge so as to include the past as well as the present, to comprehend things and happenings beyond his immediate environment. It also enables individuals to interact more freely with others; it is man's most important means of self-expression and self-realization. The development of the child's language follows the principles of development set forth in Chapter 2 and closely parallels other aspects of development, although the child's language development will be limited by the quality of his sensory equipment and by his language environment.

Language furnishes the child with a set of visual and auditory symbols which may refer to parts of a thing or the whole (Sigel, 1963). The acquisition of labels is a part of an individual's sociocultural experience. The child who refers to his teacher as "an old punk" is reflecting his cultural background at home and in his community. Likewise, the child's dialectic usage reflects his cultural background, and frequently the geographical area in which he has had most of his experiences. One's language is a revealing type of behavior; it identifies a person with considerable effectiveness. One's language habits reflect his past experiences, the geographical area where he spent his childhood, the cultural background of his associates, and the kindly or critical attitude of the speaker. Language may best be thought of as a reservoir of symbols or combination of symbols which represent experiences, thoughts, or feelings of an individual. Language is received through the modes of listening and reading; language is expressed through the channels of speaking and writing.

Factors Influencing Speech Development

Speech is affected by maturation because its development must await the growth of teeth, changes in the size and shape of the vocal mechanism, and improved muscle coordination. Other factors that were treated in earlier chapters that have a bearing on speech development include intelligence, prematurity, brain dysfunctions, emotional stress, and motivation. Some factors that will be given special consideration in the presentation that follows are: sex differences, social class influences, parent-child relations, siblings, and bilingualism.

Parent-Child Relations.   Observations reveal that infants respond to speech with speech and to intonation with intonation. The infant child is stimulated by the adult's response to his babblings. Infants in institutions make slower progress even during the first six months after birth than those in homes (Broderick and Irwin, 1946). The findings of Broderick and Irwin have been verified by subsequent research. The language development of the child at all stages in his development is directly proportional to the amount of conversation he has with his parents. (May, 1966).

Parental discipline also has an effect on the child's language development. Studies comparing the parents of stutterers and nonstutterers show that the parents of stutterers are usually more authoritarian, more demanding in language performance, less consistent in discipline patterns, and less conversant with their children (May, 1966). There is evidence from Koch's study (1954), referred to later in this chapter, that intrafamily factors which contribute to speech stimulation contributes to language development.

Influence of Siblings.   Children tend to use longer sentences when adults and children are present than when only children are present. Analysis of children's speed in the presence of adults and children shows that they use longer sentences and ask more questions with adults than with children. In the light of these and other findings about children's language development, any generalizations must take into consideration the situation where the language was observed. The interaction of children with children and children with adults will contribute to language development. There is evidence that the language development of twins is slower than that of singletons. That the slower language development of twins is a result of their social environment is shown in an early study by Davis (1937), who compared the language development of twins and singletons after they had been subjected to school experiences. Davis used as subjects children age 5½ to 9½. Toys and picture books suitable to the interest of children of these age levels were selected and used as means for eliciting language responses from the children. Her findings revealed that the language inferiority of twins is soon erased after school entrance as far as average sentence length is concerned. The greatest residual effect of twin association seems to appear in articulation even to the age of nine and one-half years.

Davis also compared the speech development of "only" children with that of singletons and twins. Her assumption was that if the poor articulation of twins was a result of hearing and imitating each other's faulty speech, only children whose association has been mainly with adults should, on the average, be advanced in their language development. The graphs presented in Figure 6-1 show only children to be superior to both single-born children of families of more than one child and twins in number of different words used. Since care was taken to eliminate errors that might result from unequal sampling of cases from

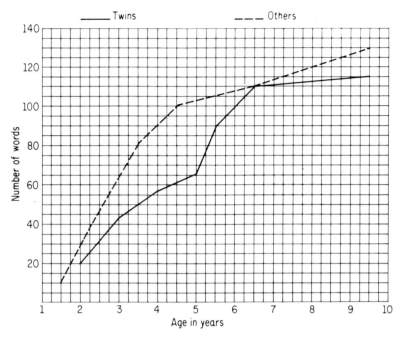

Figure 6-1. Mean number of different words used by twins and other children. (Davis, 1937, p. 136.)

different socioeconomic levels, Davis concludes that the assumption made relative to the superiority of only children in language development is a result of their interaction with adults, especially their parents.

Intelligence.   Speech defects are frequently encountered among children diagnosed as mentally retarded, indicating that there is a close relation between language development and intellectual development. According to Gens (1950), 70 to 75 percent of institutionally mentally retarded children have some sort of speech defect. In a survey of the articulation profile of 209 mentally retarded school children from ages 7 years 3 months to 17 years 5 months, Russell (1952) noted that the mentally retarded group seemed to make more infantile articulatory sounds and a larger number of defective articulatory sounds than did the normal group.

Even children who are slightly retarded may have more speech difficulty than normal children. Moskowitz (1948) suggested that the subnormal child with an IQ of between 75 and 90 will be inferior to the average child in speech and writing skills. He tends to have few ideas, make incomplete sentences, and phrase his statements poorly. The fact that the mildly retarded are found to sit, stand, and walk at approximately the same age level as normal children makes it difficult for parents to accept an early diagnosis of mental retardation.

Language acquisition may appear rapidly after the accomplishment of gait, but then development seems to level off or slow down, resulting in a very prolonged period during which very few further words if any are acquired. Very gradually it becomes clear that the child is falling behind in language development, and although progress in most cases will continue throughout childhood, the process will be slow and tedious. (Lennenberg, p. 157.)

Listening.   Listening is taken for granted, the assumption being that this appears with maturation in the child with normal hearing. Listening is an active process and involves a degree of physiological tension on the part of the listener. It is closely related to attention, for without attention there is no listening. In listening, an individual gives attention to a situation or condition, and this involves varying degrees of comprehension. It is true that the child acquires his oral language through listening to the models he encounters. Yet there is evidence that the listening ability of elementary school pupils will benefit from a program aimed at its improvement (Pratt, 1955-56). The ability to give attention to the speech of others (listening) is a product of maturation and experience. Since the small child is to a large degree egocentric in nature, guidance may be necessary for him to acquire skill in listening. However, listening ability at different stages of development is perhaps an aspect of the child's mental and educational development.

During the preschool years, the child's ability to express himself seems to lag behind his comprehension ability, but during the elementary school years his listening ability appears to fall behind speaking and reading skills. In a study of approximately 2,000 pupils, Young (1936) noted that by the sixth-grade level, reading comprehension exceeds aural comprehension. Using sixth-grade pupils as subjects, Pratt found a correlation of .42 between listening ability and reading ability, and a correlation of .66 between listening ability and measures of intelligence.

The purpose of a study by Peisach (1965) was to (1) evaluate the extent to which information is successfully communicated from teacher to pupils, and (2) evaluate the degree of effective communication among children from different social backgrounds. The subjects consisted of 64 first-graders, and 127 fifth-graders. The entire sample was matched for social class level, race, and sex. The task of the subjects was to restore words deleted from samples of the teacher's speech and the speech of children from diverse social backgrounds.

No significant differences were found in the performance of first-grade children from the lower class and the middle class. IQ similarities reduced social class differences, supporting the conclusions of Pratt that intelligence is an important factor in listening efficiency. She noted that sex differences varied with social class. She states (pp. 479-480): "In virtually all cases where sex differences were obtained, it was demonstrated that middle-class boys and girls were equal in performance; however, lower-class boys were inferior to lower-class girls." This finding suggests that sex differences in listening may reflect differences in motivation and training related to social class.

Bilingualism.   The results of studies of the effect of bilingualism upon language development reveal that, generally, children from homes in which two languages are spoken are retarded in the rate and extent of either language development in comparison to children reared in monolingual homes. It appears that in the development of two languages at once, there is first a stage in which the child uses the elements of both languages at random. As he matures, there is a gradual separation and parallel formation of the two languages. One of the writers observed this over a period of eighteen months in a Spanish speaking family from Panama. There were three boys, ages 5, 9, and 11. The writer frequently conversed with the three boys as well as their parents. Rickey, the five-year-old boy, found it difficult to move from his Spanish, which was spoken in the home, to English. However, Rickey frequently used English words in referring to his toys, although he was talking to his mother in Spanish. The nine- and eleven-year-old boys used English at all times when playing games with boys from English-speaking homes, although when talking with their parents, they spoke in Spanish. The eleven-year-old boy showed greater maturity in his language usage, and was actually a leader among a group of nine or ten boys in touch football and other games requiring skill, alertness, and teamwork.

In an early study by Smith (1949), a group of bilingual children ranging in age from approximately three years to six and one-half years were given English and Chinese vocabulary tests in order to compare the language development of bilingual and monolingual children. Despite the fact that the parents of bilingual children were slightly above the average in occupational status, the vocabulary in each language was below the average for monoglot children of the same chronological age. When the vocabularies of the two languages were combined for each child, the scores were, on the average, near the norms; two-fifths of the individuals exceeded the norms. Although, when duplicate meanings were eliminated, the group fell to about 80 percent of the estimated norm and only one-sixth of the children exceeded it.

In a carefully controlled study of teaching Japanese to second-, third-, and fourth-grade pupils, Grinder and others (1962) found that fourth-graders learned Japanese more effectively than did the second or third-graders. This superiority in the learning of the fourth-graders can best be attributed to their greater maturity and to the fact that the English language is better established, thereby avoiding the confusion that may appear at an earlier period. The results of this and related studies suggest a second language can more effectively be learned after the native language is well established.

Social-Class Influences.   There is evidence from many studies of preschool children that those from an impoverished environment are seriously handicapped in their language development. For the middle-class child, there is a progressive development toward verbalizing experiences, while this is not usually the case for the lower-class child. This is not a result of a deficiency of potential ability to learn, but results from the social environment and the social relationships acting through the linguistic medium. The shift of emphasis from nonverbal to verbal signals occurs earlier in the middle-class mother-child relationship than in the lower class. Inherent in the middle class mother-child situation is a pressure placed upon the child not only to verbalize his experiences but also his feelings in a relatively individual manner, and development at this stage is guided largely by models that the child confronts in his home. However, a child from a priviliged home may be handicapped in his language development by parental neglect or lack of stimulation.

Contrasts in language development of lower and middle-class children and the divergence in modes of thinking and comprehension of the two groups were studied by Bernstein (1962). He noted that lower-class children predominantly acquire a form of speech characterized by concreteness, few speech modifiers, and a dependence upon nonverbal cues in communication. On the other hand, the language of middle-class children was more elaborate, enabling them to make use of language in more exact communication and in comprehending finer discriminations in meaning.

The results of an early study by Dawe (1942) show that a stimulating environment has a beneficial effect upon the language development of young children. Her subjects consisted of 22 orphaned children. These were divided into two equivalent groups—experimental and control—on the basis of school group, age, sex, mental age, scores on a spoken vocabulary test, IQ, and answers to the "home living and general science" part of an information test. Special training involving experiences designed to improve comprehension of words and concepts was given to the experimental group; no such training was given to the control group. Both groups were retested following the training period. The results showed that the group given the special training and enriched experiences made significant improvements on the different tests; whereas the control group showed much less improvement. The results presented in Figure 6-2 show that the experimental group surpassed the control group in all areas tested. The results of this study support the hypothesis that an enrichment of an impoverished environment will have a beneficial effect upon language development. Recent studies in which enriched programs have been provided for preschool children from impoverished environments have given considerable support to earlier theoretical viewpoints regarding the deleterious effects of an impoverished environment on the child's linguistic, mental, and educational growth.

Physical Conditions. Children born with serious hearing loss or who lose their hearing before speech develops will not develop speech unless given special instruction. The spontaneous speech sounds of deaf-born, five-year-old children were studied at the Iowa School for the Deaf over a period of more than two years (Carr, 1953). The results showed that these deaf-born children used many spontaneous speech sounds in their undirected vocalizations. These speech sounds were natural in quality; however, the development of vowel and consonant sounds did not continue much beyond the level of hearing of infants of twelve to thirteen months.

Any severe or prolonged illness, injury, coma, spasm, or convulsion during the first two years after birth or during the speech readiness period will likely

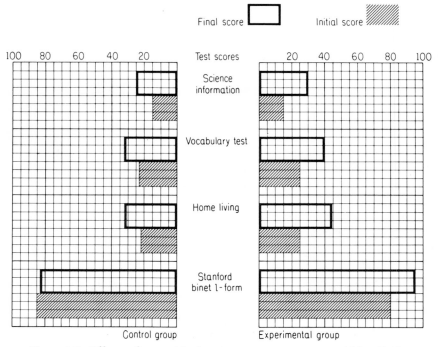

Figure 6-2. Effects of an enriched environment on test scores. (After Davis, 1942, p. 203.)

interfere with the development of early speech. Childhood diseases such as measles, mumps, whooping-cough, and chicken pox can greatly retard speech development, especially for a relatively short period of time (Lupker, 1960). Because of the widespread use of DPT shots and vaccines, these childhood diseases do not present the serious problem that they formerly presented.

In children with severe brain damage, there may be a disturbance of language development, referred to as aphasia. In the past twenty-five years more and more children with delayed speech development and aphasic symptoms have been observed. Examination of case histories has indicated that many of these children are "antibiotic babies" saved by modern medicine after very severe illnesses in early childhood. In other cases there are indications of prenatal or birth damage (Kent, 1957).

Childhood Psychosis. Children with severe disorders in oral language caused by severe emotional disturbances need to be differentiated from mentally retarded and brain damaged children. A large category of children with extreme communicative disorders are those classified as schizophrenic. The symptoms of these have been described by Lennenberg (p. 161) as follows:

A common psychiatric symptom is mutism. The patient fails to address anyone for periods that may extend over years. Yet these children are rarely incapable of saying something. Usually they can be heard to mumble a word or two and sometimes even phrases and sentences, for instance while standing in a corner staring blankly into space or while engaged in their favorite pastime. These utterances may be muttered under their breath; but even so, they can be understood clearly since their phonology and syntax are well developed. . . . It is common experience in psychotherapy that the patient gives frequent behavioral evidence of having understood commands and sometimes even elaborate explanations.

Sex Differences. Students of child development frequently refer to the superiority of girls in language development without careful attention to various conditions that must be considered in making comparisons and generalizations. McCarthy (1954) summarized the results of fourteen studies, each of which compared the mean length of language response of boys and girls, and found that in 64 comparisons, 43 favored the girls, 3 were similar for each sex, and 18 favored the boys. These and more recent studies show that there is a slight language superiority of girls over boys during the early years. At the first-grade level the average girl seems to articulate clearly and has a larger vocabulary than the average boy. In contrast to the girl's slight superiority in fluency, there is evidence from studies by Koch (1954) that boys exceed girls in their understanding of words.

A plausible explanation for sex differences in language ability is that of social environmental forces. Support for this lies in studies by Davis (1937) and Young (1941); it was noted that sex differences are most marked in children of parents engaged in unskilled or semiskilled manual labor, where sex roles tend to be more sharply contrasted. It seems most likely that the play and recreational activities of girls which involve dolls, storybooks, and other people are more conducive to language development than the play and recreational activities of boys.

Koch (1954) explains that the superiority of boys in understanding the meaning of words as resulting from questions boys more frequently ask about causal relationships. In the study by Koch, the *Thurstone Primary Mental Abilities Test,* which includes a vocabulary subtest was administered to 360 five- and six-year-olds. It was noted that though sex differences consistently favored the boys, they were statistically significant only when the boys were first-born children with a sibling two to four years younger. A study by Edmonds (1964) included materials from 1,239 eleventh-grade students from 63 high schools in socioeconomically disadvantaged areas. Results were obtained from the students on the *Cooperative School and College Ability Test* and the *Otis Mental Ability Test.* No significant differences were found between the measured verbal ability of boys and girls when the factor of socioeconomic status was held constant. The major differences noted were between the scores of students from more advantaged and those from the most disadvantaged high schools.

A study by Murray (1953) of the written and tape-recorded oral language activities of fourth-, fifth-, and sixth-grade pupils revealed no significant sex differences. This seems to be supported by a study of Peisach (1965), a study involving listening, referred to later in this Chapter.

In the study by Griffin (1966), boys were superior to girls in the handling of syntax in all grades studied (grades 1, 2, 3, 5, and 7), except grade 5. Griffin concludes, "Over-all grades, boys used significantly longer T-units, and they used fewer such units shorter than nine words in kindergarten, grade 2, and grade 7. The incidence of sentence-combining transformations was also higher in the speech of boys than in that of girls, though at no point was the difference significant" (pp. 6-7). Gains in the use of adverbial clauses were not significant at any one particular point when one grade group was compared with that immediately below it.

Prespeech Communications

The child learns to communicate when someone understands and responds to his sounds or gestures. The early forms of language are actually expressive sounds—consisting of the cries, motor activities, and bodily movements of the infant. It was pointed out in Chapter 3 that the infant learns at an early age to use crying as a means for gaining attention and for relieving distress. During the early months, the baby makes use of three preliminary forms of communication; crying, babbling, and gestures.

Crying. Generally, the first response to distress and violent stimuli is the birth cry, which starts the infant breathing. Although all newborn infants cry, individual differences in the amount of crying may be observed at the end of the second week.

Hunger is the most common cause of crying during the first two months, while older babies cry because of pain and discomfort, sharp noises, sleep disturbances, fatigue, hunger, and restriction of movements. By the time the baby is three months old, he has usually learned that crying is a sure method of getting attention. Among nursery school children, crying is predominantly social, with girls crying more than boys. The most common causes of crying in nursery school in order of frequency, according to Landreth (1958) are attack on child's person, attack on child's property, accidental injury, frustrated by another child, frustrated by inanimate objects, conflict with adults, and fear.

By the end of the second month the baby's crying varies in intensity, tonal quality, and rhythm. All babies appear to have a large repertoire of cries, with each child's repertoire more or less distinct. When the child has acquired a sufficient vocabulary or other means to make his wants, thoughts, and feelings known, his crying tends to go down. There should be a reciprocal relation between the development of speech and crying. However, the young child who has learned that crying is a simple and effective method of coping with his wants and may be slow in giving it up in favor of speech.

Babbling. The earliest noncrying speech sounds consist of vowels, which usually appear by two months. In an early study of 25 babies, Shirley (1933) notes that some babies combine vowels and consonants by the age of five months, frequently repeating some sounds several times in succession, as "da-da-da, mum-mum-mum." Most children are able to make a variety of babbling sounds by the time they are eight or nine months old. By combining these sounds, they produce some sounds similar to those heard in their environments.

Babbling is a form of "play" in that sounds are uttered as part of the infant's general activity. Babbling occurs most frequently in periods of contentment, when the baby is alone rather than when he is with others who give him special attention. Babbling is not real speech. It is engaged in for enjoyment and will likely be continued until he develops another, a more complete, form of play that is more enjoyable. The value of language sound in relation to speech development is not clear. It appears, according to Simon (1957) that the babbling sounds of infants are part of his total repertoire of behavior and have little relevance for later language acquisition.

The pattern of learning to speak closely parallels the pattern of the development of postural control (Mysak, 1961). Cooing and vocalization in response to social stimulation come about at the time the baby is able to hold the head erect; babbling begins soon after the baby has developed the ability to sit alone. However, the pattern of speech development is marked by spurts and plateaus—times when no apparent improvement appears. These plateaus appear whenever a new motor act is being established such as grasping, sitting alone, standing, and walking.

The baby shows evidence of being able to comprehend the meaning of words before he is able to reproduce them, a condition found among most people at all stages of life. This may be observed in the infant's response to the mother in such situations as feeding, bathing, snuggling, and toilet care. This is also observable in the response of the infants to words related to familiar objects in his environment. Through continued trials he succeeds in reproducing certain sounds, tones, and rhythms. The response of those around him serves to reinforce his learning to respond to sounds and to reproduce the sounds he hears.

Gestures. Gestures as a form of communication may be observed in the infant child. Through the use of gestures, the infant is able to communicate with others in his environment. Their failure to respond to his gestures produces frustrations and crying. Without this form of communication many of the child's needs would remain unsatisfied, since he hasn't acquired speech as a means of communication.

The continued use of gestures will depend upon such factors as (1) the extent of the development of the ability to communicate with speech, (2) gestures used by parents and others who serve as models, and (3) motivation to discontinue the widespread use of gestures.

Oral Language Skills

Pronunciation. Articulation or learning to formulate sounds that make up words is an important task of early childhood. The quality of a child's articulation depends upon a number of factors including (1) degree of maturation of the nerves and muscles of the speech mechanism, (2) level of native intelligence, (3) quality of hearing, and (4) the language environment.

A child's pronunciation of words will lag behind his understanding of them. This is to be expected, since this learning is more complex than one realizes, unless he considers the difficulty of learning to pronounce correctly the words of a foreign language. Many errors made by children are due to their perceiving words as lumps of sounds. Children frequently omit sounds that are of low intensity. They say "ump" for "jump," "way" for "away;" they often omit the final "s" sounds from plural words; they may omit a whole syllable if it is unstressed in the word (Van Riper, 1950).

Maturation plays an important role in the pronunciation of newly acquired words. Strayer (1930) noted a maturational advantage of five weeks had a significant influence on the effectiveness of vocabulary, and pronunciation training during early childhood. Using identical twins as subjects, it was found that the twin whose practice was delayed had a more mature pattern of response as revealed in better pronunciation of newly acquired words.

The effect of poor hearing on the pronunciation of newly acquired words has been demonstrated by several investigators.

From Words to Sentences. The young child beginning to talk uses words, each of which, with varying inflections and gestures, serves as a thought unit. There is a gradual and continuous increase in the mean number of words per response. The increase in sentence length during the early years follows the pattern for increase in vocabulary; it is according to McCarthy (1954) the best single index of the growth in linguistic ability of children.

Some model sentences spoken by a mother and the imitations produced by her two 30-month-old children are presented in Table 6-1. One of the most important things to observe is that the imitations follow the word order or language structure of the model utterance. Although some words are missing and others slightly altered, words of the child are in the order of the model utterance. This preservation of order suggests that the model sentence is preserved by the child as a total construct rather than a list of words. Concerning the importance of this, Bellugi (1964, p. 37) states:

> Order is used to distinguish among subject, direct object, and indirect object and it is one of the marks of imperative and interrogative constructions. The fact that the child's first sentences preserve the word order of their models partially accounts for the ability of the adult to 'understand' these sentences and so to feel that he is communicating with the child.

One frequently finds the major grammatical constructions appearing in the simple sentences of preschool children. This was observed by Bellugi (1964). She states: "By the age of thirty-six months some children are so advanced in the construction process as to produce all the major varieties of English simple sentences up to a length of ten or eleven words" (p. 133). There is, however, a significant increase with age in the ratio of complex and compound sentence

TABLE 6–1

Some Imitations Produced by Two 30-Months-Old Children*

Model Speech	Child's Imitation
then	den
that	dat
thank	tank
coat	coke
school	kool
scare	care
scream	scream (same)

(a) Thirteen-month-old children frequently are able to pronounce certain relatively difficult words as noted in the case of *scream*.

(b) Three-year-olds sometimes confuse a new word with a familiar one for awhile:

(*new word*) clipper ship   (*familiar*) paper clip

(c) Children frequently have a few words they mispronounce even until they are four or five years old.

animal	animule
molasses	maglasses

*Data furnished by Nancy Garrison based on observations of two of her children.

length to simple sentence length. Tagruchi (1962) noted a significant increase in complex sentence structure in both Japanese children and American children between third and fifth grades.

Quantitative and Qualitative Growth.   The early stage of the child's language has been described as the word stage. The child attaches labels to activities and things during this period so as to make better use of them. There is a preponderance of nouns in the child's speech during the early stage. With an increased awareness of the self, the child makes use of pronouns involving the self. The self pronouns, include "I," "me," and "my." Davis (1938) noted that by age 4 most children seem to have acquired the commonly used pronouns. Likewise, prepositions and conjuctions are frequently used.

The number of nouns used increases throughout life. Nouns and verbs constitute about 70 percent of the different words used after age 5½.

The purpose of a study reported by Di Vesta (1965) was to determine the modes of qualifying used by children of five age levels. Modifiers were elicited from 100 subjects in each of grades 2 through 6. The frequency and diversity of each modifier used by each subject in a word-association task was recorded and studied.

Differences among age groups were found in the frequency data for the more popular modifiers. For example, the general use of the words "good" or "bad" is inversely related to the developmental level of the group. Conversely, modifiers that are less popular with the 7-year-old group are used progressively more often in the older groups, as illustrated by the data for the modifiers "tiny," "delicious," "sharp," and "faithful." Essential agreement in the usage of modifiers across grade levels was found. Differences among age groups existed in the manner in which substantives were qualified. The author noted a clear-cut preponderance of the use of evaluative words among 7- and 8-year-old subjects and a rapid (linear) decline in the use of evaluative words in the intermediate ages 9 through 11.

A study by Menyuk (1963) was concerned with a description of the changing processes of the child's language system or structure as he matures. The population studied was composed of 48 private nursery school children. Children with a physical disability, including impaired speech and those with an IQ under 90 as measured by the *Full Range Picture Vocabulary Test*, were not included in the study. Menyuk concludes from his study that the basic structures used by adults to generate their sentences can be found in the grammar of the nursery school children. However mean sentence length has long been used as a valid quantitative measure of increased verbal maturity (p. 418). In this study it was found that in the same stimulus situations the total sentence output increases significantly with age, and that as the child matures, syntactic structures are added to syntactic structures leading to increased length, but without adding to the basic structures used.

Vocabulary Development.   Once the child is speaking, the size and content of his vocabulary becomes important in determining his ability to communicate. A number of investigators have furnished data showing different age levels. It should be pointed out, however, that what is obtained from a vocabulary test is a vocabulary index. This index is useful in comparing vocabulary development in children and in studying the influence of different factors and conditions on vocabulary development.

There is considerable recent evidence that underpriviledged children have vocabularies at age six which are so limited that they cannot learn to read unless given special preschool language experiences. On the other hand, many six-year-old children have vocabularies far beyond that found in most basic first-grade readers. This was noted in a study by Hughes and Cox (1949) in which the free conversation of a group of first-grade children during their first two months of the school year was analyzed and compared with the vocabulary contained in first-grade reading books. A large percentage of common words appeared in both the children's speech and in the basal readers. The investigators concluded that the first-graders talked about more different things, used a greater variety of descriptive words, employed more verbs and verb forms of speech than the first-grade books included.

There is a continuous growth of the size of the vocabulary with additional experiences involving words. The vocabulary continues to grow throughout the school years, and afterward as long as the individual is confronted with new words in learning situations. In general, the number of words known by adults, as measured by the synonym type of vocabulary test continues to rise throughout most of the life span (Birren and Morrison, 1961); however, there seems to be a decline with age in verbal fluency or in the number of words associated in a fixed period, such as the number of words beginning with a particular letter of the alphabet (Schaie, 1958). There seems to be a decline with age in speed of both written and spoken word associations (Birren et al., 1962). This is in harmony with the findings presented in Chapter 4 relative to the decline in reaction time and speed in motor skills.

Riegel and Birren (1966) gave two tests of syllable associations to 30 young subjects with an average age of 14 years and to 23 elderly persons from age 60 to 80. The subjects were instructed to name a word which begins with the same syllable as shown. The older subjects were slower in responding, but their responses were more randomly distributed. The older subjects, by restricting their responses to the most common ones and by avoiding unique and original answers, increased their speed during continued performance. They finally reached the latency level of the younger subjects.

Content of Speech. The speech of children was classified by Piaget (1926) into two major categories: *egocentric speech* and *socialized speech.* In egocentric speech the child talks only for his own satisfaction. No attempt is made to exchange ideas or to consider the ideas of others. Most speech during early childhood is egocentric.

Socialized speech occurs when social contacts are established, and is subdivided into (1) *adapted information,* involving an exchange of ideas or a common purpose; (2) *criticism* of the activities of others, directed to a group; (3) *commands, requests,* and *threats;* (4) *questions;* and (5) *answers.* Concerning this stage of a child's speech Piaget (1926, p. 19) states, "The child speaks from the point of view of his audience. The function of language is no longer merely to excite the speaker to action, but actually to communicate his thoughts to other people."

Based on observations and studies of children's speech, Piaget noted that while the early responses were primarily egocentric, socialized speech prevailed largely between ages five and six. On the other hand, Vigotsky (1939), although agreeing in part with Piaget, contended that most of the three-year-old child's speech is social in general function. By the age of seven, he believed the child's speech was almost completely social in both structure and function.

Since speech reflects the child's development and personality, we would expect the speech of the socially mature child to be more socialized in nature than that of the child less mature. Furthermore, in harmony with the principle that growth is gradual, we would expect the transition from egocentric speech in early childhood to be a continuous one, but changing at a faster pace in the child who is advanced in his emotional and social development.

Speech Disorders

Surveys of the prevalence of speech disorders are not in agreement because of the populations studied, standards used in identifying speech disorders, and

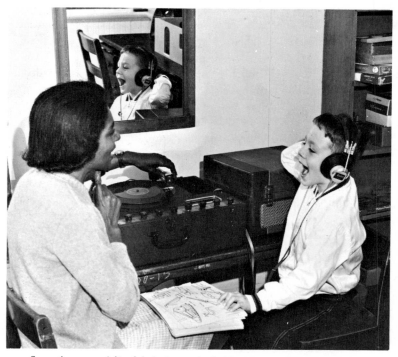

Sometimes specialized help is required. (Courtesy Kirk-Cone Rehabilitation Center—Chesapeake, Va.)

methods of classifying disorders. Surveys have reported from 7 to 10 percent of
school-age children with impaired speech. It has been estimated that a minimum
of 5 percent of school-age children have speech problems sufficiently serious to
warrant speech correction or therapy and an additional 5 percent noticeable but
less serious defects. A classification and estimated prevalence of speech problems
and accompanying disorders by the American Speech and Hearing Association is
presented in Table 6-2 (1961).

It may be noted from Table 6-2 that articulatory defects comprise over
80 percent of the estimated school-age children with speech or hearing problems.
Under disorders of articulation are those characterized by the substitution, omission, addition, and distortion of speech sounds (Lubker, 1959).

One form of articulation defect that frequently appears among preschool
and first-grade children is *immature speech*—when the substitution of one sound
for another frequently occurs. This may be observed when Jane substitutes *w* for
r as "wail woad" for "rail road." The normal process of maturation along with
correct examples usually remedies this condition.

Another articulation difficulty frequently observed among preschool and
early elementary school children is *lisping*—the inability to pronounce certain
letter sounds or combinations of sounds and a tendency to omit, transpose, or

TABLE 6-2

Distribution of Speech Defects of Various
Types and Causes in Public School Children*

Type of Defect	Percentage
Articulatory defects	81.0
Stuttering	6.5
Delayed speech	4.5
Hard-of-hearing	2.5
Voice problems	2.3
Cleft palate	1.5
Cerebral palsy	1.0
Bilinguality Mental retardation Aphasia	0.7
Total	100.0

*Data from American Speech and Hearing
Association (1961).

make slurring sounds. These sounds require tongue-tips and fine coordination of movements. Tongue-thrust on the part of the child frequently interferes with the correct production of a particular sound. The frequency of lisping decreases rapidly in the upper grades of the school; its persistence beyond five or six should demand special attention.

Cleft lip and cleft palate are also responsible for certain articulation faults; some of these approximate lisping, while others are more serious in nature. About one out of every 850 children are born with these congenital abnormalities and at least 50 percent of these need surgery and/or extensive therapy during childhood.

A multiple of special conditions frequently appears among children with articulation difficulties. This was observed in a study reported by FitzSimons (1958) involving two matched groups of children: a control group of 70 children with normal speech and an experimental group of children with diffuse, non-organic articulatory problems. Significantly more members of the problem group had experienced abnormal birth conditions, bottle feeding, early weaning, early implementation and accomplishment of toilet training, delay in locomotion, and emotional upsets.

A study by Solomon (1961) had as its purpose to test the possible relationship between functional articulatory defects and personality and behavior disorders. A group of 49 boys and girls with functional defects of articulation was matched with a control group of 49 children with normal speech. Mothers of both groups were requested to describe the behavior of their children over the previous two years in nine areas: (a) eating behavior, (b) sleeping behavior, (c) toilet training, (d) fears and anxieties, (e) comfort patterns, (f) tension, (g) aggression, (h) dependency, and (i) peer relations. The four areas in which there were significant differences between the two groups were sleeping, fears and anxieties, peer relations, and tension. Solomon concludes that children comprising the speech-defective group tended to be passive; they internalize their responses and were characterized by submissiveness, timidity, and a need for approval (p. 734).

Delayed Speech. Delayed speech, as the name implies, is characterized by retarded speech development. There is usually a deficiency in vocabulary, a retardation in the development of conventional sentence structure, and often a marked inadequacy in the formulation and expression of ideas through the use of words.

It is not possible to state a precise time at which delay in speech development is significant, since this will vary with different circumstances in the life of an individual. Morley et al. (1955) reported data on the main conditions associated with delayed speech in 278 children referred to them supposedly for this condition. These causes or conditions are presented in Table 6-3. It will be noted that deafness accounts for almost 40 percent of the cases.

TABLE 6-3

Causes of Delayed Speech in 278 Children
(After Morley)*

Cause	Numbers
Deafness	110
Developmental aphasia	72
Transient	49
Prolonged	23
Mental deficiency	71
Cerebral palsy	22
Mental illness	3

*Reprinted from the *British Medical Journal*, (1955), Vol. 2, pp. 463-467, by permission of the editor and publisher.

Aphasia. Aphasia accounts for the second largest group in Table 6-3. According to Barger (1953), aphasia is a generic term "indicating faulty functioning of one or more faculties in the cerebral areas concerned with specialized language culture" (p. 167). According to Gordon (1967) aphasia involves a neurological lesion, usually in the left hemisphere. In a left-handed person there is not as marked right cerebral dominance as for the right-handed person; therefore, aphasia of the left-handed child is of shorter duration than that of the right-handed child.

Among children, the process is mainly a failure to develop the central process of speech, or sometimes to understand languages as a result of brain injury. The aphasic children of the study by Morley et al. did not develop any recognizable words until two years or later, or phrases until four years or later. Those referred to in Table 6-3 as transient aphasia developed fairly quickly and successfully after the age of four years. The group of children referred to as prolonged aphasia should be given special therapy. It is most likely that these children have a real cerebral disorder. The prognosis for aphasia is good for dividing under ten and twelve. Little improvement can be expected after the second year of recovery for late teen or adult patients.

Certain speech problems characterized in part by delayed speech are associated with bulbar poliomyelitis, cerebral palsy, and other impairments involving the central nervous system. A study by Miller (1953) of a sample of 165 cerebral palsy cases showed that 27 percent had no speech; 62 percent had speech sufficient for communication at their mental age level.

Speech Problems of the Deaf and the Hard-of-Hearing. The congenitally deaf child will remain without speech until he is given special training. The differences in the sounds made by the congenitally deaf and hard-of-hearing child and the child with normal hearing can be detected by the trained observer by the sixth month; although the differences in sounds are in quantity rather than in quality. Concerning the prognosis of the deaf child, Lenneberg (1964, p. 155) states:

> A deaf child should encounter no difficulty in the acquisition of language through the graphic medium: reading and writing are established in due course, though stylistic and grammatical mistakes commonly persist in some measure throughout life. Skill in lip reading and vocal communication varies greatly from individual to individual, the overall success being well correlated with the age at which hearing is lost and the profoundness of the loss. It is interesting to note that when the child is about three years of age, an important milestone is passed. The child who has had normal hearing up to the age of three and who has started on its course towards language acquisition and then suddenly becomes deaf (for instance due to meningitis) has a significant headstart in the language arts in comparison with the congenitally deaf.

Stuttering. The child's speech reflects his emotional, physical, neurological, and social characteristics; this may be observed in stuttering. During the preschool years, most children stutter a little—that is, they repeat words until they can think of another word or the next word needed, although this is sometimes called "stammering." A factor in stuttering during the preschool years may be disturbances in auditory feedback. It has long been known that interference with natural relationships between ongoing speech and consequent feedback of information could lead to serious disturbances in the smooth process of speech (Cherry and Sayers, 1956).

Cross-cultural studies lend support to Johnson's (1942) "diagnosogenic" notion of the origin of stuttering. According to Johnson, parental anxiety concerning the child's speech during the period when he is learning to speak leads to additional blockings and limitations labeled as stuttering. In certain cultures where there is a tolerant and accepting attitude toward stuttering, little, if any, stuttering appears; whereas, in cultures with strict standards of speech, there is a high incidence of stuttering (Lamert, 1962). Moncur (1952) concluded from his study that there is a syndrome of environmental factors that cause and aggravate the stuttering condition. This syndrome involves such conditions as parental domination, overprotection, excessive expectation, and too much adverse criticism.

There is an increase in stuttering when the child enters school. This increase was observed by Malmivaara and Kolho (1962) in their studies of five- to seven-year-old children in Helsinki, Finland. Those children who stuttered were found to have trends toward rigidity, inhibition, and immaturity. The flare-up of stuttering upon entering school may best be attributed to the new pressures at school. Those cases that have not appeared before may disappear as adjustments to school are made. At this stage, teachers should not compel the child to read or recite before the class until he can be helped to develop the necessary self-confidence; however, it is imperative that he be offered opportunities to recite.

Other Conditions. Mongolism, mechanical injury at birth, and prenatal infections are usually damaging to patterns of verbal communication, whereas a greater number of normal components in communication patterns may be found in children who have suffered postnatal cerebral accidents and in mental retardation resulting from adverse environmental conditions. Gross deviations from normal anatomy of the lips, teeth, palate, or tongue will interfere with the development of normal speech (Blanchard, 1964). Concerning the effect of tongue-tiedness, Lennenberg states (p. 173): "In the most extreme cases of tongue-tiedness no greater interference could be produced than a mild lisp, or defective pronunciation of certain speech sounds, none of them severe enough to render speech unintelligible."

The loss or impairment of the voice resulting from organic or psychic conditions is known as *aphonia*. This condition, according to Travis (1967), is a result of the failure of the vocal folds to vibrate properly. The two most common causes of aphonia during childhood are trauma and vascular accidents. In most cases, the individual's disturbance in production is the same as that for understanding, although occasionally a child seems to have more difficulty in speaking than in understanding. The prognosis is good for individuals under ages 10-12. Little improvement can be expected after the second year of recovery for late teen and adult patients.

Visual Language

Prior to the child's entering school, almost all of the language he has mastered is oral. He has learned to discriminate among a large number of sounds and to attach meanings to them. And, although speech remains his most important medium of social interaction, learning to read provides him with an ability that will enable him more nearly to fulfill his potential mental ability. It is through reading that he will be able to broaden his understanding of his social, physical, and biological world. The development of visual language has enabled man to pass on accumulated knowledge from generation to generation. Reading provides the individual with a key to unlock great storehouses of knowledge accumulated throughout the centuries.

Prereading Experiences.   Soon after birth, the typical American child begins to encounter experiences essential for learning to read. Preschool children reared in a favorable environment frequently listen to stories read to them; they encounter books containing pictures of people, animals, and familiar objects (McCarthy, 1960). The child should be stimulated to discriminate sounds and objects, to look at pictures and talk about them, and to listen to and use words. Such early experiences are very important in preparing the child for reading activities. Under favorable circumstances the child with normal mental, emotional, and social development will not only be ready to begin reading but also will be eager to read.

The value of these prereading experiences for the child to learn to read cannot be overemphasized; the importance of reading skill to academic success and to remaining in school is well known. Appell (1966) had this in mind when he stated this in relation to dropouts. He says: "It isn't 16-year-olds that drop out of school but rather six-year-olds." School readiness may mean verbal and visual development through special experiences involving the use of vision in looking at pictures and words. It seems that largely because of the nature of their experiences six-year-old girls are more likely to be what Appell terms visual-verbal, whereas, many six-year-old boys are termed auditory-active. Because a child may not be ready for school, we should not conclude that he is not ready for learning.

There is evidence that children who are exposed to books and who are read to between the ages of 12 and 30 months develop significantly larger vocabularies and an interest in books at an early age. Preschool educational programs that furnish the child with language experiences related to field trip experiences, stories read to them, and interaction with others are most helpful to the underprivileged child. Home experiences have also been found to influence children's use of language in play behavior and in their interaction with peers (Marshall, 1961). With the acquisition of language, the child turns from overt behavior to language behavior in friendly and aggressive interactions with playmates and others.

The Reading Process.   All language processes are complex. The acquisition of reading language skills is dependent on the interaction of many factors. Readiness and motivation are essential conditions for growth in reading. However, vision is to reading what hearing is to speaking. The complexity of the visual aspects of the reading act has been shown by eye-movement photographs made during the reading process. Spache (1961) states:

> These graphs show that reading is done by a series of sweeps and stops across each line. At each stop, the eyes must come to a sharp focus, and perceive a half-word or so on either side of the point of fixation. During the sweep to the next fixation, the eyes diverge and relax and nothing is seen clearly. Then the accurate convergence and focusing must occur again at the next stop, which is

usually a word or so further along the line. At the end of the line, a long sweep to the left brings the eyes back to the next line, where they focus again close to the margin. The duration of the fixation during which reading actually occurs is a quarter to a third of a second. The number of these fixations in 100 running words usually ranges from about 90 at the college level to more than two hundred at the first grade level.

Writing. The ability to discriminate between letter forms is fairly well developed by most five-year-olds, and many children recognize many letters of the alphabet when printed in large forms before they enter school. Also, some children can print the letters of their own names in staggering sizes and alignment at this time. Children should not be given special training, nor should they be pushed in developing these abilities, although if they display a special interest in writing at this age they should be encouraged, but not expected to show special ability at so early a period. Even six- and seven-year-olds have considerable difficulty in making some written forms. An observation of these children reveals that certain letters with common features such as "d" and "b" are frequently confused. Likewise, some words such as "tap" and "top" or "dig" and "big" are easily confused.

Differentiation is an important aspect of learning, and children make rapid progress in visual discrimination of small differences in the size and shape of letters from one grade level to another. There is, however, a need for continual guidance and instruction in written language throughout the elementary school years, and in some cases into the high school years.

Ford (1954) and Harrell (1957) found a gradual development in the quality of written language among children at the different grade levels. An analysis of the compositions of New Zealand school children age 7-13 by Ford, revealed consistent improvements in unity, continuity, clarity, and complexity. No significant differences were found at age seven, but in later years girls wrote more than boys. Their compositions portrayed less action than the composition of boys, but more descriptive materials.

An investigation by Griffin (1966) had as its purposes to explore the validity of certain indexes proposed as measures of children's development toward maturity in the control of English syntax, and to identify characteristic differences in the exploitation of syntactic resources (1) by boys and girls, (2) at various age-grade levels, and (3) in speech and writing. Subjects for the study consisted of 180 white middle-class children, 30 in kindergarten and 30 each in grades 1, 2, 3, 5, and 7. Sexes were approximately equally divided in each grade group.

The language productions to be studied consisted of reports and discussions of stories enacted in two eight-minute, silent, animated-cartoon films. Oral responses were recorded on tape for later transcription. Children in grades 3, 5, and 7, produced written compositions immediately following their oral discussions. Mean length of total responses in both speech and writing increased with each advance in grade level. In speech, increases were notably greater in grades 2,

3, and 5 than in grades 1 and 7; in writing, the greatest increase was in grade 5. Written compositions were less than half as long as oral responses in grade 3; were about six-tenths of the length of oral responses in grade 5, and were about seven-tenths as long as oral responses in grade 7. Griffin states (p. 5): "Children in grade 3 had much firmer control of speech than of writing, but fifth- and seventh-graders demonstrated far greater maturity in writing than in speech."

While noun and adjective clauses were found to have varied greatly in rate of use over the grade-span studied, similar studies by Harrell (1957), Templin (1957), and Hunt (1964) revealed impressive grade-to-grade increases in the relative frequency of adverbial clauses. In writing, seventh-graders used such clauses nearly twice as often as third-graders.

Studies of child development have emphasized that the stages of the child's drawing closely parallel those found in the development of oral language. The drawings of the school-age child take on the characteristics of compositions, with a relationship between the different parts of the drawing. The drawings of the child are seldom marked by extreme incongruities in design or color, although they frequently appear to be caricatures when viewed by adults (Goodenough and Harris, 1950).

The development of the ability of children to draw parallels other aspects of the child's motor and mental ability. The early "scribble" drawings do not reveal recognizable designs; they do have meaning to the child as indicated when the observer questions the child about his "scribble" drawings.

Summary

The development of language skills is an outgrowth of one's sociocultural experiences. It is man's most important means of interacting with others; it is also man's most important means of self-expression. It has its beginning in the cries, motor activities, and bodily movements of the infant as means of communicating to others. The ability to hear and to listen is important at this early stage of the child's development.

Children from an impoverished environment are handicapped in their language development; a stimulating environment has a beneficial effect upon the language development of the young child. At the first-grade level, the average girl seems to enunciate more clearly than the average boy, and she has a slightly larger vocabulary. However, sex differences decrease with age so that by the fourth, fifth, and sixth grades, no significant differences appear.

After the first few years, it seems that comprehension of meanings from others exceeds the ability to produce and express meanings to others; this may be observed in the child's early articulations. The small child begins to talk by using single words. There is a gradual and continuous increase in the mean number of words per language response. Mean sentence length has frequently been used as a measure of increased verbal maturity.

Piaget classified the speech of children into two categories: *egocentric speech* and socialized speech. Most speech during the early years is *egocentric;* socialized speech, according to Piaget, prevails between ages five and six. Speech is affected by maturation so that the emotionally and socially mature child is likely to be more advanced in socialized speech.

The speech development of only children is slightly advanced over that of singletons and twins. Generally, children from homes where two languages are spoken are retarded in the rate and extent of either language development. An important condition affecting language development is the nature and extent of parent-child relationships.

Some of the major causes of speech disorders are: (1) deafness, (2) brain damage, (3) emotional disturbances, (4) poor models, (5) immaturity, (6) physical conditions, (7) unfavorable environmental conditions, (8) lack of motivation for good speech, and (9) miscellaneous conditions and disorders.

The role of visual language is noted in the importance of reading and writing. Both reading and writing depend upon readiness, which involves maturation, experiences, and dynamic factors. Growth in reading is closely related to the total development of the school child. As in speech, the mean length of total responses increases with each advance in grade level.

During the elementary school years, listening ability seems to fall behind speaking and reading skills. Intelligence is an important factor in listening ability. No sex differences appear among middle-class children; lower-class girls are superior to lower-class boys.

References

American Speech and Hearing Association, "Public School and Hearing Services," *Journal of Speech and Hearing Disorders,* Monograph Supplement 8, 1961.

Apell, R. J. "Visual Problems in Reading," Reading Conference, Old Dominion College, October 1966.

Barger, W. C. "An Experimental Approach to Aphasia and Nonreading Children," *American Journal of Orthopsychiatry,* Vol. 23 (1953), pp. 158-170.

Bellugi, R. B. U. "Three Processes in the Child's Acquisition of Syntax," *Harvard Educational Review,* Vol. 34 (1964), pp. 133-151.

Bernstein, B. "Linguistic Codes, Hesitation Phenomena and Intelligence," *Language and Speech,* Vol. 5 (1962), pp. 31-46.

Birren, J. E., and D. F. Morrison. "Analysis of the WAIS Subtests in Relation to Age and Education," *Journal of Gerontology,* Vol. 16 (1961), pp. 363-369.

Birren, J. E., K. F. Riegel, and J. S. Robbin. "Age Differences in Continuous Word Associations Measured by Speech Recordings," *Journal of Gerontology,* Vol. 17 (1962), pp. 95-96.

Blanchard, I. "Speech Pattern and Etiology in Mental Retardation," *American Journal of Mental Deficiency,* Vol. 68 (1964), pp. 612-617.

Broderick, A. J., and O. C. Irwin. "The Speech Behavior of Infants without Families," *Child Development,* Vol. 17 (1946), pp. 145-156.

Carr, J. "An Investigation of the Spontaneous Speech of Five-Year-Old Deaf-Born Children," *Journal of Speech and Hearing Disorders,* Vol. 18 (1953), pp. 22-29.

Cherry, C., and B. McA. Sayers, "Experiments upon the Total Inhibition of Stammering by External Control and Some Clinical Results," *Journal of Psychosomatic Research,* Vol. 1 (1956), pp. 233-246.

Davis, Edith A. *The Development of Linguistic Skill in Twins, Singletons With Siblings, and Only Children From Age Five to Ten Years.* Institute of Child Welfare Monograph Series No. 14. Minneapolis: U. of Minnesota Press, 1937.

———. "Developmental Changes in the Distribution of Parts of Speech," *Child Development,* Vol. 9 (1938), pp. 309-317.

Dawe, Helen C. "A Study of the Effect of an Educational Program upon Language Development and Related Mental Functions in Young Children," *Journal of Experimental Education,* Vol. 11 (1942), pp. 200-209.

Di Vesta, J. "Developmental Patterns in the Use of Modifiers as Modes of Conceptualization," *Child Development,* Vol. 36 (1965), pp. 185-213.

Edmonds, W. S. "Sex Differences in the Verbal Ability of Socio-Economically Depressed Groups," *Journal of Educational Research,* Vol. 58 (1964).

Fitzsimons, R. "Developmental, Psychological and Educational Factors in Children with Nonorganic Articulation Problems," *Child Development,* Vol. 29 (1958), pp. 481-489.

Ford, C. T. "Developments in Written Composition during the Primary School Period," *British Journal of Educational Psychology,* Vol. 24 (1954), pp. 38-45.

Gens, G. W. "Speech Retardation in the Normal and Subnormal Child," *Training School Bulletin,* Vol. 42 (1950), pp. 32-36.

Goodenough, L., and D. B. Harris. "Studies in the Psychology of Children's Drawings, II, 1928-1949," *Psychological Bulletin,* Vol. 47 (1950), pp. 369-433.

Gordon, R. "Neurological Factors in Speech Development," Spring Meeting Speech and Hearing Association of Virginia, May 13, 1967.

Griffin, W. J. "A Transformational Analysis of the Language of Kindergarten and Elementary School Children," paper read at a meeting of the American Educational Research Association in Chicago, Feb. 19, 1966.

Grinder, R. E., A. Otmo, and W. Toyota. "Comparison between Second, Third and Fourth Grade Children in the Audio-Visual Learning of Japanese as a Second Language," *Journal of Educational Research,* Vol. 56 (1962), pp. 191-197.

Harrell, L. E. "A Comparison of the Development of Oral and Written Language in School-Age Children," *Monographs of the Society for Research in Child Development,* Vol. 23, No. 3 (1957).

Hughes, M., and K. Cox. "The Language of First Grade Children," *Elementary English,* Vol. 26 (1949), pp. 373-380, 406.

Hunt, K. W. *Differences in Grammatical Structures Written at Three Grade Levels, the Structures to be Analyzed by Tranformational Methods.* Report to the U. S. Office of Education, Cooperative Research Project No. 1998. Tallahassee, Florida, 1964.

Irwin, O. C. "Infant Speech: the Effect of Family Occupational Status and of Age on Sound Frequency," *Journal of Speech and Hearing Disorders,* Vol. 13 (1948), pp. 224-226, 320-323.

Johnson, W. "A Study of the Onset and Development of Stuttering," *Journal of Speech and Hearing Disorders,* Vol. 7 (1942), pp. 251-257.

Kent, M. S. "The Aphasic Child in a Residential School for the Deaf," Maryland School for the Deaf, Frederick, Md., 1957.

Koch, H. L. "The Relation of 'Primary Mental Abilities' in Five- and Six-Year-Olds to Sex of Child and Characteristics of His Sibling," *Child Development,* Vol. 25 (1954), pp. 209-223.

Landreth, C. *The Psychology of Early Childhood.* New York: Knopf, 1958.

Lemert, E. M. "Stuttering and Social Structure in Two Pacific Societies," *Journal of Speech and Hearing Disorders,* Vol. 27 (1962), pp. 3-10.

Lennenberg, E. H. "Language Disorders in Childhood," *Harvard Educational Review,* Vol. 34 (1964), pp. 152-177.

Lubker, B. B. "Defective Speech as a Handicap," *Bulletin of Ophthalmology and Otolaryngology,* Vol. 5 (October 1959), pp. 38-44.

———"Factors in Delayed Speech in Children," *Bulletin of Ophthalmology and Otolaryngology,* Vol. 1 (1960), pp. 52–56.

McCarthy, Dorothea. "Language Development," *Monographs of the Society for Research in Child Development,* Vol. 25, No. 3 (1960).

———"Language Development in Children," in L. Carmichael (ed.), *Manual of Child Psychology,* 2nd ed. New York: Wiley, 1954.

Malmivaara, K., and P. Kolho. "The Personality of 5- to 7-Year-Old Enuretics in the Light of the Sceno and Rorschach Tests," *Ann. Paediat. Fenniae,* Vol. 8 (1962), pp. 166-172.

Marshall, H. R. "Relation between Home Experiences and Children's use of Language in Play Interactions with Peers," *Psychological Monographs,* Vol. 75, No. 5 (1961).

May, F. B. "The Effects of Environment on Oral Language Development," *Elementary English,* Vol. 43 (1966), pp. 587-595.

Menyuk, P. "Syntactic Structure in the Language of Children," *Child Development,* Vol. 34 (1963), pp. 407-422.

Miller, M. "An Investigation of Secondary Defects Potentially Affecting the Educability of Children Crippled by Cerebral Palsy," unpublished Ph.D. dissertation, University of Southern California, 1953.

Moncur, J. P. "Parental Domination in Stuttering," *Journal of Speech and Hearing Disorders,* Vol. 17 (1952), pp. 155-165.

Morley, M., D. Court, H. Miller, and R. F. Garside. "Delayed Speech and Developmental Aphasia," *British Medical Journal* (August 1955), pp. 463-467.

Moskowitz, M. "Teaching the Slow Learner," *School Review,* Vol. 16 (1948), p. 477.

Murray, T. "A Study of the Oral and Written Language of Children in the Fourth, Fifth, and Sixth Grades in Various Social Situations," Ph.D. dissertation, University of Southern California, 1953.

Mysak, E. D. "Organismic Development of Oral Language," *Journal of Speech and Hearing Disorders,* Vol. 26 (1961), pp. 377-384.

Peisach, C. "Children's Comprehension of Teacher and Peer Speech," *Child Development,* Vol. 36 (1965), pp. 467-480.

Piaget, J. *The Language and Thought of the Child.* New York: Harcourt, 1926.

Pratt, E. "Experimental Evaluation of a Program for the Improvement of Listening," *Elementary School Journal,* Vol. 56 (1955-56), pp. 315-320.

Riegel, K. F., and J. E. Birren. "Age Differences in Verbal Associations," *Journal of Genetic Psychology,* Vol. 108 (1966), pp. 153-170.

Russell, H. K. *Articulation Profile of 209 Mentally Retarded Children.* Seminar in Special Education Report, San Francisco State College, 1952.

Schaie, K. W. "Rigidity-Flexibility and Intelligence: a Cross-Sectional Study of the Adult Life Span from 20 to 70 Years," *Psychological Monographs,* Vol. 72, No. 9 (1958).

Shirley, M. M. *The First Two Years: A Study of Twenty-five Babies. Vol. II: Intellectual Development.* Institute of Child Welfare Monograph No. 7. Minneapolis: U. of Minnesota Press, 1933.

Sigel, I. E. "The Need for Conceptualization in Research on Child Development," *Child Development* Vol. 27 (1956), pp. 241-252.

Simon, C. T. "The Development of Speech," in L. E. Travis (ed.), *Handbook of Speech Pathology.* New York: Appleton, 1957.

Smith, Madorah, E. "Measurement of Vocabularies of Young Bilingual Children in Both of the Languages Used," *Journal of Genetic Psychology,* Vol. 74 (1949), pp. 305-310.

Solomon, A. L. "Personality and Behavior Patterns of Children with Functional Defects of Articulation," *Child Development,* Vol. 32 (1961), pp. 731-737.

Spache, G. D. "Children's Vision and Their Reading Success," *Journal of California Optometric Association,* Vol. 39, No. 5 (1961).

Strayer, L. C. "Language and Growth: the Relative Efficacy of Early and Deferred Vocabulary Training Studied by the Method of Co-Twin Control," *Genetic Psychology Monographs,* Vol. 8 (1930), pp. 209-319.

Tagruchi, T. "A Study of the Structure of Colloquial Japanese from the Standpoint of Developmental Psychology," *Japanese Journal of Psychology,* Vol. 33 (1962), pp. 193-201.

Templin, Mildred. *Certain Language Skills in Children: Their Development and Interrelationships.* Institute of Child Welfare Monograph Series, No. 26. Minneapolis: U. of Minnesota Press, 1957.

Travis, L. E. *Handbook of Speech Pathology.* New York: Appleton, 1957.

Van Riper, C. *Teaching Your Child To Talk.* New York: Harper, 1950.

Vigotsky, L. S. "Thought and Speech," *Psychiatry,* Vol. 2 (1939), pp. 29-54.

Young, F. M. "An Analysis of Certain Variables in a Developmental Study of Language," *Genetic Psychology Monographs,* Vol. 23 (1941), pp. 3-141.

Young, W. E. "The Relation of Reading Comprehension and Retention to Hearing Comprehension and Retention," *Journal of Experimental Education,* Vol. 5 (1936), pp. 30-39.

Chapter 7

Concept Formation and the Cognitive Process

The concepts, generalizations, and principles learned at different stages of development become an integral part of one's personality. These differences, resulting from different kinds of concept formation and cognitive processes, vary among cultures and societies and among individuals within the same society. A child growing up in an area of the United States bordering Ontario, Canada, will have a very different concept of his country, Canada, and Mexico from that of an American child growing up along the U. S.-Mexican border. These and other environmental-oriented concepts tend to produce and shape different personalities.

The six-year-old child at school has already developed a system of concepts and characteristic ways of perceiving and organizing the various environmental stimuli he encounters. The mental growth of the child includes cognitive processes—those processes by which he organizes, interprets, and interrelates the data of sensory experiences.

The Formation of Concepts

The mental life of the child has its beginnings in the experiences he encounters through his senses. However, no mental activity would be possible if the individual were unable to record and retain the impressions he receives and at a later time recall those necessary for making discriminations and comparisons. The formation of a concept involves more than the retention and recall of sensory impression. A concept is a classification of impressions of stimuli according to certain common characteristics.

Verplank (1957) suggests that concepts are typically statements. He states: "Most concepts are statements that refer to the common property: 'blue,' 'square,' 'velocity,' 'beauty,' 'length.' Pseudoconcepts may depend on a number of partially overlapping common property: 'honesty,' 'virtue,' 'rigidity.'" One would deduce from this definition that concepts refer to common properties rather than a broad class of objects or events, the numbers of which have a single quantifiable property in common.

According to McDonald (1965, p. 162) two processes are involved in acquiring a concept: discrimination and generalizations. These may be observed in the child's acquisition of the concept of "airport" to repeat a verbal definition of "airport" is insufficient. The formation of the concept of "airport" requires the child to go beyond a definition or brief description of the only "airport" is established when the child's classification or categorization extends beyond a single "airport" to other examples of airports. This requires the child to first make discriminations and second to generalize the concept to other examples.

Perception. The child's mental life involves thought processes or thinking. Thinking involves perceptions of form, size, shape, color, intensity, texture, and other meanings developed through interacting with environmental stimuli. Russell (1956 p. 70) defines perception as "the process of organizing and interpreting the sensations the organism receives from external and internal stimuli." Through the sense organs and the central nervous system stimuli from the environment are received and interpreted. This becomes the basis for his reactions to the objects and conditions about him. The infant's early learnings are largely perceptual; they involve elements from his immediate environment.

The importance of the early years is emphasized by Bloom, Davis, and Hess (1965). They state (p. 13): "Perceptual development is stimulated by environments which are rich in the range of experiences available; which make use of games, toys, and many objects for manipulation: and in which there is frequent interaction between the child and adults at meals, playtime, and throughout the day." However, perceptual learning emerges into concept formation. This may be illustrated by the development of the concept, roundness. This concept developed out of a wide range of perceptual learning involving roundness. The concepts which the child develops from his early perceptions are the meanings and understandings which he will carry, with some modifications throughout life. They are basic to his attitudes, beliefs, ideals, and values.

Significance of Early Learning. It has been noted that the ease of concept learning is a function of the discriminability of the stimuli. This suggests that the degree of previous learning of the differentiating response has a bearing on the ease of concept attainment. The idea of enhancing human cognitive development through an early environment that provided rich and stimulating experiences and to counteract two fairly well-entrenched assumptions: the one that intelligence is fixed and the second that the unfolding of cognitive abilities resulted from a predetermined maturational sequence.

Recently attention has been given to providing preschool children with stimulating and enriched concrete language experiences. This may be noted in Head Start and related programs, the results of which show that the early years are extremely important to the optimum development of a child's potential abilities.

Results of Cultural Deprivation. The outcome of cultural deprivation is well known: children from deprived backgrounds score well below middle-class children on standard individual and group measures of intelligence (a gap that increases with age); they come to school without the skills necessary for coping with the first grade curricula; their language development is poor. Studies of culturally deprived children seem to point to the following general conclusions: (1) The behavior which leads to social, educational, and economic poverty is socialized in early childhood i.e., it is learned. (2) The central quality involved in the effects of cultural deprivation is lack of cognitive meaning in the mother-child communication system. (3) Growth of the cognitive process is fostered in family control systems which offer and permit a wide range of alternatives of action and thought and such growth is constricted by systems of control which offer predetermined solutions and few alternatives for consideration and choice.

In a study by Hess and Shipman (1965) 160 Negro mothers and their four-year old children, selected from four different social status levels, were studied. The mothers were taught three simple tasks, which they in turn taught their children. The mothers were also interviewed twice in their homes and tested at the university. The results indicate that the influence of the mother's pattern of interaction and communication with the child plays an important role in cognitive skill development. Using the observational situation approach, Hess (1965) conducted a series of studies of the interaction of the preschool child and the mother in problem-solving situations. Special consideration was given to the way in which the mother assists the child in solving problems and the nature of the cognitive environment provided. The results indicate that when mothers provide a limited or restricted language code in the solution of the problem, the child's problem-solving ability is decreased.

Lower levels of achievement motivation and expectation have been observed among lower-class children (Rosen, 1956). This seems to result from long-term social depirvation by parents and is passed on to the child. These are closely related to differences in the ways the child has learned to perceive his environment and its rewards for achievement. For example, Terrell and others (1959) noted that lower-class children performed more effectively for a material incentive, whereas a nonmaterial incentive was as effective as one of materials for the middle-class child.

Early studies of institutionalized children by Goldfarb (1953) showed that they, as contrasted with rejected children, showed greater defects in their intellectual processes. They seemed to have greater difficulty in organizing their experiences in a meaningful way and to abstract relationships from them. However, in human development, the ability to recover from the handicap of different forms of perceptual deprivation indicates that, despite the importance of early environmental experiences, maturational components cannot be ignored (Dennis and Najarian, 1957).

The Role of Language.   Words are not concepts, although they are useful formal properties of concepts. Nouns represent concepts. Many adjectives also embody concepts. Large, small, rough, smooth, and round represent adjectival concepts. Concepts are also present in other parts of speech including some verbs, such as read, write, and play. There is also a close relationship between

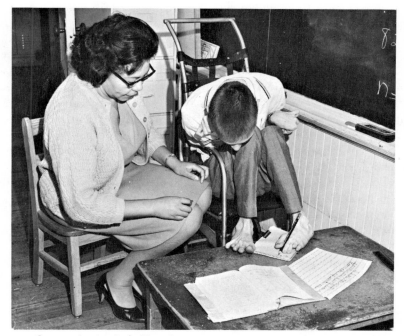

Communication is facilitated in a unique manner. (Courtesy Kirk-Cone
Rehabilitation Center—Chesapeake, Va.)

language and thinking, especially in the more complex types of thinking involving abstractions and in making finer distinctions. Language includes the most
complex organization of perceptual and motor skills and the most abstract,
symbolic processes of which the organism is capable. The interaction of language, thought, and environment appears in all types of concept building, problem solving, and creative thinking.

The development of language enables the child to move out beyond the
present both temporally and spatially; it permits productive operations in the
absence of what is represented. This accomplishment enables the child to delay
gratification and to bring forth ideas outside his immediate environment. Bruner
(1964, p. 4) states: "Once the child has succeeded in internalizing language as a
cognitive instrument, it becomes possible for him to represent and systematically
transform the regularities of experience with far greater flexibility and power
than before."

Some Attributes of Concepts.   Three closely related attributes of concepts
are abstractness, inclusiveness, and generality. The continuum of abstractness
ranges from direct sensory impressions with actual objects or events to purely
verbal representations of objects or events. Concepts also range in inclusiveness
from one example to an unspecified number of examples. There is only one *me*, a
number of continents, many nations, an indefinite number of stars. Concepts

range in generality from applicability to people in a small minority group to applicability to all people.

In addition to the attributes of abstractness, inclusiveness, and generality, concepts have the attributes of structure and function. According to structure, concepts may be conjunctive, disjunctive, and relational (Klausmeier and Goodwin, 1966, p. 218). In a conjunctive concept all the attributes are present at the same time. For example, a baseball team may be conceived of as a conjunctive concept and is composed of a pitcher, catcher, infielders, and out-fielders. If any of these are lacking it is not a complete team. Many concepts which involve classification are of the conjunctive type, such as river, fruit, mammal. Disjunction implies separation. The attributes are not present in all the exenokars if a disjunctive concept. For example, a foul called in a basketball game can occur in many ways, although each is called a foul. Relational concepts involve dependencies and are embodied in such words as larger, older, heavier, upward, downward. Geographic concepts such as north and south are relational. Relational concepts develop out of a wide range of experiences and are not usually present to any widespread degree among preschool and early elementary school children.

According to Klausmeier and Goodwin (p. 219) concepts serve two main functions in human behavior: as responses to objects and events by which they are classified and as mediators between stimulating events and subsequent be-havior. If one has the concept *shoe,* then one treats all objects which fit his concept of shoe as belonging to the same classification or set. Knowing the attributes of a class helps one to recognize other examples belonging to that class. Some concepts by their nature influence our behavior, the exemplars of the concept. This may be noted in concepts that bear on the sacred for an individual.

Stages in Concept Formation

It was suggested in Chapters 6 and 7 that language abilities as well as other intellectual abilities change with learning and maturation. The problem-solving behavior of children becomes more complex and more flexible as they grow older. Each stage of development depends upon the previous stage and leads to a higher operational level. The schools must take into consideration the learning abilities and characteristics of children at different stages of their development. Considerable research has accumulated relating to stages in conceptual develop-ment. Such materials should be most helpful in the development of a sound educational program. The question remains: How extensively can the conceptual processes in the young child be modified? Bruner and others (1956) contend that almost any subject matter, if properly organized, can be taught at the grade-school or preschool level. At the other extreme we note that Inhelder and Piaget (1958) claim that specific levels of cognitive development must be achieved before certain conceptual strategies can be learned. An examination of these and other viewpoints should give us a better understanding of stages in conceptual development.

Piaget's Conceptions.   For many years the ideas of Piaget concerning ontogenetic development of intellectual abilities were ignored by a large percentage of students of child development. This was to a marked extent due to the methods used in gathering data, which were characterized by presenting certain material to an unclassified number of children and securing their responses without attempting to standardize the questions, integrating the results obtained with his theory. Despite limitations in his method of collecting and evaluating data, Piaget has made substantial contributions to our understanding of the stages of the child's intellectual development, as shown in the verification of many of the developmental trends in replication studies (Danziger and Sharp, 1958; Elkind, 1961, 1964; Lovell, 1961; Smedslund, 1963).

Piaget's ideas are of widespread interest, due in part to Flavell (1963), who translated and summarized a number of his publications. Piaget has set forth the following chronological order of the development of mental processes involving cognition (Berlyne, 1957):

>   Birth to two years—the period of sensorimotor adaptation.
>   Two to four years—the period of preconceptual thought.
>   Four to seven years—the period of intuitive thought.
>   Seven to eleven years—the period of concrete operations.
>   Eleven to fifteen years—the period of formal operations.

Birth marks the beginning of the sensorimotor period, and involves little or no thoughtful response. At first only reflexes are manifested; these undergo separate modifications with experience. During this stage actions are started that are oriented toward objects and events in one's external environment. Out of jumbled sensations the child creates an organization. Size, color, and pattern that are experienced together come to be distinguished as objects, and these objects are formed into an organization which approaches the boundary of meaning. At first the world is a succession of visual patterns, sounds, and sensations. Gradually the child builds up a view of the world as a collection of objects that exist even when they are not in his immediate environment. This development goes hand in hand with the formation of a less "egocentric" and a more "sociocentric" conception of conditions and objects in his world.

During the second stage (two to four years) the child extracts concepts from his experiences, thus relearning on a conceptual level some of the lessons acquired earlier on a sensorimotor level. However, the child is unable to take the viewpoint of another at this stage. The three-year-old must use something between the concept of an object and that of a class. When watching the birds in the yard he is unable to determine whether he is seeing a succession of different birds or whether the same bird continues to reappear. Around age four, egocentrism tends to be replaced by increased social interaction. "Preconcepts that are formed are action ridden, imaginative, and concrete, rather than schematic and abstract" (Klausmeier and Goodwin, P. 223). During this period vague relational concepts such as "bigger," "stronger," and "more" are constructed from experience and can be formed without verbal instruction. Piaget contends that until age 7 or 8 a child's language and thought are largely egocentric, that he depends upon intuition and trial and error, and that he arrives at conclusions from a single case. The child at this stage (four to seven years) is dominated by his perceptions. If he sees his father use the water hose to wash his car he then perceives the water hose as a means for washing the car, overlooking any other meanings that might be attached to the water hose. In his thought processes at this third stage "centering" causes one element in a situation to be overemphasized while all other elements are in the main ignored, a characteristic frequently present in the thought processes of adults when dealing with emotionally toned problems in the areas of politics or religion.

Around age 7 the child begins making use of concrete operations. This enables him to solve simple, concrete problems. According to Piaget, operational thoughts emerge during this period. In order for operational thoughts to appear the child must first have acquired a basic stock of concepts, and secondly these concepts have been organized into coherent systems. These concepts are called "operations" because they are internalized responses.

The period of formal operations begins at age 11. The eleven-year-old is able to apply operational thinking to concrete situations and practical problems. The child who has reached the period of formal operations still possesses the nine groups of concrete operational thought. At this stage they are more fully developed, more flexible in nature, and can be handled with increased facility. A complete array of logical possibilities can be considered, since relations involving more than one variable can be dealt with. The child or adolescent who has reached the formal operations level will systematically attempt more complex combinations in an effort to solve a particular problem. He looks for different ways or combinations to employ in dealing with a problem. The individual at this stage is concerned with the possible, not just the real. The adolescent has acquired the capacity for abstract thought. This opens to him the deductive procedures of science, mathematics, and logic. His theorizing about the problems around him stems from his ability to see possibilities and alternatives.

Since a variety of new intellectual techniques are available at this time, the individual can, through guided instruction, plan scientific investigations, carry on logical thinking in areas other than the sciences, and develop theories and models as guides.

Age Changes.   As with other phases of development, significant changes take place with age, although there is much overlapping of the different age groups. The understanding of individual properties and attributes proceeds from simple to complex, general to specific, vague to clear, and in a sequence that is fairly stable from child to child. This was noted by Weinstein (1957, pp. 171-172) in his study of the development of the concept of the flag and a sense of national identity. At ages 5 and 6, the flag is a name for a class of objects that has certain common physical characteristics. At this stage it belongs rather than identifies. At age 7, the flag identifies proprietorship. Nations are different on the basis of different geographical areas and different flags identified with them. The notion of multiplicity of flags appears at age 8, when the full extent of the symbolism associated with the flag is understood. By age 9, the flag is understood as a conventional symbol; a country is regarded as a geographical area with a particular governmental administration, with the group of people in a particular country having common purposes and allegiances.

Marked changes appear in concepts relating to time from age 2½ to 8 (Ames, 1946). According to Ames it was not until age 8 that all children studied were able to answer correctly the day of the week, while all the children were able to tell time by age 7. Children's concepts of, "What season is it?" "What year is it?" and "What day of the month is today?" were poorly developed prior to age 8. There is evidence for a sequential order of time concepts in data presented on children ages 6-11 by Uka (1956). He noted that some concepts develop early, some show a slow start with a sudden spurt, and some develop gradually over a relatively long period of time. This is illustrated in Figure 7-1, showing the growth in understanding of the following problems related to time:

(15)   What day comes before Friday?

(22)   In what month is Christmas?

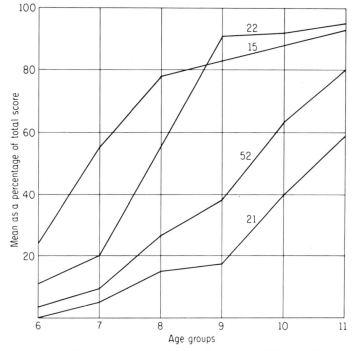

Figure 7-1. Growth curves showing the nature of the growth of certain time concepts. (After Ngwobia Uka.)

(52)   How long does the summer last?

(21)   Name the months of the year.

The results of a study by King (1961) of the development of scientific concepts among children age 6-11 support results obtained for growth in time, quantity, word, and space concepts. In the study by King, children were presented questions and problems involving (1) length, weight, time, and direction; (2) volume and weight; (3) mechanical principles; and (4) living things, seasons, and the like. The responses to these questions indicated a steady increase in correct solutions with age, although the increase was slower for the more complex concepts. There was a significant relationship between the level of the intellectual ability of the pupils and the development of time and science concepts. The development of time, space, number, science, and word concepts closely correlate with other aspects of the child's intellectual development. The guidance of the child in the acquisition of concepts insures more meaningful concepts and increased transfer.

An experiment by Mosher (1962) was concerned with strategies used by children age 6-11 for getting information in a game of twenty questions. Their task was to determine by "yes-no" questions what caused an automobile to go off the road and hit a tree. Mosher found that children age 6-11 progressively used more and more constraint in their explanations and in locating connecting questions. Only 29 percent of the six-year-olds used constraint; they were more inclined to follow an impulse in answering questions, frequently displaying little regard for the problem.

Piaget's pioneering work in studying the development of children's concepts of causality stimulated additional research on different problems involving scientific concepts (1932). He found a sequence of distinct types of causal explanations, each of which was characteristic of different stages of the child's development. The first and second stages were classed as precausal, while a third stage appeared around age 7-8 which he regarded as truly causal. He related these stages to the child's progress from egocentrism to socialization. He noted a tendency for children to endow physical objects with human qualities; this animism developed in four distinct stages. Johnson and Josey (1931) repeated Piaget's experiments in logical thinking and failed to find the distinct stages of development described by Piaget. Oakes (1947) in a detailed study of children's explanation of natural phenomena found no evidence to corroborate Piaget's contention that there is a definite stage in the child's thinking characteristics at each age level. He concluded that each individual, regardless of age, mental ability, or grade level, gave explanations of a wide variety. In general, understanding of relationships improved with age. He further noted that the answers given by a child were influenced by the nature of the problem, the way the question was worded, the child's relation to the interviewer, and by the child's background of experience to a much greater degree than by a particular mental structure at a given age level.

Evidence from a wide variety of controlled studies seems to lead to the following conclusions about the development of scientific and nonscientific concepts, and relationships between such concepts. Development is gradual in nature and is closely related to a number of factors, especially the child's experiences and maturation. A child reared in an environment where superstition is used to explain natural phenomena or unusual happenings will have many more faulty concepts of causality than he would have if his learning experiences had been more realistic. Likewise, a child who has read books and watched television programs with a fairy-tale content will have a less realistic viewpoint of causation, and will place considerably more stress on magic as a cause of many things where the cause is not apparent. Although different experiences have an important bearing on the development of concepts of causality, a general pattern of development may be observed. There is little indication that children below age 7 or 8 understand cause and effect, especially in complex situations. Thus their concepts of cause and effect relations are frequently illogical, inaccurate, and magical in nature.

The purpose of a study by DiVesta (1965) was to conduct a systematic investigation of the qualifying modes used by children at five different age levels. In studying the development of affective meaning systems, modifiers (or adjectives) were elicited from 100 children in each of grades 2 through 6. Differences were noted among age groups in the manner in which substantives were qualified. There was a clear-cut preponderance of the use of evaluative words among the seven- and eight-year-old children and a rapid decline in the use of evaluative words in the intermediate ages nine through eleven.

In a study by Elkind (1966), 32 children and 32 adolescents were tested for their ability to shift from a functional to a perceptual and from a positive to a negative similarity orientation in the course of a concept attainment task. Two sets of 24 cards containing outline drawings of things used for transport, six of which were wheeled (car, wagon, truck, trailer, bicycle, and bus) and six of which were nonwheeled (steamship, sailboat, horse, camel, skiis, and ice skates). The remaining 12 drawings were of tools, six of which were wheeled and six of which were nonwheeled. For both the level and the similarity shift conditions the two decks were paired. The adolescents (average age 166.84 months) were significantly more successful than the children (average age 120.37 months) on the tasks requiring a shift from a functional task figural level of conceptualization and on a task requiring a shift from a positive to a negative similarity orientation.

In a study by Hill (1965) children age 1, 4, 6, and 12 were tested on object discrimination, oddity, and conditional-oddity problems. Two restrictions were placed on the selection of subjects with the different age groups; subjects must have average or better ability as judged by the teacher and must be willing to participate in the experiment. The object-discrimination task consisted of selecting a green triangle or a red cylinder, one of the objects being consistently rewarded. The oddity task entailed selecting one of three objects, two alike and one odd, the odd stimulus object always being rewarded. The conditional-oddity problem was more complex, the subject selecting from three objects, two alike and one odd, the odd object being rewarded when on a blue tray, the nonodd object on the outside position being rewarded when on a yellow tray. The results revealed that both the availability of problem-solving response tendencies and the control and direction of attention appear to underlie the performance of older as well as younger children. Young children appear to have a preferred response; older children appear to have a variety of responses available for their use, once their attention is directed to the relevant aspects of the problem.

The results of a study by Blackwell (1962) confirm the developmental theory of concepts postulated by Piaget. Seventy children, ten in each of seven age groups, were studied. The children were given sets of material developed for measuring the degree and level of concept formation. The results were in general agreement with the following hypotheses:

1. The mean number of choices required to attain the concept is an inverse function of age.
2. The mean number of attribute changes is an inverse function of age.
3. The mean number of choices more like the original focus card than like any preceding card choices is an inverse function of age.
4. The mean number of redundant choices is an inverse function of age.

The Cognitive Process

The word *cognition* is derived from the Latin word *cognitive* meaning "knowing." Cognitive psychology is concerned with those processes by which an individual acquires knowledge. The information included in a body of knowledge is usually tied together in some way, involving some kind of relationships. "Cognition," according to Klausmeier and Goodwin (1966, p. 39), "refers to immediate discovery, awareness, rediscovery, or recognition of information that has been discriminated, synonymous for cognition are comprehension and understanding." Most of the learning which takes place at school is accounted for through cognition. Interest in cognitive behavior has brought into focus the problem of organizing subject matter and learning tasks.

The Role of Learning.   It should be borne in mind that human behaviors are learned. For example, the individual who has a complex higher mathematical repertoire has learned an extremely complex set of S-R mechanisms in a training program that include many conditioning trials stretching over a period of many years. And while it is generally believed that only individuals with special genetically based qualities, such as average or above average intelligence, can acquire such complex repertoires in view of the lack of evidence, we have to entertain the possibility that any normal person can acquire such a repertoire if exposed to the appropriate learning circumstances (Staats, 1968, p. 385).

The naturalistic evidence that a complex set of training circumstances is essential to the development of complex cognitive repertoires is all around us.

Staats states: "Peoples and groups who do not receive appropriate training circumstances do not evidence members with the highly developed cognitive repertoires—nor does the people as a whole produce the products of such cognitive repertoires" (p. 385).

In Table 7-1 we note a hierarchial arrangement of cognitive abilities involved in problem solving (Harootunian and Tate, 1960). Note the high correlations of reading with problem solving, problem recognition, and IQ, and the lower correlations between problem solving and word fluency, closure, and ideational fluency. However, we should not conclude from this that problem solving can be performed only by people who can read, although the use of symbols is essential for solving abstract problems.

TABLE 7-1

Correlations between Problem Solving and Other Variables
(After Harootunian and Tate)

Variable	Problem Recognition	Word Fluency	Ideational Fluency	Closure	Judgment	IQ	Reading
Problem solving	.62	.42	.29	.40	.71	.68	.73
Problem recognition		.40	.56	.30	.55	.52	.60
Word fluency			.46	.33	.37	.40	.49
Ideational fluency				.17	.28	.32	.36
Closure					.27	.36	.35
Judgment						.54	.64
IQ							.56

Cognitive Styles. The contemporary theorists contend that learning is essential for the development of cognitive structures and processes. The meaning of cognitive structure and some related terms is described by Ausubel (1963, p. 76) as follows:

> Cognitive structure refers solely to the stability, clarity, and organization of a learner's subject-matter knowledge in a given discipline. The actual ideas and information embodied in this knowledge are "cognitive content." "Cognitive style" refers to the self-consistent inter-individual differences and idiosyncratic trends in cognitive organization and functioning.

Cognitive styles differ depending upon many phenomenological (individual) factors; however, according to Witkin, various styles can be categorized into two dimensions known as "field-independent" and "field-dependent" (Scheerer, 1964). Field-independent refers to performances which reflect the ability to perceive objects apart from the context in which they occur or to overcome an embedded content. Field-dependent relates performances which refer to the prevailing field or relative inability to separate item from the field. There is no intention on the part of Witkin to suggest a complete dichotomy into fields.

In evaluating field dependence in perceptual situations we find a continuum of performances, with most people falling in the middle of the range.

There is now considerable evidence that people we call field-independent do significantly better at problems in which the essential element required for solution must be isolated from the content in which it is presented and used in a different kind of relation to the rest of the problem material. A study by Goodenough and Karp (1961), using factor analysis, was conducted with groups of ten- and twelve-year-old boys as subjects. The boys were given a special series of cognitive tasks including perceptual and field dependence tests and the subtests of the *Wechsler Intelligence Scale for Children*. Three main factors emerged which are: (1) verbal factor, (2) attention-concentration factor, and (3) analytic factor. An analysis of the tasks presented by the block design, picture, completion, and object assembly suggests that they require the same kind of analytic functioning as do the perceptual tests. Apparently, children with a more field-dependent or field-independent way of perceiving are not significantly different in overall tested intelligence.

Sequencing Cognitive Operations.   It has been noted that the ease of concept learning is a function of the discriminability of the stimuli. This suggests that the degree of previous learning of the differentiating response has a bearing on the ease of concept attainment. The idea of enhancing human cognitive development through an early environment that provided rich and stimulating experiences is a relatively recent one. To arrive at this notion it was essential to gather evidence showing the values of early environmental experiences and to counteract two fairly well-entrenched assumptions: the one that intelligence is fixed and the second that the unfolding of cognitive abilities resulted from a predetermined maturational sequence.

A study by Wolman and Baker (1965) dealt with Piaget's theory of the development of cognitive functioning in children, which suggests that there is a pronounced qualitative change in the child's defining of words in harmony with development levels of thought. A sample of 117 children ages 4–12 drawn from the middle to upper middle class, was used as subjects. Each child was presented a list of 43 carefully chosen words to be defined by answering the question: "What does z mean?" or "What is an x?" An important finding was that as age increases, the percent of *use definitions* tends to decrease. This is shown for three age groups:

Four-year-olds	78 percent
Eight-year-olds	63 percent
Twelve-year-olds	25 percent

The investigators conclude, ". . . the transition from the infantile mode of defining words to the more mature form is gradual and slow. It was also found that intelligence and sex play no important role in this development. Factors that do correlate with the mode of defining are (a) age and (b) number of words known" (p. 165).

Kofsky (1966) employed the scalogram analysis to test Piaget's theory that there is a fixed order in which classification concepts are learned. The subjects used in this study consisted of 122 children age 4–9. Tasks were developed that required the subjects to demonstrate their understanding of each of eleven classification operations. Each testing session lasted approximately one-half to three-quarters of an hour. The data from this study confirm the findings of earlier studies by Dodwell (1960), Lunzer (1960), and Lovell et al. (1962) that individuals vary in the sequence of mastery of cognitive tasks and the steps by which they master a particular cognitive task.

Bruner (1964, p. 1) contends that

> . . . the development of human intellectual functioning from infancy to such perfection as it may reach is shaped by a series of technological advances in the human mind. Growth depends upon the mastery of techniques and cannot be understood without reference to such mastery. These techniques are not, in the main, inventions of the individuals who are "growing up"; they are, rather, skills transmitted with varying efficiency and success by the culture, language being a prime example. Cognitive growth, then, is in a major way from the outside in as well as from the inside out.

Older children are able to gather information by asking questions in a directed sequential order leading to a goal or solution to a problem. Bruner (1964) noted that older children are capable of recognizing visual displays in a manner governed by a dominated frame of reference that transcends momentary and isolated pieces of information. It seems then that as children mature they are able to use information processing other than pointing to what is presently referred to. They are able to make remote references to states and conditions not given in the immediate environmental situation, and are able to go beyond the information given. Second, they seem to be able to gather and organize information into a structure that can be operated upon by rules that go beyond associations based upon similarity and contiguity.

According to Bruner (1960) the child acquires symbolic modes of representing and transforming the world mainly by actively manipulating his environment. Bruner concedes the importance of stimulus-response-reinforcement sequences in the development of the young child, but contends that their influence wanes with age. However, according to Bruner (1960) when behavior becomes more long-range and competence-oriented, it comes under the control of more complex cognitions. In such a case behavior is directed from within in accordance with aspirations, standards, and values. In such a case symbolic systems such as language are important in mediating and even in giving shape to mental life.

The Operation of Perceptual Cues. Developmental studies of perceptual exploration, such as the one reported by Zaporozhets (1965) suggest that the preschool child scans a figure in a global but unsystematic manner, whereas by the age of five or six, there is much more systematic patterning of exploration. This has been found to be true for both the visual and manipulatory type of exploration. The older preschool child brings some perceptual cues to bear upon his understanding of elements in his environment. This was also noted by Elkind, Koegler, and Go (1964) in their studies of perceptual development. They pointed out that perceptual performance is determined both by the nature of the stimulus configuration and the child's level of perceptual development.

Milgram and Furth (1963) noted that mentally retarded children performed reasonably well when compared to average children in attaining concepts on the basis of perceptual cues; however, they found concept attainment more difficult for the mentally retarded on transfer tasks which did not lend themselves readily to a solution based on perceptual cues. This is in harmony with findings of many studies of learning. Transfer of training involving abstract materials is to a marked degree a function of intelligence and mental development. Since intelligence and mental development are an ultimate part of maturation, one necessarily concludes that everything else being equal, there is an optimal time for learning (or sequence) which serves economy and efficiency, notwithstanding statements of Bruner which obviate need for readiness as it relates to maturational age.

With normal children, the lower the chronological age and the lower the mental age, the less able they are to demonstrate concept verbalization, conceptual control, and other operations which mature only with increasing age. By the age of nine, these abilities have matured significantly for normal children to develop proficiency in conceptual control (Milgram and Furth, 1967, pp. 541–542).

Early Experiences and the Cognitive Process.   The importance of an enriched and stimulating early environment was emphasized earlier in this chapter. The inquiry by Hess and Shipman (1965) dealt with the question: How does early cultural deprivation act to shape and depress the development of cognitive abilities? The investigators noted that in all of the tests used, one of the most striking and obvious differences between the environments provided by the mothers of the research group was in their patterns of language use. In the entire testing session, Hess and Shipman believe that the most obvious social-class variations was in the total amount of verbal output in response to questions and tasks asking for verbal response. For example, mothers from the upper-middle class gave protocols that were consistently longer in language productivity than did mothers from the other three groups.

Most of the structural tests that Hess and Shipman utilized that differences in verbal products indicate the extent to which the maternal environments of children in different social-class groups tend to be mediated by verbal cues and thus were found to offer (or fail to offer) opportunities for labeling, for identifying objects and feelings and adult models who can demonstrate the usefulness of language as a tool for dealing with interpersonal interactions and for ordering stimuli in the environment. In addition to this gross disparity in verbal output there were differences in the quality of language used by mothers in the various class groups.

Hess and Shipman maintain that in their findings, the mothers of the four groups differed relatively little, on the average, in the effective elements of their interaction with their children. The gross differences appeared in the verbal and cognitive environments that they presented.

The objective of their study was to discover how teaching styles of the mothers induce and shape learning styles and information-processing strategies in their children. The picture that seemed to emerge is that the meaning of deprivation is a deprivation of meaning. This involves a cognitive environment in which behavior is controlled by status rules rather than by attention to the individual characteristics of a specific situation and one in which behavior is not mediated by verbal cues or by teaching that relates events to one another and the present to the future.

In a study of transposition in the two-stimulus problem in young children, Kuenne (1946, p. 488) suggested that "there are at least two developmental

The Child Constructs His World. Through the Whopper Blocks, the child is able to construct his world as he perceives it, thus furthering his educational development. (Courtesy Schoolcraft, Inc.)

stages so far as the relation of verbal responses to overt choice behavior is concerned. In the first place, the child is able to make differential verbal responses to appropriate aspects of the situation, but his verbalization does not control or influence his overt choice behavior. Later, such verbalization gains control and dominate choice behavior."

There is some evidence that inadequately learned stimulus names, when used for rehearsal, actually produce interference. This was noted by Reese (1960) in his studies of four-, fifth-, and sixth-grade children and by McCormack (1958) in studies of college students. It seems likely, then, that with a well-learned concept there is no necessary deficiency in mediation as a function of age, while with a poorly established concept there is a deficiency at any age.

Going Beyond the Information.   The most characteristic feature of mental life and man's intellectual process, over and beyond the fact that one acquires an understanding of the events and situations in the world, is that one constantly goes beyond the information given. This was early suggested by Spearman (1923) and more recently emphasized by Bruner (1964) and other students of learning and of the thought processes. Some examples of different ways in which people go beyond information that is given should furnish us a better understanding of information processing (Bruner, 1964, pp. 294-295). The first form suggested by Bruner is that of going beyond sensory data to the class identity of the object being perceived. Given the presence of a few properties of the object as cues, we are able to go beyond them to the inference of identity. For example, given the shape, size, texture, and uses of an object not present, that it is an edible fruit grown in certain specific areas of the world, we infer that it is a banana. The act of identifying the banana as a fruit, placing it in an equivalency classification, is one of the simplest forms of going beyond the information given.

A second form of going beyond the information given, presented by Bruner (1964), involves learning the redundancy of the environment. The missing word in the sentence, "George Washington was the first _____ of the United States," is easily recognized by most school boys and girls; however, the word "ps*ch**ogy" is not readily recognized except by students familiar with the word psychology. Once one learns the probability texture of the environment, he is usually able to go beyond the given by predicting its likely concomitant. This is commonplace and characterizes the behavior of the fast reader when reading.

A third form of going beyond the information given appears in the omission of parts in a serial order, such as "3, 5, 8, 12, **, 23." Formal codes and probability codes are frequently combined in making inferences. Kendler and Tracy (1956) noted that three- and four-year-olds were capable of making inferences essential for problem solving. The use of syllogisms involves the learning and interpreting of certain formal schemes. The usage enables man to derive interpretations from given statements. This may be illustrated by the following syllogism:

> All of the states of the United States have a state capital.
> Nevada is one of the states of the United States.
> Nevada has a state capital.

The potential capacity of an individual to acquire the ability for equivalence is enormous. Without this capacity man would be required to respond to each event or situation as a unique one. This would require learning the specifics of each event or situation, thus overwhelming one with the wide range of differences existing in a single situation such as rivers, mountains, and so forth. Bruner (1964, p. 294) states: "Equivalence categories or concepts are the most basic currency one can utilize in going beyond the sensory given. They are the first steps toward rendering the environment generic."

Relation Between Cognition and Overt Behavior. In a study by Grinder (1964) of the relation between cognition and behavioral measures of conscience development, no significant associations were found between the temptation task and Piaget-type stories of moral judgment. Whiteman (1967, p. 154) concludes: "The relation between age and conceptions of psychological causality appears stronger than the relation between age and conceptions of physical causality." One would expect further that the growth of understanding psychological causality to parallel the growth of moral judgments. Data gathered seems to increase with age, the behavioral and cognitive dimensions of conscience develop independently. The results of a subsequent study by Medinnus (1966) support findings of Grinder in showing "little association between a child's actual behavior and his verbally expressed attitudes" (pp. 149-150). However, it appears that at any age level behavior is a function of the strength of motivation. Thus Grinder's conclusion that we should speak of consciences rather than conscience seems to be an accurate appraisal of the levels of conscience development during childhood and adolescence.

The Thinking Process

One reason why there seems to be so many varieties of thinking is that the word has become an omnibus word, carrying with it many ideas. It is frequently used as a catchall and includes such terms as guessing, predicting, remembering, reflecting, creating, opinion, imagination, and judgments. Russell (1956, p. 27) states: "Thinking is a process rather than a fixed state. It involves a sequence of ideas moving from some beginning, through some sort of pattern of relationships, to some goal or conclusion."

Many students of child development believe that thinking begins before the child has acquired a spoken vocabulary. Evidence of the thinking processes may be observed in the activities of the baby in a crib as he reaches for the different objects about him. An attention response resembling thinking may also be observed in the responses of the child to the sound of his mother's movements in an adjoining room. In these responses the child makes use of nonverbal cues. As he matures and acquires language skills, his dependence upon nonverbal cues decreases and he progressively depends more and more on words. Thereafter, language involving words is for the normal child his chief medium for thinking.

In the psychology of thinking, regardless of the approach, these questions or problems appear.

1. What is the nature of the rules by which the thinker operates?
2. What can be discovered about the structure within which these rules hold sway?
3. What gives thinking its directional character and how does it operate? (Whitaker, 1965, p. 324)

The Nature of Thinking. Outside of the view that thinking is involved in problem solving and creative behavior there is little agreement among psychologists as to what thinking does involve. Anderson (1965, pp. 535-539) has described a number of positions on the nature of thinking. The first is one held by Skinner (1957, p. 449) who has stated:

> The simplest and most satisfactory view is that thought is simply *behavior*—verbal or nonverbal, covert or overt. It is not some mysterious process responsible for behavior but the very behavior itself in all the complexity of its controlling relations.

The second viewpoint is that thinking refers to essentially subverbal and nonverbal events within the organism. "There is a continuum of opinion regarding the role of verbal behavior in thinking, beginning with the assignment of a small role for verbal processes and ending with the position that thinking is nothing but verbal behavior" (Anderson, p. 536). The latter can be called the third view of the nature of thinking. According to this view thinking is an inner language and is so closely related to outer forms of expression that it is impossible to separate the one from the other.

A fourth position identifies thinking with awareness and consciousness. The content of consciousness, although largely verbal, includes nonverbal imagery. This viewpoint is held by those psychologists who emphasize consciousness as central to their psychological theories. A fifth viewpoint of thinking emphasizes thinking as a mediating process. This viewpoint was developed by Maltzman (1955) among others. Thinking is regarded as a name for some of the formulas that permit one to predict future behavior from antecedent events. This is a behavioristic viewpoint in which thinking is characterized as a temporal sequence, a chain of events, or train of thought.

It is possible to make a distinction between the materials of thinking, the different stages in the development of thinking, conditions influencing thinking, and the thought process. Thinking may vary considerably with the nature of the situation eliciting it, the nature of the goal sought, the maturity of the person doing the thinking, and the experiential background of the person doing the thinking. These different influences combine in such a way so as to suggest that one may speak of the events in thinking as well as the materials of thinking. A convenient method of classifying thinking into events is according to the amount of direction present. Russell (1956, p. 28) has described the different types, moving from relatively nondirected to relatively directed thinking as "perceptual thinking, associative thinking, thinking leading to concept formation, creative or imaginative thinking, critical thinking, and problem solving." Most thinking cannot manipulate the concrete objects present in one's environment, but will depend upon symbols which may be far removed from reality. This may be noted also in abstractions used in thinking, where symbols are usually involved.

Mediating Responses. Individuals differ widely in their capacity to perform certain internal processes, some of which may best be described as thinking processes. These internal processes are referred to by Travers (1963) as "Mediating responses," since they mediate between the stimuli through which the learning situation is presented and the response. Significant individual differences exist in the capacity to perform different types of mediating responses, so that a response that is easy for one person may be quite difficult for another person. One person learns to solve mathematics problems but finds it difficult to interpret certain phases of literature. Differences between individuals in their ability to perform various mediating processes represents a class of variables referred to by Travers as "intervening variables," since they are characteristics which intervene between stimuli and response.

Kendler, Kendler, and Wells (1960) suggested from their studies of reversal and nonreversal shifts in discrimination learning in preschool children that there is a stage in human development in which verbal responses do not readily mediate between external stimuli and overt responses (p. 87). A subsequent study by Kendler (1963) involving discrimination made use of similar stimuli requiring a shift in response. One type of shift was the *reversal shift,* which requires the subject to respond to the previously relevant dimension but in an opposite way. In another type of shift, called the *nonreversal shift,* the subject was required to respond to the previously irrelevant dimension. In the reversal shift, the initial dimension maintains its relevance, hence so does the mediating response. Only the overt response needs to be changed. In the nonreversal shift the previously acquired mediation is no longer relevant, consequently both the mediating and overt response must be changed, making the task more difficult than the reversal shift task. Thus it is to be expected that for subjects who mediate, a reversal shift will be acquired more easily than a nonreversal shift. Results from different studies led to the conclusion that the single unit S-R model adequately explains the behavior of the majority of children. However, the mediating response is helpful in explaining the more mature behavior within the S-R framework. It seems that mental maturity and wide range of experiences are important to the generalization or transfer of verbal responses to overt behavior.

The mediated response is frequently used to find a common theme between simple and complex behavior. "The mediator is a response, or series of responses, which intercede between the external stimulus and the overt response to provide stimulation that influences the eventual course of behavior. These responses may be overt, but they are usually presumed to be covert." (Kendler, 1963, p. 34.) It has been observed that preschool children frequently verbalize spontaneously the correct solution to a problem while simultaneously making an incorrect response. This sort of behavior is explained in the following way (p. 116): In the early stages of child development, speech is only a means of communication with adults and other children. . . . Subsequently it becomes also a means whereby one organizes his own experiences and regulates his own actions. So the child's behavior is mediated through words." Concerning the role of language in cognitive growth, Bruner (1964, p. 14) states:

> Once language becomes a medium for the translation of experience, there is a progressive release from immediacy. For language, as we have commented, has the new and powerful feature of remoteness and arbitrariness: It permits productive, combinatorial operations in the *absence* of what is represented. With this achievement, the child can delay gratification by virtue of representing to himself what lies beyond the present, what other possibilities exist beyond the clue that is under his nose. The child may be *ready* for delay of gratification, but he is no more able to bring it off than somebody ready to build a house, save that he has not yet heard of tools.

Teachers usually assume that pupils have a sufficient repertoire of mediating responses available to enable them to acquire the knowledge, understandings and generalizations involved in the cognitive process. Thus, they attempt to use what the child has already learned to mediate new learning. Sometimes the child's personal experiences can only be related by analogy; or his experiences may be so limited that it becomes well-nigh impossible for him to acquire certain concepts without additional experiences. This is the case of many disadvantaged children who enter school at age 6 without special preschool experiences.

The relevance of the variable of "familiarity" was demonstrated in an early study by Brownell and Stretch (1931) on problem solving. Children were given the same arithmetic problem in four different forms. In Form A, the problems were written in terms familiar to children. In Form B, relatively less familiar terms were used. In Form C, the terms used were unfamiliar to the children, and artificial terms were employed in Form D. The children were tested on the problems written in each of the four forms. The percentage of problems solved correctly for each of the forms were as follows:

Form A	Form B	Form C	Form D
64	58	57	51

Although these differences are small, they are statistically significant and suggest that familiarity is an important variable in cognitive behavior.

Developmental Stages in Thinking.   Most attempts to define developmental stages in thinking draw on studies by Piaget. Though most students of language development do not distinguish the different stages as clearly as Piaget, they recognize his important contributions to our understanding of the language and thoughts of children.

According to Piaget (1937), the language and thoughts of the child are aspects of the cognitive process. There is evidence from many sources that the intellectual development of the child can best be understood through a study of his language and thought processes. In this account, three levels of intellectual activity (2) egocentric thought and language; and (3) rational thought.

During the first stage of thinking, the child is exploring his world, and he gradually learns to differentiate important elements in his world. He learns that his world includes others who play different roles in relation to his needs. He learns that symbols are closely related to the different things in his environment as well as different happenings in his life. During the preschool years he acquires a vocabulary, which grows rapidly during the preschool and early school years. However, the world of people, things, and events is interpreted largely in terms of the self. Language and thought during the preschool years are in general egocentric in nature.

Through egocentric speech, according to Piaget (1926), the child "does not bother to know to whom he is speaking nor whether he is being listened to. . . . He does not attempt to put himself at the point of view of his hearer." Thus the second stage of language development may best be described as egocentric, although the child's speech gradually passes from egocentricity to a stage of egocentricity. At this stage he likes to converse with others, even though the self is projected into most of his language and thought.

The third stage which involves rational thought appears during the seventh to eleventh years, although preschool children frequently display rational thought in their attempts to solve problems within their mental abilities. After the child reaches school, his language and thought becomes more social and logical in nature. Increased mental maturity, broader experiences, and adult guidance during the early school years lead to an increase of logical thinking and a decrease of egocentric thinking.

One should not look upon these stages as discrete. Egocentric thought appears at all stages of life. Logical thought frequently appears among preschool children. Studies by Deutsche (1937) showed that different kinds of explanation of causal relations were offered at the various age levels. The results of her study indicate that children's thinking cannot be separated into specific types for certain stages of development, although some types were more frequent at a particular age level while others were more frequently found at another age level. It was noted that logical thinking tends to increase during the school years.

Operational Thought. Operational thought develops as a result of organizing one's concepts into a more systematic and meaningful pattern. Many of the preschool child's concepts are isolated vague impressions. Some operational thought appears by the age of five, while some concrete operations are not yet under control in adulthood. This gradual emergence may be observed in connection with the data presented in Figure 7-2 (Braine). The more irrelevant information presented along with relevant information, the more difficult it is to attain the concept (Haygood and Bourne, 1964). This may be observed in history,

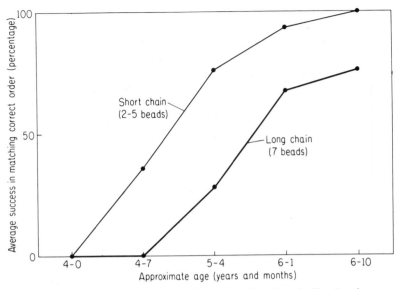

Figure 7-2. The operation of ordering is achieved gradually. Results were nearly the same for sequences of 2, 3, and 5 beads. (Data from Braine, 1958.)

science, or other areas where information must be carefully selected in a correct solution to a problem. It is at this point that guidance in problem solving can be very helpful to the learner.

In concrete operational thought, a person reasons successfully about things that he has previously encountered in a concrete manner. Sharp distinctions between related properties such as *weight* and *volume* are a necessary preliminary to success in operational thought. A person unable to distinguish true *distance* from *distance-as-it-appears* will not be able to think accurately about distances, and even here estimates of distance will depend upon environmental cues acquired through earlier experiences, which may not operate successfully when present in a different configurational pattern. When the learner is able to connect each concept with a unique operation, he can separate concept and attend to one at a time (Elkind, 1961). This ability is closely related to age and experience. In art and history, as well as in different areas of science, one deals with relations of properties and facts. The ability to keep two facts or properties in view becomes possible for most normal children at ages five and six.

When operational thought emerges, a child can understand principles, such as *conservation*—that piling blocks up in different ways so as to produce different patterns does not change the number of blocks, or that changing the shape of plasticine does not change its weight. In drawing, the parts are first seen as a global mass; later they are coordinated to fit into an overall theme, which is closely identified with meaning.

Age Changes. In a study by King (1961) 1,811 children ranging in age from five to twelve years were tested for the development of scientific concepts. He was especially concerned with the questions: Two what extent are scientific concepts acquired with age and on the basis of past experience? What is the role of instruction and guidance? Questions and problems dealing with length, time, volume, weight, direction, night, and sky were used. The results agreed with those obtained in an earlier study by Oakes (1947) who found no evidence to corroborate Piaget's interpretation that there is a definite stage of the child's thinking characteristic of a given age. King concludes:

> There is evidence that children behave like adults, that is they lack in their early years the correct words and use a limited range of words to verbalize in the same way as adults would meet the same difficulties in describing or attempting to understand some of the modern scientific discoveries.

Elkind (1961) attempted a systematic replication of Piaget's studies of the development of quantitative thinking. Comparisons were made for three types of quantity for three age groups. The scores presented in Table 7-2 show that the majority of the four-year-old children succeeded only with gross quantities; the majority of the five-year-old group succeeded only with gross and intensive quantities; most of the six- and seven-year-olds succeeded with all three types of quantity. These results are in agreement with Piaget's findings of three age-

TABLE 7-2

Comparison Score Means and Fractions for Three Types of Quantity for Three Age Groups (After Elkind)

N	Age Group	Quantity Compared			F
		Gross	Intensity	Extensive	
18	4	5.88	1.77	0.11	221.10[*]
40	5	6.00	3.20	0.75	220.76[*]
22	6–7	6.00	5.49	3.95	4.78

[*]Significance beyond the 0.01 level.

related hierarchially ordered stages of success in the development of quantitative thought. Piaget assumes that success in comparing quantity earmarks developmental changes in both the form and content of children's quantitative thinking.

In a study of orientational shifts in children and adolescents Elkind (1966) found that adolescents were significantly more successful than children in a task requiring a shift from a positive- to a negative-similarity orientation. These findings indicate that the thought of the adolescent is not only more logically elaborate than that of the child, as Inhelder and Piaget (1958) maintain, but also that it is more flexible in nature.

The gradual emergence of operational thought may be noted in the results of a study by Braine (1951), shown in Figure 7-2. Braine asked children to match sets of beads in such a way that they were required to hold in mind the order of colors. The results show that the child can match a short chain significantly earlier than a long chain. No attempt is made to determine the role of maturation and the role of experiences in the growth of this ability, although one might infer that maturation and learning are important in such operational thought, since there is little likelihood that instruction entered significantly into the solution of such a problem.

Summary

The mental life of the child has its beginnings in the experiences he encounters through his senses. No mental activity would be possible if the individual were unable to record and retain the impressions he receives. The child's mental life involves thought processes or thinking, perceptions, and concepts. Learning is essential for the development of perception and cognitive structures and processes. Much emphasis has been given to the importance of rich and stimulating experiences in early life for cognitive development. The development of language enables the child to move out beyond the present in time and space; this development is most important to the development of cognition.

Piaget has offered a very complete description of the stages of conceptual development. Inhelder and Piaget claim that specific levels of cognitive development must be achieved before certain conceptual strategies can be learned. Considerable controversey and research, dealing with the development of cognition, appeared following the early theory proposed by Piaget. These studies seemed to support certain aspects of Piaget's views related to the development of cognition, although many studies failed to support his contention that a certain type of thinking characterizes a particular stage of life. According to Bruner, cognitive growth is in a major way from the outside of the individual as well as from the inside out, the child acquires symbolic modes of representing and transforming the world mainly by manipulating his environment. Burner places central importance on symbolic systems such as language in mediating and giving shape to mental life.

Significant cognitive changes take place with age, although there is much overlapping of the different age groups. There is evidence for a sequential order of time concepts. Evidence from a wide variety of studies seems to lead to the following conclusions: (1) Development is gradual in nature and is closely related to maturation and learning. Faulty concepts, like correct concepts, develop out of one's experiences. (3) A general pattern of development may be observed, especially in the development of concepts of causality. (4) Young children appear to have a preferred response; older children seem to make use of a variety of responses available to them.

Significant individual differences exist in the capacity to perform mediating responses. Mental maturity and a wide range of experience are important to the generalization or transfer of verbal responses to avert behavior. Perhaps the most characteristic feature of man's mental life and intellectual process is that of going beyond the information given, which appears in a number of different ways.

Thinking is defined as a process rather than a result. There is little agreement as to what it involves, and the term is used in different ways. Piaget describes several stages of thinking, which he regards as quite distinct from each other. Significant age changes appear in the development of thinking and the thought processes. Also, instructional media are important in the development of concepts and the cognitive process. Increased mental maturity, broad experience, motivation, and adult guidance during the growing years lead to better habits of thinking.

References

Ames, Louise B. "The Development of the Sense of Time in the Young Child," *Journal of Genetic Psychology,* Vol. 68 (1946), pp. 97-115.

Anderson, R. C. Introduction, in R. C. Anderson and D. P. Ausubel (eds.), *Readings in the Psychology of Cognition.* New York: Holt, 1965.

Ausubel, D. P. *The Psychology of Meaningful Verbal Learning.* New York: Grune and Stratton, 1963.

Berlyne, D. E. "Recent Developments in Piaget's Work," *British Journal of Educational Psychology,* Vol. 27 (1957), pp. 1-12.

————. "Recent Developments in Piaget's Work," R. C. Anderson and D. P. Ausubel (eds.), *Readings in the Psychology of Cognition.* New York: Holt, 1965.

Blackwell, Amelia A. "The Development of Concept Formation in Children," Boston University Graduate School, 1962. Dissertation Abstracts, Vol. 23, No. 4 (1962), pp. 1416-1417.

Bloom, B. S., A. Davis, and R. Hess. *Contemporary Education for Cultural Deviation.* New York: Holt, 1965.

Braine, M. D. S. "The Ontogeny of Certain Logical Operations: Piaget's Formulation Examined by Nonverbal Methods," *Psychological Monographs,* Vol. 75, No. 5 (1959).

Brownell, W. A., and Laura B. Stretch. *The Effect of Unfamiliar Settings on Problem Solving.* Durham, N.C.: Duke University Studies in Education, No. 1, 1931.

Bruner, J. S. "The Course of Cognitive Growth," *American Psychologist,* Vol. 19 (1964), pp. 1-15.

————. "On Going Beyond the Information Given," in R. J. Harper, C. C. Anderson, C. M. Christensen, and S. M. Munka (eds.), *The Cognitive Process: Readings.* Englewood Cliffs, N.J.: Prentice-Hall, 1964.

————. *The Process of Education.* Cambridge, Mass.: Harvard U. P., 1960.

Bruner, J. S., S. J. Goodnow, and G. A. Austin. *A Study of Thinking.* New York: Wiley, 1956.

Danziger, C., and N. Sharp. "The Development of Children's Explanation of Growth and Movement," *Australia Journal of Psychology,* Vol. 10 (1958), pp. 196-207.

Dennis, W., and P. Najarian. "Infant Development under Environmental Handicap," *Psychological Monographs: General and Applied,* Vol. 71, No. 7 (1957).

Deutsche, J. M. *The Development of Children's Concepts of Causal Relations.* University of Minnesota, Child Welfare Monograph Series, 1937, no. 13.

Di Vesta, F. J. "Developmental Patterns in the Use of Modifiers as Modes of Conceptualization," *Child Development.* Vol. 36, No. 1 (1965), pp. 185-213.

Dodwell, P. C. "Children's Understanding of Number and Related Concepts," *Canadian Journal of Psychology,* Vol. 14 (1960), pp. 191-205.

Elkind, D. "Children's Discovery of the Conservation of Mass, Weight, and Volume: Piaget Replication Study II," *Journal of Genetic Psychology,* Vol. 98 (1961), pp. 219-227.

————. "Conceptual Orientation Shifts in Children and Adolescents," *Child Development,* Vol. 37 (1966), pp. 493–498.

————. "The Development of Quantitative Thinking: A Systematic Replication of Piaget's Studies," *Journal of Genetic Psychology,* Vol. 98 (1961), pp. 37–46.

————. "Discrimination, Seriation, and Numeration of Size and Dimensional Differences in Young Children: Piaget Replication Study VI," *Journal of Genetic Psychology,* Vol. 104 (1964), pp. 275-296.

Elkind, D., R. R. Koegler, and Elsie G. "Studies in Perceptual Development, II: Part-Whole Perception," *Child Development,* Vol. 35 (1964), pp. 81-90.

Flavell, J. H. *The Developmental Psychology of Jean Piaget.* Princeton, N.J.: Van Nostrand, 1963.

Goldfarb, W. "The Effects of Early Institutionalized Care on Adolescent Personality," *Journal of Experimental Education,* Vol. 12 (1953), pp. 106-129.

Goodenough, D. R., and S. Karp. "Field Dependence and Intellectual Functioning," *Journal of Abnormal and Social Psychology,* Vol. 63 (1961), pp. 241-246.

Grinder, R. E. "Relations between Behavioral and Cognitive Dimensions of Conscience in Middle Childhood," *Child Development,* Vol. 35 (1964), pp. 881-891.

Harootunian, B., and M. W. Tate. "The Relationship of Certain Selected Variables to Problem-Solving Ability," *Journal of Educational Psychology,* Vol. 51 (1960), pp. 326-331.

Haygood, R. C., and L. E. Bourne. "Forms of Relevant Stimulus Redundancy in Concept Identification," *Journal of Experimental Psychology,* Vol. 67 (1964), pp. 392-397.

Hess, R. D. "Effects of Maternal Interaction on Cognitions of Pre-School in Several Strata," paper read at the American Psychological Association Meeting, Chicago, Sept. 1965.

Hess, R. D., and Virginia C. Shipman. "Early Experience and the Socialization of Cognitive Modes in Children," *Child Development,* Vol. 36, No. 4 (1965), pp. 869-886.

Hill, Susanne D. "The Performance of Young Children on Three Discrimination-Learning Tasks," *Child Development,* Vol. 36, No. 2 (1965), pp. 425-435.

Inhelder, B., and J. Piaget. *The Growth of Logical Thinking from Childhood to Adolescence.* New York: Basic, 1958.

Johnson, E. C., and A. Josey. "A Note on the Development of the Thought Forms of Children as Described by Piaget," *Journal of Abnormal and Social Psychology,* Vol. 26 (1931), pp. 338-339.

Kendler, T. S. "Development of Mediating Responses in Children," *Monograph of the Society for Research in Child Development,* Vol. 28, No. 86 (1963), pp. 33-48.

Kendler, T. S., H. H. Kendler, and D. Wells. "Reversal and Nonreversal Shifts in Nursery School Children," *Journal of Comparative Psychology,* Vol. 53 (1960), pp. 83-88.

Kendler, H. H., and S. K. Tracy. "Inferential Behavior in Preschool Children," *Journal of Experimental Psychology,* Vol. 54 (1956), pp. 311-315.

King, W. H., I. "The Development of Scientific Concepts in Children," *British Journal of Educational Psychology,* Vol. 31 (1961), pp. 1-20.

Klausmeier, H. J., and W. Goodwin. *Learning and Human Abilities: Educational Psychology,* 2nd ed. New York: Harper, 1966.

Kofsky, E. "A Scalogram Study of Classificatory Development," *Child Development,* Vol. 37 (1966), pp. 191-204.

Kuenne, M. R. "Experimental Investigation of the Relation of Language to Transposition Behavior in Young Children," *Journal of Experimental Psychology,* Vol. 36 (1946), pp. 471-490.

Lovell, K. "A Follow-Up Study of Inhelder and Piaget's 'The Growth of Logical Thinking,' " *British Journal of Psychology,* Vol. 52 (1961), pp. 143-154.

Lovell, K., B. Mitchell, and I. R. Everett. "An Experimental Study of the Growth of Some Logical Structures," *British Journal of Psychology,* Vol. 53 (1962), pp. 175-188.

Lunzer, E. A. "Some Points of Piagetian Theory in Light of Experimental Criticism," *Journal of Child Psychology and Psychiatry,* Vol. 8 (1960), pp. 27-31.

McCormack, P. D. "Negative Transfer in Motor Performance Following a Critical Amount of Verbal Pretraining," *Perceptual Motor Skills,* Vol. 8 (1958), pp. 27-31.

McDonald, F. J. *Educational Psychology,* 2nd ed. Belmont, Calif.: Wadsworth, 1965.

Maltzman, I. "Thinking from a Behaviorist Point of View," *Psychological Review,* Vol. 62 (1955), pp. 275-286.

Medinnus, G. R. "Behavioral and Cognitive Means of Conscience Development," *Journal of Genetic Psychology,* Vol. 109 (1966), pp. 147-150.

Milgram, N. A., and H. G. Furth. "Factors Affecting Conceptual Control in Normal and Retarded Children," *Child Development,* Vol. 38 (1967), pp. 531-543.

Milgram, N. A., and H. G. Furth. "The Influence of Language on Concept Attainment in Educable Retarded Children," *American Journal of Mental Deficiency,* Vol. 27 (1963), pp. 733-739.

Mosher, F. A. "Strategies for Information Gathering," paper read at the Eastern Psychological Association, Atlantic City, N.J., April, 1962.

Oakes, M. E. *Children's Explanation of Natural Phenomena.* New York: Teachers' College Press, *Contributions to Education,* No. 926 (1947).

Piaget, J. *The Child's Conception of Physical Causality.* (trans. M. G. Gabain). New York: Harcourt, 1932.

———. *Factors Determining Human Behavior.* Cambridge, Mass.: Harvard U. P., 1937.

———. *The Language and Thought of the Child.* New York: Harcourt, 1926.

Reese, H. W. "Motor Paired-Associate Learning and Stimulus Pretraining," *Child Development,* Vol. 31 (1960), pp. 505-513.

Rosen, B. C. "The Achievement Syndrome: A Psycho-Cultural Dimension of Social Stratification," *American Sociological Review,* Vol. 21 (1956), pp. 203-211.

Russell, D. *Children's Thinking.* Boston: Ginn, 1956.

Scheerer, Constance. *Cognition: Theory, Research, Promise.* New York: Harper, 1964.

Skinner, B. F. *Verbal Behavior.* New York: Appleton, 1957.

Smedslund, J. "The Acquisition of Transitivity of Weight in Five- to Seven-Year-Old Children," *Journal of Genetic Psychology,* Vol. 102 (1963), pp. 245-255.

Spearman, C. *The Nature of Intelligence and The Principle of Cognition.* London: Macmillan, 1923.

Staats, A. W. *Learning, Language, and Cognition.* New York: Holt, 1968.

Terrell, G., K. Durkin, and M. Wiesley. "Social Class and the Nature of the Incentive in Discrimination Learning," *Journal of Abnormal and Social Psychology,* Vol. 59 (1959), pp. 270-272.

Travers, R. M. *Essentials of Learning: An Overview of Students of Education.* New York: Macmillan, 1963.

Uka, N. *Sequence in the Development of Time Concept in Children of Elementary School Age.* Ph.D. dissertation, University of Southern California, 1956.

Verplank, W. S. *A Glossary of Some Terms Used in the Objective Science of Behavior.* Washington, D.C.: American Psychological Association, 1957.

Weinstein, E. A. "Development of the Concept of Flag and the Sense of National Identity," *Child Development,* Vol. 28 (1957), pp. 167-174.

Whitaker, J. O. *Introduction to Psychology.* Philadelphia: Saunders, 1965.

Whiteman, M. "Children's Conceptions of Psychological Causality," *Child Development,* Vol. 38 (1967), pp. 143-155.

Wolman, R. N., and E. N. Baker. "A Developmental Study of Word Definitions," *Journal of Genetic Psychology,* Vol. 107 (1965), pp. 159-166.

Zaporozhets, A. V. "The Development of Perception in the Preschool Child," in P. H. Mussen, "European Research in Cognitive Development," *Monographs of the Society for Research in Child Development,* Vol. 30, No. 2 (1965), pp. 82-101.

Chapter 8

Patterns of Intellectual Development

The task of maximizing the intellectual potentials of our children and adolescents has acquired a new urgency. Three of the top challenges of our day lie behind this urgency. First, worldwide competition in science, including the space age, makes it imperative that we develop all our human resources to meet the worldwide challenge. Second, the role of technology, now appearing in increased automation, decreases opportunity for people with limited competence and skills, while it increases the opportunity for those competent in the use of language, in mathematics, in science, in creative thinking, and in problem solving. Third, the challenge of providing equality of education and employment opportunity is most important if we are to make the maximum use of *all* our human potential and abilities in meeting the problems of today.

Several factors in the cognitive domain affect learning efficiency at school. Three of these are general intelligence, specific abilities, and previous experiences related to the learning task. These are perhaps interrelated in all learning tasks. The role of experiences in the development of language, concepts and the cognitive process was presented in Chapters 6 and 7. This chapter is particularly concerned with patterns of intellectual development.

Introduction: Concepts of Intellectual Abilities

Few terms in psychology have been so generally used with functional meaning and yet are so difficult to define operationally as is the term intelligence. Binet, among the earliest investigators, conceived of intelligence as a unitary character and regarded it as directness of thought capacity to make adaptations, and autocriticism (Peterson, 1925). Others have described it as the ability to learn, to solve problems, or to adjust to new or complex situations. One of the most complete definitions of intelligence is presented by Wechsler (1960). He states: "Intelligence is the aggregate or global capacity of the individual to act purposefully, to think rationally, and to deal effectively with his environment" (p. 7).

Early Notions about Intelligence and Intelligence Tests.   Following early developments of intelligence testing, the idea prevailed that intellectual ability as measured by available tests could not be improved through educational experiences. Since World War II, psychologists and other students of human behavior have carefully reviewed earlier notions about such basic concepts and intelligence, including the older nature-nurture controversy.

The roots of the notion of fixed intelligence may be observed in Darwin's theory that evolution takes place through variations in strains and species enabling certain ones to survive and reproduce. This led to the notion that man survived because he had intelligence that enabled him to survive. Francis Galton, a cousin of Charles Darwin, reasoned that the improvement of man's traits lies in heredity or eugenics, not education. This had a tremendous impact on early students concerned with the measurement of intelligence.

The Concept of Primary Mental Abilities.   Beginning in the 1930's the Thurstones, among others, questioned the validity of the concept of general mental ability. It was conceived that five or more tests may correlate with one another because of group factors common to the different tasks rather than a "g" or general factor, as posed by Spearman (1927). Consequently, L. L. Thurstone worked out a mathematical technique for what he termed factor analysis. By this method he found it possible to find a *set* of separate factors that accounted for the correlations in a battery of tests. The multiple-factor methods have been sufficiently accepted so that they are the basis for many studies bearing on the abilities that are to be included among the primary mental abilities.

In 1938, Thurstone assembled a battery of 56 psychological tests for use in a study to determine factor loadings. The tests consisted of a wide variety such as mechanical relationships, computations, reasoning from syllogisms, perceptual speed, word fluency, vocabulary, memory, and reasoning. These tests were administered to 240 college students; "nine primary abilities were identified in this phase of the study." In a later study 1,154 eighth-grade children were given a similar battery of tests designed to determine whether the same "primary abilities" would appear in a younger and less selected group of subjects. Seven of them did (Thurstone and Thurstone, 1941). Later evidence was presented for the existence of six of the same factors in kindergarten children (T. G. Thurstone, 1941).

The primary mental abilities found among both college and eighth-grade students were as follows:

Space.   Visualization of geometrical figures in different positions in space.

Perceptual speed.   Quick observation of details.

Number.   Quickness in making arithmetical computations of all sorts.

Verbal meanings.   Grasp of ideas and meanings of words.

Word fluency.   Speed in manipulating single and isolated words.

Memory.   Ease in memorizing words, numbers, letters, and other materials.

Induction. Ability to extract a rule common to the materials of a problem or test.

In a study by Travis (1965) the *Wechsler Intelligence Scale for Children* (WISC) test was given to 163 preschool children, and one year later to 153 of the same children. Six factors extracted at the six-year level were stable and congruent with those found at the preschool level, indicating that by age 6 differential mental abilities are discernible.

Guilford's Structure of the Intellect.   Our knowledge of the components of intelligence has come about largely since the momentous work of Thurstone in the development of Primary Mental Abilities, referred to in the previous chapter. Three kinds of classifications of the factors of the intellect were formulated by Guilford (1959, 1967). These are represented by a cubical model, as shown in Figure 8-1. This model is referred to as the "structure of the intellect"; each

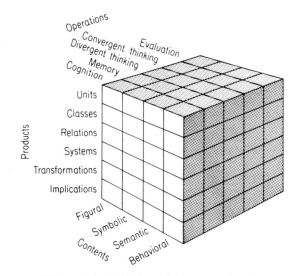

Figure 8-1. Cubical model representing the structure of the intellect (Guilford).

dimension represents one of the models of variation of the different factors. One dimension presents the different kinds of operations; a second one shows the various kinds of products, and a third one gives the various kinds of content.

The three kinds of classifications of the factors of intellect, formulated by Guilford, have been most helpful in eliminating the concept of intelligence as a single ability accounting for all differences in learning abilities among school children. A recent concept of intelligence is that presented by Wallach and Kogan (1967, p. 38):

> The psychological concept of *intelligence* defines a network of strongly related abilities concerning the retention, transformation, and utilization of verbal

and numerical symbols; at issue are a person's memory storage capacities, his skill in solving problems, his dexterity in manipulating and dealing with concepts.

The Origins of Intellectual Abilities.   It was pointed out in earlier chapters that the individual, even at birth, is a product of the interaction of hereditary and environmental forces. In Chapter 2 it was suggested that the closer the genetic relationship between two persons, the greater the similarity in observable traits. Burt (1958) studied the effect of genetic relationship on tested intelligence. The correlations presented in Table 8-1 range downward from the 90's for identical twins reared together to the 20's for unrelated children reared together.

TABLE 8-1
Correlations between Mental Assessments (After Burt)

	Group Intelligence Tests	Individual Intelligence Tests
Identical twins reared together	.944	.921
Identical twins reared apart	.771	.843
Nonidentical twins reared together	.542	.526
Siblings reared together	.515	.491
Siblings reared apart	.441	.463
Unrelated children reared together	.281	.252

The reason for the high degree of similarity between closely related persons is understandable; although one notes that correlations are significantly reduced when children are reared separately rather than in the same home. Sontag and others (1958) noted that "close genetic relationships tend to have somewhat similar patterns of mental growth" (p. 134). The structure that makes possible the development of intellectual abilities is the brain and central nervous system. The foundation for this is set forth at the time of the fertilization of the egg cell. The role the environment plays begins with the embryo following the period of fertilization. Some of the effects of an adverse environment during the prenatal and infancy stages were presented in Chapter Three. Some effects of different environmental conditions on the development of the child's intellectual abilities will be presented in the forthcoming discussions.

Mental Growth

Through data collected from intelligence tests of single individuals over a number of years, investigators have been able to plot mental growth curves which furnish useful information about the nature and rate of different aspects of intellectual development during childhood and adolescence. The curves show that there is a gradual and continuous growth in mental abilities from birth to maturity, with the various abilities maturing at different periods. In general,

One measure of cognition—the individual psychological examination. (Courtesy of Chesapeake City Schools, Chesapeake, Va.)

those mental abilities that developed rapidly during early childhood tend to reach their full development during adolescence. However, the reader should distinguish between mental abilities and intelligence as measured by intelligence tests, which is the ability to use these abilities. Whereas the various functions tend to reach their fullest power coincidentally with physical maturity, certain aspects of intelligence seems to continue to grow as long as one remains mentally active and vigorously pursues learning as a student. Additional materials bearing on this are presented later in this chapter.

Mental Growth Curves.   Growth curves for four of the eleven tests in the *Wechsler Intelligence Scale for Children* are presented in Figure 8-2 (Wechsler, 1950). These curves show roughly the proportion of fifteen-year-old mental maturity attained at the different age periods 5-6 to 15-6. The average score for digit span increases rapidly until age 11, after which little increase occurs. On the other hand, vocabulary development follows a steadier and a more gradual course. The ability to memorize also improves rapidly until around the fourteenth year. The curves for memorizing poetry and nonsense syllables are similar and are roughly parallel to the curve of general intelligence.

Individual growth curves reveal a wide variety of patterns, although they follow the same basic pattern. Growth during the early years is very rapid; this rapid rate of intellectual growth continues through childhood, although at a continuously decelerated rate. Plateaus frequently appear during adolescence, and growth continues at a decelerated rate until maturity is reached.

The Stability of Mental Growth.   An issue that arose in early studies of mental growth is referred to as the *constancy of the intelligence quotient.* Early

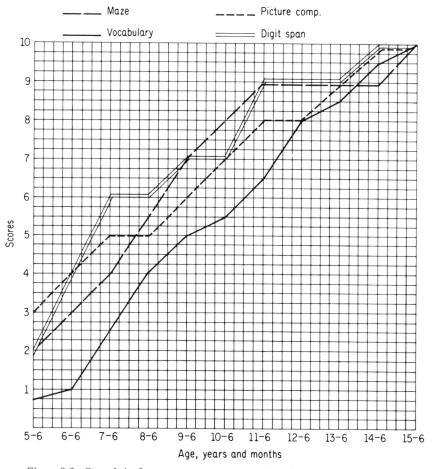

Figure 8-2. Growth in four components measured by the WISC Test. Weighted scores at the mean of each age when base of comparison is the equivalent standard score of 15-4 to 15-7. (After Wechsler, 1950, p. 46.)

studies by Baldwin and Stecher (1922) and Garrison (1922) supported the notion of the constancy of the IQ. Garrison, using 42 middle-class and upper-class children enrolled in a private school found a correlation of .83 between scores on the Stanford Revision of the Binet Tests after an interval of three years. These studies were made with privileged children as subjects from a favorable environment. Adverse environment during childhood has an injurious effect upon mental growth that cannot be completely overcome at a later stage.

Long-term predictions of intelligence-test scores based on earlier scores are unreliable (Bayley, 1949). This was clearly shown by Jones (1954, p. 169) in which data from many different studies were brought together and analyzed. The curve plotted in Figure 8-3 shows the correlation between test scores ob-

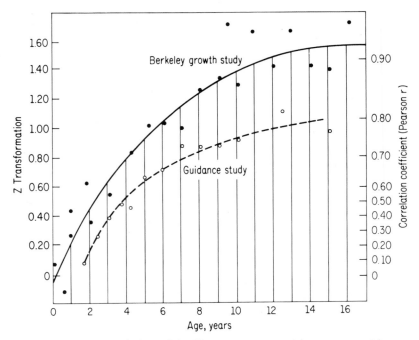

Figure 8-3. Correlation of intelligence scores at eighteen years with scores at successive earlier ages. (From Jones, based on data from Bayley and from Honzik, Macfarlane, and Allen.)

tained at successive ages with those obtained at 18 years of age. Note the low correlations between scores obtained during the early years and scores at age 18. The correlations become increasingly higher between scores obtained at ages closer to 18.

Lorge-Thorndike Intelligence Tests. These tests were administered by Eagle (1966) to 115 eighth-grade boys and 150 eighth-grade girls who had previously taken the test when they were in grades three or four. The correlations obtained between the verbal IQ scores secured earlier and those obtained in the eighth grade was .592 for boys and .777 for girls; the correlations between the nonverbal IQ scores obtained earlier and those secured in the eighth grade was .494 for boys and .666 for girls. These results indicate that verbal IQ scores are more stable during the period from the third to the eighth grade than nonverbal IQ scores and that the scores for girls were more stable than those for boys. In an earlier study, the *Primary Mental Abilities*, Intermediate Form was administered to a sample of eighth-grade pupils. The test was readministered when they were completing the eleventh grade (Meyer and Bendig, 1961). Correlations obtained between the grade 8 and grade 11 scores show that there is considerable stability of academic abilities during the period; there is, however, less stability in word fluency, and nonacademic ability.

The Effects of Age.   An early investigation by Jones and Conrad (1933) made use of the Army Alpha intelligence test in studying the growth and decline of intelligence. Scores were obtained from a sample of 1191 subjects from rural New England. Developmental curves were obtained for each of the eight subtests of the Army Alpha. Significant variations appear in the curves shown in Figure 8-4. The adolescents were superior to the adults in some tests such as numerical, completions, and analogies; in other tests such as oral directions, dissecting sentences, opposites (vocabulary) and general information, the adults, on the average, surpassed the adolescents.

An examination of the developmental curves for the individual subtests shows considerable variation. Note that the peak performance for analogies was reached in the teen years and was followed by a relatively rapid decline. No discernible decline was noted for opposites (vocabulary) and general information. On most of the subtests there was a leveling off of ability in the late teens or early twenties, followed by a slow but accelerated decline of scores with age. However, certain longitudinal studies have shown gains in intelligence tests scores with age. Two studies in particular may be cited in support of continued gains in intelligence. One study reported by Bayley and Oden (1955) involved subjects from Terman's gifted population; the other study by Owens (1953) included former college students.

The results of studies dealing with age and mental abilities are confusing, due in part to the nature of the samples studied, the nature of the tests used, and the method of administering and scoring the tests. Early studies, such as the one reported by Wechsler (1942), showed a gradual, constant decline in intelligence test scores with age. He noted that during the age span 25-69 verbal abilities showed less decline than nonverbal abilities. This is in harmony with findings presented in Chapter 4 showing a decline in certain types of motor performances with age. Anastasi (1956), using the *Wechsler Adult Intelligence Scale*, noted a decline in scores with age, but suggested that the results might have been influenced by the population on which the scale was standardized.

A psychometric study of aging twins was conducted by Jarvik (1962) with 134 pairs of twins at least age 60 being tested at the time of the first testing. The same battery of tests was administered again to 207 of the subjects after a period of two years; the test was administered to 78 survivors six years later; and a fourth test was given to 17 subjects of the original sample after a period of two and a half years. The results furnished interesting information on intellectual changes in relation to aging. Different tests showed varying rates of decline as shown in Table 8-2. A definite decline was noted on the two speeded motor tests only—tapping and digit symbol substitution.

Jarvik (p. 199) noted that "a positive relationship emerged between test scores and survival for most of the tests. In other words, the original test scores were lower for subjects who died before 1955 than for those still alive at that time." This finding is supported by an earlier study by Sanderson and Inglis (1961). Vocabulary scores tended to show a positive correlation with age and on

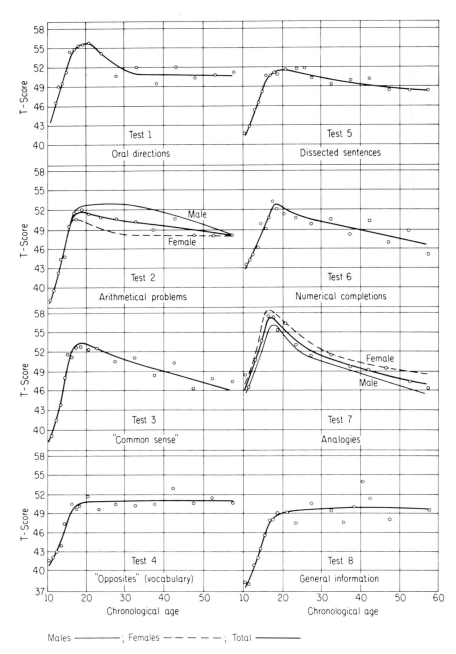

Males —————; Females — — — — —; Total —————

The T-score values for each test are given at the left; chronological age is given at the bottom; original data for total group are plotted as small circles.

Figure 8-4. Growth and decline of ability in the individual subtests of the army alpha.

TABLE 8-2

Mean Scores of 17 Aged Subjects on Four Successive Testings (1947–1957)

(After Jarvik)

	Number of Subjects	Test Session							
		First		Second		Third		Fourth	
Vocabulary	14	30.4	(5.9)[*]	31.1	(5.9)	31.9	(4.4)	30.0	(5.3)
Tapping	16	73.9	(15.2)	74.5	(16.8)	56.4	(15.1)	61.4	(16.6)
Digits forward	15	6.4	(0.9)	6.3	(1.2)	6.4	(1.3)	6.5	(1.4)
Digits backward	15	4.8	(1.4)	4.9	(1.0)	4.6	(0.9)	4.3	(1.0)
Digit symbol	15	30.3	(7.6)	28.1	(10.7)	27.2	(8.3)	25.9	(8.7)
Similarities	17	11.1	(4.1)	10.5	(3.9)	11.4	(4.6)	11.1	(3.6)
Block designs	13	15.4	(4.8)	16.0	(6.6)	12.5	(5.1)	13.2	(3.2)
Age	17	67.5	(6.8)	68.3	(6.8)	74.2	(6.1)	76.3	(6.3)

[*]Standard deviations in parentheses.

a longitudinal basis only 32 percent of the aged subjects decreased their scores, while the digit symbol test score tended to show a negative correlation with age. A greater similarity was observed between the scores of one-egg than of two-egg twins even after age 60, indicating the persistence during adult life of gene differences in specific mental functioning.

The contention that there is a marked deficit in memory functioning with increased age is supported by folklore, clinical reports from professional people who care for institutionalized elderly people, statements from elderly people based on their experiences, and some empirical studies questionable as to how much of the observed deficit is a function of variables other than memory which influence the amount of material recalled. Canestrari (1963), in a paced and self-paced learning exercise, noted that the deficit in learning attributable to age is considerably reduced if such variables as health status, interest in material, and rate of presentation and responding are controlled. A study reported by Hulicka (1964, 1966) showed that when materials are learned to the same criterion, recall scores do not decline as a result of age.

Influences Affecting Intellectual Development

So long as it was believed that the intellectual development of a child is fixed and the rate is constant, the intellectual inferiority of children from families of low cultural and socioeconomic status had to be considered as an unalterable consequence of heredity. The vast amount of research showing the ill effects of adverse conditions upon intellectual development has altered our notion about the nature and growth of intellectual abilities and furnished hope for combating such inferiority by altering certain conditions under which some children develop.

Influences of an Impoverished Environment. An impoverished environment during childhood will adversely affect the development of intelligence to the extent that it can never completely overcome the ill effects, whereas an enriched environment will most likely accelerate its development (Bloom, 1964). The early years are most critical as shown by Bloom in Table 8-3. The materials

TABLE 8-3

Hypothetical Effects of Different Environments on the Development of Intelligence in Three Selected Periods (After Bloom)

Age Period	Percent of Mature Intelligence	Variation from Normal Growth in IQ Units			
		Deprived	Normal	Abundant	Abundant Deprived
Birth–4	50	−5	0	+5	10
4–8	30	−3	0	+3	6
8–17	20	−2	0	+2	4
Total	100	−10	0	+10	20

presented are based on the assumption that 100 percent of mature intelligence is achieved by age 17. Based on this assumption, Bloom estimates that 50 percent of mature intelligence is reached by age 4; consequently, an impoverished environment during the first four years will be quite detrimental to the child's intellectual development. Although one would not defend the materials of Table 8-3 as scientifically accurate, they do indicate the importance of a favorable environment during the early years.

The results of research conducted by Steadman and a team of researchers at Durham, N.C. show that the first three years are crucial to the child's optimum intellectual development (1967). The investigators first tested a group of four-, five-, and six-year-old children from an impoverished background and found that they operated at an IQ range from 70 to 85. Next the investigators worked with a group of young children from a similar background. The young children were tested at ages three, six, nine, twelve and fifteen months. At these ages the disadvantaged children demonstrated above average IQ. They also demonstrated better motor skills—the ability to perform tasks requiring coordination of intellectual and sensorimotor abilities. Thus somewhere between the fifteenth month and age 4, children from deprived backgrounds undergo a considerable reduction in intellectual functioning.

A study by Deutsch and Brown (1964) dealt with some aspects of experience that affect the development of intellectual functions in children. Data were collected on cross-sectional samples involving first and fifth-grade children. The Lorge-Thorndike, Levels 1 and 3, essentially nonverbal tests was administered during school hours to the children, while socioeconomic status data were gathered by mailed questionnaires and home interviews.

The results revealed (1) a linear relationship between socioeconomic status and performance level for both Negro and white groups, and (2) within this relationship the IQ increase was greater for the white group than for the Negro group. The hypothesis advanced for this is that while the lower-class status, which is a deprived status, operates to a more similar degree for both Negro and Whites than does the middle or upper-middle class status, where it is most difficult for the Negro to attain similar advantages and status.

Studies of the effects of educational treatment of disadvantaged children show such a treatment at an early age can accelerate rate of mental growth of children reared in psychosocially deprived homes. At the University of Illinois in Urbana, psychologists report raises in the IQ of deprived children from 96 at age 3 to 120 when they entered the first grade, as a result of intensive language and arithmetic drills and strict discipline (*Newsweek*, 1968). Without special educational consideration, children from disadvantaged homes tend to retain their slow rate of mental development or drop in rate of development as they grow older. When compensatory environments are introduced such as a preschool program, a reversal of this tendency is accomplished. (Kirk, 1966, p. 125) concludes:

> The results of recent research, my own as well as others, indicate that the intellectual development of some retarded children is partly contingent upon child-rearing practices and the extent of educational treatment at an early age. Furthermore, among the higher grades of the retarded, the evidence points to a cultural etiology rather than a genetic one for many of the retarded children in our society.

Influences of Parent-Child Relations. The influence of parent-child relations upon the IQ was brought forth many years ago in a study by Baldwin, Kalhorn, and Breese (1945). They found that the IQ's of four to seven-year-old children tend to increase when parental-discipline consists of responsive and realistic explanation; they tend to decrease when discipline consists of non-chalant unresponsiveness or of demands for obedience for its own sake, with punishment as the alternative.

A study by Crandall and others (1964) showed that certain specific attitudes and behavior of the parents toward their children's intellectual achievements were predictive of the children's academic-test performances, while others were not. More significant relations were found between the parents' attitudes and behaviors and their daughters' academic proficiency than occurred between these parental attitudes and behaviors and the boys' performances. In particular, they noted that "the more proficient girls had fathers who more often praised and less often criticized their everyday intellectual-achievement attempts than did the less academically competent girls" (p. 66).

Bing (1963) noted that a close relationship with a demanding and intrusive mother facilitates the development of high verbal abilities, whereas a causal relationship enhances the development of nonverbal abilities. The subjects were 60 mothers of fifth-grade children of either high or low verbal ability with similar total IQ, the compensating nonverbal ability being spatial or numerical ability.

A comparison of the mothers of the high with those of the low verbal ability groups on an interview questionnaire and a mother-child interaction situation showed some significant differences. In general, high-verbal-group mothers, whose children were low in either spatial or number ability, gave their children more verbal stimulation during infancy and early childhood, remembered a greater number of their children's early accomplishments, let their children participate more in conversations, punished them less for faulty speech, bought more story books for them, and criticized them more for poor achievement at school. They used anxiety arousal more in training, showed less permissiveness with object experimentation, had more restrictions, and perceived their husbands as stricter than themselves. Contrary to predictions, the father's rather than the mother's reading rate was significantly higher for the high-verbal girl's group.

Regarding the interaction session, high-verbal-group mothers were found to be higher than low-verbal-group mothers in all categories of helping behavior, in pressure for improvement, in giving help when requested by the child, in asking the observer more questions, in giving more physical help, and in giving such help sooner. High-verbal mothers were also higher on withholding help and disapproval than low-verbal mothers.

Another experience variable studied by Deutsch and Brown was the presence or absence of the father. The data presented in Table 8-4 show that the IQ

TABLE 8-4

Comparison of the IQ's of Children from Homes Where the Father Is Present with Those from Homes Where the Father Is Absent (after Deutsch and Brown, 1964)

Grade	Father Present			Father Absent		
	Mean IQ	S.D.	N	Mean IQ	S.D.	N
SES I						
Grade 1	95.24	14.51	41	87.78	20.40	33
Grade 5	92.77	13.89	47	85.73	9.81	37
SES II						
Grade 1	96.68	12.33	41	92.80	18.64	10
Grade 5	92.92	15.89	39	92.05	14.65	21

is more depressed in homes where the father is absent. Perhaps some of the differences between scores of Negro and white children may be accounted for by the greater proportion of broken Negro homes.

Motivation. It was pointed out in Chapter 5 that the achievement motive develops during early childhood and appears in varying degrees among children. This has been shown to be responsible for some of the differences in intelligence test scores and in the variability and direction of IQ changes. Sontag and associates (1958) noted that eagerness to learn or "learning to learn" was closely related to an increase in IQ throughout childhood; lack of an interest in learning or low achievement need was related to a deceleration of the IQ during the elementary school years. The degree to which a child possesses the achievement need or motivation to learn depends upon a number of factors, including certain parent-child relations, referred to earlier in this chapter. The child's self-concept and aspirations are part of the make-up that affects the development of his intellectual abilities.

Overstimulation may have an adverse effect upon problem solving and other behavior patterns requiring continued attention and effort. Scheerer (1963) refers to a study by Birch, who noted that when a chimpanzee was very hungry he would fixate on a stimulus such as a banana to satisfy his hunger, and strive in vain to reach it. His behavior was more rigid than a less hungry chimpanzee who was able to find a way to obtain food by a less direct method. Applying this to human motivation Scheerer stated: "On the human level there is some evidence that strong ego-involvement in a problem makes for overmotivation and is detrimental to a solution" (p. 128). Inner motivation, based upon interest and the achievement need, is a condition or feeling that needs preservation rather than further stimulation.

Sex Differences.   In a previous chapter dealing with language development, it was noted that there were significant sex differences in language development during the early years. This is usually attributed to the more rapid physical maturation of girls; although there is evidence that the early environment of the average boy is less conducive to language development than that of girls, with the environmental difference being greater for children from the lower social class. Since there is a high correlation between vocabulary test scores and verbal intelligence test scores one would expect girls to excel boys during the early years in their performance on verbal intelligence tests.

A study by Ames and Ilg (1964) dealt with sex differences in test performance of matched girl-boy pairs in the five-to-nine-year-range. The subjects consisted of 81 kindergarten children, 26 first-grade children, and 29 second-grade children. The subjects were given a battery of tests including the Incomplete Man test, the Rorschach, the Lowenfeld Mosaic, and Visual III from the *Monroe Reading Aptitude Test* annually for three successive years.

The findings from this study confirmed those of earlier investigations that the average test performance of girls in the five-to-nine-year range is considerably advanced over boys in the same age range. Although the boys made lower mean scores than the girls, in seven out of nine test groups boys were more accurate than the girls on both mean and median percent correct out of those attempted.

Achievement—Creativity

The limitations of our definition and measurement of intelligence to classroom learning is a historical happenstance—a consequence of the fact that early studies in this field were especially concerned with students having learning difficulties at school. This has been pointed out by Getzels and Jackson (1963, p. 371) in their descriptions of giftedness. They state:

> If we moved the focus of inquiry from the classroom setting, we might identify qualities defining giftedness for other situations just as the IQ did for the

classroom. Indeed, even without shifting our focus of inquiry, if we only modified the conventional criteria of achievement, we might change the qualities defining giftedness even in the classroom. For example, if we recognized that learning involves the production of novelty as well as the memorization of course content, then measures of creativity as well as the IQ might become appropriate in defining characteristics of giftedness.

Intelligence and School Achievement.   Group intelligence tests have recently been referred to as scholastic-aptitude tests. Although the correlations between intelligence-test scores and achievement-test scores seldom exceed .70, intelligence test scores are perhaps the best single basis for predicting school achievement. There is evidence from different studies to confirm the hypothesis that a well-designed test of verbal and mathematical ability furnishes useful information relative to a student's future academic performance. However, variables such as motivation, other interests, and unreliability of grades make prediction unreliable. Colleges have been able to reduce the failure rate among students through their selective (testing) admission policies; although this procedure has no doubt eliminated many students who would have succeeded, if given the opportunity, because of certain extraneous factors. It is quite safe to conclude that intelligence test scores serve as a sounder basis for predicting scholastic success than in predicting personal and social adjustments or vocational success.

The Academically Gifted and the Talented.   It seems likely that the portrait of the personal and social characteristics of the gifted obtained from early students did not take into consideration their educational, socioeconomic, and cultural backgrounds. In a study by Smith (1962), religion, socioeconomic level, and nationality background were controlled. A comparison of the "bright" and average children in this study revealed no significant differences in various personal and social traits studied.

The study by Cicirelli (1965) was an attempt to clarify the nature of the relationships between IQ, creativity, and academic achievement. He found an interaction between IQ and creativity as they affect academic achievement. Beyond a certain IQ level, higher IQ will not usually distinguish individuals in terms of their academic achievement. However, he noted that within a critical range, both IQ and creativity distinguish individuals in terms of their academic achievement. In a study of seven- and eight-year-olds Ward (1968) found a clear separation of creativity and intelligence. This problem of the relation between creativity and intelligence was also studied by Cropley (1966). He concludes from his studies: "It is inacceptable to think of creativity as a separate basic intellectual mode." He suggests further that high scores on tests of divergent thinking will usually be accompanied by high scores on tests of convergent thinking and vice versa, although the two kinds of thinking are not identical.

A consideration of the relation between intelligence and creativity must take into consideration the age level of the subjects being tested and the nature of the tests used. Both divergent and convergent thinking of an abstract nature involve reflective thinking and the higher mental processes, even though the two kinds of thinking are not identical. With maturation and experience there is most likely to be an unevenness of the development of these abilities by most individuals. Since most intelligence tests involve convergent thinking rather than divergent thinking, it seems likely that the relationship between these abilities might decline with the age level of the subjects being tested. Thus the tendency to equate high IQ with superior creative ability still persists, despite evidence to the contrary. Concerning this, Getzels and Jackson (1960) state:

> Despite this recognition of relative independence at the theoretical level, when turning to practical problems involving the assessment of the two qualities, one finds that the well-established intelligence test is most frequently used as *the* indicator of creativity. Individuals are grouped by IQ, and generally there is disappointment if the high IQ person is not also creative. Sometimes, he is not. There is also bewilderment when the creative individual has a relatively low IQ, as is often the case.

Teachers have constantly observed some students who are academically superior and other students who are especially talented in one or more of the arts—painting, drama, music. Juniors and rising seniors selected from high schools in North Carolina for the Governor's School, an eight-week residential summer program, were studied by Welsh (1966). There were two major divisions in the school: the Academic Division and the Arts Division. The Academic Division students were selected on the basis of outstanding scholastic records; the Arts Division students were selected on the basis of demonstrated talent in a special area.

The two groups were given the *Terman Concept Mastery Test* (Terman, 1956), *D-48* (Black, 1963), a non-verbal test, and the revised *Art Scale* (RA) of the *Welsh Figure Preference Test* (Welsh, 1959). The results for the three tests are shown in Table 8-5. The Academic Division students averaged higher on both

TABLE 8-5
Comparisons of Scores of Two Groups of Gifted
Adolescents on Intelligence and Creativity
Measures (After Welsh)

Tests	Academic Division (N = 207)		Arts Division (N = 161)
CMT	M	67.35	41.55
	SD	26.88	26.89
D-48	M	32.15	27.07
	SD	4.89	7.09
RA	M	29.53	34.22
	SD	15.72	14.12

intelligence tests while the Arts Division students average score was higher on the creativity measure. Correlations obtained between scores on the three tests showed that the intelligence tests are significantly correlated with each other, but that neither correlated with the creativity measures.

Academic Achievers and Nonachievers.   Children with high IQ's have great potential for academic achievement, but many of them fail to fulfill their promise. There is evidence that the difference lies in the way parents treat bright children. In a study bearing on this, Norman (1966) used the *Gordon Survey of Interpersonal Values,* which measures how highly one values being treated with kindness, doing what is socially acceptable, being recognized and admired, being free to make one's own choices, doing things for other people, and being a leader. The tests were given to the parents of 49 Albuquerque school children with IQ's over 130 who did well on an achievement test. Norman found that fathers of boy achievers and the mothers of girl achievers give independence values a higher score and conformity values a lower score than do the counterpart parents of the nonachieving children.

The Development of Special Abilities.   Wolfe (1960) proposed "that it is advantageous to a society to seek the greatest achievable diversity of talent, diversity within an individual, among the members of an occupational group, and among the individuals who constitute a society." Such a diversity results from a culture that permits and reinforces the development of special abilities from early childhood, so that variability in different traits increases rather than decreases. Few individuals can develop to a high level of achievement in more than one or two human talents, even under favorable conditions (Miles, 1954).

Pressey (1955) noted in his study of the nature and nurture of genius that individuals who reached a preeminent level in their field started upon their special career very early in their lives, and were continuously saturated with experiences in their special field. This development from early childhood may be observed in the case of musicians in Europe beginning about two hundred years ago, or in the case of ice skaters in Sweden today, or in the case of many athletes in the United States. These adult stars received special training and practice from early childhood, were rewarded for achievement in their special fields, and were brought into close association with others of similar talent and interest. They spent considerable time and effort in study and practice in their special fields (Reynolds, 1963).

The absence of achievement in some area is not a sure sign of lack of talent in that area. The school program is especially necessary for learning to read and to acquire understandings in different academic areas. Creative abilities and ability in art, mechanics, and human relations are not as yet recognized and reinforced in a strictly academic environment.

Creativity.   Studies of creativity by Lehman (1964) show that young thinkers frequently demonstrate memorable creative achievements. He has collected a total of more than 200 significant attainments by individuals less than 21 years old. Frequently we read of prodigies in various fields of endeavor. Thus Lehman suggested a number of years ago that the highest creative production rate occurs prior to age 40. The appearance of such a high rate of creative productivity at so early an age leads to the thesis that creative youngsters should be identified in the teen years and given special training in their fields so that they can reach the highest level of achievement and have a long period of productivity.

We should not, however, conclude that all creative productions appear during the early years of one's life. Again, Lehman (1953) has pointed out from his studies that highly significant creative work has been done during the late years of life as well. Lehman cites cases where the thinker was largely unknown during the early years of life. Individual differences and peculiar environmental circumstances combine to produce creative thinkers in different fields and at different age periods. Furthermore, there are many individuals who have had the ability, health, motivation, and opportunities that enabled them to continue throughout their lives doing notable creative work.

High Versus Low Creative Ability.   An important question about creativity is: What differences do we observe between children who are high and children who are average or slightly above the average in creativity? Another question of importance to parents and teachers relates to the background of creative individuals. Datta and Parloff (1967) attempted to determine the kind of home in which the creative individual is likely to develop. The investigators noted that both creative young scientists and their equally bright but less creative controls describe their parents as moderately affectionate, nonrejecting, and high in encouraging intellectual independence. The creative subjects more often perceived both parents as furnishing a "no rule" situation in which the integrity and responsibility of the children were assumed rather than one in which expectations were enforced by authoritarian controls and punishment.

A study reported by Trowbridge and Charles (1966) sheds some light on the question about the differences between children who are high and those who are average in creative ability. The investigators observed 75 youngsters attending classes at a municipal art center. Paintings produced by the children over a semester were saved and evaluated. The first hypothesis that creativity and competency could be separated was supported. The developmental pattern for technical competency was gradual and steady throughout the age range studied; the pattern for creativity remained relatively constant from 3 to 15 years with a sharp rise from 15 to 18 years.

The behaviors differed in the students judged most and least creative in all of the age groups. In comparison to the low creative group, the high creative group displayed less conformity, showed more universality in their creativeness, showed more self-direction and inner motivation, and used more free time alone reading, working, playing, and daydreaming.

In a study of outstanding scientists, Bloom (1963) found these individuals had a tremendous amount of energy, had difficulty establishing close relationships with others, and tended to retreat from a social and personal world into a world of ideas and objects. These findings are similar to those of Drevdahl and Cattell (1958), who studied artists and writers. There is no evidence, however, that these traits characterize children and adolescents who show considerable scientific ability.

A study by Cashdan and Welsh (1966) dealt with the personality correlates of creative potential in talented high school students. The subjects of the study were 311 academically gifted or talented adolescents. The adolescents were classified on the basis of the RA scale into high and low creative groups. The high-creative adolescent emerged as a very different person from his low-creative contemporaries, although the high-creative persons were quite similar to one another, regardless of their speciality or sex. On the other hand, the low-creative adolescent, particularly the male, was found to be a somewhat compulsive, eager-to-please person who views himself as dominant and self-confident. He is in general less independent that the high-creative persons and shies away from change; he is overly concerned with maintaining order in the universe. He is not an interpersonal recluse; females score higher on heterosexual relations. In general, talented males seem to be very similar to males in general; talented females seem to be similar to females in general. As suggested earlier for eminent scientists, it seems that with advanced age and increased specialization, significant differences appear between individuals high in special abilities.

Summary

Three factors in the cognitive domain affect learning efficiency at school—intelligence, special abilities, and previous experiences related to the learning tasks. Much controversy has existed and presently exists about the nature and measurement of intelligence. The idea that intelligence as measured by tests was fixed and not subject to improvement prevailed during the early period of intelligence testing, although results from later studies disproved such a notion.

The concept of primary mental abilities, developed by the Thurstones, brought forth a broader concept of intelligence, emphasizing different types of intellective processes. Additional research revealed that although close genetic relationships tend to have somewhat similar patterns of mental growth, intelligence-test scores are affected by environmental conditions. Longitudinal data collected from single individuals over a number of years show that there is a gradual and continuous growth in mental abilities, with the various abilities maturing at different periods. However, the influences of an adverse environment during childhood cannot be completely overcome at a later stage.

Long-term predictions of intelligence-test scores based on scores obtained during the preschool years are hazardous. Developmental curves for the different mental abilities show considerable variation, with a leveling off of ability on most tests during the late teens or early 20's. However, certain longitudinal studies indicate an increase in information and vocabulary with increased age.

Some of the major influences affecting intellectual development are (1) an impoverished environment, unfavorable parent-child relationship, (3) lack of motivation, and (4) sex. Most studies show that girls are slightly superior to boys in language development during the early years.

Correlations between intelligence-test scores and school achievement seldom exceed .70. Early studies of the personal and social characteristics of the gifted failed to take into consideration their educational, socioeconomic, and cultural background. Beyond a certain IQ level, high IQ does not generally distinguish individuals in terms of their academic achievement; although within a critical range, both IQ and creativity distinguish individuals in terms of their academic achievement. Differences between pupils with high IQ's who are achievers and those who are nonachievers seems to lie in the way parents treat bright children. Parents of high achievers give independence values a higher score and conformity values a lower score than parents of low achievers. The absence of achievement in some area is not a sure sign of lack of talent in that area. Although young thinkers frequently demonstrate creative achievements, highly creative work may appear at a later stage, even in the absence of earlier creative thinking. During the adolescent years talented males seem to be very similar to males in general; talented females seem to be similar to females in general. Significant differences appear during later years.

References

Ames, L. P., and Florence L. Ilg. "Sex Differences in Test Performance of Matched Girl-Boy Pairs in the Five-to-Nine-Year-Old Range," *Journal of Genetic Psychology,* Vol. 104 (1964), pp. 25-34.

Anastasia, Anne. "Age Changes in Adult Test Performance," *Psychological Reports,* Vol. 2 (1956), p. 509.

Baldwin, A. L., Joan Kalhorn, and F. H. Breese. "Patterns of Parent Behavior," *Psychological Monographs,* Vol. 58 (1945).

Baldwin, B. T., and L. I. Stecher. "Additional Data from Consecutive Stanford-Binet Tests," *Journal of Educational Psychology,* Vol. 13 (1922), pp. 556-560.

Bayley, N. "Consistency and Variability in the Growth of Intelligence from Birth to Eighteen Years," *Journal of Genetic Psychology,* Vol. 75 (1949), pp. 165-196.

Bayley, Nancy, and M. H. Oden. "The Maintenance of Intellectual Ability in Gifted Adults," *Journal of Gerontology,* Vol. 10 (1955), pp. 91-107.

Bing, E. "Effect of Child-Rearing Practices on Development of Differential Cognitive Abilities," *Child Development,* Vol. 34 (1963), pp. 631-648.

Black, J. D. *Preliminary Manual the D-48 Test.* Palo Alto, Calif.: Consulting Psychologists Press, 1963.

Bloom, B. S. "Report on Creative Research at the University of Chicago," in C. W. Taylor and F. Barron (eds.), *Scientific Creativity.* New York: Wiley, 1963, pp. 251-264.

————. *Stability and Change in Human Characteristics.* New York: Wiley, 1964.

Burt, C. "The Inheritance of Mental Ability," *American Psychologist,* Vol. 13 (1958), pp. 1-15.

Canestrari, R. E. "Paced and Self-Paced Learning in Young and Elderly Adults," *Journal of Gerontology,* Vol. 18 (1963), pp. 165-168.

Cashdan, S., and G. S. Welsh. "Personality Correlates of Creative Potential in Talented High School Students," *Journal of Personality,* Vol. 34 (1966), pp. 445-455.

Cicirelli, V. G. "Form of Relationship between Creativity, I.Q., and Academic Achievement," *Journal of Educational Psychology,* Vol. 56 (1965), pp. 303-309.

Crandall, V., R. Dewey, W. Katkovsky, and Anne Preston. "Parents' Attitudes and Behaviors and Grade-School Children's Academic Achievements," *Journal of Genetic Psychology*, Vol. 104 (1964), pp. 53-66.

Cropley, A. J. "Creativity and Intelligence," *British Journal of Educational Psychology*, Vol. 26 (1966), pp. 259-265.

Datta, Lois E., and M. B. Parloff. "On the Relevance of Autonomy: Parent-Child Relationships and Early Scientific Creativity," paper read at the Seventy-fifth Annual Convention of the American Psychological Association, 1967.

Deutsch, M., and B. Brown. "Social Influence in Negro-White Intelligence Differences," *Journal of Social Issues*, Vol. 20 (April 1964), pp. 24-35.

Drevdahl, J. E., and R. B. Cattell. "Personality and Creativity in Artists and Writers," *Journal of Clinical Psychology*, Vol. 14 (1958), pp. 107-111.

Eagle, N. "The Stability of Lorge-Thorndike I.Q. Scores between Grades Three and Four and Grade Eight," *Journal of Educational Research*, Vol. 60 (1966), pp. 164-165.

Garrison, S. C. "Additional Retests by Means of the Stanford Revision of the Binet-Simon Tests," *Journal of Educational Psychology*, Vol. 13 (1922), pp. 307-312.

Getzels, J. W., and P. W. Jackson. "The Highly Intelligent and the Highly Creative Adolescent: A Summary of Some Research Findings," in R. G. Kuhlen and G. G. Thompson (eds.), *Psychological Studies in Human Development*. New York: Appleton, 1963, pp. 370-381.

―――――. "The Study of Giftedness: A Multidimensional Approach," *The Gifted Student*. Cooperative Research Monograph No. 2, United States Department of Health, Education, and Welfare, Office of Education, Washington, D.C., 1960, p. 6.

Guilford, J. P. "The Structure of Intellect," *Psychological Bulletin*, Vol. 33 (1956), pp. 267-293.

―――――. "Three Faces of Intellect," *American Psychologist*, Vol. 14 (1959), pp. 469-479.

Hulicka, I. "Age Differences in Wechsler Memory Scale Scores," *Journal of Genetic Psychology*, Vol. 109 (1966), pp. 135-146.

―――――. "Short-Term Learning-Retention Efficiency as a Function of Age, Health, and Type of Task," paper presented at the Eastern Psychological Association meeting, Philadelphia, April 1964.

Jarvik, L. F. "Biological Differences in Intellectual Functioning," *Vita Humana*, Vol. 5 (1962), pp. 195-203. S. Karger Basel, New York.

Jones, H. E. "The Environment and Mental Developmennt," in L. Carmichael (ed.), *Manual of Child Development*, 2nd ed. New York: Wiley, 1954.

Jones, H. E., and H. S. Conrad. "The Growth and Decline of Intelligence: The Study of a Homogeneous Group between the Ages of Ten and Sixty," *Genetic Psychology Monographs*, Vol. 13 (1933), pp. 223-298.

Kirk, S. A. "Effects of Educational Treatment," in J. L. Frost and G. R. Hawkes, (eds.), *The Disadvantaged Child*. Boston: Houghton, 1966, pp. 120-125.

Lehman, H. C. *Age and Achievement*. Princeton, N.J.: Princeton U. P., 1953.

―――――. "Young Thinkers and Memorable Creative Achievements," *Journal of Genetic Psychology*, Vol. 105 (1964), pp. 237-255.

Meyer, W. J., and A. W. Bendig. "A Longitudinal Study of the Primary Mental Abilities Tests," *Journal of Educational Psychology*, Vol. 52 (1961), pp. 50-60.

Miles, C. C. "Gifted Children," in L. Carmichael, ed., *Manual of Child Psychology*, 2nd ed. New York: Wiley, 1954, pp. 984-1063.

Newsweek (Jan. 29, 1968), pp. 47-48.

Norman, R. D. "The Interpersonal Values of Parents of Achieving and Nonachieving Gifted Children," *Journal of Psychology*, Vol. 64 (1966), pp. 49-57.

Owens, W. A. "Age and Mental Abilities: A Longitudinal Study," *Genetic Psychology Monographs*, Vol. 48 (1953), pp. 3-54.

Petersen, J. *Early Conceptions and Tests of Intelligence*. New York: Harcourt 1925.

Pressey, S. L. "Concerning the Nature and Nurture of Genius," *Scientific Monthly,* Vol. 81 (1955), pp. 123-129.

Reynolds, M. C. "Some Research-Related Thoughts on Education of the Gifted," *Exceptional Children,* Vol. 30 (Sept. 1963), pp. 6-12.

Sanderson, R. E., and Inglis. "Learning and Mortality in Elderly Psychiatric Patients," *Journal of Gerontology,* Vol. 16 (1961), pp. 375-376.

Scheerer, M. "Problem Solving," *Scientific American,* Vol. 208 (April 1963), pp. 118-128.

Smith, D. "Personal and Social Adjustment of Gifted Adolescents," *Council for Exceptional Children Research Monograph,* Vol. 1, No. 4 (1962).

Sontag, L. W., C. T. Baker, and V. Nelson. "Mental Growth and Personality Development: A Longitudinal Study," *Monographs of the Society for Research and Child Development,* Vol. 23, No. 2 (1958).

Spearman, C. *The Abilities of Man: Their Nature and Measurement.* New York: Macmillan, 1927.

Steadman, D. J., Director of Research, The Durham Education Improvement Program, Durham, N.C., 1966-1967.

Terman, L. M. *Manual, The Concept Mastery Test.* New York: Psychological Corporation, 1956.

Thurstone, L. L. "Primary Mental Abilities," *Psychometric Monograph No. 1,* Chicago: U. of Chicago Press, 1938.

Thurstone, L. L., and Thelma G. Thurstone. "Factorial Studies of Intelligence," *Psychometric Monographs,* No. 2 (1941).

Thurstone, T. G. "Primary Mental Abilities of Children," *Educational and Psychological Measurements,* Vol. 1 (1941), pp. 105-116.

Travis, O. R. "Factor Structure of the Wechsler Intelligence Scale for Children at the Preschool Level and after First Grade: a Longitudinal Analysis," *Psychological Reports,* Vol. 16 (1965), pp. 637-644.

Trowbridge, N., and D. C. Charles. "Creativity in Art Students," *Journal of Genetic Psychology,* Vol. 109 (1966), pp. 281-289.

Wallach, M. A., and N. Kogan. "Creativity and Intelligence in Children's Thinking," *Transaction,* Vol. 4 (1967), pp. 38-43.

Ward, W. C. "Creativity in Young Children," *Child Development,* Vol. 39 (1968), pp. 737-754.

Wechsler, D. "Intellectual Changed with Age," *Mental Health in Later Maturity.* Supplement No. 168 to Public Health Report, Federal Security Agency, United States Public Health Service, 1942, pp. 43-52.

———. "Intellectual Development and Psychological Maturity," *Child Development,* Vol. 21 (1950), pp. 45–50.

———. *The Measurement of Adult Intelligence.* Baltimore: Williams and Wilkins, 1960.

Welsh, G. S. "Comparison of D-48, Terman CMT, and Art Scale Scores of Gifted Adolescents." An extended report of a brief report with the same title published in the *Journal of Consulting Psychology,* Vol. 30 (1966), p. 88.

———. *Preliminary Manual, The Welsh Figure Preference Test* (research edition). Palo Alto, California: Consulting Psychologists Press, 1959.

———. "Verbal Interests and Intelligence: Comparison of Strong VI B, Terman CMT, and D-48 Scores of Gifted Adolescents," paper presented at the Southeastern Psychological Association meeting, New Orleans, March 31, 1966.

Wolfe, D. "Diversity of Talent," *American Psychologist,* Vol. 15 (1960), pp. 535-545.

Chapter 9

Acquiring Attitudes, Ideals, and Values

Attitudes, ideals, and values are "soaked up" from the milieu in which one lives; they are a fundamental part of the milieu. At home, in the community, and at school the child has many meaningful experiences, most of which are emotionally toned. Out of these experiences he acquires attitudes, ideals, and values. These learnings take place at all age and grade levels, but their learning is more pronounced during childhood than during adolescence or adulthood. Membership in primary groups, such as the family, and informal neighborhood groups markedly influence their development.

Attitudes, Ideals, and Values: Their Meaning and Development

Attitudes, ideals, and values are among the most important outcomes learned at home, in the community, and at school and work; they are important determiners of how the individual reacts at different stages in his development to situations about him. Thus they serve both as responses and as motivational forces. Some attitudes are learned early and become firmly fixed during the early years; others are learned later and become more firmly established as a result of further learning and experiences.

Affective Processes and Outcomes. Affect refers to the feeling aspects of behavior. The affective processes have usually been regarded as subjective in nature and have only recently come under scientific scrutiny. A classification scheme of the affective processes that has important implications for educational objectives was developed by a national committee composed of Krathwohl, Bloom, and Masia (1964). In the scheme developed, the investigators attempted to order and relate the different kinds of affective behavior and made use of the concept of internalization—the process of incorporating something into one's behavior as his own. Internalization is not only characterized by the dimensions of the external and the internal, it also has dimensions of the simple and the complex, and the concrete and the abstract. These may be noted in the order of the classification scheme here presented (Krathwohl et al, 1964).

The Taxonomy of Educational Objectives:
Handbook II: Affective Domain

1.0 Receiving (attending)
- 1.1 Awareness—the person is aware of the feelings of others, whose activities may be of little interest to him.
- 1.2 Willingness to Receive—the person listens to others with respect.
- 1.3 Controlled or Selected Attention—someone being alert toward human values and judgments on life as they are recorded in history.

2.0 Responding
- 2.1 Acquiescence in Responding—someone obeying playground regulations.
- 2.2 Willingness to Respond—the person practices the rules of safety on the playground.
- 2.3 Satisfaction in Response—the person enjoys participation in activities and plays according to the rules.

3.0 Valuing
- 3.1 Acceptance of a Value—the person accepts the importance of social goals in a free society.
- 3.2 Preference for a Value—the person assumes an active role in clarifying the social goals in a free society.
- 3.3 Commitment—the person is loyal to the social goals of a free society.

4.0 Organizing
- 4.1 Conceptualization of a Value—the person judges the responsibility of society for conserving human resources.
- 4.2 Organization of a Value System—the person develops a plan for conserving human resources.

5.0 Characterization by a Value or Value Complex
- 5.1 Generalized Set—the person faces facts and conclusions that can be logically drawn from them with a consistent value orientation.
- 5.2 Characterization—the person develops a philosophy of life.

According to the taxonomy classification, internalization begins with an awareness of some phenomenon in one's environment. This is followed by a willingness to receive or give attention to the phenomenon. This is the lowest level of the hierarchy. A second level is that of responding first by acquiescence, then willingness, and finally by satisfaction. The next level, valuing, implies an increased internalization.

As values become more internalized and the level of commitment is reached, they embrace deeper experiences. Organization is now involved. This requires conceptualization, and the organization of a value system. When the value complex level is reached, the person is willing to face facts and draw conclusions from them. The individual's philosophy of life develops out of groups of organized values that are internalized. In this brief description of processes in the affective domain, relationships between the cognitive and affective elements are evident. The principal outcomes cannot be classified as cognitive and affective;

rather, the outcomes can best be thought of as interests, attitudes, values, and personality integration.

Attitudes and Early Experiences.   An attitude consists of the meaning one associates with an object or condition. Attitudes established in early life serve as a basis for the acquisition of later attitudes. Early definitions of attitudes emphasized the notion of acceptance or rejection. Subsequent studies revealed that attitudes go beyond mere acceptance and rejection; it was found that there was a basis for acceptance and rejection, although frequently not a sound one. Thus the element of meaning was introduced in addition to acceptance and rejection. We speak of one's attitudes toward religion, race, education, individuals, and fundamental social or economic issues.

Attitudes arise out of one's experiences, both consciously and unconsciously. The child in the United States is born into a culture or perhaps many cultures. His early experiences with people will largely determine later attitudes toward people, so that by the time he reaches school he has acquired favorable or unfavorable attitudes toward people and conditions. Materials presented later in this chapter help in charting the course of development of attitudes. The influence of early experiences may be noted from the results of a study by Garrison (1967, p. 210) of Missouri Synod Lutheran Clergy showing that "a higher proportion of clergy with childhood experiences with non-whites tended to have highly favorable attitudes toward (racial) integration."

The Development of Ideals.   Ideals, like attitudes, are developed from the total environment in which the child lives and learns. They differ from attitudes in their ever-present, imperative nature. During the early years of life, ideals are closely associated with the unconsciously expressed ideas and feelings of those with whom he is closely associated. They develop simultaneously with conscience, although the moral compulsion of right and wrong is not present. The child's early experiences are frequently quite narrow, and his ideals are limited to his immediate environment involving the self and those with whom he is closely identified.

Ideals, like other learnings, are dependent upon maturation, stimulation, and experiences. This may be noted in the care of two children from similar socioeconomic backgrounds, but from homes with different ideals. The one child may come from a home where kindness and consideration of others pervades the life activities of other members of the home. A child from such a home unconsciously acquires ideals of kindness and consideration of others. Another child from a home where independence and self-concern pervades the home atmosphere will lack the ideals of consideration of others and will display ideals of independence in his actions at an early age. Changes in ideals with maturation and experiences will be discussed later in this chapter and in subsequent chapters dealing with personal-social development and adjustment through the life span.

The Nature and Origin of Values.   Part of the controversy about the meaning of value results from terminology. Students of personal values have not always distinguished between *what is desired* and *what is desirable*. The two viewpoints may converge, or they may diverge considerably. The values of an individual are closely related to and interwined with his attitudes. This may be observed in connection intergroup attitudes. The individual who places a high value on "the worth and dignity of man" is not likely to possess deep-rooted prejudice towards certain groups. A man's values may refer to all his attitudes, *for or against* anything. His values include his likes and dislikes, his desires and goals, his ideals, his interests, what he regards as right and wrong, good and evil, beautiful and ugly, useful and useless, his approval and disapprovals, his standards of judgment, and so forth. Each individual acquires his own system of values, and some of these take precedence over others. For some individuals health becomes an all-important factor to consider in all aspects of life; while others may regard friendships as the factor most important in life.

Man has throughout history sought human fulfillment through the pursuit of values. The role and importance of values are recognized by students of human behavior. The importance of values in human affairs is stated by Julian Huxley (1960, p. 94) as follows: "In lower organisms, the only ultimate criterion is survival; but in man some experiences and actions, some objects and ideas, are valued for their own sake." We are able to evaluate our own values, as we observe and accept them uncritically in the behavior of others. Values are integrated with other learnings and are very important in relation to attitudes, character, and personality. Lecky (1945) set forth four prevailing sets of conditions relating to the development and extension of values; (1) new values in opposition to those already present may be rejected; (2) new values may be modified in such a way that they are no longer in opposition to the accepted values; (3) new values that are in opposition to accepted values may be ignored and thus not integrated into the existing value system; and (4) old values may be so modified that the new values are integrated into the existing value system.

Values are a product of society, and the acquisition of values by the child is part of his total learning. Values exist in all societies and will vary with different social groups. Everyone develops some form of value system which is subject to modification at later stages through learning.

Values and Needs. Needs are basic to the development of values. Values develop in certain directions, designed to serve individual needs. The boy interested in his pet dog and the girl interested in her doll have the same needs for love, security, and self-realization. It seems likely that the manner in which the child's needs at home are satisfied will have an important bearing on his attitudes and values. The girl whose achievement in early reading activities is rewarded or reinforced through parental approval satisfies a need for achievement and comes to sense the value of learning. Thus her value system becomes partially learning-oriented. The boy whose achievements in athletics are rewarded may develop a different value system from that of the boy whose efforts in science are rewarded.

Need satisfaction operates in all areas of life. One way a child has of satisfying his needs is through interaction with others having similar interests and needs. Myers (1950), for instance, noted that honor students generally chose their friends on the basis of good work habits, favorable attitudes toward school, and interests in things related to educational achievement.

The Emergence of Conscience. Learning to accept and internalize rules and regulations is dependent upon the child's ability to trust his parents or some other adult figures. Very early the child learns that pleasing those adults responsible for his behavior is rewarding, while displeasing such people is unpleasant. As he develops physically and mentally, he comes to comprehend that acts associated with pleasing his parents are good, while those associated with displeasing his parents are bad.

The young child controls his actions in order to obtain rewards and fewer punishments. His behavior is controlled by external standards—of selected adults. With practice certain reactions become somewhat automatic; the standards of others are almost completely adopted. His internalizing of the rules and standards of adults who surround him marks the emergence of conscience.

In a study of moral judgments, Morris (1958) asked pupils what they would do in fourteen problem situations of the following type:

Someone in J's class at school has broken the schools rules and the teacher wants to find out who did it. He asks the pupils to own up; but no one does. Then he asks anyone who knows anything about it to come and see him afterward. J. knows who did it. What should he do?

The pupils' responses were tabulated and the following conclusions were drawn: (1) Marked discrepancies were found between what pupils thought should be done in the problem situations and what they thought would actually be done. These discrepancies increased with age. (2) There was a slow decline with age in judgments based upon self-interest, with the greatest decline on the level of actually expected behavior. (3) There was a decline in moral dependence upon authority and an increase in independence, both subject to considerable fluctuations at the 13-15-year age level. These results indicate a change from judgments purely egocentric in nature to those involving the welfare of others.

The Development of Self-Esteem. Children who have high self-esteem have the push and confidence to make their way. They make friends easily and take things as they come. On the other hand, children with low self-esteem downgrade themselves psychologically by thinking such things as "I'm not very important," "I don't see why anyone should like me," "I can't do the things I'd like to do," "I'm not sure my ideas are good," and "I don't think I have the ability."

Self-esteem, like attitudes toward others, is learned and continuously modified as a result of varied experiences. The importance of reinforcement in the acquisition of self-esteem may be observed in everyday experiences of children and adolescents. The child who experiences success and receives approval from parents or others develops a feeling of well-being. On the contrary, continuous failure leads toward lack of self-esteem. In a study by Coopersmith (1959), 102 fifth- and sixth-grade children were administered a test of self-esteem and an anxiety scale. He found a close relationship between high self-esteem and low anxiety scores. The youngsters with high self-esteem were also more popular with their peers. In a further study (1960), Coopersmith found that fifth- and sixth-graders who have high self-esteem recall their failures, while those with low self-esteem tend to suppress or deny their failures.

In the 1959 study Coopersmith selected two groups for special study. One group was made up of children of high self-esteem whose teachers thought poorly of them; the other group consisted of children who thought poorly of themselves but who were highly regarded by their teachers. A comparison of these groups showed that the children in the latter group were more popular, better academic achievers, although more critical and more ambitious. These youngsters appear to take it out on themselves, although they are well regarded by their teachers and peers, and are successful in their school work. Youngsters who have a high self-esteem and are highly regarded by their teachers seem to get along very well in school and are less critical of themselves than youngsters who have a low self-esteem yet are highly regarded by their teachers. The group of youngsters who had low self-esteem and were poorly regarded by their teachers were least popular, achieved less, were more anxious, and held lower self-ideal concepts than those of the other groups.

Developmental Trends

Although much remains to be learned about the acquisition and modification of high attitudes, ideals, and values from infancy into and throughout adult life, information available shows that some acquired in early childhood remain fairly stable, while others change considerably under certain conditions. Furthermore, some attitudes, ideals, and values are acquired in early life, others during adolescence, and still others during different adult periods of life. Attitudes, ideals, and values appear to follow the fundamental principles of development set forth in Chapter 2; they are rarely related to other aspects of development. It was pointed out earlier that pleasantness and unpleasantness appear in infancy and are quite discernible by the second year of life. Parents report that their preschool children expressed favorable or unfavorable attitudes toward school prior to starting the first grade (Stendler, 1951). Materials presented subsequently should furnish a basis for making inferences about the formation of attitudes, ideals, and values at different stages of life.

Changes in Self-Concept with Age. According to Redl and Wattenberg (1951, pp. 102-103), one's self-concept goes through a succession of stages in development. It begins with the experiences of infancy, when the individual is the center of a very limited universe; by adulthood the individual has established the fact that he is a distinct person and has learned the boundaries of his influence upon the world about him, and which parts of this world he is closely related to and what parts are of little or no concern to him. Success or failure in need satisfaction, and consequently the type of self-concept which one forms, is largely dependent upon the effectiveness of relationships with others.

The self-concept of an individual growing up in our culture will be affected by his relations with parents, siblings, peers, teachers, and others.

One's self-concept is developmental in nature. A more exact understanding of developmental changes occurs when specific changes are studied. This may be observed when comparisons are made between self-concepts at different life periods. Sixth-graders have a better understanding of the influences of external environment and causative factors and are able to separate these from the self better than second- and third-graders. Phillips (1963) noted that the self-perceptions of sixth-graders are more realistic and less influenced by egocentrism than third-graders.

In a study by Washburne (1961), significant sex differences were noted in patterns of self-conceptualization in high school and college students. College men exhibit more mature responses than high school boys as indicated by inner controlling and self-actualization responses; the difference between college women and high school girls were less marked. The more mature responses of high school girls as compared to high school boys is perhaps closely related to their earlier physiological maturity.

Attitudes Toward Sex and Social-Sex Role. Significant changes in attitudes toward sex that occur with the onset of adolescence is presented in a later chapter. The way in which a child reacts to sexual information and sexual stimulation which he receives depends upon earlier attitudes which it developed. Attitudes toward nudity, physiological differences between the sexes, behavior expectations of males and females, as well as other aspects of sex and sexual behavior are developed progressively during the early years. This century has seen a broadening in the range of prevailing attitudes toward social-sex roles for men and women and appropriate sex behavior for boys and girls. Research indicates an increasing similarity in parents' relations with boys and girls as well as a lessening of separate sex-typed expectations on the part of parents concerning the interests, abilities, and personality characteristics of their sons and daughters. These trends are more evident in the middle than lower classes, and more prevalent among the well-educated. They also vary within the educated middle class, seemingly due to degree of traditional or modern orientation of the home and/or school.

A study by Minuchin (1965) was designed to assess the effects of different educational and home environments on the psychological development of children of similar backgrounds in all aspects other than relative traditional or modern philosophy. Traditional middle-class schools and homes were defined as stressing socialization toward general standards, and the modern viewpoint was defined as fostering the individual development of the child through more varied methods and toward more complex and individually relevant standards. The subjects of the study were 105 fourth-grade nine-year-olds from four schools, two being selected as traditional and two as modern—57 boys and 48 girls. The pupils were from middle or upper-middle class. The results were obtained from an interview with the children, the Stick Figure Scale (a self-scaling technique), a play session, and the children's picture story test.

The results obtained for social-sex attitudes were as follows:

1. A group trend was noted toward stated preference for one's own sex and toward conventional role imagery; this trend is more consistently characteristic of children from traditional backgrounds.

2. A less rigid attitude toward sex-role preferences is more characteristic of girls than the boys. It is particularly characteristic of the girls from schools and homes with modern orientations and from families of higher socioeconomic status.

3. A clearly stated preference for opposite sex roles is rare in this sample and not systematically related to either modern or traditional backgrounds.

4. Both school and home orientation seem to influence sex-role attitudes.

The Development of Prejudice. There are two types of prejudice, equally troublesome in their effects but different in their origins. An understanding of the development of prejudice requires us then to consider the origins of prejudice. The first type has been termed *pathological prejudice*. In this form of prejudice, the individual displaces his own conflicts and frustrations onto some convenient "scapegoat," and thus reduces his hostile feelings and anxieties about his problem or problems. All groups seem to be able to find a scapegoat, which is frequently a minority or helpless group.

The other type of prejudice is regarded as *normal*. Such type of prejudice will be found among individuals growing up in a culture where derogatory ideas and attitudes exist toward certain individuals or groups. A child growing up in

Peers reinforce and shape attitudes.

this culture assimilates the negative attitudes toward certain groups just as he learns other aspects of his culture. These attitudes are conceptualized with certain words or labels used to describe those belonging to certain groups.

According to Cole (1964), p. 459), the course of prejudice runs about as follows:

> (1) An individual is frustrated in his efforts to satisfy his basic needs, is rejected and neglected; (2) he feels insecure and defenseless, he wants at least enough power to defend himself and, by preference, enough to compensate for his past and present low status; (3) he feels hostile toward almost everyone, but he cannot express his hostility toward those who are more powerful than he is. . . . . (4) The individual then displaces his hostility from its natural object to his victim. (5) The prejudiced person is now ready to commit an act of aggression, and will do so when outside stimuli prompt him. . . . (6) As a final stage, the fanatic adds reason and justification for his intolerance.

A study by Gough and others (1950) disclosed that children who were most fearful and sucpicious, least confident and secure, displayed the greatest intolerance toward Jews and Negroes. According to the investigators, such personality traits developed most frequently in authoritarian homes where prompt obedience was demanded. Also, in authoritarian homes the attitudes of the parents are usually highly rigidly tinged with prejudice toward groups of people who differ from them.

The child's attitude toward religion is an outgrowth of experience, but limited by his lack of maturation and experience. His attitude is characteristically egocentric and selfish. To the young child prayers may be a means of getting things you want; if he is good, his prayers will be answered. Since he is accustomed to having things done for him, he regards God as a person who will do things for him (Lenski, 1953).

In a study by Garrity (1961), approximately 4,000 secondary school pupils in England were administered a religious-attitude scale. The highest score indicated a more favorable attitude toward religious education. The score of the adolescent girls was lower (3.66) than that of the boys (4.40), indicating a more favorable attitude toward religious training by the girls. There was a steady rise in the scores from the first to the fourth year for both boys and girls—a change in the direction of a less favorable attitude toward religion.

The results of a study of rigidity and religious participation by Appleby (1957) are interesting because of the generalization one might make of the findings to areas of life other than religion. In his study, the participation in religious activities of 200 Jewish college students, all of whom had been reared in the traditional Jewish faith, was classified as high, middle, or low in present observance, or else entirely without participation. The students then completed an attitude test involving tolerance. Those students classified as "middle" were the most tolerant, and the low participation group was next most tolerant. The two extremes were equally rigid or nontolerant. It seems that rigidity in attitudes is most likely to be found among people at the extreme on issues—in politics the extreme right and extreme left.

A number of investigations have been concerned with changes in religious activities and beliefs of students during their years at college. Argyle (1958) summarized the results of a number of these studies and noted that religious activities become less frequent and religious beliefs more liberal among college students during their early years at college. The results of studies conducted among students in England by Poppleton and Pilkington (1963) give support to the findings among college students in the United States.

A stratified random sampling of students at the University of Sheffield, including 141 in their first year at the University, was administered a scale for measuring religious attitudes and a questionnaire about typical religious practices and beliefs. In the third year at the University, the test and questionnaire were administered again to a group of students who had completed the test and questionnaire during their first year at the University. Perhaps the most interesting result from this study was that over the two-year period the women moved away from religion more than the men—moving in the direction of the behavior and beliefs of men students. The general religious rank between the three religious groups—Roman Catholic, nonconformist, and Church of England—was still preserved. However, at the later date there were no significant differences between median attitude scale scores of the three groups.

One of the factors that accounts for deep-seated continuous prejudice is the stereotype viewpoint toward a particular group. There is empirical evidence that this stereotype is best overcome through democratic living involving members of different groups on a similar level, rather than at different levels. One notices this in the army, on the athletic field, and in the entertainment world. As long as the inferior and superior roles involving a complete group is assumed, a sort of prejudice is fostered. It is interesting to note that Southern white children who favored desegregation during the early days of school integration had a more favorable stereotype of the Negro than did the majority of white children. (Grossack, 1957). It was further noted that not all Southern adults were equally prejudiced. The white college-educated professional person who has worked closely with his Negro peers on an equal basis, such as serving on committees, panels, cooperative research, is not likely to hold any significant prejudice toward the Negro. The same principle would be true for prejudices toward any other group or groups. Bogardus (1958) provides a hopeful note when he points out that measurable progress was made in the decade prior to 1958 in decreasing prejudice. One would expect this to be continued at an accelerated rate since 1958, due to increased enlightenment about human development, general respect for legal sanctions, and increased contacts between individuals on a similar level rather than a superiority-inferiority level.

Concerning the elimination of prejudice, Cole (1964, p. 460) points out:

> The deep-rooted prejudice that is based primarily upon fear of some sort is based primarily upon fear of some sort is often impossible to eradicate, because the fear prevents its possessor from seeing any new fact clearly and produces so much distortion of new data that little, if any, progress can be made. To the true

fanatic, prejudice is a way of life, to which he clings because he feels his safety and success are too involved for him to change.

Changes in Authoritarian Responses. Children reared by authoritarian parents at an early age are authoritarian in their responses to others. Their attitudes and ideals reveal their authoritarian nature. If they identify closely with their parents, they tend to treat their children somewhat like they were treated during childhood (Zeligs, 1966).

There is some evidence that there is a carry-over from some fundamentalistic religious teaching to an authoritarian attitude. Parents with a fundamentalist background seem to feel that they have the answers to most problems, especially if such problems can be related in some way to their religious beliefs. Perhaps this accounts for the greater percentage of authoritarian responses found by Williams (1966) to intergroup problems. The materials presented in Table 9-1 show the students in the southern area of the United States gave the largest

TABLE 9-1

Percentage of Authoritarian Responses to F-Scale Items by
Region and by Education (After Williams)

Item	Region	Eighth Grade, percent	Some High School or High School Graduate, percent	Some College or College Graduate, percent
1. Think that the most	S	90.9	64.2	52.4
important thing to teach	NC	86.2	57.9	38.6
children is absolute	NE	84.9	65.3	30.6
obedience to their parents	W	72.5	52.4	26.9
2. Think that any good	S	75.2	57.7	61.9
leader should be strict	NC	69.6	46.6	38.6
with people under him	NE	63.9	47.9	32.3
to gain their respect	W	67.5	47.6	36.5
3. Think that prison is	S	47.9	40.7	23.8
too good for criminals;	NC	39.9	32.4	14.3
that they should be publicly	NE	40.3	32.3	12.9
whipped or worse	W	40.0	31.7	9.6
4. Think that there are	S	74.4	63.4	59.5
two kinds of people in	NC	68.8	50.0	35.7
the world: the weak	NE	70.6	51.5	25.8
and the strong	W	65.0	49.2	34.6
5. Think that no decent	S	49.6	40.7	40.5
man can have respect for a	NC	39.1	32.4	28.6
woman who has had sex	NE	28.5	21.0	14.5
relations before marriage	W	42.5	25.4	3.8

South (8th grade) 121; (high school) 123; (college) 42;
North Central (8th grade) 138; (high school) 176; (college) 70;
Northeast (8th grade) 119; (high school) 167; (college) 62;
West (8th grade) 40; (high school) 63; (college) 52.

percentage of authoritarian responses to five problems, while the students from the West gave the smallest percentage of authoritarian responses.

Williams (1966) noted a decline in authoritarian responses among students as they advanced from the eighth grade to college. The results presented in Table 9-1 also show a regional difference with students from the South making the highest average authoritarian scores.

Attitudes Toward World Problems. The elementary school child shows little concern with world problems, except in cases where he is directly or indirectly involved. With increased age a greater concern is shown for world problems. In a study by Adams (1963), approximately 4,000 boys and girls, ranging in ages from 10 to 19, were asked what they considered to be the major problem of their country. About two-thirds of them cited international problems and one-fourth domestic problems. The remainder gave no answer; or if an answer was given, it could not be classified. There was a decrease with age in the concern with international problems and an increase in concern with domestic problems. Other changes with age cited by Adams were as follows:

> Realistic answers for domestic problems tend to increase with age; while, although this latter trend is not as certain, realistic solutions for international problems tend to decrease with age. Unrealistic solutions to international problems definitely decrease with age, while they remain relatively constant for domestic issues.   (p. 400)

Garrison (1961) found a small but significant increase in world-minded attitude test scores of college students at the University of Georgia as one progresses from the freshman to the senior level. The average score of the girls at each class level was higher than the average for boys at that class level. This is in harmony with earlier results obtained by Sampson and Smith (1957).

Persistence and Change. The question is sometimes raised about the persistence of attitudes. A follow-up study by Nelson (1954) of over 900 college students who were administered an attitude test for conservatism and liberalism in 1936 provides a partial answer to this question. These adults were administered the same test in 1950. In 18 percent of the cases there was no change; in 31 percent of the cases there was a change in the direction of conservatism; and in 51 percent of the cases there was a change toward liberalism or radicalism. These data seem to contradict the idea that people become more conservative with age. However, it is likely that in later years these people now in their 30's will become more conservative. Perhaps part of the notion of the greater liberalism of youth than their parents stems from the fact that youth, is on the average, better educated than their parents. Also, the attitudes of youth are more in harmony with changes taking place than their parents are. Thus when we compare youth and adults at the same decade we tend to find youth more ready to accept change than their adult contemporaries.

It is likely that changes in attitudes of college students are related to their later occupational, economic, and social status. An early study by Centers

(1949), showed that heads of large businesses tended to be ultraconservative or conservative, even to a greater degree than heads of small businesses. However, one must be cautious in the use of the terms conservative, liberal, and radical. An individual may be conservative in one area and quite liberal in another. It would be better to refer to specific attitudes rather than make broad generalizations. Professional people are in general more liberal than industrial workers and white-collar workers on matters pertaining to world problems (Garrison, 1961), although Centers found the professional people conservative on tests he used for measuring these qualities.

One's early childhood, education, and present status are primary determiners of one's attitude toward a particular problem. Attitudes, ideals, values, and self-concepts are important motivationally; they are interwoven with conscience. One has no feelings of guilt so long as one acts consistently with these internalized systems (conscience). Scott (1960, p. 154) noted "that an individual's attitude toward an event, X, tends to be consistent with his values and the way he sees X as relevant to his values. " That is, one's attitude toward X can be predicted from the strength of one's values and the degree to which X is deemed relevant to them. Thus there is a tendency for one to act consistently with his attitudes, ideals, and values. This tendency is to a marked degree responsible for the persistent and consistent behavior or reactions toward families of related persons, situations, and objects.

Over 2,400 children age 9-17 from Minnesota participated in a study by Anderson (1959) dealing with long-term prediction of children's adjustment. The children completed scales measuring attitudes toward family, sense of responsibility, work and attitudes toward work based on experience in home duties and chores, interests and play activities, and favorable attitudes toward experience.

The change with age in work habits and in attitudes toward the family is shown in Figure 9-1. The dotted line shows a growing capacity of the child to meet the demands of work. The solid line shows the changes in attitudes toward the family. The graph shows a rapid improvement in attitudes from age 9 to age 12, with little change noted after age 12 through the adolescent years. The graphs indicate significant progress in family and work attitudes, which is contrary to the general notion that adolescence is usually a time of rebellion against parents and deterioration of work habits.

The typical middle-aged person has to a large degree become a slave to habit. This applies to attitudes and attitude change as well as other aspects of his life. Even though information may change attitudes that are not deep-rooted or highly emotionalized, it is unlikely that he will be confronted with such information.

A problem frequently ignored in propaganda studies is that of the captive audience. We recognize the captive audience when we speak of the "Iron Curtain," or of censorship in Red China. We fail to notice that, although we may not have an imposed limit to our freedom in connection with the news media,

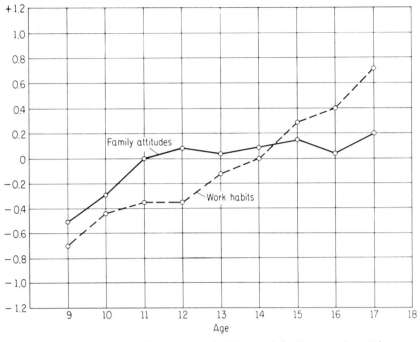

Figure 9-1. Changes with age in work habits and family attitudes. (After Anderson, 1959.)

we have as a result of habit patterns selective audiences. Republicans read newspapers oriented toward Republican viewpoints; Democrats read newspapers oriented toward Democratic viewpoints. Wall Street bankers are not likely to read the *Daily Worker;* the typical union worker is not likely to give careful attention to the more conservative newspaper attitudes on labor problems. An interesting aspect of this selection is found in the ease with which a person is able to learn a set of arguments contrary to his beliefs, if these arguments are quite implausible (Jones and Kohler, 1958). Such arguments are no threat to the individual's attitudinal structure and will not produce conflicts in his beliefs and judgments.

Perhaps most of our attitudes are, in each case, the immediate result of prejudgment, the distinctly human process of generalization which involves labeling and categorizing. Studies of cognition in children, referred to in Chapter 8, deal with conceptual categorization of the external environment at different stages of development. Concerning categorizing Allport (1954, p. 20) states: "The human mind must think with the aid of categories. Once formed, categories are the basis for normal prejudgment. We cannot possibly avoid the process. Orderly living depends upon it." Throughout life, beginning in early childhood, people, objects, situations, and conditions of living are classified, labeled, and thus categorized. It is in this process that attitudes are learned. The acquisition of attitudes is largely a matter of incidental learning. The labels applied by parents and other significant persons in one's life are the ones adopted by the growing individual.

Developing Adequate Values. The present scientific age is one in which many ready-made values and beliefs are seriously questioned. The problem of developing an adequate set of values in ourselves as well as in the children and youth of today is a difficult one. Bühler (1964, pp. 520-521) has given us a good description of this problem as follows:

> To begin with, we do not get, as people in previous times did, a ready-made set of values, with which we can unquestionably identify. Although there still are many divergent groups of people who try to go on living by the religious and moral traditions of the past, which they were taught, an ever increasing number feel that they have to think things through for themselves. They want to get to a new unbiased understanding of human existence. Yet when attempting this most people find that they are not really equipped to do this job in an adequate manner. They do not have the training to think about principles of living in a logical and systematic way. Nor do they know all the facts that they should be informed about, to reach any kind of valid conclusions. . . .
>
> One is that at the time when we begin to think consciously and deliberately about our values and beliefs, we have already been influenced and formed in many directions. We have picked up from or have been taught or even been indoctrinated by our environment. That includes our family, our neighbors, friends and the whole subculture in which we grow up. From at least about four years of age on, children begin to form opinions on values. From five years on, they are known to identify with prejudices of their environment. After that time, it becomes increasingly difficult for an individual to think about values without bias. Besides being brought up within the confines of some subculture, an individual's situation of life may be such that he cannot possible free himself. He may be economically too dependent, too restricted in social opportunities, too much hampered by poor education, to be able to work on his development as a person.

Influences Affecting Attitudes, Ideals, and Values

Since attitudes, values, and ideals are learned, any forces or conditions affecting one's life will have a bearing on his attitudes, values, and ideals. Although the child's early identification is normally with his parents, in his development certain adult figures stand out and are accepted as examples to follow. Identification occurs throughout childhood and perhaps adulthood. This may be observed in adults who accept the ideals, values, and ways of behaving of certain people whom they admire. The changed self that appears with age has an important bearing on attitudes, values, and ideals at different stages of life. This will be emphasized in the subsequent chapters of Part III dealing with socialization and personal adjustment at the different stages of life.

The child's first identification is normally with his parents. A child brought up in a home where there is warmth reacts favorably to his parents and other members of the family. The parent-child relationship is the most important factor in producing a close identification on the part of the child toward his parents.

Influence of the Home.   The influence of the home is the acquisition of attitudes, values, and ideals. This may be observed in the child's and adolescent's religious, political, racial, and social attitudes. Likewise, it appears in the child's values and ideals. By the time of puberty the individual has absorbed many social attitudes from his parents, teachers, and peer groups. Such media or mass communication as radio, television, and books have an important bearing on the attitudes of growing boys and girls. The child or adolescent is not likely to change his social attitudes significantly unless he finds that his present attitudes interfere with his social relations with others, especially his peers. The individual who isolated himself from the group during childhood because of unhappy early experiences will not readily enter into social activities with his peers when he reaches adolescence. Growth at each stage is but an extension of earlier learnings, all of which are integrated into the new learnings. These are not easily and readily modified unless the individual is aware that his established attitudes are interfering with his socialization.

An early study by Newcomb and Svehla (1937) furnished data that seemed to indicate a substantial relationship between parent and child's attitude toward war, communism, and church affiliation. A child's attitudes are imitative rather than based on reason. It has been observed that church membership and membership in one or another political party is usually based upon an early established emotional attitude rather than upon a real understanding of supporting factual data or the basic principles involved.

An early study by Frenkel-Brunswik (1948) was designed to throw light on the determinants of susceptibility to racial or ethnic prejudice and allied forms of undemocratic opinions and attitudes in children. From a total of 1,500 boys and girls of varied socioeconomic backgrounds, age 11-16, 120 children found to be extremely prejudiced or unprejudiced were selected for study. These were classified as ethnocentric (prejudiced) and liberal (unprejudiced). Based on a comparison of these two groups of children and their parents, the investigator arrived at the following overall conclusions:

> The parents of the ethnocentric child are highly concerned with status. They use more harsh and rigid forms of discipline which the child generally submits to rather than accepts or understands. . . . On the surface the ethnocentric child tends, especially in his more general statements, to idealize his parents. There are, however, indications that the parent-child relationship is lacking in genuine affection. In many ethnocentric children underlying feelings of being victimized are revealed by specific episodes, told by the children, of neglect, rejection and unjust punishment. The pressure to conform to parental authority and its externalized social values makes it impossible for the child to integrate or to express his instinctual and hostile tendencies. The lack of integration make for narrow and rigid personality. . . .
>
> By contrast, the liberal child is more oriented toward love and less toward power than is the ethnocentric child. He is more capable of giving affection since he has received more real affection. He tends to judge people more on the basis of their intrinsic worth than does the ethnocentric child who places more emphasis on conformity to social mores. The liberal child, on the other hand,

takes internal values and principles more seriously.... By virtue of the greater integration of his instinctual life he becomes a more creative and sublimated individual. He is thus more flexible and less likely to form stereotyped opinions about others. The interview ratings point toward a better developed, more integrated and more internalized superego. The unprejudiced child seems to be able to express disagreement with, and resentment against, the parents more openly, resulting in a much greater degree of independence from the parents and from authorities in general.

There is much evidence that children's perceptions and attitudes toward certain minority groups develop out of adult values in their home and the status quo; many children have opportunity for only the kind of learning about such groups which involves stereotypes and rejection, especially of groups that they have little or no personal contact with in their environment (Radke-Yarrow, Trager, and Davis, 1949). This is an important educational problem if we are to eliminate prejudices and intolerant behavior manifested toward certain groups.

Cultural Influences.   The dynamic role of culture was emphasized in Chapter 1. There it was pointed out that American children grow up and live in a highly technical and urban-oriented culture. They live in relatively small nuclear families in sharply differentiated neighborhoods, whose design follows certain social-economic patterns. Because of the wide differences in subcultures present in our society significant differences appear in the attitudes, ideals, and values of children, which may be observed at an early age. A number of these differences are discussed in the present chapter.

There are some universals in our culture that influence attitudes, ideals, and values at different age levels. This may be noted at an early age in attitudes toward material possessions. In the United States, early identification with possessions is so strong that a major preschool task is learning to share. Ugurel-Semin (1952) noted that selfishness is at its height at the four-to-six-year age level and only gradually diminishes thereafter. Children from large families are inclined to be slightly more generous than those from small families. The former get earlier practice in the art of sharing; they probably receive their sense of identity largely through intrafamily relationships. Americans, especially the middle class, value success and assume that each generation will outstrip the previous one. There is little sympathy for failure, the ne'er-do-well, the dropout, and the unemployed.

While Americans hail progress of a scientific, technical, and material nature, they are conservative in their attitudes toward social change. This accounts for the inconsistencies and incongruities in their moral codes as noted in their economic, social, and religious attitudes. For example, most children are taught something approximating the Christian ethic, with stress on charity, compassion, humility, altruism, love of fellowman, and cooperation. Yet the child may develop racial prejudice, aggressiveness, competitiveness, selfishness, and shrewdness bordering at times on ruthlessness. There are, however, forces at work today that lean toward a new set of changed ethics among many young people. In terms of attitudes, it may be that we are approaching a period of significant changes in certain universal attitudes and values.

Influences of Certain Background Factors. Attitudes of high school and college students toward national and world problems reflect the background of the students. Students from homes predominantly conservative on national problems will most likely reveal conservative characteristics, while students from homes with a liberal outlook toward national problems tend to display a liberal outlook.

In a study by Garrison (1961), of the world-minded attitudes of college students, it was noted that attitudes varied with the occupation of the father. The results presented in Table 9-2 show the average scores for world-minded

TABLE 9-2

Average Scores of College Students Residing in the Southeast
According to Occupation of Father (After Garrison)

Father's Occupation	Average Total Score
Farmer	100.4
Industrial and semi-skilled	105.5
Skilled	106.2
Clerical and sales	107.9
Business	106.6
Professional	114.4

attitudes for the six occupational groups studied. The lowest average world-minded attitude score was that of students from an agricultural background, while the highest average score was that from a professional background.

There is evidence from studies as well as general observations that one's perception and attitudes concerning interracial socialization are affected by racial membership and individual relationship with persons of other races. This is borne out in a study by Marascuilo and Levin (1966) with seventh-, eighth-, and ninth-grade students as subjects. Data were obtained from questionnaires completed by the students, designed to measure their attitudes toward a major reorganizational program, the purpose of which was to improve racial balance within the school. The data were obtained one year after the initiation of the program. The students were also requested to indicate the amount of interracial association in which they participated. The responses showed that students who had made friends from other racial groups were significantly more favorable toward interracial mixing than those who had not formed interracial friends.

A number of investigators have attempted to measure bigotry. Using attitude scales of the Likert type, Maranall (1967) studied the relation between some religious and political attitudes and two bigotry variables—anti-Semitic attitudes and anti-Negro attitudes. The subjects of the study consisted of four populations of college students:

1. Students with urban backgrounds at a Midwestern university.

2. Students with rural backgrounds at a Midwestern university.

3. Students with urban backgrounds at a Southern university.

The dividing line between rural and urban was drawn between communities of over 2,500 and those under 2,500.

Correlations ranging from .62 to .84 were obtained between anti-Semitism and anti-Negro attitudes. The correlations between bigotry score and other attitudes lead to the following conclusions:

1. The results show that most of the attitudes of political conservatism are significantly and positively correlated with both aspects of bigotry in all four populations studied.

2. In general, the religiosity variables are not highly or positively correlated with bigotry. An analysis of the populations studied suggest that a religious belief which stresses the more superstitious aspects of religious attitudes will yield higher positive correlations with bigotry or prejudice than one emphasizing the theistic or altruistic aspects.

3. Fundamentalist religious attitudes correlate positively and significantly with bigotry only in the Southern populations studied.

4. Mysticism, theism, ritualism, and altruism are positively correlated with both aspects of bigotry in only the Southern urban student population.

5. Fundamentalistic religious attitudes correlate positively and significantly with bigotry in only the Southern population.

6. Church-oriented attitudes are significantly and positively correlated to bigotry in only the Midwestern rural and Southern urban population.

Influence of Sex.   The attitude of peers toward school will vary with the sex and socioeconomic status. In the elementary school girls are expected to conform and display an interest in reading and other school activities; boys may assume an indifferent attitude toward studying while displaying an interest in sports, scouts, or some other outdoor activity. By the time boys and girls reach high school, certain changes occur. Older girls in junior high school become interested in boys and clothes, and socializing; boys are expected to show an interest in school in preparation for college and a vocation.

It has been noted that lower-class boys who belong to a peer group of middle-class boys show an interest in school and in going to college. On the other hand, middle-class boys in a predominantly lower-class group at school accept the values and attitudes of the lower class; they tend to assume an indifferent attitude toward school and show little interest in going to college (Pitt, 1956; Keisler, 1955).

Hallworth and Waite (1966) compared the value judgments of 155 boys and girls in the fourth year of secondary school in England on each of 36 concepts. The similarities and differences in the value judgments are in harmony with findings relative to the attitudes of adolescent boys and girls. The investigators conclude:

> For the boys, the most important cluster of concepts centers around success, ambition, reward and the future, and includes both games and study. For the girls,

the principal cluster is concerned with a feminine image and the future. Girls are apparently more concerned with themselves as women; games are prominent in this cluster, study is not; dress and home are important. . . . Boys also develop a cluster of attitudes identified with authority; girls develop a cluster identified with security. (p. 207.)

Educational Values and Class Status. An important differentiation of adolescents is that based on social class or socioeconomic status. Studies show that lower socioeconomic class adults generally place less value on formal education than do middle- and upper-class persons. This devaluation of education on the part of adults from the lower class is frequently reflected in the adolescent's lack of interest in school achievement; this then leads to withdrawal from school prior to graduation. Such a decision is anchored in the value system of the lower-class culture; it is not a rejection of parental values, and may be an affirmation of them.

With universal education, the widespread use of radio, television, and other educational media one would expect class differences to diminish considerably. However, there is ample evidence that there are class differences in attitudes and values. Considerable overlapping may be found. For example, many parents from the lower class are anxious that their children attend school regularly and perhaps go on to college. There are also parents from the middle class who display little concern for their children to attend school regularly and go on to college. Thus, we should be careful in making broad generalizations about differences between the attitudes, ideals, and values of children and adults from the lower and middle classes. These are some of the major differences usually found between parents and children from the lower class and middle class:

1. The motivation of lower-class children toward school instruction is generally low (Milner, 1951). He experiences more conflicts than his middle-class school mate with teachers. He lacks language facility and experiences more difficulties in reading and in learning abstract subject matter (Bernstein, 1959).
2. The lower-class child comes from a home background that seldom places much stress on education and remaining in school. He seldom receives encouragement from his parents as he progresses through the school program.
3. In a study by Griffith (1952), middle-class children conformed more closely to middle-class values, as usually found in the school program. Lower-class youngsters were more aggressive in their behavior. The lower-class child has more opportunities to learn physical aggression; he encounters more physical aggression with his siblings and peers.
4. The lower-class child sees little esthetic, theoretical, or social value in education. Intellectual attainment is usually unimportant to him, unless it can be used to satisfy his basic need for making money.
5. The lower-class child does not usually share the middle-class teacher's feelings about filthy talk, poor enunciation, and faulty grammar. The

speech of the child from the slums may be almost incomprehensible to a middle-class teacher, but it tends to satisfy the speech needs of most children from the slums.

6. The lower-class child seldom sees a reason for thrift; he has always lived on a marginal living standard. "For the typical lower-class child, faith in the future has received little support. He has learned instead that he had better grab while the grabbing is good. . . . ." (McCandless, 1967, p. 587.)

7. The lower-class adolescent usually has a low aspiration level in his educational and vocational goals—he is more realistic than his younger brother or sister.

Since the lower-class parents are usually more authoritarian than the middle-class parents, and children experience more physical punishment, we would expect them to have different attitudes toward disciplinary measures. This was noted in a study by Dolger and Ginandes (1946-47). The children were chosen from two schools in New York City which differed widely in their educational practices and in the socioeconomic and cultural status of the pupils. Attitudes were obtained from the children regarding what action should be taken against Jimmy, a six-year-old problem child. Also, the pupils were interviewed about disciplinary measures that would be appropriate for ten situations involving problem behavior.

Important differences were noted in the attitudes of the two groups of children relative to appropriate measures that should be taken for certain types of problem behavior. Children from low socioeconomic backgrounds were more inclined to hold the child himself responsible for the problem behavior and were more concerned with punishing such children than were children from high socioeconomic status and cultural background. The latter group of children seemed to sense an environmental factor associated with behavior to a greater degree than did the low-status children. Children from the low-status group expressed the opinion that a truant officer should see that a child who played "hookey" from school is punished; while the high-status children were inclined to blame the misconduct on circumstances at home, school, or elsewhere over which the problem child had no control. Children from the low-status group frequently referred to reform schools, truant officers, and jails, while children from the high status showed little or no familiarity with these guardians of the law.

The Influence of Schools. The schools are both directly and indirectly concerned with the molding of character—a process through which individuals take on the attitudes, ideals, and values of the society of which they are a part. Although the fundamental pattern of many attitudes, ideals, and values is laid down during the preschool years in the culture of the home and immediate environment, many of these early behavior patterns are altered as a result of experiences at school.

The accent on differences in attitudes and values of children from the lower and middle class grew out of a series of studies focusing attention on such differences. The data cited supported the viewpoint that the school was largely a middle-class institution with personnel and curriculum materials that stressed middle-class attitudes, ideals, and values. More recent studies indicate that the gap may be narrowing, especially in relation to educational needs. Medinnus (1962) found no significant differences between scores of lower- and middle-class adults on an Attitude Toward Education Scale.

The increased demand for education and skill is prolonging the period of education. Today as never before individuals from the different social class groups finish high school and continue their education in a technical school or college. Differences between attitudes of youngsters from rural areas or small towns and those from large urban areas are frequently as great or greater than those between social classes. Our criteria for success force the socially different youngsters to relinquish attitudes and values developed at home and in their immediate community and adopt broader and usually more liberal attitudes about different problems and issues. Teachers should be aware of social class differences, so that they can deal more effectively with children and adolescents from a social background that fosters attitudes and values different from those adhered to at school. However, teachers should be cautious in stereotyping or labeling children on the basis of social class. The common element among children from different backgrounds is likely to be far greater than differences that appear.

According to results obtained by Plant (1962), college attendance acts as a catalyst to speed up personality changes, including attitudes and values, that would ordinarily occur as the individual matures. This may well be noted in the weakening of an authoritarian attitude on the part of most students as a result of increased knowledge and maturity associated with college attendance. In harmony with this, Lehmann and others (1966) concluded from their study of changes in attitudes and values associated with college attendance, all groups tended to become less stereotypic in their beliefs, less dogmatic, and more receptive to new ideas. In some groups the males changed most; whereas in other groups the females changed.

Influence of Personality Structure. Perceptual research has furnished evidence that attitudinal changes are closely related to personality structure. Katz et al. (1956) advanced the idea that attitudes may serve to protect and enhance the ego of the individual. Resistance to attitude changes may arise from the possibility that a change would deprive the individual of an important defense mechanism. For example, negative attitudes of many Americans toward the Negro may stem from feelings of inadequacy. An anti-Negro attitude enables such individuals to automatically feel superior to a large segment of our population.

A study reported by Katz, McClintock, and Sarnoff (1957) was designed to test the hypothesis that the giving of insight into defense mechanisms will produce more attitudinal change in medium ego-defensive persons than in high and low ego-defensive persons. The procedure used was to test-measure attitude toward the Negro before and after exposure to experiences designed to give insight into the defensive and repressive mechanisms. The results of the study verified the hypothesis. The middle ego-defensive group showed the greatest attitudinal change. The low ego-defensive person showed very little changes, since his attitudes are not primarily defense mechanisms. The high ego-defensive person has such a strong need for maintaining his attitudes as a defense mechanism that he is not affected by experiences furnishing insight into such defense mechanisms.

In an earlier study by Katz et al. (1956) it was found that the development of insight into the self and the operation of defense mechanisms was more likely to produce attitudinal changes than was the furnishing of additional information which was contrary to exising attitudes. This has important educational implications and reveals the irrational nature of attitudes.

Summary

Attitudes, ideals, and values are among the most important outcomes learned at home, in the community, and at school. They develop out of experiences and are closely related to the culture with which the individual is identified. Ideals differ from attitudes in their ever-present imperative nature. Values are closely related to both attitudes and ideals; they refer to the importance one attaches to things or conditions. Needs are basic to the development of values.

The child identifies with adult figures, the first identification normally being with parents. The emergence of conscience is closely related to the child's early identification. This involves the internalization of the rules and standards of adults with whom he closely identifies. Self-esteem, like attitudes toward others, is learned and continuously modified by varied experiences.

Attitudes, ideals, and values are closely related to other aspects of development. One's self-concept begins with experiences of infancy; the nature of its development will depend upon interpersonal relations with parents, siblings, peers, teachers, and others with whom one is associated. The problem of developing sound attitudes and values is an educational one beginning at infancy and extending throughout the school program.

Two types of prejudice may be observed—pathological and normal. Labeling and categorizing are important to normal prejudgments. Children tend to adopt the labels used by parents in referring to different people. Deep-seated prejudices are most frequently found in authoritarian homes. In pathological prejudice the individual displaces his own conflicts and frustrations onto some convenient "scapegoat," and thus reduces his anxieties. It is very difficult to eradicate this kind of prejudice. Prejudices that are simply an outgrowth of the nature of one's culture are more easily eradicated.

Attitudes, ideals, and values are influenced by (1) the home, (2) sex, (3) class status, and (4) schools. The lower-class child is likely to be faced with conflicting attitudes, ideals, and values at school. Most teachers adhere fairly close to middle-class attitudes, ideals, and values. Both home and school orientation influence sex-role attitudes. There is considerable evidence that through education favorable attitudes toward peoples, institutions, and world affairs can be developed.

References

Adams, J. F. "Adolescent Opinion on National Problems," *Personnel and Guidance Journal*, Vol. 42 (1963), pp. 397-400.

Allport, G. W. *The Nature of Prejudice*, Reading, Mass.: Addison-Wesley, 1954.

Anderson, J. E. *A Survey of Children's Adjustment over Time, A Report to the People of Nobles County*. Minneapolis: Institute of Child Welfare and Development, University of Minnesota, 1959.

Appleby, L. "The Relationship between Rigidity and Religious Participation," *Journal of Pastoral Care*, Vol. 11 (1957), pp. 78-83.

Arglye, M. *Religious Behavior*. London: Kegan Paul, 1958.

Bernstein, B. "Social Class and Linguistic Development; a Theory of Social Learning," *British Journal of Sociology*, Vol. 9 (1959), pp. 169-174.

Bogardus, E. S. "Racial Distance Changes in the United States during the Next Thirty Years," *Sociology and Social Research*, Vol. 43 (1958), pp. 127-134.

Bühler, Charlotte. "Values and Beliefs in Our Time," *Educational Leadership*, Vol. 21 (1964), pp. 520-522, 541.

Centers, R. *The Psychology of Social Class*. Princeton U. P., 1949.

Cole, Luella. *Psychology of Adolescence*, 6th ed. New York: Holt, 1964.

Coopersmith, S. "A Method for Determining Types of Self-Esteem," *Journal of Educational Psychology*, Vol. 59 (1959), pp. 87-94.

_____. "Self-Esteem and Need Achievement as Determinants of Selective Recall and Repetition," *Journal of Abnormal and Social Psychology*, Vol. 60 (1960), pp. 310-317.

Dolger, L., and J. Ginandes. "Children's Attitude toward Discipline Related to Socioeconomic Status," *Journal of Experimental Education*, Vol. 15 (1946-47), pp. 161-165.

Frenkel-Brunswik, Else. "A Study of Prejudice in Children," *Human Relations*, Vol. 1, No. 3 (1948), pp. 295-306.

Garrison, Karl C. "A Comparative Study of the Attitudes of College Students toward Certain Domestic and World Problems," *Journal of Social Psychology*, Vol. 34 (1951), pp. 47-54.

_____. "Worldminded Attitudes of College Students in a Southern University," *Journal of Social Psychology*, Vol. 54 (1961), pp. 147-153.

Garrison, Karl C., Jr. "The Behavior of Clergy on Racial Integration as Related to a Childhood Socialization Factor," *Sociology and Social Research*, Vol. 51 (1967), pp. 209-219.

Garrity, F. D. "A Study of the Attitude of Some Secondary Modern School Pupils toward Religious Education," *Religious Education*, Vol. 56 (1961), pp. 141-143.

Gough, H. G., D. B. Harris, W. E. Martin, and M. Edwards. "Children's Ethnic Attitudes: I. Relationship to Certain Personality Factors," *Child Development*, Vol. 21 (1950), pp. 83-91.

Griffiths, W. *Behavior Difficulties of Children as Perceived and Judged by Parents, Teachers, and Children Themselves*. Minneapolis: U. of Minnesota Press, 1952.

Grossack, M. M. "Attitudes toward Desegregation of Southern White and Negro Children," *Journal of Social Psychology,* Vol. 46 (1957), pp. 299-306.

Hallworth, H. J., and G. Waite. "A Comparative Study of Value Judgments of Adolescents," *British Journal of Educational Psychology,* Vol. 36 (1966), pp. 202-209.

Huxley, J. *Knowledge, Morality, and Destiny.* New York: Mentor, 1960.

Jones, E. E., and T. Kohler. "The Effects of Plausibility on the Learning of Controversial Statements," *Journal of Abnormal and Social Psychology,* Vol. 57 (1958), pp. 315-329.

Katz, D., I. Sarnoff, and C. McClintock. "Ego Defense and Attitude Change," *Human Relations,* Vol. 9 (1956), pp. 27-45.

————. "The Measurement of Ego Defense as Related to Attitude Change," *Journal of Personality,* Vol. 25 (1957), pp. 465-474.

Keisler, E. R. "Peer Group Ratings of High School Pupils with High and Low School Marks," *Journal of Experimental Education,* Vol. 23 (1955), pp. 375-378.

Krathwohl, D. R., B. S. Bloom, and B. B. Masia. *Taxonomy of Educational Objectives: Handbook II: Affective Domain.* New York: McKay, 1964.

Lecky, P. *Self-Consistency.* New York: Island Press, 1945.

Lehmann, I. J., B. K. Sinha, and R. T. Harnett. "Changes in Attitudes and Values Associated with College Attendance," *Journal of Educational Psychology,* Vol. 51 (1966), pp. 89–98.

Lenski, G. E. "Social Correlates of Religious Interest," *American Sociological Research,* Vol. 18 (1953), pp. 533-544.

Maranall, G. M. "An Examination of Some Religious and Political Attitude Correlates of Bigotry," *Social Forces,* Vol. 45 (1967), pp. 356-362.

Marascuilo, Leonard A., and Joel R. Levin. "Inter- and Intra-racial Group Differences in the Perception of a Social Situation," paper read at the Fiftieth Anniversary Meeting of the American Educational Research Association, Chicago, 1966.

McCandless, B. R. *Children Behavior and Development,* 2nd ed. New York: Holt, 1967.

Medinnus, G. R. "The Development of a Parent Attitude toward Education Scale," *Journal of Educational Research,* Vol. 56 (1962), pp. 100-103.

Milner, Esther. "A Study of the Relationship between Reading Readiness in Grade One School Children and Patterns of Parent-Child Interaction," *Child Development,* Vol. 22 (1951), pp. 95-112.

Minuchin, Patricia. "Sex-Role Concepts and Sex Typing in Childhood as a Function of School and Home Environments," *Child Development,* Vol. 36 (1965), pp. 1033, 1048.

Morris, J. F. (ed.), II. "The Development of Adolescent Value Judgments," *Journal of Educational Psychology,* Vol. 28 (1958), pp. 1-14.

Myers, R. C. "The Academic Overachiever: Stereotyped Aspects," *Journal of Experimental Education,* Vol. 18 (1950), pp. 229-238.

Nelson, E. N. P. "Persistence of Attitudes of College Students," *Psychological Monographs,* Vol. 68, No. 373 (1954).

Newcomb, T. M., and G. Svehla. "Intra-Family Relationship in Attitude," *Sociometry,* Vol. 1 (1937), pp. 180-205.

Phillips, B. N. "Age Changes in Accuracy of Self-Perceptions," *Child Development,* Vol. 34 (1963), pp. 1041-1046.

Pilkington, G. W., P. K. Poppleton, and G. Robertshaw. "Changes in Religious Attitudes and Practices among Students during University Degree Courses," *British Journal of Educational Psychology,* Vol. 25 (1965), pp. 150-157.

Pitt, A. B. "An Experimental Study of Children's Attitudes Toward School in Auckland, N.Z.," *British Journal of Educational Psychology,* Vol. 26 (1956), pp. 25-30.

Plant, W. T. *Personality Changes Associated with a College Education.* U.S. Office of Education, Cooperative Research Branch Project No. 348, 1962.

Poppleton, P. K. and G. W. Pilkington. "The Measurement of Religious Attitudes in a University Population," *British Journal of Social and Clinical Psychology,* Vol. 2 (1963), pp. 20-36.

Radke, Yarrow, Marian, Helen Trager, and H. Davis. "Social Perceptions and Attitudes of Children," in R. G. Kuhlen and G. G. Thompson (eds.), *Psychological Studies in Human Development,* 2nd ed. New York: Appleton, 1963.

Redl, F., and W. Wattenberg. *Mental Hygiene in Teaching.* New York: Harcourt, 1951.

Sampson, D. L., and H. P. Smith. "A Scale to Measure World-minded Attitudes," *Journal of Social Psychology,* Vol. 45 (1957), pp. 99-106.

Schorr, A. *Social Security Bulletin,* February 1966.

Scott, W. S. "Personal Values and Group Interaction," in Dorothy Willner (ed.), *Decision, Values, and Groups,* Vol. I. New York: Pergamon, 1960.

Shimberg, B. "Information and Attitudes toward World Affairs," *Journal of Educational Psychology,* Vol. 40 (1949), pp. 206-222.

Stendler, C. B. "Social Class Differences in Parental Attitudes toward School and Grade 1 Level," *Child Development,* Vol. 22 (1951), pp. 36-46.

Stevenson, H. W., and E. C. Stewart. "A Developmental Study of Racial Awareness in Young Children," *Child Development,* Vol. 29 (1958), pp. 399-409.

Stoughton, M. L., and A. M. Ray. "A Study of Children's Heroes and Ideals," *Journal of Experimental Education,* Vol. 15 (1946), pp. 156-160.

Ugurel-Semin, R. "Moral Behavior and Moral Judgments of Children," *Journal of Abnormal and Social Psychology,* Vol. 47 (1952), pp. 463-474.

Washburn, W. C. "Patterns of Self-Conceptualization in High School and College Students," *Journal of Educational Psychology,* Vol. 52 (1961), pp. 123-131.

Williams, J. A. "Regional Differences in Authoritarianism," *Social Forces,* Vol. 45 (1966), pp. 273-277.

Zeligs, Rose. "Children's Favorable Attitudes toward Home and School," *Journal of Educational Research,* Vol. 60 (1966), pp. 13-21.

Part III

Psychosocial Development and Adjustment

Chapter 10

Socialization:
The Preschool Years

In Part II of this volume the emphasis was upon different aspects of growth —physical, motor-language-cognitive, intellectual—and attitudes and values. The interaction of the individual organism and his environment has been emphasized. All these aspects of growth are involved in socialization. The infant is born into both a physical and social world. What he becomes depends to a marked degree upon the nature of his socialization. This chapter emphasizes socialization during the preschool years. These are the critical years in the socialization of the child, since they are the formative years and provide the framework for later development. However, socialization can best be thought of as a major lifelong task. This is suggested by a definition offered by Hoffman and Hoffman (1966, p. 222): "Socialization may be defined as the process by which an individual learns the alternative modes of behavior available in various social situations and the consequences of adopting each mode."

Introduction: The Child in America

The Child Population. The increase of our child population is phenomenal. The task of caring for and educating these children presents a challenge to our adult citizens. Based on fertility levels somewhat lower than prevailed in 1960-63, the child population under 15 in the United States in 1980 may reach 75.7 million. This is a 35 percent increase as compared with 56.1 million children in 1960. By 1985, children under 15 would number 84.1 million, according to projections of the population by the U.S. Bureau of the Census in 1964. The same projections indicate a 50 percent increase in size of the maternal and newborn infant populations from the middle 1960's to the middle 1980's. (U.S. Bureau of Census, 1964) Births in the fiscal year 1984-85 are estimated at 6.33 million as compared with the estimate for 1964-65 at 4.26 million.

With growth of the child population based on these projections, the ratio of children to adults would increase from 73 children under 15 per 1,000 adults 25 to 64 years of age in 1960 to 737 per 1,000 in 1985, an increase of nearly

10 percent in children to be cared for by adults during their most productive years.

Child-Rearing Practices.   Child-rearing practices in the United States are being influenced more and more by results of scientific studies. A large percentage of mothers rely upon expert opinion to help them meet different problems. Benjamin Spock's famous child-rearing book has almost replaced the Bible for many mothers since 1950. The gap in differences in child-rearing practices of different social classes has become smaller, due to the increased homogeneity of our culture and its widespread educational media. Also, members of the lower class receive a higher income and have greater security than formerly, and thus are better able to plan their lives and the care and education of their children.

There is today an upward mobility in our society. Better incomes and increased education have combined to produce parents who have greater concern for the education and welfare of their children, and as a means for improving their status in life. It is within the culture of the "American type" that the child is being reared and prepared for school. The school has become in the minds of most parents the one relatively sure way to a better and richer way of life for their children.

Increased Attention to the Preschool Years.   Following World War II, there was set in motion a social revolution in this country which it is hoped will give real meaning to our concept of a democratic society. The revolution has entered into the organization and practices of our schools. The task of our schools has been difficult because of traditional barriers to new innovations. Also, differences between schools are so great that we cannot apply the same policies or set forth the same objectives, or make use of the same instructional materials.

Out of the awareness of the educational, psychological, and social effects of a deprived environment has come forth much experimentation and a changed philosophy of preschool education: increased recognition of the preschool years as important years for certain learnings. The purpose of the kindergarten is to prevent the tragic and continuous failure of millions of American children to develop their learning potentials during the early years, when there is the greatest promise. If failure and dropouts are to be reduced, beginnings must be made in the preschool years so that children will have completed those learning tasks essential for successful work in elementary and secondary grades.

Early Social Behavior

During the preschool years the child develops into a distinctly socialized individual. Most of the important types of social behavior essential to adjustment to others begin to develop in infancy, and are expanded and enriched during the preschool years. The ill effects of an inadequate social environment have been recognized in recent years and major steps are being taken on a national basis to provide children from such environments richer experiences and broadened social experiences.

The Beginnings of Emotional Behavior. The infant's first developmental task is the organismic one of recovering from the crisis of birth and adapting to conditions of living in a particular type of environment where as a helpless being he is cared for by adults. The involuntary actions of bodily mechanics enable the neonate to maintain a balanced state and meet emergencies. The reflexes and responses that become differentiated into emotional behavior are part of the homeostatic system that protects him from certain dangers and enables him to meet varying emergencies. This may be observed in the startle response of the infant to a sudden, violent auditory or visual stimuli, loss of support, and physical restraint. The startle response is characterized by generalized mass activity and gross motor movements, including muscular flexion of the fingers, kicking, squirming, and crying. The mass activity restores an internal balance and within a few months after birth it seems to express a feeling of delight. Out of this state of general excitement that appears in early infancy other emotional responses subsequently develop through the process of differentiation and control.

Although students of child psychology continue to study the emergence of emotional behavior, there is general agreement concerning certain aspects of emotional development:

1. The differention of emotional behavior appears early and becomes more pronounced as the individual develops.
2. Individuality of emotional behavior appears in early infancy, and increases throughout childhood.
3. The specific patterns of emotional behavior are learned ways of responding to needs. They follow the principles of learning set forth for other forms of behavior.
4. There is a relationship between the nature of a child's emotional responses and the level of his maturation.

Initially, the child responds primarily to external stimuli. Later through the process of conditioning a behavior pattern is set forth whereby the child responds not only to the original external stimulus but also to a stimulus that has been repeatedly associated with the original stimulus. This may be noted in connection with the hungry child who cries both at the sight of his bottle of milk and at the sight of the mother who feeds him. Also, the reaction pattern to an external stimulus may be so learned that the response can be evoked by symbolic representation of the original stimulus.

Early Affection Pattern. The infant's enjoyment of the mother's careful handling of him, her soft warm body, her smiles, and her soothing voice is the beginning of affectionate behavior. In the early stages there is little differentiation and he will smile in answer to a smile. At this stage everyone can share in the delight of the infant. During the second half of the first year he frequently stares at strangers, then begins to cry. (However, once the infant has completely scrutinized the face of the stranger without being required to respond, he will display less anxiety and fear. By gently helping him pick up one of his toys, a friendly relationship may be established, followed by a smile.)

Affection Breeds Affection.   The mother who smiles at her infant child will soon be greeted with a smile. The stranger who bides his time and then displays affection toward the infant will most likely be greeted with affection. Institutional care, with its lack of motherly love, is apt to have definite ill-effects upon early childhood development. Rheingold (1956) noted that when institutional children were given more caretaking by an adult they showed an increase in their smiling rate to that caretaker as well as to other adults.

Several characteristics are notable in children who have been deprived of love. These have been grouped by Hymes (1963) as follows: (1) usually very silent (2) smaller in height and weight than would normally be for their age, (3) have little emotional drive, (4) have poor intellectual ability, (5) have a limited vocabulary, and (6) generally unable to mix with others and be accepted by others.

The importance of infancy for the optimum development of the preschool child is indicated by many studies. Recently Stewart and others (1966) interviewed mothers of 37 children with the "hyperactive child" syndrome, and of 36 normal first-grade children, relative to the difficulties of these children during infancy. Comparisons were made of the frequency of difficulties among the hyperactive children and those among a group of control children. The results, presented in Table 10-1, show that hyperactive children displayed difficulties

TABLE 10-1

Comparisons of the Frequency of Certain Difficulties of "Hyperactive" Children with Those of a Controlled Group. (Copyright, the American Orthopsychiatric Association, Inc., reproduced by permission.)

	Hyperactive	Control
Infant feeding problems	10	3
Infant sleeping problems	8	1
Colic	9	3
Poor health in first year	9	1
Delayed speech development	13	2

during infancy to a much greater degree than the normal first-graders. Closely related to this researchers from the Institute of Child Health in Birmingham, England (1966) noted that when infants become fat they tend to stay over-weight. Among 269 school children treated for obesity, 118 had been over-weight since infancy. Prevention of obesity should begin in infancy.

Passivity and Dependence.   There is evidence from studies reported by Kagan and Moss (1962) that early passivity may be linked with direct forms of passivity during late childhood and adolescence. The investigators state (p. 79):

> . . . Intensive study of the observations on the school-age children who fell at the behavioral extremes of this dimension suggested that the tendency toward passivity during preadolescence was already apparent during the first two years of life. Passivity during the first three years was significantly associated with a con-

sistent cluster of school-age behavior (ages 6 to 10): avoidance of dangerous activity, absence of physical and verbal aggression, conformity to parents, and timidity in social situations.

A study by Gottesman (1960) involving 34 pairs of identical and 34 pairs of fraternal twins (same sex) indicated that a dimension of social withdrawal versus social extraversion may have a genetic component. This finding combined with the evidence that differences in passivity and dependency appears at an early age suggest a likely constitutional correlate of a passive approach to environmental stress.

Passivity was found by Kagan and Moss (1962) to be more characteristic of girls than of boys and more stable for females than for males. It is frequently assumed that this difference is largely a by-product of training. However, studies by Bell (1960) and Knop (1946) indicate that even neonatal girls are more likely than neonatal boys to display motoric passivity. Also, Harlow (1962) found from studies of the activities of infant monkeys that infant male *macaques* tended to make threatening gestures and were less inclined to withdraw in the face of attack than the female infants. This suggests that constitutional differences in activity level do exist between males and females during infancy and early childhood.

Aggressive Behavior.   Aggression is another behavior system that begins its growth during early childhood. The early display of aggression is a regular concomitant of development. The hitting and pushing of a playmate, the destruction of a sibling's doll house, and the nasty verbal attacks on the mother may be noted in the behavior of a large percentage of preschool children.

Data presented by Kagan and Moss (1962, p. 100) support the hypothesis that preschool aggression in girls is met with more punishment than similar behavior in boys. Thus the potential for conflict over aggression is greater for females than for males, since the pattern of social rewards and traditional sex-role standards of behavior act to discourage direct aggression in girls, even during the preschool years. We would accordingly expect that aspects of aggression would be more stable for males than for females. Kagan and Moss found this to be true. Overt aggression during the preschool years is related to adult aggression for men but not for women.

Emergence of the Self-Concept. The importance of one's self-concepts has been emphasized in recent years. The total behavior of the preschool child is greatly influenced by the concepts he has of himself. The infant is born with a physiological self. He is born into an environment to which he reacts. However, the distinction between the self and environment is not clear during infancy, and true personality in all its aspects does not begin its unique functioning until the child has learned to discriminate between the self and nonself. Only then can the child start developing those inner patterns of emotions, reactions, ideas, and feelings or attitudes toward objects, people, and forces in his environment.

The self, characterized by many researchers as highly complex and primarily perceptual, is actually built from many perceived experiences. The child learns about his selfhood from his experiences and the reactions of others to him. Gradually the raw perceptual materials regarding the self are transformed by the mind into a conceptual material and thus, as Staines implies, the self is both perceptual and conceptual (Staines, 1965, p. 406).

The psychiatrist Abram Blau has traced the emergence of the self to three separate levels or stages of development. The first stage, he claims, is the one of *no self,* the stage occupied by the newborn infant, who is one step removed from being a physical part of his mother. In the infant's yet naïve view he is still one with her, and like his mother's breast which he suckles, the whole world is part of him. He is at this stage, says Blau, totally devoid of objective reality (Blau, 1956). As the infant grows and develops he enters the second stage where he begins to develop a sense of *I* as separate from *you.* It is in this highly self-centered stage that the child's parents assume major importance as his protectors. Additional development brings the child into a third stage—his relationship with others. He begins to see himself as a person apart from and different from others, and he gains a gradual awareness of his weaknesses and his strengths.

It is during this first year of life, in that transitional period between no-self and first awareness of self, that the child needs a sense of physical and emotional closeness to his mother. It is the feeling of security and confidence gained during this period that will make it possible for him to stand alone eventually. In the earliest stages the self-concept develops in the interaction of the individual with those whom he has labeled as "significant others" (his mother, father, nurse, siblings) the earliest and most crucial being the child's interaction with his mother. The self-concept, Blau claims, is made up of the reflected appraisals of these "others" who intimately provide the rewards and punishments in a person's life. If these reflections are salutory, a healthy self will be produced, if the appraisals are negative the result would be an unhealthy self.

Anderson (1961) suggests that what is demanded by significant people is considered valuable by the child and what the significant others reject is considered bad. For every bad portion located in the self-concept there are good portions erected and emphasized and enhanced in order to pull a balance (for example, "I'm not smart, but I'm honest"). To the extent that the child will find himself threatened (afraid of losing security or love) or inadequate, or unacceptable (not smart) to those he depends on, to that extent will he restructure such traits (honesty) within himself and even overemphasize them in order to restore a balance toward safety, security, and survival. Thus we see how character traits become part of the structure of the self, and may be employed by the self as compensatory or defense mechanisms in order to insulate the self against psychological discomfort. Anderson maintains that trait functions are established only after experience has shown its usefulness (that is, it will have brought a certain result from a significant person). She cites as an example the feeling of security and freedom from threat experienced by the self-structure of obedience. From this it is possible to conclude that those structural traits which have not produced interpersonal functions, or for those that will have produced painful consequences, will not be accepted as part of the pyschological image of the self.

A child's self-concept rises in an interpersonal setting and feelings about the self are established early in life and modified by subsequent experience. It is the significant people, with their pressures, attitudes, demands, and feelings, who bestow the self-structure and content in the self-concept so that the growing child and later the adult will have guideposts to measure up to or rebel against. Without the interactionary experiences which set up expectancies or anticipations in the child, namely that this kind of act will bring that kind of response, life would be chaotic.

Self-love, according to Banham (1950, p. 288) does not usually occur until the second year. She states:

> During the second year, among the objects of the child's affections may be included himself. He clings to his toys, clothes, or chair, and collects small objects. He attracts attention to himself and cries at interference. From this phase, within the second and third year, he passes to one where affectionate behavior is shown largely to adults, but also to other children as well as himself.

Blau (1956, p. 90) indicates that growth of the self strives from semidependence to complete independence and reaches its epitome with the ability of the individual to give himself freely in love to others. Staines (1965, pp. 406-407) sees the self in three different phases:

1. *The cognized or known self*—which comprises all of the characteristics of the person recognized as part of the *"Me."* (This may or may not be related to objective reality or to the view held of the self by others.)
2. *The other self*—what the individual thinks others think of him, (e.g., the teacher thinks I'm no good in English).
3. *The ideal self*—consists of part wish and part ought and refers to a standard the individual has set for himself.

Thus we have seen that all selves start out as no-selves and become at first narcissistically self-centered. Consequently, the infant can only receive. As love and attention are received, the infant develops an awareness of self which later matures in a capacity to give love to others. The important point to make here, and which will be referred to in a later section, is that a person has to have had experienced adequate love before he can expend it on others.

Individuality in Behavior. It was pointed out in Chapter 3 that differences in behavior are observable in infants soon after birth. Some infants are very active, turning a great deal even while asleep; others are considerably less active. The question may be raised: Do differences that may be observed during the early months tend to persist? According to Chess and Birch (1959), individuality in behavior appears early in life and tends to persist. A longitudinal analysis of the continuity of behavioral reactivity from early infancy was made by Chess and others with 74 children as subjects. The data gathered consisted of six detailed interviews with the mothers during this period. An analysis of the interview data indicated that a passive approach to new situations was relatively stable over this period. A striking consistency in the child's reaction pattern to a new situation was noted, whether it was a bath, the introduction of solid foods, vaccinations, reaction to strangers, or the first contact with the nursery school at three years.

Social Development

Social development during the preschool years follows the principles of development set forth in Chapter 2. There is a gradual and continuous development of social behavior consistent with the needs, abilities, and opportunities of each child. The quality of the child's behavior becomes more appropriate for different situations, indicating increased differentiation of responses. The roles of maturation and learning may be observed in each social response.

Aggression During Early Childhood. Aggression appears during infancy, and develops as a result of maturation and learning. It appears when the child's normal behavior pattern is blocked. A study by King (1966) involving a small group of kindergarten children showed that the ratio of unfriendly acts to the total number of acts made by one child to another during free play was strongly related to the mean distance maintained by the second child from the first. The mean distances, however, were found to reduce in most cases when a prized toy was juxtaposed with the first.

Aggressiveness is especially strong among children who are highly frustrated and want to dominate or who are identified with an aggressive adult (Levin and Sears, 1956). Boys are usually more aggressive than girls as illustrated in Figure 10-1 (Sears, 1951). Aggression varies according to the time of the day, the setting of the play situation, and the degree of familiarity with the other children. The better the child knows the other children in his play group, the more likely he is to display aggressive behavior. Also, children tend to be more aggressive when there is an adult around whose attention they want to attract (Siegel, 1957). There is an increase in aggression from two to four years followed by a decline (Walters, 1957).

Cooperative Behavior. Since children of two or three years of age are self-centered and quarrelsome, there is little cooperation in their play with other children. Even with adults they cooperate little because the adult has a tendency to give in to the child and to allow him to have his own way. By the end of the third year, however, cooperative play and group activities are more frequent and longer in duration. With practice, the child learns to cooperate with other children and to play in an increasingly harmonious manner. The stronger the ties of friendship between young children, the more cooperative is their play.

Almost all young children show a strong tendency to be "bossy." The child attempts to secure materials that he wants from other children, and to direct and influence the behavior of his playmates. From three years of age on, ascendancy increases with the increase in opportunities for social contacts. This reaches its

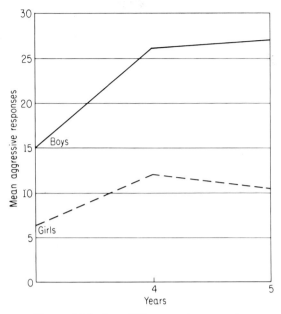

Figure 10-1. Sex differences in aggression
during the preschool years. (After Sears.)

peak around the fifth year. While ascendant behavior is increasing, there is a
marked decrease in isolate behavior, but submissive behavior changes little.

Where authoritarian child-training methods are used in the home to force
cooperation, children frequently develop negative attitudes and tend to be un-
cooperative or aggressive when parental authority is absent; while children
brought up in more democratic homes tend to be more friendly and cooperative
(Highberger, 1956).

Friendships During the Preschool Years.   For the most part, the young
child's friends will consist of the adults in the family, siblings, and children in
the immediate neighborhood. Only if the child attends Sunday school, nursery
school, or kindergarten does the circle of his companions enlarge. The young
child's relationships at home play an important role in his adjustment to children
outside the home. Only children or those with siblings widely separated in age or
of a different sex are likely to be withdrawn when they are with other children.
When the siblings are of the same sex, the child has more difficulty in associating
with peers of the opposite sex. The child who is younger than the playmates
available for him to play with strives to keep up with them and is dominated by
them. If he is older than his playmates and his siblings, he generally is "bossy"
and becomes their leader. This early play experience with siblings and companions outside the home has a marked influence on how successfully the child
makes the transition to school.

Young children show far less stability in their friendships than older children. Because their companions are, in reality, playmates rather than true friends, children are likely to lose interest in their companions when their own play interests change. Kindergarten children sometimes change friends many times during a weekend period. Boys usually change their friends more often than girls. The child's need for friends is best met by those who are similar to him in interests and like to do the things he likes to do. Similarity in interests facilitates expressions of affection and provides him an outlet for self expression. In a study of Oriental and Caucasian children, McCandless and Hoyt (1961) observed that the children preferred as their companions children of their own race and sex, since they felt more "at home" with children from a background similar to theirs, not because of prejudice at an early age.

Imaginary playmates are common among young children, especially when parent-child relationships are unfavorable or when the child has few opportunities for real playmates. It is a natural developmental phenomenon in many children and is especially characteristic of the age period 2½-4½ years. This is the time when the craving for friendship with other children begins to appear. The child who is unable, for one reason or another, to satisfy this craving frequently compensates with imaginary companions. This, however, is not a satisfactory solution to the lonely-child problem. Having learned to play with an imaginary companion, the child does not get the training in social cooperation essential to satisfactory adjustment to real children. He is likely to acquire the habit of dominating his playmates, which is possible with an imaginary playmate but frequently is not possible with a real child. When he discovers that the technique that worked so successfully with his imaginary playmate does not work with real children, the child is likely to become a maladjusted member of the group.

Personal-Social-Cultural Development.   The preschool child's self-concept has an important bearing on his personal-social-cultural development. The child reared in poverty with its accompanying handicaps experiences failure wherever he meets middle-class norms. These experiences have an adverse effect upon his personal development, social development, intellectual development, and self concept.

The poor in America, who are largely of lower-class social status, are seldom part of this cultural world. They live largely in isolation from the middle class, residentially, culturally, and socially. In response to their deprived lives they develop ways of coping with problems of their lives that lead to distinctive styles of living. Their mode of living may best be characterized as a subculture of poverty. The child reared in such a culture acquires the attitudes and behaviors of that culture. Such a child is at a distinct disadvantage in a society dominated by middle-class cultural norms. In the typical American middle-class culture certain forms of behavior are acquired at different age levels. Various attempts have been made to determine the forms of behavior characteristic of the different age levels. Based on the different studies bearing on this, the writers have formulated a list of behaviors characteristic of ages 1 through 5 years. These are presented in Table 10-2.

The development of the self is realized through satisfying experience. (Courtesy Eliot Pearson—Tufts Univ.)

TABLE 10-2

Personal-Social-Cultural Development

Age	Behavior
One year	Cooperates in dressing. Gives toy when asked. Finger feeds. Mastering use of cup. Eats a wide variety of table foods. Sleeps 14 hours a day. Aware of strangers and often balky at being handled by them.
Two years	Can play alone. Grabs toys away from other children. Plays mama and daddy, feeding teddy bears and dolls and wiping their noses. Can be stubborn and strong-willed.
Three years	Uses spoon well. Puts on shoes but cannot fasten them. Takes turns and can sometimes wait and share.
Four years	Can wash and dry face and hands. Goes on errands. Plays cooperatively.
Five years	A "little man" or "little lady." Dresses self, eats well, can help set table or clear off. Can dry dishes. Plays organized games, taking different roles. Believes anything he is told.

Sex Identification. During the preschool period children identify with their own sex, which is, of course, dependent upon their ability to discriminate sex differences. In the study by Katcher (1955) four-, five-, and six-year-olds readily assigned the correct sex to adults based upon clothing, hair style, genitals, and breasts, in that order. In an earlier study Rabban (1950) compared the sex discrimination ability of nursery-school and lower-elementary-school from two different social classes. He concluded:

> (a) Three-year-old boys and girls of both groups show incomplete recognition of sex differences and as a group are unaware of any appropriateness of sex-typed toy objects. (b) The fourth and fifth years are periods of growth in clarification of sex rôle for working class boys, while the sixth year is particularly significant for middle class boys. (c) Working class girls accept the sex-appropriate pattern by six years of age, but middle class girls do not fully acquiesce to the definition of appropriate sex-patterning even by the eighth year, when all other groups have accepted the social expectations.

An investigation by DeLucia (1963) made use of a toy preference test for studying sex-role identification. The subjects were from five school grades, kindergarten through the fourth grade. Photographs of 52 familiar toys were judged by a panel of young adults and rated on a nine point scale from 1—masculine to 9—feminine. From these were taken 24 pairs which were used in this study. Then, a pair of pictures was presented to the child and the child was asked which toy shown in the picture he would most like to play with.

Sex differences were manifested in toy preferences. The principal finding of this study was that with increasing age, boys made more appropriate responses than girls, supporting the Freudian hypothesis of sex-role identification. These results are in harmony with those obtained by Rabban, and reveal that sex identification may be manifested at an early age.

The Development of Role-Playing Ability. In any social group different roles appear. The preschool child cannot assume the role of a school-age child, adolescent, or adult. However, in his imaginative games he frequently assumes a specific role. This "role playing" is commonly considered an important rehearsal device for the development of fully socialized behavior. The results of a study reported by Bowers and others (1965) revealed that verbal intelligence contributes to role playing ability during childhood, while age contributes significantly to dramatic acting test scores, that is, the ability to portray others.

Children's descriptions of their age-mates' behavior show that they ascribe roles to each other, such as being a fast runner, a "crybaby," a toy-grabber, a hitter, or a sulker. No age trends were noted by Radke-Yarrow and others (1963) in their study of social perception and attitudes of 250 kindergarten, first-grade, and second-grade children, although many misconceptions and distortions of facts appeared among the older as well as the younger children. The investigators concluded that changes with age indicated an increasing crystallization of attitudes (p. 423). (a) Where picture interpretations are made in racial or religious terms rationalizations are given for the behavior projected. (b) The attitudes expressed by the child toward a given group tend to be the same each time that group appears. (c) A philosophy of behavior toward persons or groups is expressed. (d) The group labeled and its "meaning" become attached to people rather than to symbols or institutions or behavior. (e) The child shows personal involvement in responding to the pictures, sometimes through identifying himself with the child pictured, sometimes in showing emotional reactions to groups other than his own.

Social Acceptance–Popularity.   When the child begins to play with other children, his acceptance or rejection by them soon becomes apparent. Whether he is popular or not is not necessarily determined by his activity in the group. Sometimes the aggressively bossy child, who pushes himself into everything, is thoroughly disliked by other children. The outstanding trait that makes for popularity among young children is the acceptance of a situation, such as willingness to do what others do, offering no resistance, complying with requests, and accepting gracefully what happens. The popular child is conscientious in his conformity to the group ways. Girls at this age are more popular than boys with members of both sexes. Bright children are generally more popular than less bright. The child who is less dependent on adults and who participates more in social activities is more popular than the dependent child. However, as children learn to function in a group, they become less dependent on adults. There is no marked sex difference in dependency on adults or in social participation.

The unpopular child at the preschool age, on the other hand, is one who attacks vigorously, who strikes frequently, or pushes and pulls. Personal affronts and lack of respect for the property rights of others do not win friends for him. Added to the aggressive behavior of unpopular children are frequent attempts to escape responsibility, such as clinging to an adult or running away, dawdling; refusals to comply to the requests of others; failure to conform to the routine. Furthermore, the unpopular child usually has objectionable personality traits. The child who is rejected by others often tries to force himself into the group, and this increases his unpopularity. The child who is handicapped, as is true of children with hearing problems, often fights to become a member of a group and its leader. However, if challenged by the group he will usually withdraw and play alone. Being rejected by others tends to make a child "self-bound," which sets up barriers that intererfere with possible acceptance as the child grows older.

Influences Affecting Early Social Development

The early identification of the child with a parent or other adult figure has been emphasized by many students of child development. This identification may be thought of as having two aspects—emotional and behavioral. Emotional identification involves the nature of the relationship of the child with his parents or other adults, and may be observed in the warm, positive relationship of a parent or other adult to a particular child. Or the relationship may be one of indifference or hostility, especially when the child was unwanted or when the adult either consciously or unconsciously uses the child for his own selfish purposes or goals.

The behavioral aspect of identification may be observed as the child attempts to imitate some adult. This usually happens in good parent-child relations, and is sufficiently evident that others refer to this as an hereditary characteristic.

The Role of the Mother.   In Western culture the tasks of satisfying the infant's needs for food, cleanliness, and physical comfort are regarded, under normal conditions, as being the responsibility of the mother. Usually mothers spend more time with their children than do other members of the family; therefore, any adequate study of children, particularly infants and the very young, has been and must be concerned with the relationships between mother and child. Although this relationship is essential for the infant's survival, it is also important for normal development. Concerning this Sears, Maccoby, and Levin (1957, p. 15) have stated:

> The mother plays a central part, for she is the most common element in her child's experience. She it is who does the changing—or tries to. In so doing, she must not only establish in her mind what new behavior is to be added to the child's repertory of acts, but she must devise ways of training him. Not all her interactions with him are purposefully designed to this end, of course. Much that she does, day in and day out, is simply caretaking or enjoyment of him as another human being whom she loves. Sometimes, too, she reacts to him as an annoying person, and she hurts or frustrates him.

Mothering consists of responding to the infant when he cries, feeding him when he is hungry, protecting him from cold and excessive light and sound. Montagu (1963) has presented evidence that physical contact—petting, patting, cuddling—has an impact on degrees of contentedness, alertness, and vigor in the infant and increases the ease with which the infant's demands may be satisfied. Interestingly enough, much speculation about baby care has been stimulated by Harlow (1957, 1962), who has reported that baby monkeys show a distinct need for care involving warmth and contact comfort.

The Role of the Father.   Just as the mother's personality and adjustments are important to her ability to care for her children, the father's personality and his adjustments are important to the mother's happiness and to other family experiences to which a child is exposed. Usually, it is the father's interests, educational background, occupation, socioeconomic status, and place in a community that determine the geographical location of the home, its size, its furnishings, and the amount and quality of play space, toys, books, playmates, and recreations available to the child. When the father does not reside in the home with his children, because of divorce, affiliation with the armed services, or an occupation that keeps him away from the family most of the time, the amount of financial support he lends to his wife determines the amount and quality of his children's earliest life experiences. An important developmental task that appears even during early childhood is that of learning appropriate sex-role behavior. The absent father cannot adequately give his children a model of maleness, and, as we have indicated, this developmental task is one of the most important ones in the socialization of the child. To both boys and girls, a father is the supreme authority on everything objective and factual. (Children generally turn to their mothers on subjective matters and the subtleties of social relationships.) The influence of a father's maleness is exerted not merely through interactions between himself and his child but also through his attitudes toward other members of the family and his general behavior patterns. A boy will observe the ways which his father treats elderly people, the politeness extended to a woman, the protective attitudes toward girls in the family. One father, described by Pitcher (1963, p. 90), spoke—probably unconsciously—with a high voice when talking to his daughter but used a deep bass voice when speaking to his son.

Influence of Social Class.   The social class of the child's parents has an important bearing both directly and indirectly on his social development. The education of the parents, income-level of the home, goals and values of the parents are closely related to their social class and thus the social development of the children. These influences may be observed in the behavior and self-concepts of children during their preschool years.

Using 112 three- and four-year-old children as subjects McKee and Leader (1955) studied the relation of social-culture background to competitive behavior. The children were equally divided as to age, sex and middle or lower socioeconomic status. Two judges acting independently rated each child on a four-point rating scale for both aggression and competition. The results showed considerably more competition among children from low socioeconomic backgrounds. Likewise, more aggression was observed among the low socioeconomic children. In all subgroup comparisons significantly more competition was found among children from low socioeconomic status than among children from upper-middle-class backgrounds; however, clear-cut sex and age differences in aggression did not appear. The lack of clear-cut sex differences may be a result of records obtained by the judges of both overt behavior and verbalizations. There is evidence that as children develop boys tend to display more overt aggression, whereas girls display more verbal aggression (Durrett, 1959).

Influence of Nursery School Experiences.   It is evident that individuals "see" different things in the same social situation. These perceptions (that is, interpretations of a situation based on previous knowledge and experience) vary from one individual to another. The Estvans (1959) conducted a study to determine how a child's social perception is related to urban and rural differentials, sex and intelligence. They established two questions to serve as guidelines for their study.

1. Is social perception related to variables such as sex, race, and social status among three-year old and four-year old children?
2. Does social perception develop rapidly during nursery school years or is that a period of relative stability?

Estvan's (1965) study covered a two-year period in which 78 nursery school children were involved in 129 interviews. One-half of the children were selected from the housing project in which Wayne State University (origin of the study) was located; the other half was selected from various surrounding areas in order to balance the representation of racial and socioeconomic groups.

Interviews were conducted of individual and projective type based on a series of fourteen life-situation pictures. These pictures were created to reflect three social backgrounds.

1. A community depicting rural life and urban life situations,
2. A social status block contrasting upper class and lower-class situations,
3. A child-adult block presenting situations commonly associated with the child-adult or age differentials.

The results of this study indicated that nursery school children's perceptions are related to sex, race, and social status. Differences were evident in each group comparison. The greatest difference appeared in the area of values and attitudes, while the fewest occurred in the awareness of a space-time setting or field. Specific differences are:

1. Boys and girls differ in social perceptions. Girls exhibit more cognitive aspects and a more positive approach to life situations. Boys are more neutral. Although boys and girls share interest in home, the patterns are more consistent for the girls. Girls are more aware of social status (rejected two low socioeconomic life situations included in the series).
2. Caucasion and Negro children differ in social perceptions. Negro children display more cognitive aspects of perception. In their mode of response the Negro is more noncommittal; he takes longer to become involved to the point of expressing feelings. The Caucasion child reacts more definitely to the whole interview. Both groups share preference for a nice home and both reject low socioeconomic living. The Negro has a greater recognition of the church; the identification of the girls with life situations may reflect the place of religion and matriarchal family patterns in the Negro subculture.
3. Low-status and high-status children differ in their social perceptions. The higher status children are more superior in recognition. Lower-class children do not seem concerned over lower status living. Children from the higher class are more boy conscious, while the lower class is oriented toward the girl. This may reflect class differentials regarding the role of the male in the family.

The nursery school period is one of rapid development in social perception. There are significant changes between the three- and four-year olds. The greatest gains occur in the recognition of life situations and the development of feelings about them. What most educators are trying to do is to lay a broad and firm foundation for further learning by developing social perception, curiosity, open-mindedness, self-assurance, and showing children how to learn. "The attempt must be made," according to Deutsch, "to engage the child as an active participant in the learning, rather than as a passive recipient of a school experience" (Special Report, 1966).

Continuity and Stability of Social Development.   Two questions may be raised about social development: (1) Does a pattern of social behavior appear during the preschool years? (2) If a pattern of social development appears during the preschool years, to what extent is this a continuous and somewhat stable pattern? Results from studies by Kagan and Moss (1962), cited earlier in this chapter, indicate that passivity and aggression (especially among males) tend to persist from the preschool years into the adult years.

In a short-term longitudinal study of continuity and stability of early social development Emmerich (1966) used as subjects 53 middle-class children who attended four consecutive semesters of nursery school. The average age of the children at the beginning of the first semester was 3.1 years. The children were rated at the end of each semester by the head and assistant teachers independently on 34 social-behavior scales. Through the application of statistical procedures the number of factors were reduced. The same basic factor structures emerged in all four time periods. These were *aggression-dominance, dependency,* and *autonomy.* These three factors exhibited considerable individual stability as well as behavioral continuity through the four semesters. This is suggested by the stability coefficients presented in Table 10-3. Emmerich concludes (p. 26):

> Aggression-Dominance, Dependency, and Autonomy are salient personality dimensions having high stability from ages 3 to 5, supporting the view that personality differences arise early in life and are maintained in essentially their original form. However, because of certain methodological limitations, these generalizations should be accepted with caution.

TABLE 10-3

Factor-Stability Correlations (After Emmerich)

Semester	Aggression-Dominance				Dependency				Autonomy			
	Semester				Semester				Semester			
	1	2	3	4	1	2	3	4	1	2	3	4
1												
2	.84				.83				.78			
3	.47	.64			.61	.56			.44	.63		
4	.47	.66	.81		.48	.45	.69		.54	.67	.80	

Summary

Socialization is a lifelong task, beginning in early childhood and extending throughout the life span. Child rearing practices have an important bearing on the individual's social development. A recognition of the importance of learning during the preschool years has led to an increased attention to these years, especially for disadvantaged children.

The beginnings of emotional behavior are intimately related to social development. This may be noted in the early affectional pattern displayed by the infant toward the mother and other adult figures. Passivity and dependence during early childhood may be directly linked with passivity and dependent behavior during late childhood and adolescence. The early display of aggression is a regular concomitant of development.

The child learns about self from his experiences and the reactions of others to him, especially those who provide the punishments and rewards in his life. Individuality in behavior appears early in life and tends to persist. Social development during the preschool years follows the principles of development set forth regarding other aspects of development. This may be noted in cooperative behavior, which seems to go through several stages. Friendships during the preschool years are confined largely to the members of the family and children in the immediate neighborhood. Imaginary playmates are common among young children.

References

Anderson, C. M. "The Self Image: A Theory of the Dynamics of Behavior," in L. D. Crow and A. Crow (eds.), *Readings in Child and Adolescent Psychology.* New York: Longmans, 1961, pp. 407-418.

Banham, Katharine M. "The Development of Affectional Behavior in Infancy," *Journal of Genetic Psychology,* Vol. 76 (1950), pp. 283-289.

Bell, R. Q. "Relations between Behavior Manifestations in the Human Neonate," *Child Development,* Vol. 31 (1960), pp. 463-478.

Blau, A. "Self-Acceptance: A Psychiatric View," in S. Novek (ed.), *Judaism and Psychiatry,* New York: United Synagogue Press, 1956, pp. 87-93.

Bowers, Patricia, and L. London. "Development Correlates of Role-Playing Ability," *Child Development,* Vol. 36 (1965), pp. 499-508.

Chess, S., A. Thomas, and H. Birch. *American Journal of Orthopsychiatry,* Vol. 29 (1959), pp. 791-802.

DeLucia, Lenore. "The Toy Preference Test: a Measure of Sex-Role Identification," *Child Development,* Vol. 34 (1963), pp. 107-118.

Durrett, Mary E. "The Relationship of Early Infant Regulation and Later Behavior in Play Interviews," *Child Development,* Vol. 30 (1959), pp. 211-216.

Emmerich, W. "Continuity and Stability in Early Social Development," *Child Development,* Vol. 35 (1964), pp. 311-332.

——— . "Continuity and Stability in Early Social Development: II, Teacher Ratings," *Child Development,* Vol. 37 (1966), pp. 17-27.

Estvan, F. J. "Relationship of Nursery School Children's Social Perceptions as to Sex, Race, Social Status, and Age," *Journal of Genetic Psychology,* Vol. 107 (1965), pp. 295-308.

Estvan, F. J., and E. W. Estvan. *The Child's World: His Social Perceptions.* New York: Putnam, 1959.

Gottesman, I. I. "The Psychogenetics of Personality," unpublished doctoral dissertation. University of Minnesota, 1960.

Harlow, H. F. "The Heterosexual Affectional Response System in Monkeys," *American Psychologist,* Vol. 17 (1962), pp. 1-9.

——— . "Love in Infant Monkeys," *Scientific American,* Vol. 200 (June 1957), pp. 68-74.

Highberger, R. "Maternal Behavior and Attitudes Related to Behavior of the Preschool Child," *Journal of Home Economics,* Vol. 48 (1956), pp. 260-264.

Hoffman, Lois W., and M. L. Hoffman. *Review of Child Development Research.* New York: Russell Sage Foundation, 1966.

Hymes, J. L., Jr. *The Child Under Six.* Englewood Cliffs, N.J.: Prentice-Hall, 1963, pp. 29-30.

Kagan, J., and H. A. Moss. *Birth to Maturity: A Study in Psychological Development.* New York: Wiley, 1962.

Katcher, A. "The Discrimination of Sex Differences by Young Children," *Journal of Genetic Psychology,* Vol. 87 (1955), pp. 131-144.

King, M. G. "Interpersonal Relations in Preschool and Average Approach Distance," *Journal of Genetic Psychology,* Vol. 109 (1966), pp. 109-116.

Knop, C. "The Dynamics of Newly Born Babies," *Journal of Pediatrics,* Vol. 29 (1946), pp. 721-728.

Levin, H., and R. R. Sears. "Identification with Parents as a Determinant of Doll Play Aggression," *Child Development,* Vol. 27 (1956), pp. 135-153.

McCandless, B. R., and J. M. Hoyt. "Sex, Ethnicity, and Play Preference of Preschool Children," *Journal of Abnormal and Social Psychology,* Vol. 62 (1961), pp. 683-685.

McKee, J., and Florence Leader. "The Relationship of Socioeconomic Status and Aggression to the Competitive Behavior of Preschool Children," *Child Development,* Vol. 26 (1955), pp. 135-142.

Montagu, A. "The Awesome Power of Human Love," *Reader's Digest* (Feb. 1963), pp. 80-82.

Pitcher, Evelyn G. "Male and Female," *The Atlantic Monthly,* Vol. 211 (March 1963), pp. 87-91.

Rabban, M. "Sex-Role Identification in Young Children in Two Diverse Social Groups," *Genetic Psychology Monographs,* Vol. 42 (1950), pp. 81-158.

Radke-Yarrow, M., H. G. Trager, and H. Davis. "Social Perceptions and Attitudes of Children," in R. G. Kuhlen and G. G. Thompson (eds.), *Psychological Studies in Human Development,* 2nd ed. New York: Appleton, 1963.

Rheingold, H. L. "The Modification of Social Responsiveness in Institutional Babies," *Monographs of the Society for Research in Child Development,* Vol. 21, No. 2 (1956).

Sears, P. S. "Doll Play Aggression in Normal Young Children: Influence of Sex, Age, Sibling Status, Father's Absence," *Psychological Monographs,* Vol. 65, No. 6 (1951).

Sears, R. B., Eleanor E. Maccoby, and H. Levin. *Patterns of Child Rearing.* New York: Harper, 1957.

Siegel, A. E. "Aggressive Behavior of Young Children in the Absence of an Adult," *Child Development,* Vol. 28 (1957), pp. 371-378.

Special Report, *Newsweek,* May 16, 1966, p. 110.

Staines, J. W. "The Self-Picture as a Factor in the Classrooms," in D. E. Hamchek (ed.), *The Self.* Englewood Cliffs, N.J.: Prentice-Hall, 1965, p. 404.

Stewart, A., F. N. Pitts, A. G. Craig, and W. Dieruf. "The Hyperactive Child Syndrome," *American Journal of Orthopsychiatry,* Vol. 36 (1966), pp. 861-867.

U. S. Bureau of the Census, "Projection of the Population of the United States by Age and Sex to 1985," *Current Population Reports,* Series P-25, February 1964, p. 279.

Walters, J., D. Pearce, and L. Dahms. "Affectional and Aggressive Behavior of Preschool Children," *Child Development,* Vol. 28 (1957), pp. 15-26.

Chapter 11

Psychosocial Development During Late Childhood

Personality development is more than a complex interaction of physical growth, motor development, physiological changes, language concepts, and intelligence. There is also the social aspect. At each stage of the child's development, he is faced with adjustments made necessary by the different people in his environment. It was pointed out in Chapter 9 that attitudes and values have their beginning in home situations involving adults. The present chapter is concerned with the psychosocial development of the school-age child, the child from age six to the early adolescent period, which is marked by the beginning of sexual maturity.

Interpersonal Relationships

In the preceding chapter, we stated that the preschool years, to a marked degree, are years when the child identifies closely with members of his immediate family. The relationships within the family are important socializing influences and continue to play an important part throughout childhood. However, during late childhood there is a gradual decrease of emotional dependence on family ties and an increased dependence upon peers as well as a greater degree of self-sufficiency.

Identification with Parents. Preschool children frequently perceive their parents as the ideal. During late childhood they often look to figures outside the home as their ideal, but tend to identify closely with their parents. Children identify with the parent whom they perceive as being the more rewarding and affectionate (Payne and Mussen, 1956); the relationship is closer when the child sees himself as being similar to the parent of the same sex. The nature of the identification is very important to the socialization of the boy, since peers are more likely to regard favorably the boy who sees himself as similar to his father (Gray, 1959).

According to psychoanalytic theory, the identification process for girls is more complex than that for boys. The reason seems to be that the role of the girl is less well defined. It appears that it is more important for adolescent boys to identify with their fathers than for girls to identify with their mothers. Working with upper-middle-class pupils in the fifth through the eighth grade, Gray (1959) found that there was no significant difference in the adjustment of girls with high or low mother identification. The reason for these differences seems to lie in the masculine prestige factor in Western culture; the feminine role of the mother or the work role of women usually lacks this prestige factor.

Relationships within the Family. School-age children find within their homes continuing love and security along with increased freedom and encouragement to develop their potential abilities. Investigators have found relative close relationships between certain attitudes and practices on the part of one or both parents and similar behavior in their children. Lyle and Levitt (1955) reported a positive correlation between the punitiveness of parents and that of their children. If a boy received distinctive punitive measures from his father, he displays increased aggression toward his peers and others. Likewise, the daughter whose mother is overly submissive is likely to identify with the mother and display submissive behavior in her relations with others outside her home.

The responsibilities of parents will vary in the many societies of our world, although in Western civilization these responsibilities have been divided between the father and mother, with the father providing for the material needs of the family and the mother ministering to their emotional and social needs. Increasingly, the two roles are becoming less clearly defined, especially in the middle-class America (Babchuk and Bates, 1963). There is good evidence that the fusion of parental roles has in general been beneficial to children (Slater, 1961).

The importance of the mother during the early years was emphasized in the preceding chapter. The role of the mother does not end when the child enters school. Koppitz (1957) used 75 boys with an average age of 12 years in a study of the relationship of parental attitudes and characteristics to the attitudes of children toward themselves and others. She concluded from her study that a child will be inclined to feel anxious and guilty and have an unfavorable self-concept if his mother is unstable during the early years. A fearful, resentful, impatient mother will produce children lacking in self-confidence and emotional control.

Within the past decade there has been an accumulation of evidence that the father is extremely important to the development of the child during the elementary school years. For the boy, his father is a primary source for learning the role of the adult male and concepts related to male interests and activities. From the father the boy frequently learns many things later useful to him in his role as a male adult. To both boys and girls, a father is the supreme authority on factual matters, a disciplinarian, and love object. Just as the boy learns the male role from his father, the girl has in the father a model for her concept of the male role in life.

The question has been raised about the effects on the adjustments and behavior of elementary school children of the mother's employment outside the

Adapted from "Dennis the Menace."

home. There is no evidence that mothers' employment, so widespread today, has a harmful effect on school-age children (DuVall and DuVall, 1964). In some homes the general family spirit improves, and the children cooperate to a greater degree in the performance of household activities. It is the quality rather than the quantity of relationships in the home that is most important.

Interactions at School.   Whether a school-age child likes school or not, he spends the largest part of the day there. At school he constantly interacts in the classroom and on the playground with his classmates. Based on findings from the Robbers' Cave Experiment, Sherif and others (1961) proposed that in social interaction involving a common goal, definite group structures appear involving relatively stable status hierarchies and group norms. On the other hand, the constructive or destructive nature of the between-group interactions was largely determined by whether the goal was available to all; strong in-group loyalties developed along friendly and helpful intergroup interactions and appeared when the groups worked cooperatively toward a goal available to all.

The studies by Schmuck (1962, 1963) show the effects of classroom structural organization on the child's self-perceptions and academic performance. Two kinds of sociometric structure were differentiated—central and diffuse:

> Centrally structured peer groups are characterized by a large number of pupils who agree in selecting only a small cluster of their classmates as pupils they like. Along with this narrow focus on a small number of pupils, many other pupils are neglected entirely. Diffusely structured peer groups, on the other hand, are distinguished by a more equal distribution of liking choices; by no distinct subgroups whose members receive a large proportion of preference; and by fewer entirely neglected pupils." (Schmuck 1963, p. 341)

Diffusely structured peer groups have a more positive and helpful attitude toward each other and display greater sympathy; however, pupils seem to be more accurate in estimating their own status in the centrally structured groups, particularly low-status children.

Changing Views of the Self.   The child brings to school certain concepts about the self acquired during the preschool period. He has some self-confidence or none at all, a degree of being worthy or unworthy, a degree of friendliness or hostility, and a fair degree of eagerness or lack of eagerness. This basic view of the self may be modified as a result of experiences at school where he meets other boys and girls, comes into contact with others of his age, tests his abilities and skills against theirs, and receives approval from his teachers for his accomplishments. He then acquires a better understanding of the self.

This period of development may be thought of as one in which the child learns to face certain realities about himself. Amatora (1956), Green (1948), Webb (1952), and Wylie (1957) found from their studies that the accuracy of self-evaluations is a function of the variables being evaluated. The child is likely to be most accurate in his self-evaluation on traits that can be relatively objectively evaluated, such as height, weight, strength, speed of reading, and the like. However, Bledsoe and Garrison (1962) found that self-overestimation is more common among fourth- and sixth-grade children than self-underestimation. They also observed consistent individual tendencies toward accuracy, overstimulation, or underestimating themselves. This finding of Amatora may stem in part from the greater amount of failure in school activities by school-age boys as compared to that of girls.

Accompanying changing views of the self are changes in personal values, although values in general tend to remain constant during the elementary school years. The data presented in Figure 11-1 show that while most values remain relatively constant there is an increased interest in self-improvement and family

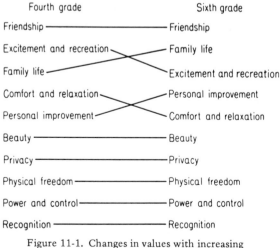

Figure 11-1. Changes in values with increasing
age. (Adapted from G. R. Hawkes.)

life during this period, accompanied by a slight decline in the categories of excitement and relaxation and in comfort and relaxation (Hawkes, 1952).

Behavioral Characteristics at Different Stages.   Piaget observed boys in games of marbles, questioned them on their conceptions of the game, and found a progression of patterns of social thinking and behavior during the period of late childhood (1932, 1951). According to Piaget, social maturation is in large part dependent upon the genetic growth of perceptual ability. The child's view of others and of his environment progresses from subjectivity to objectivity, from lack of autism to realistic awareness of self and others (Bobroff, 1960). Using the framework set forth by Piaget, Bobroff investigated the stages of maturation in socialized thinking and ego development. Games of marbles were used as the media through which a child's performance in social situations would be observed. This enabled the investigator to determine and compare the child's level of social maturation and level of ego development. A correlation of .64 was obtained between ego development and *practice* of rules; a correlation of .55 was obtained between ego development and *consciousness* of rules. Generalizing further from the data, Bobroff noted that the groups of children studied proceeded through concomitant stages in both areas studied. The following are some of the characteristics typical of the normal child at different stages:

Stage I—age 6

1. The child acts upon his impulses with apparently little or no deliberation.
2. The child does not differentiate between what are rules (which regulate the behavior of interacting individuals) and what are habits (which he practices as an individual).
3. The child's game behavior is self-oriented, even when he is joined by others in play.

Stage II—age 8

1. The child does not perceive cause and effect operating in human relations. Hence he views outcomes as fortuitous in nature and independent of purposeful action.
2. The child accepts the prescriptions of authority figures as "desirable" while showing little understanding of the roles, functions, or feelings of these persons.
3. The child wishes to behave acceptably. However, he does not yet understand why certain behaviors are expected of him and hence he often acts as if he is unaware of external demands.
4. The child prefers games of short duration, although he may play for extended periods of time.

Stage III—age 10

1. The child often tries to modify some of his *feelings* in accordance with the demands of the school, family, social group, and the like.

2. The child respects those whom he considers to be in authority and looks beyond himself for guidance in solving his problems.
3. The child wants and is able to master the details of the rules of games and to follow them correctly.
4. The child begins to seek the many values afforded by group association, and is willing to subvert some of his own inclinations in order to facilitate team activity.

Stage IV—age 12

1. The child can articulate his feelings within the alternate modes society provides for their expression.
2. The child demonstrates a belief that, in general, calculated actions produce predictable outcomes.
3. The child can view reality more objectively, and is better able to grasp causal relations.
4. The child is able to compromise some of his desires in the interest of group functioning without submerging his individuality.

In the preceding chapter, the importance of the preschool years to the child's emotional and social development was emphasized. Social and emotional development are closely related during all stages of development. This may be observed in the smiles of the infant in response to the warmth and love behavior displayed by the mother or some other adult authority figure. With a growing awareness of the self and widened social experiences, his affections are broadened and deepened with close friendships established outside the home. Increased physical maturity and wider social contacts affect the child's behavior in many ways, as revealed in the different aspects of socialization.

Growth toward social maturity results from both maturation and learning. The physiologically immature child should not be expected to display the same degree of social maturity as his more physiologically mature age-mate, although experiences will have a profound effect on the level of social maturity of each child. Doll (1947, 1965) has devised a useful test for evaluating social maturity of children and adolescents—*Vineland Social Maturity Scale*. The items making up the scale were gathered from observing youngsters over a period of years. These items are arranged in order of normal average life age progression. Illustrative items from the Scale are shown in Table 11.1.

What Children Fear. Several diverse theories have been proposed to explain the fears of school-age children. Most of these recognize the importance of learning, although it should be pointed out that learning abstractions or materials that are not significant to the child will have little effect upon children's fears. Children are not likely to fear such abstract things as the atomic bomb. In fact, first children usually display little fear for germs or automobile wrecks. This makes the task of safety training at an early age very difficult.

In a study by Maurer (1965) involving 130 children, ages 5 years and five months to 14 years and 6 months, responses were obtained about the things

TABLE 11-1
Items from the Vineland Social Maturity Scale (After Doll, 1965)

Category	Items	Life Age Mean
S	Plays simple table games	5.63
C	Uses Pencil for writing	6.15
SHG	Tells time to quarter hour	7.28
SHD	Combs or brushes hair	8.45
O	Does routine household tasks	8.53
SHE	Cares for self at table	9.03
L	Goes about home town freely	9.43
SD	Is left to care for self or others	11.45

S = socialization   SHG = self-help general
C = communication   SHD = self-help dressing
L = locomotion   SHE = self-help eating
O = occupation   SD = self-direction

feared. Fear of animals dominated the responses, with 64 percent of the children naming animals in general or some specific animal. However, fear of animals decreased significantly with age and became more realistic, with the fears being qualified by such as answer as "fear of dogs with rabies." Fear of nonexistent entities such as ghosts or monsters disappeared after age 10, while there was a decline in fear of the dark after age 7. Fears of people, kidnapping, being hurt, and giving people trouble increased with age. Maurer pointed out that as the child matures, the emotion of fear attaches more and more upon realistic objects, depending upon experience learning rather than upon verbal instruction. The nature and intensity of the child's fears depend largely upon family relationships and fears encountered in interpersonal relations within the family.

Social Compliance.   In a study by Crandall and others (1958) the interactions' of children with peers and children with teachers were observed and rated on a scale entitled "Compliance with Commands and Suggestions from Others." An evaluation of these ratings showed that the degree of social compliance between age 3 and 8 is not a function of either sex or intelligence. At age 3-6 significant correlations were obtained between children's compliance with their mothers while at home and their compliance with other adult authority figures. However, this relationship did not extend to peers. The authority of peer groups as expressed by acceptance or nonacceptance has not yet become manifested in the child's behavior. After age 6 the magnitude of compliance becomes more generalized and consistent from situation to situation and person to person.

It seems that the attitude of the mother toward compliance is an important factor in the development of conformity. The mothers' socialization attempts do seem to affect their children's general social compliance by early grade school level: before they do not—or at least there is no evidence from Crandall's study that they do. The study disclosed that, in general, maternal rewards for compliant behavior in the early years predicated the children's social compliance outside the home better than did maternal punishment for noncompliance. At a later age, the threat of peer punishment or nonacceptance behavior seems to be of equal importance in the maintenance of compliant behavior.

Sense of Responsibility.   One of the best indications of the level of a child's social development is his ability to accept responsibility. The development of such an ability does not just happen. It is a result of the acceptance of responsibility by the individual for different aspects of his behavior. This should begin during the preschool years, and advance gradually during the school years. The nine-year-old boy who has accepted responsibility for the care of his clothes or for doing his school work during previous years tends to readily accept these responsibilities, while his age-mate whose parents have carefully looked after these for him will display little responsibility in such life activities.

Experiences in responsibility must, however, be related to the child's level of physiological maturation. In an emotional climate characterized by affection and security the child will have more confidence in his worth and can be expected to assume more responsibility for his behavior, if he is given the opportunity to do so. Also, the tasks need to be closely related to his life, and he should sense the importance of these tasks in relation to his world.

The school setting offers many opportunities useful for aiding the development of initiative and responsibility; teachers vary considerably in encouraging or promoting the development of responsibility through performances in the school room. Also, pupils vary considerably in their abilities to accept responsibility. Children from homes where they have been encouraged to assume responsibility will normally be able to assume more responsibility than those from homes where they have been given little or no opportunity to accept responsibilities. The question of how much responsibility a third- or fourth-grade child should assume cannot be answered without an understanding of the child—his past and present.

Peer Friendships and Attitudes.   When the child comes into repeated contact with other children outside his home, he begins to form emotional ties with other children—his peers. Preschoolers and first-grade children frequently develop close friendships, but usually with one child at a time. Fluctuations in friendships appear at this time, becoming less pronounced at each grade level. The most common reasons given by children for changes in friends are lack of recent association, quarreling, replacement by another friend, inability to get along, bossiness, and lack of loyalty.

Although friendships appear tense during childhood, there is rarely any jealousy displayed when one of the pair forms other attachments, or grief for any long period when separated from the friend because of moving away. The notion that "You may never see the friend again" has little significance to the child. New friendships are easily formed, and at this age there is no apparent reason for selecting a friend of a particular type. Friendships are formed on the basis of mutual responsiveness.

Through the elementary grades there is a progressively greater tendency to form close ties with members of the same sex; although the antipathy toward boys is not as great today as formerly. As early as the first grade a girl may experience warm feelings and sympathetic reactions toward a single boy, but at this stage does not display overtly such an interest. Harris and Tseng (1957) used the sentence-completion method for determining the attitudes of children toward their peers. The sentences were scored by evaluating the completion items as positive, negative or neutral effect of the response. A careful study of the results showed that approximately 65 to 75 percent of the boys gave positive responses to other boys at all grade levels. In the third, fourth, fifth, and sixth grades over 80 percent of the girls gave favorable responses to other girls. There was a decline in favorable responses of girls to boys at the fifth- and sixth-grade levels followed by a rise of favorable response. When neutral attitudes were taken into consideration, boys in the intermediate grades were found to be more favorably than unfavorably disposed toward girls.

Socialization is developed through cooperative activities. (From Teacher's Edition, *Think-and-Do Book,* 1962. Scott, Foresman and Company.)

Social Acceptance. Traits that contribute to a child's social acceptance and popularity will vary to some degree from age to age, group to group, and from one socioeconomic level to another. Studies have shown that a relationship exists between a pupil's sociometric position within a group and his personal traits, school achievement, and other abilities. Tuddenham (1951) used the guess-who technique to determine the traits associated with popularity in the first, third, fifth, and seventh grades. Central among the boys traits is athletic skill, predicated upon motor coordination, strength, size, and physical maturity. The boy who is advanced in his physical development during the elementary school years generally has an advantage in peer status. The situation for girls is different. Traits characterized by less assertive behavior are valued, while more dominant, assertive characteristics are not, although there is an indistinct dividing line between the two categories. In summing up, Tuddenham states (p. 276) that the problem of securing group approval for a boy is one of conforming to a clearly defined group of traits for which he may or may not possess the requisite strength and motor skill. For a girl, the problem is more that of adapting to a continuously changing set of values which are never as clearly defined as they are for the boy.

Considerable research has been conducted on the relationship of intelligence and achievement to social acceptance and popularity. Based on a rather complete review of pertinent literature, a conclusion was drawn by Lindzey and Borgatta (1954) indicating that social acceptance is positively correlated with intelligence.

Gallagher and Crowder (1957) concluded from a study of the acceptance of gifted children that superior intellect and popularity as measured by sociometric tests were directly related. The investigators noted further that children with higher intelligence were more successful in predicting who would choose them as friends than were other children. Feinberg (1953, p. 211) described a group of accepted boys age 13-16 as follows: (a) Their marks were in the top 25 percent of their class and they received prizes of excellence in school grades. They felt that their academic achievements had been the result of hard work. (b) They received their best grades in arithmetic. (c) These boys have established good relationships with their teachers, most of whom they like and who they feel have had an influence on them—causing them, for example, to become very much interested in some particular subject.

The results from two independent studies (Morrison, 1953; Perry, 1953) verified the hypothesis that the overage child has a significantly lower choice-status among his classmates than do average and superior children. Out of the entire 21 overage children in different elementary class groups, none was found in the highest sociometric quartile of his class; 19 were found to be below the median. These results are in harmony with those obtained earlier by Johnson (1950) with mentally retarded pupils in grades 1 to 5 and by Martin (1955) with mentally retarded pupils in grades 5 through 8.

Social-Sex Development

The results of studies of widely different cultures show that sexually defined roles follow different patterns. Primitive tribes differ in defining the roles of the male and female; however, there is in all cases a clear delineation of the tasks that are the responsibility of the male and of the female. A child reared in a culture that clearly structures the role of the male and female at different age levels has very little responsibility for his sexually determined concept. His responsibility is that of accepting and fulfilling as best he can the role given him by his culture. A child reared in the United States where the sex roles are less clearly structured has some discretion and responsibility about his sexual identity at different stages of development.

The typical family in the United States helps the child at an early stage to recognize his own sex and to perceive the difference between his sex and the opposite sex. At an early age the boy is dressed in boylike clothes and his hair cut in accordance with the masculine norms of his culture. The small girl is dressed in girllike clothes and her hair allowed to grow so that she is identified as a girl at an early age.

Sources of Sexual Identity. The major sources of sexual identity that determine a person's concept of himself and of others as male or female are set forth by Josselyn (1967, p. 38) as (1) the inherent biological characteristic of each sex. (2) the conceptualization and mores of the culture in which one lives, and (3) the attitudes and behavior of those emotionally meaningful to the individual during childhood—the parents or in some cases other persons with whom the individual was closely identified during childhood.

It is self-evident that boys and girls differ in physiological structure as well as in other characteristics. These biological differences have been expanded as a result of the functional roles assigned to each sex. Attempts, however, to explain most of the differences between boys and girls on the basis of cultural forces fails to take into account biological different species of life. These differences in the case of man led to defining different functional roles to each sex. From this functional differentiation many related sex roles developed.

Children generally identify with their own sex long before they enter school. Katcher (1955) noted that four-, five-, and six-year-olds easily assigned the correct sex to adults on the bases of clothing, hair style, genitals, and breasts—in that order. Rabban (1950) compared the sex-discrimination ability of nursery school and lower elementary school children from lower-class and middle-class homes. He concluded (p. 141): (a) Three-year-old boys and girls of both groups show incomplete recognition of sex differences and as a group are unaware of any appropriateness of sex-typed boy objects. (b) The fourth and fifth years are periods of growth in clarification of sex role for lower-class boys, while the sixth year is particularly significant for middle-class boys. (c) lower-class girls accept the sex-appropriate pattern by six years of age, but middle-class girls do not fully acquiesce to the definition of appropriate sex-patterning even by the eighth year, when all other groups have accepted the social expectations.

Sex-Role Behavior. Social groups as well as society in general evaluates the child in part by his ability to play the roles expected of him. The appropriateness of role behavior depends upon whether the child is a boy or a girl. It was pointed out in the preceding chapter that differentiation in sex roles begins during infancy, and increases throughout childhood. The standards against which child behavior is measured vary from one sex to another, with certain changes taking place at different stages of the child's development.

The clearness with which sex-role behavior is exhibited varies with culture. The results of a study by Rabin and Limuaco (1959) revealed that ten- and eleven-year-old Filipino children showed a higher degree of sexual differentiation than American children of the same age. There is a tendency for American families to act as a unit, with the different members sharing duties that demand only slightly different roles. Thus American children are reared in an atmosphere characterized by sex-role convergence where sex roles are not so clearly defined. This trend appears to be more pronounced in the middle classes than in the lower; and, as might be expected, lower-class children are more keenly aware of sex-role behavior at an early age than middle-class children. Differences are especially great between girls of the two classes (Rabban, 1950).

A study by Minuchin (1965) was designed to assess the effects of different educational and home environments on the psychological development of children of similar backgrounds in all aspects other than relative traditional or modern philosophy. Traditional middle-class schools and homes were defined as stressing socialization toward general standards, and the modern viewpoint was defined as fostering the individual development of the child through more varied methods and toward more complex and individually relevant standards. The subjects were 105 fourth-grade nine-year-olds from four schools, two being selected as traditional and two as modern. Fifty-seven boys and forty-eight girls were from middle- or upper-class homes. The following results were obtained concerning sex typing in play and fantasy: (1) There is a substantial group trend toward sex-typical reactions and concerns, but this trend is more characteristic of children from traditional backgrounds. The direction of association is consistent in all measures, though the order of magnitude is not generally high. (2) Girls from modern backgrounds are particularly apt to depart from sex-typed expectations. (3) In areas where sex-typed expectations are decidely strong for one sex (aggression in boys, family orientation and dependence in girls), variability of reaction within that sex is relatively great. Higher aggression in boys and stronger family orientation and dependence in girls are associated with more traditional backgrounds. (4) The influence of family orientation is more evident in these projective data than that of the school (Minuchin, 1965).

The role of the father in the sex-typing of behavior among boys is shown in many studies (Mussen, 1961; Mussen and Rutherford, 1963; Steimnel, 1960).

The role of the mother in the development of sex role in girls is less clear, although recent studies show that the girl's feminine or masculine characteristics may be related to parental identification. In the early grades at school, girls frequently show a preference for aspects of the masculine role. In contrast to this preference by girls, boys at all grade levels beginning at the kindergarten and first-grade level show a predominantly masculine preference.

In the fifth grade a decided shift may be observed among girls toward a more pronounced acceptance of the feminine role. This is a likely result of

(1) greater segregation in playground activities and competitions, and (2) the beginning of puberty and changed attitudes toward the sexual self. The discrepancies in preferences between boys and girls with the lack of strong preferences by girls for the feminine role are almost exclusively products of cultural demands and expectations transmitted through the parents to the child. Through interviews with fathers and mothers, Pitcher (1963, p. 90) discovered an interesting differential in parents' sex-typing. She stated: Both fathers and mothers allow what appears to be tomboyishness in girls during the early years, while they try to discourage what might be feminine behavior in their sons. Their attitude seems to reflect the general pattern in America, where our culture tends to grant the female the privileges of two sexes: with impunity she can dress like a man; she can at will interchange the "little boy look" with cloying femininity. She can use any name—her own or her husband's—enter any job, any area of education, or she can make a career of motherhood. She can be independent or dependent, or both, as and when she pleases.

Preteen Romance. The literature bearing on social-sex behavior during the preteen and early teen years show that the traditional concept of an antagonism between boys and girls during these years is not true today (Broderick and Fowler, 1961). Studies show an increase in romantic interest today. In a sample of data from the Broderick and Fowler study, the majority of children in each of the grades studied (fifth, sixth, and seventh) claimed to have a sweetheart. The response to the question "Does your sweetheart like you too?" indicated that most of the sample expected reciprocation. Experiences with kissing was found to be quite common at this age, with 87.2 percent of the seventh-grade boys and 86.8 percent of the seventh-grade girls admitting to having been kissed by their opposite peers.

The most convincing evidence offered by Broderick and Fowler of the growth in interest of young adolescents for the opposite sex was in the choice of friends for three activities; walking, eating, and attending movies. The preteen-agers were asked to rank the desirability of a companion of the same sex, a companion of the opposite sex, or of no companion at all in the three activities. The majority of sixth- and seventh-graders stated that when walking or going to the movies they preferred a companion of the opposite sex to none at all or to one of the same sex. Both boys and girls were somewhat more conservative when choosing an eating companion; almost half of the seventh-graders preferred to eat with a member of the same sex.

In a study by Reese (1966) 177 boys and 141 girls from the fifth, sixth, seventh, and eight grades in a predominantly middle-class suburban school district were given a sociometric rating scale. The data from this scale were analyzed to determine the degrees of acceptance of the opposite sex. The results, presented in Table 11-2 showed that early in the school year fifth-grade boys accepted girls less than girls accepted boys. Results from testing later in the school year showed this trend to be reversed and agreed with the trend in grades 6, 7, and 8. Reese noted further from an analysis of data gathered that, "Accep-

TABLE 11-2
Mean Acceptance by Opposite Sex in Grades 5, 6, 7, and 8 (After Reese)

Grade	Sex	Level of Acceptance by Same Sex*			All Groups
		Low	Middle	High	
5	M	2.49	2.74	2.79	2.67
	F	1.77	2.12	2.34	2.08
6	M	2.46	2.90	3.31	2.89
	F	2.75	3.18	3.23	3.05
7	M	2.73	3.07	3.14	2.98
	F	3.17	3.18	3.30	3.22
8	M	2.96	3.18	3.32	3.14
	F	2.99	3.26	3.21	3.15

*A high score indicates high acceptance.

tance by opposite sex was positively related to acceptance by same sex in both sexes, in all four grades sampled, and throughout the school." (p. 162)

Socializing Influences

Increased maturity helps the growing individual to solve certain problems only to be replaced by others of a more complex nature. Additional socializing influences do not operate; rather they operate indirectly in affecting the ways an individual responds to new and more complex situations. This may be noted in the case of home influences, which appear to diminish when the child enters school.

The effect of early home influences on the development of problem behavior in children is brought forth in a study by Becker and others (1959) involving two groups of families, one with a child in need of clinical services and the other with no child in need of clinical services. It was noted that child behavior problems were loaded primarily on two factors: (1) conduct problems (aggressive, uncontrollable) in the child, (2) a factor defined mainly by personality problems in the child (shy, sensitive, inferior).

The results indicated that "in families with conduct-problem children, both parents are maladjusted, give vent to unbridled emotions, and tend to be arbitrary with the child. In addition, the mother tended to be active (tense), dictatorial, thwarting, and suggesting, whereas the father tended not to enforce regulations" (p. 117). In the case of the child with personality problems the influence of the father stood out. "The father was rated as maladjusted and thwarting of the child." The results of this study, like those of other studies suggest that more consideration should be given to the role of the father in the child's development.

Influence of Birth Order. By birth order is meant the sequential position of a person among his or her siblings with respect to order of birth. Many students of child and adolescent development have studied the effects of birth order on development. The studies indicate that first borns are bossy (Sutton-Smith and Rosenberg, 1966; Hilton, 1966; and Oberlander and Jenkins, 1966), since in their first childhood experiences they frequently displayed dominant behavior in their relations with younger siblings.

Differences in family environment for the second children as opposed to the first children seem generally known. First-born, for some period during their early life, have only adults in their family and are free of competition from other brothers or sisters. Later-born children find more competition for parental attention. The attitude of the mother toward the child tends to be more relaxed, less anxious with later-born children than with first-born (Warren, 1966).

The studies in which birth order is defined only as the oldest child versus the youngest or in some other limited way can be advantageous, especially for the total group studied. But as stated previously, clear understanding of the nature of birth order cannot be developed without refinement of the definition. All positions of birth, some relationship of ages, and some attention to sex pattern should all be included in a consideration of the influence of birth order on socialization. Koch (1955) pointed out that the child's sex, ordinal position, and sibling's sex must be considered in an evaluation of birth order. He observed that a boy with a much older sister tends to be more dependent, withdrawn, and tenacious than a boy with a much older brother, and that children with brothers tended to be more competitive, ambitious, and enthusiastic than children with sisters. Boys with sisters only are, according to a study by Brown (1956), somewhat more feminine in their preferences and activities than boys with all male or male and female siblings.

Family Relations.   The purpose of a study by Mutimer and others (1966) was to ascertain the differences, if any, in the family relationships of good and poor readers. Comparisons of interfamily relationships were made between 22 children from a reading clinic with 22 girls who were reading at their anticipated achievement grade placement according to their IQ scores. Both groups of children scored average or above on IQ tests. The "Two-House Technique" test was used to test interfamily feelings and relationships. From a statistical analysis of the data investigators conclude as follows (p. 73):

> One might infer from this study that achieving girls tend to identify with mothers and to reject siblings more than do underachieving girls, while the under-achieving girls tend to be more dependent upon siblings than do the achieving girls; that achieving boys tend to identify more with fathers than do the under-achieving boys; and that there is more sibling rivalry among achieving girls and more interacting with siblings among achieving boys than among any other group.

A number of investigators have postulated a relationship between behavior at home and school conduct and attainment (Douglas, 1964; Gildwell et al., 1963; Lapouse and Monk, 1964). Mitchell and Shepherd (1966) found a significant relationship between deviant behavior at home and the existence of problems of behavior in school, although a considerable divergence between the two areas of conduct was noted. This fact is important in making specific generalizations about the child's conduct in the one area of life alone.

Preschool Experiences.   Much emphasis is being given to preschool experiences today, especially for the child from an impoverished environment. The recognition by educators of the importance of school readiness for learning at school has brought forth considerable experimentation with preschool programs. Intellectual curiosity, a warm and friendly attitude toward others, and aspirations for learning at school are not nourished in an atmosphere of ignorance, prejudice, inadequate food and clothing, and ill health.

It is problematic as to how much can be done in a preschool environment to overcome the results of bland impoverishment of experience during the early years for most children.

If children from impoverished environments are to learn at school, they must acquire the background of concepts and eagerness to learn that make for reading and school readiness. Widespread efforts are being made to provide the needed experiences for children from impoverished environments.

The Child in Suburbia.   The child growing up in modern suburbia has the advantages of developing in a middle-class home where middle-class values exist. As he moves from the home to organizations and institutions he comes into contact with other children from middle-class homes. Thus, his early middle-class ways of behaving and middle-class values are practiced throughout his childhood. Miel and Kiester (1967) presents a fairly complete description of a shoreline suburb of New York City, centering primarily on children in the elementary schools of this suburban area, which is the chief training ground for American children today. Modern suburbia is relatively self-sufficient, with advantages, both material and otherwise, to offer its children; it is sorely lacking in providing opportunities to learn about life and "ways of living" outside their own sheltered world. There is a reasonable amount of homogeneity in the size and cost of homes in the particular suburb. Religious activities and programs of the type that appeals to the middle-class family will be found in suburbia.

The investigator concludes that growing up in an American suburb today fails the child in certain ways. The suburban child tends to be (1) materialistic, (2) slightly hypocritical, (3) competitive in school, (4) rigid in his social distinctions, and (5) a conformist. His attitude toward disadvantaged families, like that of his parents, is likely to be condescending and patronizing.

Influences of Social Class.   In the past the characteristic attitude of lower-class parents toward education was unfavorable or negativistic at least. Children from such homes brought unfavorable attitudes toward education to school with them. Such attitudes are not conducive to pleasant teacher-pupil interaction and learning at school. Hence the interaction between the pupil and his teacher reinforced his unfavorable attitude toward school. The lower-class youngster's school attitudes became progressively more unfavorable and his feelings about his teacher worsened. Thus in spite of our good intentions and platitudes about democratic ideals and equality of educational opportunity, the social-class hierarchy continued and is frequently perpetuated by unfavorable attitudes of so many children from the lower class. The unfavorable attitude toward school by children from the lower class is further evidenced by the aggressiveness frequently exhibited by lower-class children. Toigo (1965) noted a relationship between the classroom status level and its characteristic level of aggression among third-grade children. The relationship was in a negative direction with classrooms of lower-status level exhibiting higher levels of overall aggression than classrooms of upper-status children.

Other problems faced by the lower-class child at school are his low motivation toward learning school-related materials, inadequate language abilities and cultural experiences, and frequent lack of parental encouragement as a means of reinforcing his learnings at school. As a result of these and other factors, the lower-class child is less accepted by his classmates, experiences more failure at school, and tends to develop a lower self-concept. The consequences of continued failure with the accompanying lower self-concept frequently lead to dropping out of school, deprivation, and delinquency during the adolescent years.

Minority Group Membership. Being a member of a minority group frequently poses a serious threat to a child's ego, especially when the minority group is regarded by others in an unfavorable manner. This may occur when children are invited by a mother to a child's birthday party, but members of a minority group are excluded, even though they are friends of the child at school. Negro children in certain minority groups in the United States are frequently subject to outright rejection, especially by parents of other children. Such a condition promotes feelings of inadequacy and a sense of insecurity. The same phenomenon may appear with children of any minority group where a great deal of prejudice exists toward a particular minority group.

In cases where membership in a minority group has prestige value, positive rather than negative feelings toward the self is more likely to emerge. Experiences of social conflict or frustration by children from a minority group tend to give rise to ambivalent feelings toward their own group—expressions involving self-criticism and self-hatred.

If education is to prepare children for responsible adulthood in a world characterized by rapid change, it cannot simply pass to the new generation the traditional, including prejudices, which has too often been held up as the fundamental "way of life." Modern education must become more concerned with the child's learning how to learn and with developing the ability to fit into changing conditions—to expect and prepare for change. Concerning this, Margaret Mead (1967) states: "The biggest development in our education in the future will be to teach children to respect things that haven't yet happened." This does not eliminate the necessity of preparing children to live in our present culture; it does, however, emphasize cultural changes.

Influences of the Teacher. There is an abundance of evidence that a teacher's personality has a significant impact on the personal and social development of children (Torgoff, 1961). Much of what the teacher teaches is a result of her example and interactions with pupils. How she responds to pupils is more important than the actual response. The better liked a teacher is the greater will be her influence on the pupils, since pupils tend to emulate most those whom they admire.

Solomon and others (1964) point out that even the attitudes a child displays toward school and specific activities at school is to a large degree a reflection of his attitude regarding his teacher. Amatora (1955) noted that children are in considerable agreement about the teachers whom they liked, the ones they disliked, and reasons for liking or disliking a particular teacher. In general students at all age levels like a teacher who exhibits fairness, warmth, a sense of humor, and helpfulness.

In general boys experience more difficulties adjusting to the expectations and demands of teachers than girls. From early childhood girls are taught to conform, while boys are encouraged to display aggressiveness and originality—traits which frequently run counter to the demands of the classroom. According to Ullman (1957) the problems of girls at school are more frequently on an intrapsychic level, displaying adjustment difficulties involving digestive disturbances, headaches, allergies, and chronic fatigue; the problems of boys at school are more likely to be displayed through nervous habits, stuttering, hostility, and aggression. The traits displayed by boys are more likely to upset the school and classroom programs, and are less consistent with the teachers expectations and demands.

The lower-class child probably has the greatest difficulty in his personal relations with the teacher because of the differences usually found in their social class background. Although we should not generalize too readily about the social background of teachers, there is evidence that they represent in a substantial number all but the extremes of the upper and lower class (Havighurst and Neugarten, 1962, p. 465). Furthermore, because of their training, associations, and professional experiences they tend to adopt middle-class attitudes, behaviors, and values. Thus, the lower-class child finds himself at variance with the teacher in his aspirations, attitudes about academic learning, language usage, certain moral precepts, and values. Faced by these conflicts he frequently develops a hostile attitude toward his teachers and the school with which they are closely identified.

The Making of a Delinquent. One cannot say with certainty when the making of a delinquent begins. However, enough is known about the development of the juvenile delinquent to conclude that although these are adolescents, delinquency tendencies had their beginnings during childhood. Our discussion of delinquency in this chapter stems from the importance of childhood in the development of the delinquent. There are some who would suggest that this topic should be included in the previous chapter dealing with early socialization. No attempt is made to answer such contentions, since we realize that the early years are the foundation years when early attitudes toward the world of people and the world of things are being formed.

It is during childhood, especially late childhood, that the individual begins moving out from his home. It is during this period that the community, school, and peers take on added importance. It is during this period that the developmental task of learning to get along with others must be learned. At this time boys and girls learn a great deal about their sex role. The girl identifies more closely with girls; the boy identifies more closely with boys. Guidance and opportunities to learn acceptable social roles are most important during this period if junevile delinquency is to be avoided during the adolescent years.

Actually, many delinquents appear at this stage while symptoms of forthcoming delinquent behavior may be observed in others. The Gluecks (1950) studies of the background of delinquents revealed that by age 10 almost 90 percent showed definite signs of maladjusted behavior. A better answer than policemen for preventing delinquency, one advocated by the Gluecks, is to identify latent delinquency at the age 5 or 6 and help them overcome their maladjusted behavior. Primarily delinquents have personalities characterized by lack of security and a history of failure. The former resulting from home conditions characterized by lack of affection and discord; the latter from continuous failure in school resulting from failure in reading during the early school years.

Summary

At each stage in the child's development he is faced with adjustments made necessary by encounters with the different people in his environment. During late childhood adjustments must be made with the parents and brothers and sisters. The nature of these adjustments will vary with different cultures. Children tend to identify with their parents during chidhood. The identification process for girls is more complex than that for boys; it is important for the boy to identify with the father or some male authority figure.

The child's self-concept is frequently modified as a result of experiences at school. At this time he learns to face certain realities about himself. During the school years the child frequently develops an ideal self, which may be his teacher or some adult important to him. The child's ideals are closely related to the values in his culture that he regards as important. The relative position of these values remains fairly stable into and through adolescence.

Growth toward social maturity results from both maturation and learning. Social and emotional development are closely related during all stages of development. This may be noted in the case of the development of fear. The emotion of fear involves more and more realistic objects and situations related to the child's experiences. Social compliance to the demands of peers is manifested at the second- or third-grade level. The attitude of the mother toward compliance is an important factor in the development of conformity. One of the best indications of the level of a child's social development is his ability to accept responsibility. In an emotional climate characterized by affection and security the child will display more confidence and can be expected to assume more responsibility for his behavior.

Throughout the elementary school grades there is a progressively greater tendency to form close ties with members of one's sex. However, there is no evidence for a natural antipathy to members of the opposite sex during this period. Sexually defined roles will vary with culture. These roles are manifested during the preschool years in American culture.

Home influences as a socializing force appear to diminish when the child enters school, although there is a relation between deviant behavior at home and behavior problems at school. The child's sex, ordinal position in the family unit, and sibling's sex are important socializing influences. Preschool experiences are important in relation to learning and socializiation at school. The child in suburbia is likely to be competitive, materialistic, a conformist, and rigid in social distinctions. Membership in a minority frequently disposes the child to conflicts and frustrations, while the lower-class child is frequently a disadvantaged child in school learning and in socialization involving middle-class values.

References

Amatora, S. M. "Comparisons in Personality Self-Evaluation," *Journal of Social Psychology*, Vol. 42 (1955), pp. 315-321.

————. "Validity in Self-Evaluation," *Educational and Psychological Measurement*, Vol. 16 (1956), pp. 119-126.

Babchuk, N., and A. P. Bates. "The Primary Relations of Middle-Class Couples: A Study in Male Dominance," *American Sociological Review*, Vol. 28 (1963), pp. 377-384.

Becker, W. C., D. R. Peterson, L. A. Hellmer, D. J. Shoemaker, and H. Quay. "Factors in Parental Behavior and Personality as Related to Problem Behavior in Children," *Journal of Consulting Psychology*, Vol. 23 (1959), pp. 107-118.

Bledsoe, J., and K. C. Garrison. *The Self Concepts of Elementary School Children in Relation to Their Academic Achievement, Intelligence, Interests, and Manifest Anxiety.* Cooperative Research Project No. 1008, United States Office of Education, College of Education, University of Georgia, 1962.

Bobroff, A. "The Stages of Maturation in Socialized Thinking and the Ego Development of Two Groups of Children," *Child Development*, Vol. 31 (1960), pp. 321-338.

Broderick, C. N., and S. E. Fowler. "New Patterns of Relationships between the Sexes among Preadolescents," *Marriage and Family Living*, Vol. 23 (1961), pp. 27-30.

Bronson, Wanda C. "Dimensions of Ego and Infantile Identification," *Journal of Personality*, Vol. 27 (1959), pp. 532-545.

Brown, D. G. "Sex-role Preference in Young Children," *Psychological Monographs*, Vol. 70, No. 14 (1956), pp. 1-19.

Crandall, V. J., Sonya Orleans, Anne Preston, and Alice Babson. "The Development of Social Compliance in Young Children," *Child Development*, Vol. 29 (1958), pp. 429-443.

Doll, E. A. *Vineland Social Maturity Scale.* Minneapolis: Educational Test Bureau, 1947, pp. 3-8. Latest Edition, Minneapolis: American Guidance Service, Inc., 1965.

Douglas, J. W. B. *The Home and the School.* London: MacGibbon and Kee, 1964.

Duvall, Sylvanius, and Evelyn Duvall. *Let's Explore Your Mind.* Long Island Press, 1964.

Feinberg, M. "Relation of Background Experience to Social Acceptance," *Journal of Abnormal and Social Psychology,* Vol. 48 (1953), pp. 206-214.

Gallagher, J., and T. Crowder. "The Adjustment of Gifted Children in the Regular Classroom," *Exceptional Children,* Vol. 23 (1957), pp. 306-319.

Garrison, K. C., A. J. Kingston, and H. W. Bernard. *The Psychology of Childhood.* New York: Scribner's, 1966.

Gildwell, J. C., H. R. Donke, and M. B. Kantor. "Screening in Schools for Behavior Disorders: Use of Mothers' Reports of Symptoms," *Journal of Educational Research,* Vol. 56 (1963), pp. 508-515.

Glueck, S., and Eleanor Blueck. *Unraveling Juvenile Delinquency.* New York: Commonwealth Fund, 1950.

Gray, Susan W. "Perceived Similarities to Parents and Adjustment," *Child Development,* Vol. 30 (1959), pp. 91-107.

Green, G. H. "Insight and Group Adjustment," *Journal of Abnormal and Social Psychology,* Vol. 43 (1948), pp. 49-61.

Harris, D. B., and Sing Chu Tseng. "Children's Attitudes toward Peers and Parents as Revealed by Sentence Completions," *Child Development,* Vol. 28 (1957), pp. 401-411.

Havighurst, R. J., and Bernice L. Neugarten. *Society and Education,* 2nd ed. Boston: Allyn and Bacon, 1962.

Havighurst, R. J., M. Z. Robinson, and M. Dorr. "The Development of the Ideal Self in Childhood and Adolescence," *Journal of Educational Research,* Vol. 40 (1946), pp. 241-257.

Hawkes, G. R. "A Study of Personal Values of Elementary School Children," *Educational and Psychological Measurements,* Vol. 12 (1952), pp. 654-663.

Hawkes, G. R., L. G. Burchinal, and B. Gardner. "Preadolescents' Views of Some of Their Relations with Their Parents," *Child Development,* Vol. 28 (1957), pp. 393-399.

Hilton, Irma. "Differences in the Behavior of Mothers toward First- and Later-Born Children," paper read at the Annual Meeting of the American Psychological Association, New York, 1966.

Johnson, G. O. "A Study of the Social Position of Mentally-Handicapped Children in the Regular Grades," *American Journal of Mental Deficiency,* Vol. 55 (1950), pp. 60-89.

Josselyn, Irene M. "Sources of Sexual Identity," *Child and Family,* Vol. 6, No. 2 (Spring 1967), pp. 38-45.

Katcher, A. "The Discrimination of Sex Differences by Young Children," *Journal of Genetic Psychology,* Vol. 87 (1955), pp. 131-143.

Koch, Helen L. "Some Personality Correlates of Sex, Sibling Position, and Sex of Sibling among Five- and Six-Year-Old Children," *Genetic Psychology Monographs,* Vol. 52 (1955), pp. 3-50.

Koppitz, Elizabeth M. "Relationship between Some Background Factors and Children's Interpersonal Attitude," *Journal of Genetic Psychology,* Vol. 91 (1957), pp. 119-129.

Lapouse, R., and M. Monk. "An Epidemiological Study of Behavior Characteristics in Children," *American Journal of Public Health,* Vol. 48 (1958), pp. 1134-1144.

Lindzey, G., and E. F. Borgatta. "Sociometric Measurement," in G. Lindzey, (ed.), *Handbook of Social Psychology.* Cambridge, Mass: Addison-Wesley, 1954.

Lyle, W. H., and E. E. Levitt. "Punitiveness, Authoritarianism, and Parental Discipline of Grade School Children," *Journal of Abnormal and Social Psychology,* Vol. 51 (1955), pp. 42-46.

Martin, Sister Mary Aloyse. *Social Acceptance and Attitude Toward School of Mentally Retarded Pupils in Regular Classes.* Ed. D. dissertation, University of Southern California, 1955.

Maurer, Adah. "What Children Fear," *Journal of Genetic Psychology,* Vol. 106 (1965), pp. 265-277.

Mead, Margaret. "The Effects of Changing Cultural Patterns on the Process of Education," speech delivered at Old Dominion College, April 29, 1967.

Miel, A., and E. Kiester. *The Shortchanged Children of Suburbia.* New York: American Jewish Committee, 1967.

Milner, Esther. "A Study of the Relationship between Readiness in Grade One School Children and Patterns of Parent-Child Interaction," *Child Development,* Vol. 22 (1951), pp. 95-112.

Minuchin, Patricia. "Sex Role Concepts and Sex Typing in Childhood as a Function of School and Home Environments," *Child Development,* Vol. 36 (1965), pp. 1033-1048.

Mitchell, S., and M. Shepherd. "A Comparative Study of Children's Behavior at Home and at School," *British Journal of Educational Psychology,* Vol. 36 (1966), p. 254.

Morrison, Ida E. *Democracy and Interpersonal Relationships in the Classroom.* Unpublished doctoral dissertation, Stanford University, 1953.

Mussen, P. H. "Some Antecedents and Consequences of Masculine Sex-Typing in Adolescent Boys," *Psychological Monographs,* Vol. 75, No. 2 (1961).

Mussen, P. H., and E. Rutherford. "Parent-Child Relations and Parental Personality in Relation to Young Children's Sex-Role Preferences," *Child Development,* Vol. 34 (1963), pp. 589-607.

Mutimer, Dorothy, L. Loughlin, and M. Powell. "Some Differences in the Family Relationships of Achieving and Underachieving Readers," *Journal of Genetic Psychology,* Vol. 190 (1966), pp. 67-74.

Oberlander, M., and N. Jenkins. "Birth Order and Academic Achievement," paper read at the annual meeting of the American Psychological Association, New York, 1966.

Payne, Dorothy E., and P. H. Mussen. "Parent-child Relations and Father Identification among Some Adolescent Boys," *Journal of Abnormal and Social Psychology,* Vol. 52 (1956), pp. 358-362.

Perry, Ida E. *The Social Status of Overage Elementary School Children.* Unpublished master's thesis, Sacramento State College, 1953.

Piaget, Jean. *The Moral Judgment of the Child.* New York: Harcourt, 1932.

————. *Play, Dreams and Imitation in Childhood.* New York: Norton, 1951.

Pitcher, Evelyn G. "Male and Female," *Atlantic Monthly,* Vol. 211 (March 1963), pp. 87-91.

Rabban, M. "Sex-role Identification in Young Children in Two Diverse Social Groups," *Genetic Psychology Monographs,* Vol. 42 (1950), pp. 81-158.

Rabin, A. I., and Josefina Limuaco. "Sexual Differentiation of American and Filipino Children as Reflected in the Draw-a-Person Test," *Journal of Social Psychology,* Vol. 50 (1959), pp. 207-211.

Reese, H. W. "Attitudes toward the Opposite Sex in Late Childhood," *Merrill-Palmer Quarterly,* Vol. 12 (1966), pp. 157-163.

Schmuck, R. A. "Sociometric Status and Utilization of Academic Abilities," *Merrill-Palmer Quarterly,* Vol. 8 (1962), pp. 165-172.

————. "Some Relations of Peer Liking Patterns in the Classroom to Pupil Attitudes and Achievement," *School Review,* Vol. 71 (1963), pp. 337-359.

Sherif, M., O. J. Harvey, B. J. White, W. R. Hood, and C. W. Sherif. *Intergroup Conflict and Cooperation: The Robbers' Cave Experiment.* Norman, Okla.: U. of Oklahoma Press, 1961.

Slater, P. E. "Parental Role Differentiation," *American Journal of Sociology,* Vol. 67 (1961), pp. 296-311.

Solomon, D., W. E. Bezdet, and L. Rosenberyg. "Dimensions of Teacher Behavior," *Journal of Experimental Education,* Vol. 33 (1964), pp. 23-40.

Steimel, R. "Childhood Experiences and Masculinity-Femininity Scores," *Journal of Counseling Psychology,* Vol. 7 (1960), pp. 212-217.

Sutton-Smith, B., and R. G. Rosenber. "Sibling Consensus on Power Tactics," paper read at annual meeting of the American Psychological Association, New York, 1966.

Toigo, R. "Social Status and Classroom Aggression in Third-Grade Children," *Genetic Psychology Monographs,* Vol. 71 (1965), pp. 221-268.

Torgoff, I. "Parental Developmental Timetable: Parental Field Effects on Children's Compliance," paper presented at the 1961 meeting of the Society for Research in Child Development.

Tuddenham, R. D. "Studies in Reputation, III: Correlates of Popularity among Elementary-School Children, *Journal of Educational Psychology,* Vol. 42 (1951), pp. 257-258.

Ullman, C. A. *Identification of Maladjusted Children,* rev.ed. Public Health Monograph, No. 7. Washington, D.C.: Government Printing Office, 1957.

Warren, J. R. "Birth Order and Social Behavior," *Psychological Bulletin,* Vol. 65 (1966), pp. 38-50.

Webb, W. B. "Self-Evaluation Compared with Group Evaluations," *Journal of Consulting Psychology,* Vol. 16 (1952), pp. 305-307.

Wylie, Ruth C. "Some Relationships between Defensiveness and Self-Concept Discrepancies," *Journal of Personality,* Vol. 25 (1957), pp. 600-616.

Chapter 12

The Adolescent: His Personal and Social Development

Personal and social development during adolescence cannot be separated from the earlier stages of development, although profound physiological changes occur at this stage of life. Adolescence can correctly be regarded as a period of transition—physiologically, psychologically, and socially. The materials of this chapter are especially concerned with psychological and social adjustments and development during the adolescent period.

Growth into Adolescence

The growth of the individual from birth to maturity constitutes a considerable amount of time. However, this has decreased in percentage of the total life span due to two conditions. In the first place, the adolescents in the United States are maturing earlier than was the case several decades ago. Second, the life span has increased considerably during the past fifty years. Adolescence is a period of growth and transition. This may be observed in any group of boys and girls during the teen years, and should be recognized by those concerned with the education and guidance of adolescents.

Growth into adolescence is accompanied by developmental tasks that should be completed at this stage of development. These were set forth in Chapter 1; their importance has been emphasized by students of adolescent psychology. An intensive longitudinal study by Schoeppe and Havighurst (1952) furnishes evidence of the value of the concept of developmental tasks in relation to present as well as future adjustments and development. Successful achievement of a developmental task at one broad age level was followed by good achievement on the same task at subsequent age levels; in addition, successful achievement of a developmental task was generally associated with good achievement on other tasks at the same age level. One should not generalize too freely from these findings to individual cases. In some cases, good achievement on one developmental task resulted from an effort to compensate for poor achievement on certain other tasks. Two conclusions emerge from these findings that are most applicable to adolescents. First, within broad limits adolescents must acquire some learning outcomes successfully in order to deal effectively with the social and cultural forces in their present environment. Second, if boys and girls do not achieve during childhood and adolescence most of the tasks of adolescence, they are likely to experience difficulty during the early adult years.

The Meaning of Adolescence.   Adolescence is a "critical period" in development in that it is a time of rapid and profound changes in the organism and an in-between period or a period of transition from childhood to adulthood. The definition of adolescence offered by Eisenberg (1965) reveals the nature and importance of this stage of development. He states (p. 131):

> Adolescence may be defined as a critical period of human development manifested at the biological, psychological, and social levels of integration, of variable onset and duration but marking the end of childhood and setting the foundation for maturity. Biologically, its onset is signaled by the acceleration of physiological growth and the beginnings of secondary sexual development, its termination by the fusion of the epiphyses of the bones and the completion of sexual maturation. Psychologically, it is marked by an acceleration of cognitive growth and of personality formation, both of which continue to be subject to further evolution, though at a less marked rate, in subsequent stages of adulthood. Socially, it is a period of intensified preparation for the assumption of an adult role, and its termination is signaled when the individual is accorded full adult prerogatives, the timing and nature of which vary widely from society to society.

It was pointed out in Chapter 11 that the most obvious biological changes occurring in late childhood are those involving sexual development. At this period of life the hormones from the sex glands bring the reproductive organs to maturity. This point is referred to as *puberty*. The menstruation marks puberty for girls, but there is no single criterion to indicate puberty for boys. Among criteria frequently used are the occurrence of first ejaculation, the appearance of axillary and pubic hair, and other secondary sexual characteristics. Girls tend to judge a boy's sexual maturity by facial and body hair and by change of voice; boys judge girl's sexual maturity in terms of body figure, especially breast development (Garrison, 1965, pp. 3-4). Regardless of the method used for determining puberty, it is generally recognized that girls mature almost two years earlier than boys.

The adolescent period may be thought of as an in-between period or a period of transition from childhood to adulthood. Experiences with individuals reveal that during their "teen-age period" the individual resents being treated as a child and frequently rebels against rules and regulations that tend to limit his behavior. However, during this time the individual is unable to assume the responsibilities of an adult. He is unable to get a full-time job, and is required to remain in school until he is at least 16 years old. During this transition from childhood to adulthood he is referred to as an adolescent. Among families of lower status, a boy is accepted into adulthood at 16 or 17, while the girl frequently marries at an early age. In families of higher social status, boys and girls remain in school longer, and in case of marriage frequently continue to go to school. Garrison (1965, p. 6) writes: "It might be stated that the beginning of adolescence is to a marked degree a physical and physiological phenomenon, whereas the end of adolescence is mainly emotional-social."

Significant Changes in Heterosexual Interests. Although the biological characteristics of adolescents today are similar to those of adolescents several decades ago, important changes have appeared in the heterosexual interests of adolescents. These changes are closely related to changes in ways of living and changes in attitudes of the parents and other adults. The hypothesis of greater adolescent heterosexual interest today as compared to sexual interest in 1942 is supported by a study reported by Kuhlen and Houlihan (1965). The investigators compared the frequency of cross-sex choices on a sociometric questionnaire given to students in grades 6 through 12 in the spring of 1963 with the frequency of choices on the same questionnaire and in the same schools in the spring of 1942 for students in the sixth, ninth, and twelfth grades.

"But dad, when you were young there weren't many cute girls to 'run around' with."

On the sociometric test each student was asked to indicate a first and second choice of comparisons in nine activities such as occupying the next seat in a classroom and attending the movies. The results presented in Table 12-1 support the hypothesis that adolescents more frequently choose the opposite sex than was true over two decades ago. However, the results indicate that about the same percentage of adolescent boys and girls have the qualities that attract choices of the opposite sex today as in 1942. About the same percentage of social isolates appear at each age level. Data from both years show that boys display a greater frequency of cross-sex choices than girls. This is interpreted as reflecting less reticence on the part of the boys in expressing overtly an interest in particular girls, rather than as implying earlier and greater interest in the

TABLE 12-1

Percentages of Boys and Girls at Various School Grades in 1942 and 1963
Who Chose the Opposite Sex, Were Chosen by the Opposite Sex, and
Were Chosen by No One (After Kuhlen and Houlihan)

	Grades						
	6	7	8	9	10	11	12
Boys choosing girls							
1942	45.0			72.5			75.0
1963	48.8	68.9	69.2	79.9*	81.6	83.3	91.0
Girls choosing boys							
1942	39.2			59.7			63.0
1963	52.8*	46.7	69.6	72.9*	68.3	72.7	82.7[†]
Boys chosen by girls							
1942	31.2			49.1			65.8
1963	46.7[†]	40.0	40.7	47.4	54.7	69.4	74.0
Girls chosen by boys							
1942	30.8			52.4			59.7
1963	39.6	46.7	51.7	52.2	59.1	43.7	61.8
Boys chosen by no one							
1942	5.5			5.0			1.9
1963	5.9	5.8	7.1	8.2	4.7	9.2	5.7
Girls chosen by no one							
1942	2.5			3.2			4.2
1963	2.5	2.2	2.7	3.8	3.7	4.3	5.4

*Difference between 1942 and 1963 percentages significant at the .05 level.
[†]Difference significant at the .01 level.

opposite sex on their part. It is notable that the data show a greater heterosexual
interest throughout the age range and do not necessarily suggest an earlier onset
of interest.

The Idealism of Adolescents.   Perhaps the most striking attainment of adolescents is their ability to conceptualize at an abstract level. He moves beyond
what Piaget referred to as the concrete operations of childhood to that of organizing his experiences and ideas into fundamental principles (Flavell, 1963). No
longer a child, but not accepted as an adult in our culture, he tries to determine
who he is and where he belongs. His body image is no longer that of a child; his
feelings toward self and others have broadened; he now sees self and others in a
larger perspective; and he now uses standards he has acquired to guide him in his
relations with others.

Also, the adolescent at this stage faces the additional task of sexual identity
and playing a sexual role. This aspect of his development is most important in
his peer relations, which is discussed at a later point in this chapter.

Acquiring an Appropriate Sex Role.   Development tasks unique for the
adolescent period are acquiring the appropriate sex role and learning to get along
with members of the opposite sex. In an earlier chapter it was pointed out that
children learn to identify with their sex group during early childhood. This is

part of the preparation for acquiring the appropriate sex role. The father's active role in the home helps the child to identify with the correct sex role and to acquire the appropriate role (Nash, 1965).

Changes in sex-appropriateness of behavior during adolescence are related to physical maturation. Boys and girls advanced in their physical maturation attempt to play a masculine or feminine role advanced for their age level. This may be observed in their manner of dress, make-up, behavior, and growing interests in the opposite sex. Zuk's (1958) analysis of adolescent boys and girls during the postadolescent years (15-17) revealed the following (pp. 31-32):

1. Sex-appropriate behavior increased significantly in girls from 16 to 17 years. Boys showed no comparable increase during this period.
2. Sex-appropriate behavior tended to be more stable in girls from year to year than in boys. For both sexes, however, such behavior was more stable during the sixteenth year than during the fifteenth year.
3. Behavior which was sex-appropriate and more popular with boys tended also to be relatively more popular with girls, and vice versa.
4. Sex-appropriate behavior was shown to be related in reasonable directions but in low degree with social, physical, intellectual, and temperament factors.
5. The sex-appropriateness of adolescent behavior was shown to vary widely from one area to another in the case of both boys and girls.

In the study by Schultz (1965) 105 high school males and 159 high school females were selected as subjects, to study the perception of the feminine role in today's society. A feminine-role scale was constructed consisting of 39 items. The results of the study indicated that ninth-and tenth-grade subjects agreed with the female submissive roles, while the eleventh-and twelfth-grade pupils tended to agree with the male dominance of the continuum. Schultz states:

> Female subjects agree more than the male subjects that a woman should follow a career for herself whether married or single; and, if a woman works after marriage, it should be on a voluntary basis to prevent interference with homemaking. At the same time, females tend to agree more than males that women should have the same pay, working conditions, and hours as men, in the same jobs; and women should be trained as scientists, politicians, pilots, and engineers as well as men. (p. 49)

The Widened Gap Between Generations. Communication between the older and younger generation always has been a problem. The problem has been increased severalfold in the past 50 years due to rapid changing conditions. The ways of the older generation when they were teen-agers are vastly different from those of present-day adolescents. An adult generation that grew up during the depression of the 1930's is sharply separated from a generation of youth which experiences prosperity in abundance either by participating in it or being a bystander and desirous of becoming a part of it. Demands for social justice ring out to the new generation denied various opportunities. Deprived youth do not always come from homes where parents have a low income. They frequently come from a home where the parents are too much engaged in worldly affairs to give attention to their children. They grow up in a community where demands are made of them that they do not accept or appreciate. They go to school geared increasingly to the intellectually high achiever-to those who yield to the demands for learnings required at school. Those who lack the desire to learn or the ability to learn are left behind and denounced by the school and other adults as failures. These youths make up the misunderstood generation; communication between them and responsible adults is vital for their sake as well as for society in general.

Adolescent's Subculture.   Not all adolescents or postadolescents become a part of adolescent subculture. Young people or postadolescents can roughly be divided into three groups. The first group consists of those who follow a long course of educational training before moving into graduate and professional schools. Many of these marry in their late teens or early 20's, but continue their education.

A second group consists of those who finish high school or technical training and then go to work. This group enters into the adult world around age 17-20. A third group is made up of youth who come from a disadvantaged environment or a situation where stimulation for growth was lacking. These individuals are frequently frustrated; sometimes goals seem to be completely lacking. Such individuals drop out of school at an early age, after a history of frustration, failure, and frequently difficulties with school or legal authorities. Many of these become delinquents.

Although these are not discrete groups, they may be observed. Each group has problems of adjusting to the existing culture. However, their reactions vary. The confusions of adolescents exist in all civilized cultures; however, certain cultures help them to find a role in society more than others. A primitive tribe with its rituals defines for the adolescent a pattern of behavior as an adult that furnishes him a guide for action. The dynamic nature of American culture is such as to exclude adolescents from adult culture. Hsu and others (1961) compared the behavior of Chicago white adolescents with Hawaiian Mongolian (Chinese) adolescents by means of responses to items of the Rorschach test. The comparisons showed that Hawaiian Mongolian youth have a much smoother transition to adulthood than the American youth. They were also more contented and more emotionally stable. The investigators attributed this difference to the dynamic nature of American culture.

The American adolescent has outgrown childhood with its make-believe behavior. He is sufficiently mature physically to enter into adult culture, but is denied the opportunity to do so by present-day conditions and attitudes held by parents toward adolescents. Thus he is forced to develop a culture of his own distinct from the adult culture, yet an adaptation of its norms and behavior. Adolescents use various devices to maintain their subculture and to exclude adults from it. This may be noted in their style of dress, games, dance, and general conversation. Many fads appear, but since adolescence is a temporary aspect of life these fads and styles are continuously changing. This makes it even harder for adults to understand and appreciate adolescent culture.

Most adolescents either (1) drop out of school and go to work, or (2) among girls drop out of school and get married, or (3) adopt the adolescent subculture. There are some who feel secure in their home, school, and other activities and do not feel the need to adopt the adolescent subculture. There is in many of our large cities a group of apparently friendly young people who flount convention in an attempt to find their own identity. One of these groups in San Francisco is known as the hippies. Concerning these Halleck states: "Hippies are incredibly lonely people who seem almost incapable of forming intimate relations. Even their sexual contacts are more frenetic than meaningful" (Burgett, 1967). These hippies preach love. Most of them have tried LSD, marijuana, or other psychedelic drugs at least once in their life in their quest to understand themselves, God, love, or life. They are frequently unkempt in appearance, bohemian in their attitudes, and free-wheeling in their sex practices.

Psychological Changes During Adolescence

Data available about adolescents in the United States do not support the viewpoint that adolescence is accompanied by rebellion against the existing order, or that adolescence is a period of "storm and stress." It is true, as pointed out in Chapter 4, that important physiological changes occur at this stage of life; these are accompanied by changed feelings about the opposite sex and a sense of growing independence.

Attitudes Toward the Home. Although we witness the activities of rebellious youth, research findings do not support the rebellion image as the characteristic of the vast majority of adolescents. In a study by Ostlund (1957) 506 rural high school students were asked who was the most important reference point in their lives—family, chums, or someone else. Over three-fourths of the students indicated their parents. In a study by Garrison (1966) replies were tabulated from the responses of 222 ninth-grade boys and 243 ninth-grade girls to the question: "What three things or events in your life up to the present time have had the greatest effect upon your present life?" The percent of students listing the different items, presented in Table 12-2, show the importance adolescents attach to various home and school influences.

Inquiries among representative samples of English adolescents by Hancock and Wakeford (1965) as well as comparative studies sponsored by Unesco (Berge, 1964) show that close bonds exist between young people and their parents and a great appreciation of them as well as a reliance on them as counselors on personal and social problems. This has been observed at all social levels. In a study of young people between 14 and 20 in the industrial north of England, Musgrove (1966) found that the young people often stated a desire to talk over problems with their parents, and further stated that they were often able to do so. A fifteen-year-old daughter of a plumber wrote: "At home you can always

TABLE 12-2
Response of Ninth-Grade Pupils to the Exercise "Things or Events
Having Greatest Influence on Your Lives" (After Garrison)

Concern	Boys (Percent)	Girls (Percent)	Average (Percent)
School teachers	10.3	13.0	11.65
Home, family	7.2	7.6	7.4
Father	7.0	7.3	7.15
Friends, kinspeople	7.0	7.2	7.1
Mother	5.8	8.0	6.9
Success, rewards, sports	8.6	4.8	6.7
Entering school	5.2	8.0	6.6
Size, appearance, health, sickness	6.8	6.0	6.4
Love affair	1.2	9.8	5.5
Job, work, career	6.6	3.0	4.8
Death, accidents.	4.2	4.3	4.25
Travel, moving	3.8	4.0	3.9
Church, religion.	3.5	4.2	3.85
New experience, freedom	4.8	2.5	3.65
Neighborhood, clubs	3.2	2.3	2.75
Brothers and sisters.	2.6	2.7	2.65
Miscellaneous	10.0	7.5	8.75

tell your troubles to your parents and not be laughed at." A fifteen-year-old son of a laborer wrote: "At home you always have a chance to tell someone your troubles." These are the kinds of statements the writers have gotten from most young people in the United States that they have counseled. A broad picture of the home as a place of security where there is always someone to whom you can talk and be heard emerges.

In a study by Meissner (1965) 1,278 high school boys were asked to answer 217 questions on areas of interaction between themselves and their parents. The results indicated that typical perceptions of father and mother can be identified; the father's influence regarding guidance seems to become relatively more dominant as the boy grows older; and the adolescent boy increasingly calls into question his father's understanding of him. The shift in the pattern of interaction that is statistically significant is listed as follows (p. 228):

Positive

Increased feeling of adequate social opportunity.
Increased feeling of sufficient social freedom.
Increased acceptance of parental authority.
Increased valuation of father's guidance.

Negative

Increased dissatisfaction with home life.
Increased unhappiness in the home.
Decrease in amount of leisure time spent at home.
Increased conflict with parents over religion.
Decreased approval of parental guidance.

Increase in seeing friends disapproved by parents.
Increased feeling of the imposition of parents' ideas.
Decreased valuation of father's understanding of personal problems.
Increased feeling of being misunderstood by parents; more misunderstood by
    father than mother.

Pubescence and Changed Attitudes.   With pubescence there is an increase
in sex hormones, which relates to an increased interest in the opposite sex. The
maturing individual is attracted towards members of the opposite sex, and
associations with them are rewarding in that sexual tension is both produced and
relieved. This increased interest in the opposite sex leads to a greater interest in
personal grooming and increased attention to members of the opposite sex as
revealed in a comparison by Jones and Bayley (1950) of early-maturing boys
with average maturers. The early maturing boys from age 12 to 17 were more
natural and unaffected than the average maturer.

In an early study by Stone and Barker (1939) 1,000 girls from two large
high schools were matched in chronological age and social status but were significantly different in physiological development—one group postmenarcheal, the
other premenarcheal. The postmenarcheal girls as an age-group showed more interest in boys. They were also more interested in adornment and display of the
person, and displayed less interest in participating in games requiring vigorous
activity. There was no noticeable difference in the extent to which the two
groups rebelled against or came into conflict with family and authority.

Attitudes toward authority, ranging from almost complete conformity to
rebelliousness, were evaluated and studied by Tuma and Livson (1960) in three
interpersonal situations for a sample of boys and girls at ages 14, 15, and 16. In
line with results of other studies girls proved to conform more than boys, and
they consistently tended to increase their degree of conformity from age 14 to
16 in the three situations studied; no clear age trends were noted by boys,
except there was a decided decline in conformity at age 16, suggesting that
age 16 is a crucial period in the boys' growth in independence.

Effects of Time of Maturation.   Girls mature earlier than boys. Also,
within each sex there will be those in both sexes who are late in maturing, while
others mature early. Children at either extreme in rate of maturing are likely to
be handicapped in their development unless they are given special consideration
by those concerned with their guidance and training.

In the California Adolescent Growth Study ratings for "animation," "eagerness," "energy," "talkativeness," and "laughter" were obtained for early- and
late-maturing boys. The late maturers were found to be consistently above the
average in these traits (Jones and Bayley, 1950). Inferences from projective
materials, furnish additional material showing that late maturity had adverse
effects on personality during adolescence. An analysis of data from the Thematic
Apperception Test showed that late-maturing boys more frequently had negative self-concepts, feelings of inadequacy, prolonged dependency, and feelings of
being rejected or dominated by their parents and peers (Mussen and Jones,
1957).

The adult characteristics of early- and late-maturing boys were observed at an average age of 33 by Jones (1957). As was predicted at age 17 differences in gross size tend to disappear. Based on results of psychological tests, the early maturers made higher scores on "good impression" and "socialization." The early maturers seemed to have attained vocational goals which are satisfying and status conferring; a slightly higher proportion of the late-maturing have college degrees and the only college teacher is in this group. Since early maturing places the boy at an advantage in physical performances and leadership during adolescence it is but natural that this would lead toward positions of leadership in human relations during adulthood; the late-maturing boy more frequently turns to activities other than those requiring physical competition and would more likely satisfy his needs for achievement in academic pursuits or related activities.

This would not neccessarily operate for girls for two reasons. In the first place, girls mature earlier than boys of the same age. The late-maturing girl matures at approximately the same age as the average maturing boy. She is less likely to start dating and enter into heterosexual activities than her early-maturing class mates. Second, physical competition is not especially important among adolescent girls and young women. Thus early maturing does not place the girl at an advantage in performances based upon physical competition.

Effects of Peers.   The parent is not the only source of security for the adolescent; another source is his peer group. The typical adolescent is a conform-

The personality adjustment of the physically handicapped adolescent is improved by learning experiences involving tasks judged important to themselves and approved by others. (Courtesy Charlotte-Mecklenburg County Schools.)

ist to his peers. His peers structure a framework of acceptable behavior patterns. Thus close identification with peers is an important source of security.

Conformity to peer culture is frequently associated with good emotional and social adjustment. In a study by Langner (1954) designed to test this hypothesis, various clinical and social-psychological tests were administered to a sample of 600 school pupils from the fourth to the twelfth grade, one-third of whom were Indian, one-third white Protestant, and one-third Spanish or Mexican. The results showed that, although conformity to peer-group behavioral norms was positively correlated with emotional adjustment, deviance did not necessarily indicate maladjustment. There is some evidence that conformity is sometimes associated with feelings of adequacy, while lack of conformity may result from feelings of inadequacy or insecurity. Deviance from group behavioral norms leads to maladjustments mainly when such deviation separated the individual from the group, automatically cutting off an important source for the satisfaction of certain needs of the individual and perhaps producing an "isolate." Those who had friends but thought they had none were more seriously disturbed emotionally, while those who were actually "isolates" were better emotionally adjusted. The feeling of isolation seems to be the real basis for the disturbance, indicating the importance of the self-concept.

Changing Self-Concepts. The child moves into adolescence with certain concepts of the self fairly well formulated, while others are still not clear. Throughout the period of adolescence the individual keeps striving to integrate his behavior and attitude toward the self into a coherent whole. The integration is made difficult by changes in the physical self and by changes originating in his environment, especially in interpersonal contacts. The adolescent who learned during childhood to think of himself as worthless does not readily build a new self-image just because he has grown larger and stronger.

Sometimes a new picture of the self emerges along with physical or physiological changes. This may be observed when the adolescent boy or girl experiences success or when he is accepted by his age-mates. Unfortunately, adolescence may be a time when intellectual, social, or economic demands are made upon an individual that he is unable to meet. This makes it most difficult for the individual to maintain a favorable self-concept. Thus at this stage some disadvantaged adolescents develop unfavorable attitudes toward others.

Vocational Plans. Growth into adolescence brings with it an increased concern about the future—particularly marriage and employment. A survey conducted by the national Girl Scout Organization revealed that one-third of the girls wanted to go to college (Stratton, 1957). In their job plans, they expressed a desire for steady employment, interesting work, and pleasant people to work with. High pay and promotion ranked low with girls, especially when comparisons are made with expectations by boys. Only 2 percent of the girls expressed a desire to run their own business.

Adolescents from the lowest economic scale today are faced with a vocational situation uniquely different from that faced by the lowest economic classes of previous generations. According to Pearl (1965, p. 91) three paths for entering the vocational market were open to youth earlier, but have been closed or partially closed to youth of today.

The unskilled labor market was open to many, since the early technological changes took place at the expense of skilled labor, actually increasing in many cases the need for unskilled and semiskilled workers. However, today automation has eliminated the vast majority of unskilled jobs, making it difficult for the unskilled poor to enter the labor market. In the past, little capital was needed to get started in agriculture or business. Thus the free-enterprise system worked to the advantage of energetic individuals with little capital. This, too, has been eliminated—the worker with little capital who wished to go into business for himself.

In the past the ambitious boy or girl who remained in school to finish the tenth grade or more could be assured of a relatively good job on the labor market, since this was the educational standard set forth for many jobs. Youth of today must be prepared to stay in school beyond the high school years so as to receive the education and training needed to participate in the world of work. For many of the poor, this is well-nigh impossible. Thus, we are likely to find a relatively large percentage of disadvantaged youth among the unemployed or upon low-level or part-time jobs.

The study by Rehberg (1966), consisting of data gathered on 6,000 students enrolled as sophomores in the public and parochial schools of Pennsylvania revealed a close relation between educational expectations and certain social-psychological factors. The results revealed a positive relation between expectations to enroll in four-year colleges and (1) social status, (2) parental achievement pressure (3) education of each parent (4) proportion of the peer group which is college oriented. There was an inverse relation between college expectancy and family size. Youths from the lower class are usually oriented toward daily or weekly concrete goals; long-time, abstract goals are in the main meaningless or of little significance to them. Such youths need more immediate and concrete rewards to reinforce their learning efforts. However, in a longitudinal study reported by Tyler (1964) few career related differences in interests between subjects of different social class membership were noted prior to the eighth grade. After this stage of their educational development they seem to take an increasingly more realistic attitude toward a vocational career.

A comparison by Douvan and Adelson (1966) of the vocational aspirations of sixteen-year-old boys in a national sample with that of fourteen-year-old boys revealed the following:

1. Sixteen-year-old boys were more frequently able to state a vocational goal.
2. Sixteen-year-old boys more frequently listed a specific occupation (e.g., a nuclear physicist) rather than a broad occupational category such as a scientist.

3. Sixteen-year-old boys furnished more rational explanations for their vocational choices.
4. Sixteen-year-old boys have more realistic conceptions of the demands of the vocation and the preparation needed for it.

In addition Douvan and Adelson (1966) noted that the realistic and high achievement motivated, upward-aspiring subjects in their sample of fourteen-year-old boys chose vocational goals only moderately advanced in status over that of jobs held by their fathers; the unrealistic, upward-aspiring boys named occupations far different in status from their father's jobs.

The study by Kraus (1964) verified results from other studies that high aspirations among adolescents for going to college are in direct proprotion to the educational attainment of the father. Also, where the father's job is a high-status blue-collar occupation accompanied by a higher income than other manual workers, the children are likely to have middle-class educational aspirations. Kraus noted that in certain interests, values, and activities college-oriented lower-class youths were very similar to college-oriented middle-class students. As for peer associations and extracurricular activities, these influences were found to be significant "(a) College-oriented lower-class students were very likely to have acquaintances who also have college aspirations. (b) They tended to be extremely active in extracurricular activities. (c) They were more likely to be attending a predominantly middle-class than a predominantly working-class school" (p. 877).

The Adolescent and His Peers

As boys and girls move away from close emotional ties at home they tend to form close friendships with their age-mates and class-mates at school. These age-mates referred to here as peers, furnish the adolescent a source of security and satisfy their need for belongingness, which is closely related to security. These age-mates have somewhat similar needs and problems. In addition, lower-class peer groups frequently serve important status functions for adolescents who are disadvantaged according to criteria of society's institution (schools, churches, businesses). Thus peer groups become the most important status point for such teen-agers. Peer group norms and values stress for these youngsters achievement goals not easily attainable by the conventional norms and values of the larger society. For the lower class youngster, therefore, the peer group is extremely important, and as Sherif and Sherif (1964, p. 91) pointed out: "The greater the importance to an individual member of a natural group . . . the more binding for him is participation in activities initiated by the group." It is out of this social framework that delinquency frequently arises.

The results of a study by Lassigne (1963) support the hypothesis that adolescents (60 from the eighth grade and 60 from the twelfth) are influenced more by the opinions of their peer group than by the opinions of the adult group. Younger adolescents (eighth-graders) are influenced more by the opinions of their classmates than older adolescents. Also, adolescents from the lower social class are influenced more by their peers than adolescents of middle-class status. No significant differences were found between the sexes in susceptibility to peer-group influences, although there was a slight trend for the girls to be influenced more by the peer group than the boys.

The Structure of Adolescent Groups.   The social structure of an adolescent group will depend on many elements characteristic of the particular group as well as the cultural norms associated with the environments from which the different members come. The sociogram for boys and girls in the ninth grade, shown in Figure 12-1, was developed during the course of the California Adolescent Growth Study (Jones, 1943, p. 43). Each youngster is represented by a circle. A solid line connecting the circles indicated that each person mentioned the other as a best friend, while a dotted line indicates a one-way choice.

The social situation presented in Figure 12-1 is one which is typical of groups during adolescence. Some youngsters seem to have no friends (at least in a particular grade or group) and have been referred to as "isolates"; others have one close friend; others a few friends, and others many friends. Those frequently chosen as friends by peers have been referred to as "stars." Such a diagram shows only one of many ways the members of a group relate to each other. A different chart will be obtained from choices involving leaders, best students, creative individuals, and the like.

A comparison of the choice of friends by boys and by girls shows some striking differences revealing significant differences in the interpersonal relations of adolescent boys and girls. Chains of friends may be noted among groups with the chains for boys including more persons than that for girls. Also, more small cliques appear among the girls. Note particularly the three girls in number 2, an apparent self-sufficient triangle. Group 3 is the large in-group, while group 3a includes 2 girls that are apparent close self-sufficient chums. In contrast, the boys seem much less likely to limit their best friends, several "isolates" or "near-isolates" may be observed. In general, adolescent boys and adult males are considerably more democratic and accept boys outside the inner circle more readily than girls.

Formation of Cliques and Friendships.   In our culture boys tend to relate to peers in small groups that serve as the testing ground for locating norms of behavior and for standardizing their own behavior. Girls, on the other hand, seem to rely mainly upon close, personal friendships in pairs or very small cliques. The results of studies by Douvan and Adelson (1966) indicate that the peer group assumes an important place in the social development of adolescents, especially boys. The group supports the boy in his efforts to achieve emotional independence from home ties; the adolescent boy depends on this support as a basis for strength and security. Accordingly, there is a reciprocal loyalty established between the group as a whole and individual members. Girls do not seem

Best friends-boys

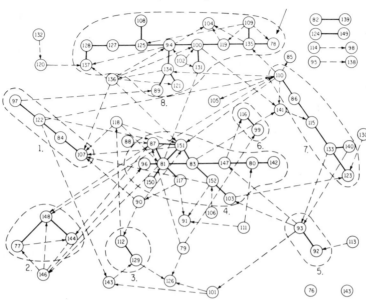

Best friends-girls

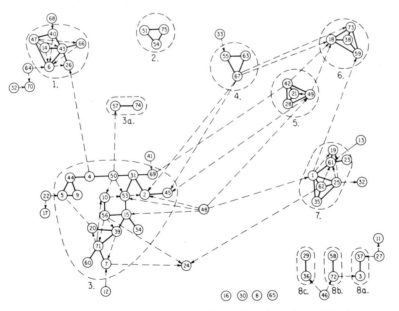

Figure 12-1. Sociogram for boys and girls based on the California Adolescent Growth Study. (From Harold E. Jones. *Development in Adolescence*. Appleton-Century-Crofts, New York; 1943, p. 43.)

to need this support to any great degree, since they are less provoked by inner striving for emotional independence from home ties. They tend to regard the group as a setting in which to find close dyadic relationships. This whole area is marked by differences in adolescent tasks of boys and girls: boys are dominated by needs for achievement and independence; girls are more concerned with developing interpersonal skills and the need for love and security. Thus the two sex groups use social relationships differently to support and express their needs and concerns.

Proximity furnishes an initial physical screen for making friendships. This determines the probability of contacts. If proximity furnishes a physical screen for contacts and friendships, peership provides a social screen. Among high school students, the year in high school is usually a prominent characteristic; it specifies how far one is toward graduation, and generally furnishes a good basis for determining age level.

The clique is by nature intolerant; it demands loyalty from its members that prevents many wholesome interactions with those who are not members of the particular clique. The spontaneous groupings of adolescents have been studied by a number of investigators. From these studies different classifications have been set forth, all of which encourage social acceptance of members of the group and exclusion of those who are not members of the group. A set of groupings set forth by Phelps and Horrocks (1958) is based upon social and economic status, preferred activities, and self-identification as to a role in the group. In almost any high school will be found the following groups:

1. A group largely from the lower class and of low ability that doesn't participate in many school sponsored activities.
2. A group from the middle class, only moderately emancipated from the home that strives for good grades and participates in most school activities as well as activities outside the school.
3. A group that is less mature socially, not emancipated from home ties, and centers its activities around the home, school, and certain community activities.
4. A group that identifies closely with lower-class behavior norms and displays little interest in school or school-related activities.

Interaction with Peers.   A study by Maccoby (1961) set forth the hypothesis that children, in their social interactions with age-mates, tended to employ the same kinds of behavior their parents used toward them in like situations. Sixth-grade pupils were used as subjects. The results showed that boys reared by parents who enforced certain rules tended to accept rule enforcement from peers when they had deviated; whereas this tendency was not noted among girls reared by such parents. The results of the study indicated that girls who insisted on rule enforcement had relatively punitive parents during early childhood.

There is evidence from many studies that peer acceptance in high school is related to intelligence and success in athletics, club work, or academic performances. The average individual in junior high school is not likely to be popular with his classmates. A study by Muma (1965) was concerned with peer evaluation and academic performance. Sociometric tests were administered to high school students in Tuscola County, Michigan. The results revealed that highly accepted individuals are academically successful, while lowly accepted individuals are average or below average in their academic performance.

A very significant finding reported by Iscoe and Carden (1961) indicated that popularity among peers is related to conformity to sex-role expectations. The investigators made use of experimental measure of field dependence and independence which had previously yielded stable sex differences in early adulthood. The investigators found that popular boys tend to be field-independent, while most popular girls were field dependent, as compared to their less popular peers. Sociometric choices clustered around those persons who had incorporated the sex-appropriate behavior that will ultimately distinguish the males and females in their group as adults. Tuddenham (1952) earlier reported similar findings based on ratings and questionnaire data. The results from these studies are impressive in that they show the importance of assuming the appropriate sex-role behavior in social adjustments during adolescence.

Dating Practices. It was pointed out in the previous chapter that dating appears among many children in late childhood. Going steady may also be frequently observed. However, the notion of earlier dating by adolescents from the lower social class than those from the middle class is not borne out in a study reported by Bock and Burchinal (1962). Data was collected from questionnaires completed by high school junior and senior students from Iowa. Occupations of fathers were taken as indices of the social-status variable. One other feature of the data may be noted. The middle-status and high-status girls began dating at a slightly earlier period than boys; the low-status boys had their first date and first steady slightly earlier than the low-status girls, although the mean differences were very small, 0.2 and 0.1 year respectively. No significant differences between ages at beginning data for boys and girls were reported in an earlier study by Lowrie (1952) involving a much larger sample.

As adolescents grow older dating frequently involves some degree of sexual experience, especially among those going steady. Adults in the United States as well as other countries within Western culture have shown considerable concern about the matter of premarital sexual relations. Dating behavior and courtship practices are related to class status and interrelations within the family. Wallin (1954) noted that circumstances or conditions that intervened so as to adversely affect interpersonal relations between parents and children tend to have an adverse affect on dating and attitude toward marriage. Some of the most obvious background factors are the absence of one parent from the family group, tension between parents, revolt against authoritarian control of the parents, an inconsistency in parental behavior and attitudes. Wallin noted that senior high school students who did not date at all generally had a less wholesome family background than seniors who dated.

There is evidence that going steady leads to sexual relations and frequently early marriages. It has been estimated that one teen-age girl in every six becomes pregnant out of wedlock (McCormack, 1967). It is likely that the birth control pill will in time reduce pregnancy among teen-agers. Scholars in different disciplines are not in agreement concerning the effect of the birth-control pill and sexual behavior among teen-agers. According to data reported by McCormack there has been a sharp rise in venereal disease, with an estimate of 300,000 being reported annually. The estimate for unreported cases exceeds one million cases.

The increased amount of petting and the frankness with which teen-agers deal with problems of sex has brought forth crys of despair from many adults. We hear of the changed sex mores, or the sexual revolution among adolescents. It seems that the so-called sexual revolution among younger people is largely a change in attitude rather than in behavior. For the vast majority of adolescents we are seeing a sort of behavior and self-control based not on guilt resulting from sin, or fear of disapproval, or fear of pregnancy, but on a concept of human relations that emphasizes self-respect, human worth, and respect for others. Adolescents are not satisfied with arbitrary standards but are demanding logical reasons for ethical standards.

Concerns about Marriage.   Marriage among teen-agers has increased sufficiently to produce changed attitudes on the part of parents and schools regarding the education and support of teen-agers and their families. It was relatively recently estimated that 600,000 babies a year were born to wives who were 18 years of age or younger (Havemann, 1965). In a study by Garrison (1966) it was noted that getting married, family life, and children were the areas of greatest concern for 18.8 percent of ninth-grade boys studied and 22.7 percent of ninth-grade girls.

According to the results of a survey by the Gilbert Youth Research Institute 40 percent of 1,155 teen-agers questioned said they expected to have families of four or more children (Gilbert, 1966). Less than 3 percent listed one child as the desired number of children, while 27 percent listed two and 32 percent listed three as the ideal number.

One aspect of a Purdue Opinion Panel (1961) on youth's attitudes toward courtship and marriage dealt with the traits desired in a future mate. The results are presented in Table 12-3. The first group of traits does not differ significantly from those desired in friends of either sex, whether or not marriage is being considered. These traits emphasize physical attractiveness, consideration, dependability, affection, cleanliness, and social maturity.

The items in the second and third group suggest that even at the adolescent period it is recognized that there is more to marriage than being a "nice" and attractive person. The realistic attitude of the adolescent is shown by his desire that his mate be able to function independently of his parents and has interests and ideals similar to his or hers.

There has been a continuous trend since World War II for adolescents to marry in many cases while still in high school. However, a large percentage of adolescents who marry young are dropouts; frequently the girl is pregnant. The

TABLE 12-3

Percentage of Boys and Girls Indicating a Trait as Being Very Desirable
for a Future Mate

Traits	Boys	Girls
Is physically attractive and good-looking	45	17
Is popular with others	46	42
Shows affection.	84	85
Takes pride in personal appearance and manners	89	90
Mixes well in social situations	51	59
Is considerate of me and others	84	95
Is dependable, can be trusted	92	96
Has a pleasant disposition	77	84
Acts his (her) age, is not childish	77	87
Is clean in speech and language	72	82
Does not pet or try to get too familiar	22	39
Does not use tobacco	42	29
Does not use liquor.	49	49
Is approved by my parents.	56	74
Desires normal family life with children	77	87
Is independent of his or her parents	45	64
Has interests similar to mine	49	48
Has ideals similar to mine	46	52
Is as intelligent as I am.	27	42
Knows how to budget and handle money	62	75
Has a job.	9	93
Is started on a professional career	8	42
Knows how to cook and keep house	79	15

boy takes the first job he can get, which is a logical decision considering the high
rate of overall unemployment in his age group. Their work history is usually
chaotic; their earnings are meager. Couples who marry in their teens and have
their first child soon thereafter are most likely to face financial difficulties,
unless they are given help by their parents. It is likely that newer contraceptive
methods, such as the pill, will produce significant changes in early marriages and
the size of the family. This is already observable among college students, where a
great many young wives are working while the husbands attend school, or where
both parties work part time and go to school.

Problems of Adolescents

Numerous techniques have been used to investigate the problems of adolescents; the most common procedure has been to use the problem inventory.
Other methods that have been used are (a) the interview, (b) projective techniques, and (c) essays. The results of the different studies reveal that between
one-third and one-half of the adolescent school population are much concerned
about grades at school and other aspects of their academic work. It has been
pointed out that this is the primary reason for the widespread cheating in school.

In a study reported by Adams (1964) approximately 4,000 boys and girls from over 30 schools were asked to report the biggest personal problem that was causing difficulty. The boys and girls were also asked to list what they thought was the greatest problem for other boys and girls of their age. The subjects ranged in age from 10 to 19 years.

Problem areas and the percent of personal problems reported by each area for self and peers by the total group of boys and girls are presented in Table 12-4. Contrary to findings of many other studies, school problems were listed by a larger percentage of boys than girls. Students from suburban communities listed more school problems than other students. Girls listed more interpersonal and family problems than boys, while boys listed more problems related to sports and recreation and finances.

TABLE 12-4

Percentage of Personal Problems Reported by Problem Area for Self and Peers by
Total Male and Female Groups (After Adams)

Problem Area	Self		Peer	
	Male	Female	Male	Female
School	35	23	21	14
Interpersonal	12	19	23	33
Maturity	2	3	2	7
Emotions	2	4	2	3
Work	6	5	7	6
Sports and recreation	4	2	5	2
Health	2	4	2	2
Ethical	1	2	1	2
Family	10	22	8	17
Habits	0	0	1	1
Finances	10	4	7	4
Unclassified	8	6	8	3
No answer	4	3	13	6
No problem	4	3	0	0

Both sexes see their peers as having fewer school problems and more interpersonal problems than they report for themselves. Otherwise, there was a close relationship between problem areas of self and of peers.

A summary by Remmers (1962) of four cross-cultural studies conducted at Purdue University in which the SRA Inventory was used revealed substantial correlations between the rankings of the seriousness of problems by the different groups studied, although the similarity was the greatest for similar cultures. What to do after completing high school was found to be a major problem of American and West Germany teen-agers. Also, many teen-agers expressed concern about grades, going to college, making new friends, and how to study better.

School Related Problems.   Adolescents' feelings about school come mainly from two sources: (1) their friendships at school and the status they have with their schoolmates, and (2) their achievement at school. For some adolescents, their relations with their teachers are also important determiners of their feelings about school. There is considerable evidence that under desirable conditions teachers have an important bearing on the adolescents' attitudes toward school. However, fewer than 10 percent of adolescents choose a teacher as their adult model (Douvan and Adelson, 1966).

Data dealing with adolescent educational expectations were obtained by Rehberg (1966) from a survey of 6,000 students enrolled as sophomores in public and parochial schools in Pennsylvania. Statistical treatment of the data led to some important generalizations about the proportion of adolescents actually expecting to enroll in a four-year college. The proportion seems to vary (1) positively with social class; (2) inversely with family size; (3) positively with intensity of parental achievement pressure; (4) positively with the education of each parent; and (5) positively with the proportion of peer groups which expect to attend college. In addition, the proportion is greater than the social stratum mean under the condition of maternal, but not paternal, educational superiority.

Among teen-agers one may find a proschool group (achievers) and an antischool group (nonachievers). In an earlier chapter dealing with motivation it was pointed out that the achievement motive in learning at school developed during childhood, and was closely related to the advantaged home where the child is continuously reinforced in the acquisition of verbal concepts.

The results of a study by Wormell (1963) indicate that communication and reinforcement of learning from parents is considerably less for the underachievers than for the high achievers of the same intelligence. This finding has been confirmed by larger studies of populations in both elementary and secondary classrooms.

The close relation between the educational expectations and the occupation of the father, which is a measure of class status, is shown in a study by Rehberg and Westby (1967). The results, presented in Table 12-5, show that educational expectations are closely related to the occupational status of the father. More than four times as many youngsters whose father's occupation is in the higher occupational scale expect to finish sixteen or more years of schooling as compared to youngsters from homes where the father is an unskilled worker.

School Failure and Dropouts.   Next to the home the school is the most potent force in the development and guidance of boys and girls into useful and worthy citizenship. And although the school is playing an increasingly important role, it frequently contributes to delinquency. Studies show that there is a close relation between truancy and delinquency. An important problem for parents and teachers is to determine the cause or causes of truancy if we are to reduce delinquency. Perhaps the outstanding characteristic of truants and dropouts is their lack of interest in school. This would seem to stem from their unpleasant experiences at school, which would involve their teachers, classmates, and school program.

The seriousness of continued school failure is supported by data from a

TABLE 12-5

Educational Expectations by Occupation of Fathers (percentages)
(After Rehberg and Westby)

| Occupation of | Educational Expectations (in years) | | | | |
Father	16+	14	12	11−	N.R.
Higher Executives, proprietors of large concerns, and major professionals	84	10	4	1	1
Business managers, proprietors of medium-sized businesses, and lesser professionals	72	15	10	3	0
Administrative personnel, small independent businesses and minor professionals	56	21	21	1	1
Clerical and sales workers, technicians, and owners of little businesses	47	22	29	1	1
Skilled manual employees	30	25	43	2	0
Machine operators and semi skilled employees	22	25	48	4	2
Unskilled employees	20	21	51	6	2

study by Zabolski (1949) in which a comparison is presented of 50 delinquent boys with a mean age of 15.5 years with a control group of 50 nondelinquent boys. The delinquent boys presented an educational and psychological deficit, which could best be attributed to a series of inadequacies or failures beginning in early life and leading to truancy and dropping out of school. If one waits to study dropouts at the time they actually drop out one will gain little that is very helpful in understanding the etiology of dropouts. It is not the sixteen-year-old that drops out of school but the sixteen-year-old who is frequently ill-prepared for school and at an early age develops an unfavorable attitude toward school (Ames and Walker, 1965).

Suicide Among Adolescents.   Suicide is the number three cause of death among those aged 15 to 19; it is the number 2 cause of death among college students (Gauzer, 1966). It has been estimated by some that the true figure of adolescent suicides in the United States may be as high as 5,000 a year. According to Stanley F. Yolles, Director of the National Institute of Mental Health in 1965, there are five categories of problems most troubling to adolescents—problems the young people do not readily discuss with parents or others who are in a position to help them arrive at a better solution than suicide. These problems center around parents, poverty, peers, broken romances, and pregnancy. Many of these problems with parents center around grades at school. Middle-class parents, especially fathers, are very demanding of their children in the maintenance of a high grade average. The demands seem to be highest for sons; therefore, the son with low scholastic ability or low motivation for school learning is likely to have conflicts with his middle-class father. The fact that most suicides involve high school and/or college students indicates that the school situation is conducive to the development of serious problems among adolescent and postadolescents.

Alcohol and Drugs.   The use of alcohol and narcotics is on the rise among teen-agers and college students. Like money and sex, the use of alcohol or drugs is often a symbol or substitute for other things. As a result, the adolescents' feelings about drinking will be determined by the role it played in his family as he was growing up. "The child who has been repeatedly told that alcohol—rather than its excessive use—is an evil thing may consider drink as a kind of rebellion. The one who has seen his parents turn to it as a form of security may find himself automatically falling into the same pattern later in life" (North American Newspaper Alliance, 1966).

The increased use of marijuana and LSD among high school students is alarming. Their use frequently stems from frustrations and conflicts along with associations with peers who are "on" these drugs. In some cases this seems to be part of the subculture of a group of teenagers, and is most frequently found in the larger high schools in our metropolitan areas, and among certain subgroups.

Juvenile Delinquency

Community, state, and national leaders have expressed a growing concern about the increase of juvenile delinquency. The rate of increase from 1940 to 1963 is presented in Figure 12-2 (*Children,* 1965). Since adolescents have not changed biologically this increase must be interpreted in terms of the social-economic-cultural conditions of today as compared with these conditions in the early part of this century.

Social and Economic Forces.   Delinquents usually come from backgrounds of social and economic deprivations. Their families tend to have lower than average incomes and social status. But perhaps more important than the individual family's situation is the area in which a youth lives. A lower-class youth has little chance of being classified as a delinquent if he lives in an upper-class neighborhood. Numerous studies have revealed the relationship between certain deprived areas and delinquency—particularly the slums of larger cities. This was shown in a Report of the Atlantic Commission on Crime and Juvenile Delinquency (1966):

> It is inescapable that juvenile delinquency is directly related to conditions bred by poverty. If the Fulton County census tracts were divided into five groups on the basis of the economic and educational status of their residents, we would find that 57 percent of Fulton County's juvenile delinquents during 1964 were residents of the lowest group which consists of the principal poverty areas of the City of Atlanta. Only 24 percent of the residents of the county lived within these tracts.

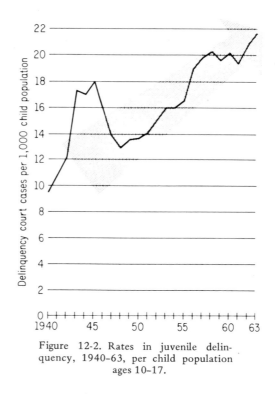

Figure 12-2. Rates in juvenile delinquency, 1940–63, per child population
ages 10–17.

However, one cannot overlook the fact that delinquents from higher income and higher status homes are less frequently brought before the courts; therefore figures based on crime data are frequently misleading.

A series of studies by Clifford R. Shaw and Henry D. McKay of the Institute of Juvenile Research in Chicago documented the disorganizing impact of slum life on different groups of immigrants as they moved through the slum and struggled to gain a foothold in the economic and social life of the city. Throughout the period of immigration, areas with high delinquency and crime rates kept these high rates, even though members of new nationality groups successively moved in to displace the older residents. Each new nationality group showed high rates of delinquency among its members who were living near the center of the city, and lower rates for those living in the better outlying residential areas of the city. Also for each nationality group, those living in the poorer areas had more of all the other social problems commonly associated with life in the slums. Thus what matters is *where* one grows up—not one's religion, race, or nationality.

Negroes who live in disproportionate numbers in slum neighborhoods account for a disproportionate number of arrests. However, when delinquency rates of whites and Negroes are compared in areas of similar economic status, the differences between them are markedly reduced. But for Negroes, movement out of the inner city and absorption into America's middle class have been much slower and more difficult than for any other ethnic or racial group. Their attempts to move spatially, socially, and economically have met with much stiffer opposition. Rigid barriers of residential segregation have prevented them from moving to better neighborhoods as their desire and capacity to do so have developed, leading to greater slum population density and stifling overcrowding of housing, schools, and recreation areas. Restricted access to jobs and limited upward mobility in those jobs that are available have slowed their economic advance.

It is likely that the official picture exaggerates the role played by social and economic conditions, since slum offenders are more likely than suburban offenders to be arrested. In fact recent studies reveal suburban and middle-class delinquency to be a more significant problem than once thought.

Delinquents from the Middle Class.   Most of the literature dealing with juvenile delinquency tends to deal with lower-class children and adolescents from the slum areas. Much less is known about the middle-class delinquent who gets into trouble with the law. In a study involving suburban secondary school students, Schanley (1967) identified a subgroup of aggressive middle- and upper-class delinquents whose pattern of police contact were generally comparable to those of a sample of Negro delinquents from a lower-class neighborhood. Elkind (1967) provides us with an elaboration of the forms of parental exploitations and the adolescents' reactions to such exploitation. He distinguishes three quite distinct groups of middle-class delinquents as follows (p. 80).

There are, first of all, adolescents whose delinquency is a direct manifestation of a long-standing emotional disturbance and for whom the remedy is usually psychiatric aid. Secondly, there are young people who come before the court almost by accident, in that they pulled some prank that turned out to be more serious than expected. A third and larger group consists of adolescents who get into trouble more or less regularly, and have a past record of being in trouble with the law. These youngsters do not appear to have serious internalized conflict, but are usually in open conflict with their parents.

An attempt to formulate a theory as to the rapid expansion of juvenile delinquency among middle-class adolescents must take into account changed attitudes and activities of the home, the nature of the school program, technological changes, and the cultural norms of our society. It appears that the joint effect of these etiological forces operating within the framework of our affluent society operate to produce widespread deviant behavior among teen-agers.

Need for Male Identification.   Juvenile delinquency rates continue to climb each decade. It is estimated that delinquency rates doubled in the decade 1950-60 and have continued to increase. It appears likely that much of the trouble lies in the mother- and feminine-dominated culture which now predominates, so that boys are not given the opportunity to identify with adult-male-oriented figures. Clinical studies and investigations of delinquents suggest that father-child relationships, especially father-son, are of considerable etiological importance to both social and psychological difficulties (Nash, 1965). Early identification of the child with adult male and female authority figures is significant in sex-role and psychosexual development, and can be understood in terms of learning theory. Warm, affectionate relationships and prolonged associations are among the more vital requirements to successful identification. It is essential in Western cultures for boys and girls to learn to get along with members of both sexes; it is very important for the boy to acquire the masculine sex role. Thus the lack of identification with the father or male authority figure fails to provide the boy with a needed adult model. Social and psychological difficulties frequently result when a child's major identification is with adult authority figures of only one sex.

Delinquent Girls.   Considerable attention has been given to delinquent boys, while the delinquent girl is frequently neglected. The problems of delinquent adolescent girls are usually misunderstood. The prevailing attitude toward delinquent boys is often attributed to the teen-age period, while the attitude toward the delinquent girl is quite critical and one of resentment, especially when the delinquency is related to sexuality. The girls are usually full of inner helplessness or hostility which they are unable to express or channel in some constructive way.

Undoubtedly, delinquent boys and delinquent girls have many similar problems. In the first place, this is a period of physiological, psychological and social transition. In some cases the problem is aggravated by the impact of economic blight, racial discrimination, difficult family relationships, parental neglect, poor housing, and personal considerations. Yet girls have problems specific to their sex, partially because of their biological make-up and partially because of the cultural lag relative to the roles of the sexes today. Girls deeply resent the "double standard" in sexual behavior. They complain that they are punished for relationships about which boys frequently boast. Konopka states (1964, p. 22): "The double standard has existed since time immemorial and there must always have been girls and women who resented it; yet in a century when the girl expects to be treated as an equal her resentment is undoubtedly more pronounced."

Government figures as of 1967 reveal there are an average of 130,000 births yearly to unmarried school girls under age 19. In 1965 there were 6,000 births to girls under 15 (*Sex Education*, 1967). Better birth control measures combined with sex education should produce desirable changes in helping both boys and girls adjust to problems related to sex and the sex drive.

Summary

Growth into adolescence is accompanied by important developmental tasks that should be learned in order to deal successfully with social and cultural forces in their present environment, and to prepare them for better adjustment as they grow into adulthood.

The adolescent period is an in-between period. Significant biological and social changes occur during this time. The adolescent faces the need for sexual identity. If he is to be successful in most developmental tasks, he must learn to adjust to his sex role. Numerous methods have been used for studying the problems of adolescents. Boys list more school problems than any other group of problems, while girls list more interpersonal and family problems. Both sexes see their peers as having fewer school problems but more interpersonal problems than they report for themselves.

The proportion of adolescents who expect to enroll in college varies with social class, family size, education of parents, and the proportion of their college-bound peers. Reinforcement of learning and college attendance from parents contributes to achievement in school.

Important physiological changes take place during adolescence which have significant bearing on the adolescent's attitude toward the opposite sex and on his interests and attitudes toward the home. Adolescent subculture develops at this time, especially when there is a wide gap between generations. The time of sexual maturation also markedly influences the interests and development of adolescents, especially boys.

Close friendships are established among adolescents as they move away from close home ties, with adolescents being affected more by the opinions of their peer group than by the opinions of adults. The sociogram is useful for showing the social structure of an adolescent group. It is in adolescence that cliques are formed. These are frequently closed groups, with the members showing great loyalty to the group and a reluctance to accept others from outside the clique. Popularity among peers is related to conformity to sex-role expectation, with each group member playing a particular role.

Dating begins earlier today than formerly. "Going steady" occurs frequently among adolescents. The greater amount of petting and the frankness with which teen-agers deal with sex problems have evoked much criticism from adults. There has also been an increase in teen-age marriages, resulting in part from premarital pregnancy. Early marriages are fraught with difficulties.

The rise in juvenile delinquency has become a national problem. Most delinquents come from backgrounds of social and economic deprivation. The importance of male identification for the adolescent boy is emphasized by students of adolescent psychology. School failure is a serious problem for many adolescents and contributes to delinquency, drug addiction, and suicide.

References

Adams, J. F. "Adolescent Personal Problems as a Function of Age and Sex," *Journal of Genetic Psychology*, Vol. 104 (1964), pp. 207-214.

Ames, Louise and R. M. Walker. "A Note on School Dropouts in Longitudinal Research with Late Adolescents," *Journal of Genetic Psychology*, Vol. 107 (1965), pp. 277-280.

Berge, A. "Young People in the Orient and Occident," *International Journal of Adult and Youth Education*, Vol. 16 (1964).

Bock, Eleanor W., and L. G. Burchinal. "Social Status Heterosexual Relations and Expected Ages of Marriage," *Journal of Genetic Psychology*, Vol. 101 (1962), pp. 43-52.

Burgett, C. "Hashberry Subculture," *Virginian-Pilot* (April 30, 1967), p. C-1.

Children, March-April 1965, p. 72.

Douvan, E., and J. Adelson. *The Adolescent Experience*. New York: Wiley, 1966.

Eisenberg, L. "A Developmental Approach to Adolescence," *Children*, Vol. 12, No. 4 (1965), pp. 131-135.

Elkind, D. "Middle-Class Delinquency," *Mental Hygiene*, Vol. 51 (1967), pp. 80-84.

Flavell, J. H. *The Developmental Psychology of Jean Piaget*. Princeton, N. J.: Van Nostrand, 1963.

Garrison, K. C. *Psychology of Adolescence*, 6th ed. Englewood Cliffs, N. J.: Prentice-Hall, 1965.

————. "A Study of the Aspirations and Concerns of Ninth-Grade Pupils from the Public Schools of Georgia," *Journal of Social Psychology*, Vol. 69 (1966), pp. 245-252.

Gauzer, B. "5,000 Adolescent Suicides, Assault on Accepted Values," *The Charlotte Observer* (Nov. 6, 1966), p. 64.

Gilbert, E. "Ideal Family Counts 4 or More Children," *The Virginia Pilot* (May 8, 1966), p. C-5.

Hancock, A., and J. Wakeford. "The Young Technicians," *New Society*, Vol. 120 (1965), pp. 13-14.

Havemann, E. "Should 17- and 18-Year-Old Girls Marry?" *McCall's* (Feb. 1965), p. 101.

Hsu, L. K. Blanche, and Edith M. Lord. "Culture Pattern and Adolescent Behavior," *International Journal of Social Psychiatry*, Vol. 7 (1961), pp. 33-53.

Iscoe, I., and J. A. Carden. "Field Dependence, Manifest Anxiety, and Sociometric Status in Children," *Journal of Consulting Psychology*, Vol. 25 (1961), p. 184.

Jones, H. E. *Development in Adolescence*. New York: Appleton, 1943.

Jones, M. C. "The Later Careers of Boys Who Were Early- or Late-Maturing," *Child Development*, Vol. 28 (1957), pp. 113-128.

Jones, M. C., and Nancy Bayley. "Physical Maturity among Boys as Related to Behavior," *Journal of Educational Psychology*, Vol. 41 (1950), p. 137.

Konopka, G. "Adolescent Delinquent Girls," *Children* (Jan.-Feb. 1964), pp. 21-23.

Kraus, I. "Sources of Educational Inspiration among Working-Class Youth," *American Sociological Review*, Vol. 29 (1964), pp. 867-879.

Kuhlen, G., and Nancy B. Houlihan. "Adolescent Heterosexual Interest in 1942 and 1963," *Child Development*, Vol. 36 (1965), pp. 1049-1052.

Langner, T. S. "Normative Behavior and Emotional Adjustment," Ph.D. dissertation, Columbia University, 1954.

Lassigne, Mary W. "The Influence of Beer and Adult Opinion on Moral Beliefs of Adolescents," Ed.D. dissertation, Indiana University, 1963.

Lowrie, S. H. "Sex Differences and Age of Initial Dating," *Social Forces*, Vol. 30 (1952), pp. 456-461.

Maccoby, Eleanor. "Role-taking in Childhood and Its Consequences for Social Learning," *Child Development*, Vol. 30 (1961), pp. 239-252.

McCormack, P. "P.T.A. Calls for Sex Education," *The Virginian-Pilot* (May 12, 1967), p. 18.

Meissner, W. W. "Parental Interaction of the Adolescent Boy," *Journal of Genetic Psychology*, Vol. 107 (1965), pp. 225-234.

Muma, J. R. "Peer Evaluation and Academic Performance," *Personnel and Guidance Journal*, Vol. 44 (1965), pp. 405-409.

Musgrove, F. "The Social Needs and Satisfactions of Some Young People—Part 1: At home, in Youth Clubs and at Work," *British Journal of Educational Psychology*, Vol. 26 (1966), pp. 61-71.

Mussen, Paul H., and M. C. Jones. "Self-Conceptions, Motivations, and Interpersonal Attitudes of Late and Early Maturing Boys," *Child Development,* Vol. 28 (1957), pp. 243-256.

Ostlund, L. A. "Environment-Personality Relationships," *Rural Sociology,* March 1957.

Nash, John. "The Father in Contemporary Culture and Current Psychological Literature," *Child Development,* Vol. 26 (1965), pp. 261-293.

North America Newspaper Alliance, "Alcoholic Teen-agers Shaped by Family Attitudes," *The Virginian-Pilot* (Dec. 15, 1966), p. 29.

Pearl, A. "Youth in Lower-Class Settings," in M. Sherif and C. W. Sherif, (eds.), *Problems of Youth.* Chicago: Aldine, 1965.

Phelps, H. R., and J. E. Horrocks. "Factors Influencing Informal Groups of Adolescents," *Child Development,* Vol. 29 (1958), pp. 69-86.

Purdue Opinion Panel, "Youth's Attitudes toward Courtship and Marriage," *Report of the Poll No. 62,* 1961.

Rehberg, R. A. "Selected Determinants of Adolescent Educational Expectations," paper presented at the Fiftieth Anniversary Meetings, American Educational Research Association, Chicago, 1966.

Rehberg, R. A., and D. L. Westby. "Parental Encouragement, Occupation, Education and Family Size: Artifactual or Independent Determinants of Adolescent Educational Expectations," *Social Forces,* Vol. 45 (1967), pp. 362-374.

Remmers, J. A. "Cross-Cultural Studies of Teen-Agers' Problems," *Journal of Educational Psychology,* Vol. 53 (1962), pp. 254-261.

Report of the Atlanta Commission on Crime and Juvenile Delinquency, *Opportunity for Urban Excellence,* 1966, p. 24.

Schanley, F. J. "Middle-Class Delinquency as a Social Problem," *Sociology and Social Research,* Vol. 51 (1967), pp. 185-198.

Schoeppe, Aileen, and R. J. Havighurst. "A Validation of Development and Adjustment Hypothesis of Adolescence," *Journal of Educational Psychology,* Vol. 43 (1952), pp. 339-353.

Schutz, J. Nell, "Adolescents' Perceptions of the Feminine Role in Today's Society," M.Ed. thesis, University of Texas, 1965.

"Sex Education Is Taught to Help Children Adjust," *The Charlotte Observer* (Dec. 3, 1967), p. 4A.

Sherif, M., and Carolyn W. Sherif. *Reference Groups.* New York: Harper, 1964.

Stone, C. P., and R. G. Barker. "The Attitudes and Interests of Premenarcheal and Postmenarcheal Girls," *Journal of Genetic Psychology,* Vol. 54 (1939), pp. 27-72.

Stratton, Dorothy C. "Interpretations of the Findings of the National Study of Adolescent Girls," *National Association of Women's Deans and Counselors Journal,* Vol. 21 (1957), pp. 18-20.

Tuddenham, R. D. "Studies in Reputation: I. Sex and Grade Differences in School Children's Evaluation of Their Peers," *Psychological Monographs,* Vol. 66, No. 333 (1952).

Tuma, E., and N. Livson. "Family Socioeconomic Status and Adolescent Attitudes to Authority," *Child Development,* Vol. 31 (1960), pp. 387-399.

Tyler, Leona E. C. "The Antecedents of Two Varieties of Vocational Interests," *Genetic Psychology Monographs,* Vol. 70 (1964), pp. 177-227.

Wallin, D. "Marital Happiness of Parents and Their Children's Attitudes Toward Marriage," *American Sociological Review,* Vol. 19 (1954), pp. 20-23.

Wormell, Helen E. "A Comparative Study of Perceptions Related to Self, Home, and School Among Selected Ninth-grade Students," Doctoral Thesis, University of Michigan, 1963.

Zabolski, F. C. "Studies in Delinquency: Personality Structure of Delinquent Boys," *Journal of Genetic Psychology,* Vol. 74 (1949), pp. 109-117.

Zuk, G. H. "Sex-Appropriate Behavior in Adolescence," *Journal of Genetic Psychology,* Vol. 93 (1958), pp. 31-32.

Chapter 13

The Early Adult Years

With the advances in civilization, the recognized adult years have been advanced so that adulthood is achieved by those in the middle class six or seven years after the individual has reached sexual maturity. Thus there is no particular age level that can be designated as the beginning of adulthood, although certain activities and responsibilities have been legalized at specific age levels.

In this chapter and the two that follow, the adult years are arbitrarily defined as beginning in the early 20's and ending with death. For purposes of convenience, the period is divided into the early adult years, the period between the early 20's and the middle 30's; the middle adult years, the period between the late 30's and the early 60's; and the late adult years, the period after the early 60's—frequently regarded as the period after age 65, when retirement usually begins. It should be emphasized that these are arbitrary divisions intended mainly to help the student study the adult years. It will be emphasized throughout this and the two subsequent chapters that these periods cover a wide range and that significant individual differences appear in each grouping. Caution should be exercised in classifying and stereotyping individuals into specific age groups, since there is a broad area of individual differences at all age levels in all aspects of development—anatomical, physiological, intellectual, emotional, and social.

Early Adulthood: Period of Adjustment

The early adult years are fraught with adjustment problems not unlike those of the late adolescent years. Perhaps the greatest changes in the adjustment problems lie in the independence and responsibility of adulthood. With adulthood comes greater independence and frequently a loss of security found in the home and among peers during the adolescent years. There is a tendency among many middle-class parents to continue to provide some economic help and security after their children reach maturity, and even after marriage. Often the pride of the young adults prevents them from seeking, and in some cases from accepting, parental help. The supervision and guidance of the adult years are largely absent during the early adult years, but problems frequently loom larger than before. The individual is now "on his own" and must make his own decisions and accept the consequences of his decisions.

From the beginning of adulthood until the early 30's, the typical American is faced with adjustment problems in different major life areas. Usually these adjustment problems appear at different times, with one adjustment problem requiring most of his attention before he proceeds to another problem. The fact that many of these problems seem to appear simultaneously frequently creates confusion and conflicts. However, by the early 30's, most adults have established a relatively stable life pattern that will not change much in subsequent years. The 30's are important years in the life of adults as indicated by a study by Meltzer and Ludwig (1967) of 143 workers in a paper-converting plant. Data on age differences in memory optimism and pessimism were gathered by interviewing each subject. A summary of the results showed that each group studied, as well as the groups as a whole, expressed significantly more pleasant memories than unpleasant. When the means for all groups were compared on memory optimism or P-U potency, the results indicated a peak of performance of pleasantness over unpleasantness at age 30-39. The mean memory optimism scores for the different age groups is shown in Figure 13-1.

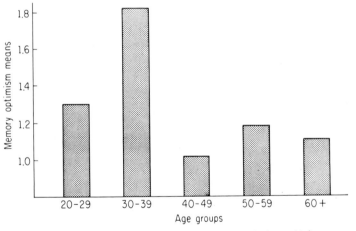

Figure 13-1. Age differences in memory optimism. (After Meltzer and Ludwig, 1967.)

Expectancy. When the individual reaches adulthood he is expected to assume the responsibilities of an adult, and his behavior is expected to conform to that required of adults. If he fails to meet adult expectations, he makes poor adjustments, since at this stage these adjustments are controlled by other adults. Expectations are perhaps as clearly defined in our culture as in any other; some of them are actually fixed by law, such as age for driving a car, discontinuing schooling, buying alcoholic beverages, obtaining a marriage license, and voting.

The adolescent is familiar with these long before he reaches maturity. These expectations have been set forth by Havighurst (1953) as developmental tasks and were presented in Chapter 1. They include selecting a mate, learning to live with a marriage partner, getting started in an occupation, beginning a family, raising children, homemaking, assuming civic responsibility, and acquiring friends.

The young adult's success in mastering these developmental tasks and thus measuring up to adult expectations will depend largely upon the foundation laid during childhood and adolescence. The child and adolescent who successfully mastered the developmental tasks of his age period is well prepared to meet adulthood and should be successful in mastering the tasks of early adulthood. The developmental tasks for each age level are not discrete; rather, the tasks of a later period are a continuation of tasks learned earlier. The adolescent did not complete the tasks of preparing for a vocation, or achieving emotional independence from parents; however, the extent to which he completed the tasks of adolescence will have an important bearing on the adjustment problems he faces as a young adult.

Ego Strength in Adulthood.   Ego strength is defined by Allen (1967, p. 53) as "one's ability to cope with one's environment—to deal adequately, directly, and realistically with problems that arise." Adult personality adjustment may be defined in terms of the strength of the ego. The importance of childhood experience in the development of personality is emphasized by clinical psychologists. A review and summary of the various positions of psychoanalytic theory indicates that excessiveness of either indulgence or deprivation during childhood results in low ego strength (Allen, 1964).

A study by Allen (1967) was concerned with the relationship of childhood experience and adult personality, by means of a cross-cultural study in which the concept of ego strength was used. Some relationships found between ego strength and early socialization variables, were: (1) Factors of childhood experience are directly related to adult personality adjustment. (2) Factors of childhood anxiety have a greater effect upon the ratings of adult ego strength than do factors of childhood gratification. (3) It is the combination of many variables rather than a single variable in the childhood experiences that is responsible for the correlations with the ratings of adult personality adjustment. (4) The sexual areas of experience correlates the strongest with the cultural measure of adult ego strength.

The success with which the individual adjusts to problems has a profound effect on his *self-concept* at all stages in his life. Many children and adolescents enter adulthood with unfavorable concepts of the self or feelings of inadequacy. Such individuals will lack self-confidence, assurance, and ego strength in meeting problems.

In a civilization where a large percentage of people have a relatively high level of education the self-concept and aspirations of the masses from the lower class is likely to be low. Margaret Mead states (1967): "We have all over this country pockets of people who have very low levels of aspirations, since they have been cut off by various devices from participation in our culture life." However, most adolescents make reasonably good adjustments to the expectancies of life. Thus the self-concept remains relatively stable throughout adulthood, with a tendency to become stronger and more permanent with age (Burgental and Gunning, 1955).

Sex-Role Attainment.   One of the developmental tasks of children and adolescents is that of attaining an appropriate sex role. Webb (1963) has suggested from studies of early adolescents that the male and female role may be in a state of confusion on the part of many adolescents. Failure to attain one's sex role frequently leads to maladjustments in early adulthood. This is suggested in a study reported by Heilbrun (1964) with college students as subjects. He found that male college students whose behavior tended to conform to cultural stereotypes of masculinity showed higher role consistency than less masculine males. Females who were either high or low feminine were more consistent than girls who were only moderately feminine. It would seem then that the college girl who combines elements of both the traditional feminine and modern masculine roles would show less role consistency. Perhaps these findings are a result of reinforcement in that certain forms of behavior are reinforced, thus producing consistency, whereas when there is a lack of reinforcement the result will be a less consistent role.

Changes in the adult pattern of living, due to science, technology, and urbanized living have brought about significant changes in the concepts of adult roles for men and women. (Materials related to these changes as they affect women in the labor force and homemaking are presented later in this chapter.)

These changes are more pronounced in the middle and upper classes than in the lower classes. The traditional concepts of the male and female roles are gradually being replaced by the developmental concept, which emphasizes the individuality of each person as a male or female, rather than the traditional concept, which follows a prescribed pattern for men and women without regard to their special interests and aptitudes.

While the changes in the concepts of adult sex roles make adjustment more difficult for some individuals, they simplify it for those who do not fit the traditional pattern. The person who knows exactly what is expected of him will find it easier to make certain adjustments than the person who is uncertain about the expectancies. Since the roles of women are not as clearly defined as those of men, their sex-role adjustment problem is perhaps more difficult, although the different roles furnish choices for the woman who does not want to follow the traditional role, while the man is expected to continue as head of the family and wage earner (Gray, 1957).

Stability of Personality Variables. It was pointed out in earlier chapters that personal characteristics and behavior ratings are relatively unstable during the preschool years. Beginning around age 6 or 7 there is considerable stability of behavior ratings with similar behavior at maturity. The results of a study by Garrison (1967) on the behavior of the clergy on racial integration strongly suggest that childhood experiences with individuals of other subcultures lead to later favorable adult behavioral expectations and involvements.

Tuddenham's (1959) follow-up of the California Adolescent Growth Study shows similarities in activity levels that persist from adolescence into adulthood over a 20-year period. The stability of intelligence-test scores was emphasized in an earlier chapter. In a study by Kelly (1955), self-ratings were obtained on a number of personality variables over a 20-year period. The retest correlations showed considerable stability over this period. Because the personality pattern of the individual is so well established during childhood and adolescence, it becomes apparent that the nature of personal and social adjustments during adulthood is largely dependent upon the personality make-up of the individual as he grows from childhood to adulthood.

An examination of the data presented in Figure 13-2 shows that there are distinct sex differences on the stability of many personality variables, especially dependence, behavior disorganization, and heterosexuality (Kagan and Moss, 1962). The changes in passivity and dependence are in the direction of the concept usually held for masculine and feminine variables, with girls and boys showing considerable variation (low correlations) between passivity and dependence at age 6-10 and at maturity. There was a relatively close correlation between heterosexuality of boys at age 10-14 and at maturity; the correlation for girls was very low or negligible.

The personality variable that correlated highest with childhood rating and adult rating was achievement, with sex-typed activity next in stability. This

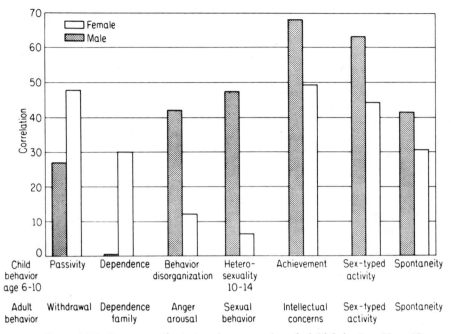

Figure 13-2. Summary of relations between selected child behaviors (6 to 10 years of age) and phenotypically similar adult behaviors. (Kagan and Moss.)

result is in line with materials presented in earlier chapters suggesting that the achievement motive and sex-role behavior are acquired relatively early.

Some Aids to Adjustment. The individual who has been successful in adjustments during adolescence will find it easier to resolve different problems during adulthood. The young adult is further aided in meeting adjustment problems that appear at this stage by being at his peak in physical and mental vigor. It was suggested in Chapter 4 that the peak of physical efficiency is complete or nearly complete in the mid-20's. It is also at this time that most people meet their most difficult adjustment problems.

With advancing age people tend to become more conservative and rigid in their behavior. This rigidity interferes with adjustments to change and to new tasks, conditions, and problems. The young adult is near the problems of everyday life. He does not have the weight of a life heritage binding him to the past. He is usually eager and ready to attempt something different—to make fresh approaches and contacts. Concerning the advantages of youth in making adjustments Karl Mannheim (1952, p. 295) stated years ago:

> Fresh contacts play an important part in the life of an individual when he is forced by events to leave his own social group and enter a new one—when, for example, an adolescent leaves home, or a peasant of the countryside for the town, or when an emigrant changes his home, or a social climber his social status or class. It is well known that in all these cases a quite visible and striking trans-

formation of the consciousness of the individual in question takes place: a change, not merely in the content of experience, but in the individual's mental and spiritual adjustment to it. In all these cases, however, the fresh contact is an event in one individual biography, whereas in the case of generations, we may speak of "fresh contacts" in the sense of the addition of new psycho-physical units who are in the literal sense beginning a "new life". . . . We can accordingly differentiate between two types of "fresh contact": one based on a shift in social relations, and the other on vital factors (the change from one generation to another). The latter type is potentially much more radical, since with the advent of the new partici- pant in the process of culture, the change of attitude takes place in a different individual whose attitude toward the heritage handed down by his predecessors is a novel one.

How conservative and inflexible the young adult is depends largely on his personality make-up, the degree of his self-confidence, the level of his education, and the extent to which he has learned to adjust through past experiences. One of the important dimensions of personality is that of rigidity versus flexibility. In general, education contributes to the development of a flexible personality—a person accepts new ideas and practices and expects change.

Dating and Courtship Adjustments

The adolescent years are extremely important to good sexual adjustment during adulthood. Good sexual adjustment is important to a happy marriage. In American culture there is an extended period of courtship beginning in the adolescent years and frequently extending into the early adult years. The social- sexual experiences of these years influence marital choice and to a marked degree marital expectations. However, expectations should extend beyond the social and sexual realm of life to the other life areas.

Friendship Formation.   An important developmental task of late child- hood and adolescence involves the formation of friends. Thus those individuals who learned to get along with their age-mates during the early years find little difficulty in forming friendships during the early adult years.

Proximity or opportunity for contact helps people to become acquainted with one another by providing opportunities for interaction. When this inter- action is mutually rewarding friendships are formed. This was brought out in the results of studies by Newcomb (1956). In one case 17 male college transfer students who met as strangers and who lived in the same student house were carefully studied during their first semester together. Through interviews, questionnaires, and tests, data were gathered relevant to their degree of attrac- tion for one another.

Students tended to be attracted to each other in proportion to their per- ceived similarities on attitudes and relevant issues. That is an individual liked those who in general agreed with his own positive and negative impressions of their self-image. After a period of time when students came to know each other better certain small-group friendships were formed; based largely upon similarity of attitudes and values. However, the fact must not be ignored that persons are frequently drawn together because their personal qualities are different and thus tend to complement one another. A timid person frequently finds a close friend who is an outgoing person.

Such friendships are like a love relationship that characterize individuals of the same or opposite sex. They are different from the sexual love relationship in that sexual behavior is not involved. When a love relationship has as one of its aspects overt sexuality, then we may categorize the relationship as sexual love relationship (Levine, 1963, p. 297).

Sexual Behavior of College Students. There has been much discussion of the sexual revolution as it affects college students. Certainly, changed conditions and ways of living are having an important effect upon the attitudes and behavior of college students. This is reflected in all aspects of their lives. Studies of the sexual life of college students tend to explode the myth which holds that the sexual appetite and powers tend to diminish sharply as the individual advances up the educational ladder.

TABLE 13-1
Responses of Freshmen and Senior College Students
to Certain Test Items Concerned with Sexual Behavior
(After Freedman)

Item	Freshmen		Seniors	
	%T	%F	%T	%F
1. I am embarrassed by dirty stories	20	80	8	92
2. No man of character would ask his fiancée to have intercourse with him before marriage	53	47	18	82
3. A large number of people are guilty of bad sexual conduct	45	51	31	61
4. In illegitimate pregnancies, abortion is in many cases the most reasonable alternative	16	82	51	49
5. People would be happier if sex experience before marriage were taken for granted	16	84	35	65
6. I never attend a sexy show if I can avoid it	39	55	12	86
7. I believe women ought to have as much sexual freedom as men	25	73	57	41
8. I like to flirt	57	43	84	16
9. I like to talk about sex	59	41	16	29

Note: The percentages are pooled means of three classes. N's for freshmen classes are 398, 404, and 39; N's for senior classes are 274, 258, and 253.

Freedman (1965) reported test data based on three freshman classes and three senior classes of college students. Most of the students came from upper-middle-class families. Results of some of the test items, presented in Table 13-1, indicate that a substantial amount of change in attitudes toward sexual behavior takes place between the freshman and senior year. The change is in the direction of moving away from the traditional norm.

Changed Attitudes Toward Sexual Behavior. Studies indicate that since the 1920's there has been a consolidation and acceptance of sexual attitudes, instead of a rapid change as some would suggest. Reiss (1966, p. 126) states:

> What was done by a female in 1925 acting as a rebel and a deviant can be done by a female in 1965 as a conformist. This is a significant change. Of course, milder forms of premarital sexual behavior have increased, and there may well have been some moderate increases in coitus rates also. But this is not the major significance of the changes during the last quarter or even half century. The major importance lies in the increasing acceptance of premarital coital behavior rather than in increased performance of this behavior.

The results of a limited study by Freedman (1965) involving the sexual behavior of American college women are consistent with the findings of other studies relative to the sexual behavior of college women. The women studied consisted of college seniors from the upper middle class who were interviewed several times a year, beginning in their freshmen year, with the bulk of the interviewing reserved for the senior year. Few of these students had engaged in behavior other than kissing and light petting before the junior and senior years of high school. The modal age for commencing extensive petting was 17. The incidence of intercourse was 22.45 percent. The findings of this and related studies suggest that when college women engage in intercourse they usually do so with men with whom they are emotionally involved; and that sexual promiscuity, in the sense of frequent sex relations of an automatic kind, is likely confined to a small percentage.

Differences in the sex attitudes of mothers and their daughters enrolled in college were brought out in a study by Bell and Buerkle (1966). These differences appear with each generation, but are perhaps more pronounced now than earlier because of the vast social, economical, and technical changes today. The investigators compared the attitudes of 217 coeds about preserving their virginity until after marriage with that of their mothers. The comparisons are presented in Table 13-2, showing that the daughters are less strict and demanding in their sexual code.

One reason girls do not respect their mother's sexual standards is the lack of realism or validity of the mother's arguments; for many girls, premarital sex is pleasurable, easily concealed, not likely (with modern devices) to end in unwanted pregnancy, and frequently does not result in marriage. The fear of pregnancy and the fear of Hell do not have their earlier force. The increased freedom of women has no doubt had an influence on changing attitudes. However, one

TABLE 13-2
Comparison of the Attitudes of Mothers and Daughters
toward Sexual Relations before Marriage (After Bell
and Buerkle)

	Response of Mother (percent)	Response of Daughters (percent)
Virginity very important	88	55
Virginity generally important	12	34
Virginity unimportant	0	11
Sexual intercourse, if engaged:		
very wrong	83	35
generally wrong	15	48
right in many situations	2	17

cannot at this time state what the attitudes of these college girls may be when they become mothers of college-age daughters.

A myth that is still rather widely prevalent is that the sexual desire and ability of the American male tends to decrease as he ascends the ladder of education and economic success. Popular writers have perpetuated the legend that the real virile male is the energetic blue-collar laborer who is both boisterous and tattooed. However, this myth has no scientific basis. In a detailed study of 152 married couples in the Midwest United States, Rainwater (1967) found that it was the lower-class couples who had the least satisfactory sex lives, the middle classes and above, the most. Of the lower-class couples interviewed, only 44 percent of the husbands and 20 percent of the wives expressed great interest and enjoyment in sexual intercourse; the figures for the middle-class couples were 75 percent for the husbands and 50 percent for the wives.

A plausible explanation offered for these findings is that the lower-class husbands and wives lead a more segregated existence—that is, the wife concerns herself largely with the home and children while the husband involves himself with his job and pals. This does not make for a continuing happy sexual relationship, since husband and wife do not share strong mutual concerns in their lives together.

Homosexuality.   Traditionally, our society has strong prohibitions against certain methods of obtaining sexual stimulation, with the only approved way being that of heterosexual contact, and this is highly restricted. One must first of all be married and have sexual relations only with his married mate. Furthermore, the marriage partner must not be a close relative, and less important but frequently present among some groups in our society, the marriage partners are supposed to be of the same race, religion, and socioeconomic background. Our belief in the rightness of these restrictions stems largely from our fixed notions about normal sexual behavior, so that people who deviate from such behavior are considered a kind of sexual pervert. This is especially true for the homo-sexual—the idea being that the normal person is not physiologically or biologi-cally capable of being stimulated by a like-sexed person. It was left to Freud to explode this myth, because of his studies of the behaviors observed in his patients.

Evidence gathered by students of behavior following the observations of Freud have supported the notion that the variability in the nature of sexual responses is a result of experiences and is therefore learned.

The studies of sexual behavior by Kinsey and others (1948, 1953) indicate that a large percentage of American adults have had and enjoyed homosexual stimulation at one time or another. Studies by anthropologists and comparative physiologists have furnished sufficient evidence for us to conclude that homo-sexuality does not constitute a genetic "sport" or perversion. Ford and Beach (1951) conducted exhaustive cross-species and cross-cultural comparisons of sexual behavior. They found homosexual behavior present in every mammalian species studied; almost all lower animals including subhuman primates engaged in both heterosexual and homosexual behavior. Of 76 societies studied they found that 28 totally disapproved of homosexual behavior. In most of the societies studied it was accepted for some of all the members, although all societies were more supportive of heterosexual behavior than of homosexual behavior. For example, the Siwans of Africa talk about their male love affairs as freely as their love affairs with the female, but they are more strongly hetero-sexual in that marriage is expected and required. In no societies studied was homosexuality found to be exclusively practiced; most individuals prefer hetero-sexual behavior. Gordon (1963, p. 241) states:

> It may be that heterosexual behavior provides stimulation which is in some way more effective or efficient in drive reduction than homosexual or other means of obtaining stimulation. On the other hand, it is possible that the prefer-ences are learned. . . . Certainly all societies are more supportive of heterosexual behavior than of homosexual in that, though they may not proscribe the latter and may even encourage it, they must demand the former if the society is to continue to exist.

Marital Adjustment

The young adult at some time either marries or contemplates marriage. America may be regarded as a marrying nation, since most young people marry before or during the early adult years. Marriages among young people take place in the context of a love relation involving the opposite sex. It is an intimate personal relationship conducted in accordance with certain social conventions. In our culture, marriage is monogamous—one man is married to one woman. Marriage confers a valued status upon its members, although about one out of ten men and one out of every seven girls in our society will never marry, both the expectations and hopes of most men and women is that they will marry and remain married (Levine, 1963, p. 307).

Early Marriages.   Following World War II there was a pronounced trend toward earlier marriages, especially on the part of girls. Teen-age marriages were formerly confined mainly to the lower socioeconomic group. However, this is no longer the case. As many as one-fifth of the undergraduate college students in this country are married, with approximately half of these having children; although it is most likely that the birth-control pill will reduce early marriage and children, since early marriages are frequently a result of premarital pregnancy. Financial difficulties are a common problem. Parental aid and working wives have been helpful in relieving the financial problem.

Although the marriage trend for several decades has been downward, most teen-agers according to Gilbert Youth Research Institute Survey in 1966, are not planning on getting married at an early period. Less than one-half of one percent of those asked about marriage were in favor of planning for marriage while still in high school; only 7 percent felt that the proper time for marriage is after high school graduation. Over half of the teen-agers surveyed said that boys and girls should wait until they had finished college, while 22 percent said that plans for marriage should be made while still in college. One should not confuse plans with what actually happens, although with increasing percentages of teen-agers finishing high school as well as going to college, we would expect a larger percentage of them to postpone marriage.

That most young couples are eager to have children is shown by interviews and by the birth rates, although dealers in children's clothes as well as statistical data available indicate a decrease in the birth rate following more widespread use of the pill. This should provide a basis for family planning and the elimination of certain problems of sexual maladjustment resulting from fear of pregnancy.

Trends and Prospective Changes.   An open marriage system, such as we find in the United States, does not reduce a set of closed networks to interaction. It was stated earlier that adolescents' dating patterns usually involve individuals from the same high school, same social-class background, and somewhat similar ethnic culture. Based on studies of marriages in America and in Oslo, Norway (Ramsey, 1966), we may conclude that marriages between persons of the same or similar occupational status occur more frequently than expected, and that marriages between persons who live close to one another occur more frequently than expected. Although there is usually found a relation between homogamy and propinquity, the conclusion set forth by Ramsey (p. 784) applies: "People marry their equals in social status; they marry their neighbors; neighbors tend to be social equals."

There is nothing immutable about the specific definition of roles in the family, the nature of the interaction within the family, or the nature of the power structure of the family. As changes take place in other institutions and as science provides more information about family practices, a faster rate of changes in family norms becomes inevitable.

One of the striking features of recent trends in American marriages is the extent to which marriage partners are becoming standardized (Parke and Glick,

1967). In the first place, nearly everyone gets married nowadays. Projections indicate that as few as 3 percent of the men and women now in their late 20's may enter middle age without having married. This is quite a change from the present, but is in harmony with the trends.

Second, to a greater extent than before, young people are getting married at about the same age. The reduction in the age of first marriage has been accompanied by a compressing of marriages into a narrower age range. American women marry men who are more nearly their own ages than is generally true elsewhere. This observation is based on data from the 1960 U.S. Census showing the median age at first marriage for men and women: "Husbands over 55 years of age in 1960 were 3.6 years older than their wives, on the average; while husbands under 35 years old were, on the average, only 1.9 years older than their wives."

Fourth, recent data from the U.S. Census show a decline in teen-age marriages. The marriage rate among teen-agers was reached soon after 1950 and is now on the decline. Comparison of the age of first marriage of different age women show that the percentage who married before they were 18 years of age is successively smaller for each younger age group.

Fifth, nearly all married couples now maintain their own household, and it is becoming ever rarer for a grandparent to live with one of his children.

Sixth, the average size of the family in terms of children will not likely change a great deal. Changes that appear in the near future are more likely to be toward smaller rather than larger families.

Seventh, a decline in the relative frequency of divorce and separation should result to the extent that there are reductions in poverty and teen-age marriages and general improvements in the economic conditions of the different marginal families. All too frequently alarmists compare the present conditions with what they regard as a "perfect society." Reiss (1966) has pointed out that "Contrary to popular expectations, there has been no major change in the divorce rate in America for the past 25 years. In fact, there is only a slight upward trend even for the past 45 years." (p. 126). However, proposals have been made that we should have different kinds of marriages, or marriages contracted for a certain period of time subject to renewal of the contract and child rearing by substitute parents especially trained in child rearing (Satir, 1967).

Work and Spending Patterns.   Young couples typically start out in apartments and have little need for extra rooms and a great deal of furniture. Among "young marrieds" under 25, work and spending follow a pattern. If the husband is still in school, the wife works, especially when there are no children. Frequently both are in college part or full time. A second group of young couples involves those living in apartments with both husband and wife working so as to have money for a budget that enables them to splurge on recreation, entertainment, travel, and "eating out," or in some cases to make a payment on a home. A third group of young couples in the 20-24 group married in their teens, frequently because of pregnancy, and are raising the family with a relatively low income. The young mother is busy caring for children and caring for the home on an income that remains low, since the mother is not working and the father's job provides only for minimum family needs.

The Marital Role. In the midst of rapid changes, many women find themselves confused and uncertain about their roles—about what is really expected of them. There is frequently a search for female esteem. Women are better educated than ever before; but all their efforts expended at school on term papers and examinations does not help them in making bread and cakes, when they can purchase bread and cake mixes so easily. Automatic washing machines, dish washers, frozen foods, prepared foods, vacuum cleaners, and other labor-saving devices have simplified home making. Thus many wives turn to pursuits outside the home to satisfy their social and psychological needs.

Many women have been conditioned from childhood to be the perfect homemaker, to care for her children, and to contribute to society. They strive to do something, to be something they aren't, so that ought's and should's weigh them down in confusion about their marital role. Their problems are magnified; they become overly concerned about themselves without really attaining any degree of self-knowledge. These are some of the problems that many married women are confronted with. A marital relation in which there is first love for the self as a unique person and love for another as one with whom there are common bonds of interpersonal relations provides a source of happiness and satisfaction.

A number of studies have shown important changes in the attitudes of teen-agers and youth about the wife working after marriage. In the Gilbert Youth Research Institute survey for 1966, nearly two-thirds of the teen-agers felt that a wife should work during the early years of marriage. One question directed only to the girls was: "Did they hope to combine marriage with a career?" Fifty-five percent of the girls indicated they did, while 35 percent stated they did not. This left 10 percent in doubt. With an increasing percentage of girls who finish college or take specialized training of a vocational nature, we can expect an increasing percentage to continue working indefinitely after marriage.

According to Sylvia Porter (1967), a full 56 percent of husbands of college graduates have a favorable attitude toward their wives' employment, and another 26 percent are neutral on the subject. Only 17 percent of the husbands actually oppose their wives' employment. In the case of those now working, more than 9 in 10 of the husbands openly approved or were neutral, and only 4 percent disapproved of their wives being in the labor force.

A significant finding from the study of "College Women Seven Years After Graduation," made by the Women's Bureau of the Labor Department, shows that attitudes are not changed by the fact that there are children involved; under these circumstances about 4 percent of the husbands disapproved of their wives working. These results reflect a marked decline in the age-old prejudice against the working wife and mother. It appears that the working wife, particularly the college-educated wife, is now commonplace and will become more so. No doubt this will have an important impact on our socioeconomic lives and attitudes.

Sources of Marital Discord.   The divorce rate is frequently used as a measure of marital discord. It should be noted, however, that there are many marriage failures that never end in divorce; these failures are best defined in psychological rather than legal terms. In a psychological sense, a marriage fails if there is not a love relationship between husband and wife. Marriage obviously involves two persons, and the relationship between these two will depend upon the individual personalities involved and the interaction of these personalities. A study reported by Pickford and others (1967) of husband-wife differences in personality traits as a factor in marital happiness made use of three groups: Group A (happily married couples), Group B (couples having trouble), and Group C (couples on the verge of separation). An analysis of the findings by traits showed that a high initial discrepancy between husband and wife on the following traits contributed to unhappy marriages: general activity, restraint, ascendancy, sociability, emotional stability, objectivity, friendliness, thoughtfulness, and personal relations. In our culture it is the similarity rather than dissimilarity of traits that contributes to marital happiness. Also, when differences in traits appear, those differences should generally be in the direction of cultural norms or expectations—for example, aggressiveness is usually regarded as more masculine. Thus differences in aggression should be in favor of the husband rather than the wife. Likewise, friendliness and sociability are regarded as feminine traits; differences in these traits should be in favor of the wife rather than the husband.

Romantic notions to the contrary, the birth of a child does not dispel discord between husband and wife. The results of a study by Feldman of 852 American couples reported at the Groves Conference on Marriage (1967) showed that the second child does not seem to fit into the family any more easily than the first. Husbands and wives reported that with the second child marital satisfaction seemed to diminish. Both husbands and wives felt less romantic, although the husbands said that they felt more needed by the wife and both spouses were more self-confident about caring for their children.

A long period of courtship, being in love, and satisfactory sexual relations does not seem to assure marital happiness. What, then, are some of the conditions and factors that produce marital dissatisfaction and unhappiness? First of all, many people experience disenchantment after marriage. Some of the major sources of this disenchantment may be listed:

1. Although there was a long period of courtship, the partners actually didn't learn each other's true nature. In most cases they merely put forth their "best behavior."
2. Dating and courtship involved "having fun," and little thought was given to accepting responsibility and showing deep concern for one another.
3. The seriousness of any faults observed were played down, the attitude

being that these could easily be corrected or that they were after all insignificant.

4. The need to be loved was sufficiently strong that actions of the partner were always interpreted as stemming from love.

5. The loved one could see in every act of the person loved the real or wished for qualities desired in a marriage partner.

The Unmarrieds. The unmarried in our society are faced with difficult social and psychological problems, despite the fact that the economic problems have largely been eliminated. The problem is more frequently found among women, since there are many more unmarried women in almost any community than unmarried men. Jokes about maiden aunts and aged spinstresses reflect the attitudes of society toward the unmarried woman. Since the woman's role in our culture is a passive one, the man is expected to take the initiative in relationships between the sexes. This places the women at a great disadvantage. If she takes too active a role her behavior is frowned upon—she must await the overtures of the man. However, many women are successful in gaining the attention of men through their attractiveness and a sort of subtle form of initiative. With altered conditions and customs, we may find significant changes occurring relative to the status and activities of the unmarried. Apartments, clubs, and certain organizations in our cities have already had an important bearing on the problems of the unmarried.

The unmarried man is in considerable social demand during early adulthood. He is in a position to "play the field." His mental and physical health does not compare favorably with that of his married contemporaries. He has much difficulty adjusting to marriage after a long period of bachelorhood with its accompanying freedom. His social position is not so serious throughout the early adult years.

Vocational success is a frequent substitute for marriage among both men and women. In a study by Ellis (1952), mobile career women, whose occupational and social levels were above those of their immediate families, were compared with nonmobile career women. Women who had moved upward either through education or geographic mobility made less satisfactory adjustments to singleness than did the nonmobile career women. Evidence from studies of single career women reveals that those who do not strive to attain a higher social status compare favorably with married women of the same age in overall adjustments. Their superiority is frequently noted in health, a sense of personal worth, fewer withdrawal tendencies, greater social participation, more complete acceptance of social standards, and fewer antisocial tendencies (Martinson, 1955). Thus it is not singleness per se that determines adjustment or lack of adjustment, but rather the personal attitudes, interests, and values found in a particular person.

Vocational Adjustment

Vocational adjustment has become increasingly difficult for each generation. This is due in part to the continuously increasing number of different types of jobs from which the individual must make a choice. There are today over 100,000 distinct occupations from which the individual must make a choice. The scientific and technological explosion is changing our lives fast. It is estimated that 50 percent of the young adult work force will be employed on types of jobs which have not yet been invented and indeed cannot be imagined.

There is also a problem of preparing for the type of work the individual chooses, which may require a long and costly education. School counselors are continuously faced with late adults who are compelled to modify their vocational aspirations due to lack of ability, lack of drive, or lack of financial means for the education required for the vocational career.

Havighurst (1964) established a six-stage schema of vocational development by merging the concepts of vocational life stages and vocational developmental tasks. The stages of vocational development for a large percentage of workers in the United States may be grouped into the following age brackets:

TABLE 13-3

Age and Vocational Development
(After Havighurst)

Age	Stage of Vocational Development
15–25	Vocational preparation and acquiring identity as a worker
25–40	Becoming a productive person
40–50	Achieving a maximum level of productivity
50–60	Maintaining a high level of productivity
60–70	Declining level of productivity leading to disengagement from the work job

Vocational Selection. Vocational values are extremely important in vocational selection and vocational stability. Work has different meaning and values for different people. It may be a source of prestige and recognition, an opportunity for service, a means of avoiding boredom, a basis for a sense of usefulness or worth, a source of creative expression, a means of satisfying a need for achievement, or just a way of earning a living. The values an individual stresses in selecting a vocation will be influenced by the socioeconomic class to which he belongs. Individuals from the lower economic class stress the earnings aspect of the job, paid vacation, salary increases, and fringe economic benefits; those of the upper economic class emphasize the satisfactions to be derived, services rendered, and the freedom of the particular job (Morse and Weiss, 1955).

There is a striking trend for sons to follow fairly closely the occupations of their father or an adjacent occupation, and for daughters to marry within the social-class position of the father's occupation. The relationship between career choice of students and the occupation of their fathers was studied by Wertz (1966), using 16,141 male and 14,417 female college freshmen as subjects. He noted that sons tended to overchoose their father's occupations as a career in cases where this was possible; the "father-model" effect generally did not hold for girls. When fathers' occupations were categorized into socioeconomic group-ings, it was found that low social class boys tended to overchoose careers as engineers, teachers, chemists, accountants, clergymen, and farmers; high-social-class boys tended to overchoose careers as physicians, lawyers, and college pro-fessors; intermediate-social-class boys tended to overchoose careers as business-men, physicists, dentists, mathematicians, and architects. In the case of girls, the low-social-class girls tended to overchoose careers as teacher, nurse, and lab technician; high-social-class girls tended to overchoose careers as social worker and psychologist.

It should be pointed out that there are college students who revealed a higher vocational aspiration than those who did not go to college. It is with the adult who dropped out of high school that problems of vocational choice has become extremely limited in this highly complex, technological age.

Thirty-two female and 85 male college students enrolled in an introductory industrial psychology course served as subjects in a study by Burke (1966) of differences in perception of desired job characteristics of the opposite sex. They were asked to rank ten job characteristics from the point of view of how impor-tant each was for himself and how important each would be for a person of the opposite sex.

The rank order of the ten job characteristics regarded as most important for the self are shown in Table 13-3. The results show considerable agreement, much larger than that frequently postulated. Importance of the job was ranked higher for males, while a good boss was ranked higher for females. Otherwise, the similarity of the rankings was very high. The four rank orders were intercor-related to determine the extent to which females and males assigned similar importance rankings to the job characteristics and the extent to which females and males could predict the rankings of the opposite sex. This matrix is pre-sented in Table 13-4. The following conclusions appear from the results of Tables 13-3 and 13-4:

1. Rank orders for female and male self-importance correlated .84, indicat-ing high real similarity of job-characteristic preferences.
2. Females correctly predicted that males had similar preferences and were able to predict the actual male rankings accurately.
3. Males incorrectly predicted that females had different preferences and were unable to predict the actual female rankings correctly.

Stability of Vocational Choice.   Stability of vocational choice increases with age. An early study by Strong (1951) revealed an 86 percent agreement

TABLE 13-4
Rank Order of the Importance for Self of Ten
Job Characteristics (After Burke)

Job Characteristics	Rank Order	
	Female	Male
Challenges ability	1	2
Opportunity for advancement	2	1
Good salary	3	3
High responsibility	4	4
Good boss	5	8
Voice in decisions	6	7
Job security	7	5
Good physical working conditions	8	9
Importance of the job	9	6
Liberal fringe benefits	10	10

between occupational interest scores of 345 college students and their occupations 20 years later. Those who had changed their occupations did not have as high scores as those who remained in their occupation. In a later study (1953) Strong noted that freshmen choosing occupations with less prestige value were most likely to change. He also noted that job changes within an occupation are more likely than occupational changes. Professional workers change occupations least while unskilled workers and those in white-collar occupations change most. Individuals who are most successful in their careers and more stable individuals in lower occupational categories are least likely to change. Women frequently are forced to shift their job or occupation to adapt to changes brought about by changes in their family status or their husband's jobs. However, with more women entering professions and other jobs requiring special training, they simply find employment in the new community where the husband is employed.

TABLE 13-5
Intercorrelations among Females and Male
Importance-for-Self and Importance-for
Opposite-Sex Rank Orders (After Burke)

Category	Female Importance for Opposite Sex	Male Importance for Self	Male Importance for Opposite Sex
Female importance for self	.66†	.84*	−.12
Female importance for opposite sex		.89*	−.07
Male importance for self			−.32

[a]N = 10 for all correlations.
*Correlation is significantly different from zero at the .01 level of confidence.
†Correlation is significantly different from zero at the .05 level of confidence.

This may be noted in the case of the beautician, office worker, nurse, and school teacher.

Many individuals will change their jobs and feel the need for additional training for the new job. Due to technology advancements many individuals will be required to pursue additional training to meet the new demands of their job. The work life expectancy, expected changes during working life, and job life expectancy for men is presented in Table 13-5 (Rice 1964-65).

TABLE 13-6

Work Life Expectancy, Expected Life-time Job Changes, and
Job Life Expectancy for Men, 1960–61. (After Rice)

Age	Work Life Expectancy at Beginning of Age Interval	Expected Job Changes During Work Life at Beginning of Age Interval	Job Life Expectancy at Beginning of Age Interval
20–24	42.6	6.6	5.6
25–34	37.0	4.8	6.5
35–44	28.6	2.7	7.7
45–54	19.7	1.4	8.1
55–64	11.9	.6	7.2
65 and over	6.3	.2	4.7

Vocational Trends and Education.   Historically, our educational system, including vocational education, was designed to prepare man for his role in a society that was relatively stable. Changes which occurred took place over a period of generations. Today we are faced with new dimensions of time and change. Some of the signs and consequences of change that begin to be apparent have been set forth by Venn (1967, p. 33):

1. The labor force six years ago moved from a majority in production to a majority in the services and distribution occupations. As of 1966, 40 percent of workers were in production jobs, which will continue to decrease because production can be done better by machines than by individuals.
2. Man will need to change his job four or five times during his life time, making continuous education and reeducation a necessity.
3. Preparation of the individual for specific job skills is no longer defensible, but wholly new concepts of preparation in broad occupational fields will be needed to give man the basic skills required to move into new occupational areas.
4. Occupational education cannot be isolated from the mainstream of education. The worker is more than a "worker on the job;" he is a family man, a citizen of a community, a living personality with basic physiological and socio-psychological needs.

Vocational preparation has become a necessity for youngsters and others entering the labor market. It is estimated that at the present rate of construction, a nationwide system of 1,865 area vocational schools should be available by 1975. These should provide vocational education opportunities for the predicted need of our technological age and will be accessible to persons of all ages (Venn, 1967). This is imperative if we are to have near-full employment, since the young adult without a skill or at least a high school education will find it well nigh impossible to find full-time employment.

There is also a continuous increase in the percentage of workers classified as professional. This increase coupled with increased educational demands has placed a great burden upon the schools and colleges. Each year a larger percentage of students enter college. The increased enrollment has been especially notable among women and among men from the lower socioeconomic class. Father's occupation was used as an index of socioeconomic status by Wertz (1966) in a comparison of sex differences in college attendance. A total of 76,015 boys and 51,110 girls entering 248 colleges were studied. Using high school grades as an index of ability, Werts found that low-ability boys were much more likely to enter college than low-ability girls; high-ability boys and girls were equally likely to enter college. Likewise, boys from low socioeconomic status were much more likely to enter college than girls from low socioeconomic status, whereas boys and girls whose fathers were closely associated with the academic community were equally likely to attend college.

The College Dropout.   The dropout problem is one with which colleges are very much concerned. Scholastic failure is frequently thought of as closely identified with dropping out of college. Although many students do drop out of college because of failure in their scholastic performances, there are many able students who drop out for other reasons. Frequently students have not been realistic in their vocational and college plans. A 1960 poll of youth's attitudes conducted by the Public Opinion Panel revealed that 58 percent aspired to enter some professional field (Franklin et al., 1960).

A four-year longitudinal study by Astin (1964) dealt with the reason for dropping out of college for 6600 Merit Scholarship Finalists. A comparison of students who dropped out with those who did not showed that (1) the dropouts tend to come from lower socioeconomic backgrounds, (2) tend to have lower ranks in high school, (3) expected initially to get lower college degrees, and (4) applied for relatively fewer scholarships. Personality measures indicated that the dropouts were more aloof, self-centered, impulsive, and assertive than nondropouts.

Professional and Managerial Occupations.   Professional and managerial positions offer many attractions for young people considering the choice of a career. These occupations offer opportunities for assuming responsibility and usually lead to relatively high earnings. As a rule, these vocational fields require a great deal of specialized education or other preparation, since a broad knowledge of one's field and judgments based upon broad understandings are required for success in these types of work. There has been a pronounced increase in the percentage of workers in professions, administrative, and related occupations. Automation has had an important bearing on industrial employment, while the greater use of the computer continues to replace the white-collar worker.

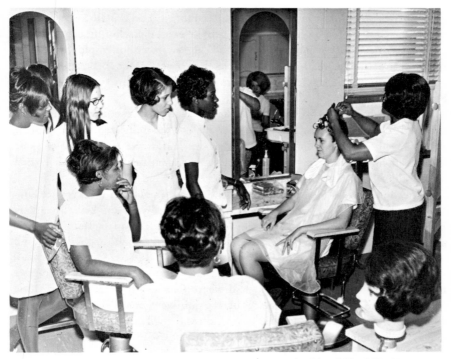

Urban Technical and Vocational Centers prepare youth with salable skills. (Courtesy Norfolk City Schools, Norfolk, Virginia.)

The largest group of professional workers includes teachers, engineers, physicians, clergymen, dentists, lawyers, and accountants. These require considerable formal education in well-organized fields of knowledge, some as long as seven to ten years. Other professions require less formal training, while some fields may not require as much training, they demand a great deal of background knowledge or creative talent and skill acquired through experience. It is not easy for the young adult to prepare for and enter professional work, since applicants are not accepted for professional training unless their school grades are high.

Closely related to the professions is a wide variety of semiprofessional and technical occupations. People in these occupations work closely with professional personnel on occupations for which they are trained. Employment in these technical occupations also require specialized training in some basic scientific knowledge and skills. Such training is obtained in technical institutions, junior colleges, and other schools and colleges, or through technical on-the-job training. Because of their limited education and training, technicians generally find it difficult to advance to professional or high-order positions. This sometimes is a source of frustration for young adults with higher aspirations, especially those from upper-middle-class homes.

The White-Collar Worker in Perspective. The white-collar worker has become increasingly more important in our economy. The United States has become the first nation in which more people earn their livelihood providing services than producing goods. Virtually all the net growth of employment since the middle of the century has occurred in the service sector so that by 1967 it comprised up to 55 percent, and their ranks continue to swell (*Newsweek,* Sept. 1967).

The widely accepted stereotype of the white-collar worker as one who clings to middle-class status with earnings below that of the unionized factory worker is challenged by some who have noted that one-half of the white-collar workers identify themselves as working class. These class identifications are closely tied in with their class of origin.

The middle-class identifiers among the clerical and sales workers are considerably ahead of both other clerical and sales employees and skilled workers with respect to income. However, they seem to show less satisfaction with their income than the working-class identifiers or the skilled, although there is no evidence that they are suffering from a status panic.

Women and Work.   Traditionally girls have entered into occupations where there is almost certain employment and where they will have little competition from men and where the demands of the job were considered more or less compatible with those of marriage. In such cases the wife readily gives up her job when her husband accepts a position at a place not within commuting distance to her work. Frequently, however, she finds employment at the new location. Equality of opportunity in employment has now been guaranteed by law. There is no physical or legal reason why women should not be trained for the professions or careers equal to those of men. It appears likely that more women will enter career professions. Some of the latent consequences that may result from this have been summarized by Nye (1963, p. 247) as follows:

1. In an increasing number of families the principal or only provider will be the wife, with the husband in some instances becoming the housekeeper in the family in a complete reversal of roles.
2. The divorce rate is likely to increase as the wife's occupation makes more demands on her time, requires her to travel, and leads to her financial independence.
3. Nurseries and day-care centers will increasingly care for children as the number of full-time homemakers decrease.
4. The sexual lives of women are likely to more nearly approximate those of men as women travel more and become less economically dependent on men.
5. The birth rate is likely to continue to decline as interesting and rewarding alternatives to rearing children develop.
6. The age of girls at marriage is likely to increase as the completion of education becomes more obviously useful to them.

The American Workers—Blue-Collar Workers.   Although the so-called blue-collar worker represents less than half of the total working force today, he plays a very important role in our economic, political, and social lives. A six-year study of employee motivation by Myers (1964) revealed that a challenging job which provides a feeling of achievement, responsibility, and growth is the most important key to motivating the workers. Most American workers are ready for the abundance and leisure time that automation is bringing to them. This is reflected in their ambitions for their children, improved living conditions, and use of leisure time.

The results of a study by Klausner of the University of Redlands upset long-held theories about the attitudes of workers toward their jobs (Bernstein, 1967). Klausner asked vacationing Kaiser Steel employees 75 questions in a detailed 10-page questionnaire (employees on vacation with pay for 13 weeks, every five years). The workers were not bored. They did not seek other employment, but were happy with the leisure time and the opportunities it afforded them. Some of the workers took this opportunity to travel; most of them stayed near their home and enjoyed their family, friends, and the free time.

Workers in better paying positions and in positions of responsibility consider themselves as belonging to the middle class. Data were gathered by Blood and Hulin (1967) from 1900 male workers located in 21 plants in eastern United States and analyzed to determine the influences of environmental factors that are presumed to produce feelings of alienation from middle-class norms. The hypotheses were confirmed that blue-collar workers in communities fostering integration with middle-class norms would report higher satisfaction on highly skilled jobs, would value retirement and plan for it, and would accept middle-class educational and many other cultural values. In communities which do not foster integration with middle-class norms the workers displayed more dissatisfaction.

Leisure.   The individual is at leisure when he is not at work—doing whatever he chooses, free of any sense of obligation. To be able and willing or ready to work is regarded as highly desirable. The Judaeo-Christian culture handed down to us made a virtue of work.

> A slack hand makes men poor: a busy hand makes men rich. He who reaps in summer is a man of sense: he who sleeps through harvest does a shameful thing.—
> Proverbs 10: 4-5   (James Moffat, *The Bible*, Harper, 1955)

The American adult regards work as a virtue. However, the amount of time spent at work continues to become less. In 1850, the average work week was about 70 hours; in 1950, this had dropped to 40 hours, and this downward trend is expected to continue (Kaplan, 1960). With the increased leisure available for the typical worker, he can engage in varied pursuits of his own choosing. Concerning the use of leisure time, Levine (1963, p. 287) states:

> During the young adult years the issue of leisure becomes clearly delineated, largely because leisure and work stand in close relationship to one another. Without work there can be no leisure, for leisure by definition has to do with nonworking and nonobligatory experience in which the individual is free to elect how he will spend his time. In conditions of unemployment or enforced idleness, there is no leisure. Most young adults first engage in full-time employment during this period of their lives, and the value of time becomes increasingly apparent to them.

The young adult gives careful consideration to how weekends, evenings, holidays, and vacations are to be spent.

Summary

The early adult years are fraught with adjustment problems not much different from those of the adolescent years, although during this period the individual must become more independent of emotional ties and of peers. Adulthood brings with it responsibilities and expectations that must be met. Responsible adulthood calls for the attainment of certain developmental tasks during childhood and adolescence, ego strength, sex-role attainment, marital adjustment, and vocational adjustment.

Dating and courtship adjustments are extremely important to most individuals during the adolescent and early adult years. Proximity or opportunities for contacts with peers help people become better acquainted, thus paving the way for friendships, dating, and marriage. High school and college students tend to be attracted to each other in proportion to their perceived similarities on attitudes and relevant issues. Changed attitudes toward sexual behavior have occurred during the past quarter-century. There is no evidence that the sexual desire and agility of the American male tends to decrease as he ascends the cultural and educational ladder. Homosexuality varies considerably in different societies, although it is disapproved of in the majority of them.

Following World War II there was a pronounced trend toward early marriage. This frequently occurs because of pregnancy, and may decrease as a result of improved and more widespread means of birth control. People usually marry their equals in social status, and are nearly the same age at marriage. Recent data show a decline in teen-age marriages. Many women find themselves confused and uncertain about their roles. Increased educational and vocational opportunities have contributed to this. A high discrepancy in certain traits between husbands and wives contributes to marital discord. The birth of a child does not usually dispel such discord. The unmarried in our society are frequently faced with difficult social and psychological problems. In their cases vocational success or a career is a frequent substitute for marriage.

Vocational adjustment has become increasingly difficult for each generation. Due to technological advancements there will continue to be a growing demand for education and training, some additional training may be required at different periods of the individual's life. The values an individual stresses in selecting a vocation will be influenced by the socioeconomic class to which he belongs, although there is some evidence that class lines may not be as rigid today as formerly. Sons tend to follow fairly closely the occupations of their father or an adjacent occupation, while daughters tend to marry within the social-class position of their father's occupation.

An important vocational trend is the larger number of workers in the services and distribution occupations and the decreased number in production occupations. Greater numbers of individuals are also entering the professions.

Professional workers change occupations least, whereas unskilled workers and those in white-collar occupations change most. There will be more vocational stability of women as a result of their better vocational preparation.

References

Allen, M. G. "Childhood Experience and Adult Personality—a Cross-Cultural Study Using the Concept of Ego Strength," *Journal of Social Psychology,* Vol. 71 (1967), pp. 53-68.

————. "Psychoanalytic Theory on Infant Gratification and Adult Personality," *Journal of Genetic Psychology,* Vol. 104 (1964), pp. 265-274.

Astin, A. W. "Personal and Environmental Factors Associated with College Dropouts among High Aptitude Students," *Journal of Educational Psychology,* Vol. 55 (1964), pp. 219-227.

Bell, R. R., and J. V. Buerkle. "What Every Mother Should Know," *Journal of Social Issues,* April 1966.

Bernstein, Harry. "Study Finds U.S. Enjoys Vacations" (Washington Post-Los Angeles Times News Service), *The Charlotte Observer* (Jan. 26, 1967), p. 16C.

Blood, M. L., and C. L. Hulin. "Alienation, Environmental Characteristics, and Worker Responses," *Journal of Applied Psychology,* Vol. 51 (1967), pp. 284-290.

Burgental, J. F. T., and E. C. Gunning. "Investigations into Self-Concept: III—Stability of Reported Self-Identification," *Journal of Clinical Psychology,* Vol. 11 (1955), pp. 41-46.

Burke, R. J. "Differences in Perception of Desired Job Characteristics of the Opposite Sex," *Journal of Genetic Psychology,* Vol. 109 (1966), pp. 27-36.

Ellis, E. "Social Psychological Correlates of Upward Social Mobility among Unmarried Career Women," *American Sociological Review,* Vol. 17 (1952), pp. 558-563.

Feldman, H. Study reported at the Groves Park Conference on Marriage, San Juan, 1967.

Ford, C., and F. Beach. *Patterns of Sexual Behavior.* New York: Harper, 1951.

Franklin, R. D., S. G. Grazino, and H. H. Remmers. *Report of Poll 59 of the Purdue Opinion Panel: Youth's Attitudes toward Industrial Relations.* Lafayette, Ind.: Purdue University Division of Educational Reference, 1960.

Freedman, B. "The Sexual Behavior of American College Women: An Empirical Study and an Historical Survey," *Merrill-Palmer Quarterly,* Vol. 11 (1965), pp. 33-48.

Garrison, K. C., Jr. "The Behavior of Clergy and Racial Integration as Related to a Childhood Socialization Factor," *Sociology and Social Research,* Vol. 51 (1967), pp. 209-219.

Gordon, J. E. *Personality and Behavior.* New York: Macmillan, 1963.

Gray, S. W. "Masculinity-Femininity in Relation to Anxiety and Social Acceptance," *Child Development,* Vol. 28 (1957), pp. 203-214.

Havighurst, R. J. *Human Development and Education.* New York: Longmans, 1953.

————. "Youth in Exploration and Man Emergent," in H. Borrow, (ed.), *Man in a World at Work.* Boston: Houghton, 1964.

Heilbrun, A. B. "Conformity to Masculinity-Femininity Stereotypes and Ego Identity in Adolescents," *Psychological Reports,* Vol. 14 (1964), pp. 351-357.

Kagan, J., and Moss, H. A. *Birth to Maturity: A Study of Psychological Development.* New York: Wiley, 1962.

Kaplan, M. *Leisure in America.* New York: Wiley, 1960.

Kelley, E. L. "Consistency of the Adult Personality," *American Psychologist,* Vol. 10 (1955), pp. 659-681.

Kinsey, A., and P. Gebbard. *Sexual Behavior in the Human Female.* Philadelphia: Saunders, 1953.

Kinsey, A., W. Pomeroy, and C. Martin. *Sexual Behavior in the Human Male.* Philadelphia: Saunders, 1948.

Levine, L. S. *Personal and Social Development: The Psychology of Effective Behavior.* New York: Holt, 1963.

Mannheim, K. "The Problem of Generations," in P. Keckskemeti, (ed.), *Essays on the Sociology of Knowledge.* London: Kegan Paul, 1952, pp. 276-321.

Martinson, F. M. "Ego Deficiency as a Factor in Marriage," *American Sociological Review,* Vol. 20 (1955), pp. 161-164.

Mead, Margaret. "The Effects of Changing Cultural Patterns on the Process of Education," speech delivered at Old Dominion College, April 29, 1967.

Meltzer, H., and D. Ludwig. "Age Differences in Memory Optimism and Pessimism in Workers," *Journal of Genetic Psychology,* Vol. 110 (1967), pp. 17-30.

More, D. M. "Social Origins and Occupational Adjustment," *Social Forces,* Vol. 35 (1956), pp. 16-19.

Morse, N. C., and R. S. Weiss. "The Function and Meaning of Work and the Job," *American Sociological Review,* Vol. 20 (1955), pp. 191-198.

Myers, M. S. "Who Are Your Motivated Workers?" *Harvard Business Review,* Vol. 42 (1964), pp. 73-88.

Newcomb, T. M. "The Prediction of Interpersonal Attraction," *American Psychologist,* Vol. 11 (1956), pp. 575-586.

Nye, F. I., and Lois W. Hoffman (eds.). *The Employed Mother in America.* Chicago: Rand McNally, 1963.

Parke, R., and P. C. Glick. "Prospective Changes in Marriage and the Family," *Journal of Marriage and the Family,* Vol. 29 (1967), pp. 249-256.

Pickford, J. H., E. I. Sigmon, and H. Rempel. "Husband-Wife Differences in Personality Traits as a Factor in Marital Happiness," *Psychological Reports,* Vol. 20 (1967), pp. 1087-1090.

Porter, Sylvia. "Men Who Won't Let Wives Work Are Growing Scarce," *The Charlotte Observer* (March 18, 1967), p. 38.

Rainwater, L. "Sex and Class," *Newsweek* (April 17, 1967), p. 100.

Ramsey, N. R. "Assortive Mating and the Structure of Cities," *American Sociological Review,* Vol. 31 (1966), pp. 773-786.

Reiss, Ira L. "The Sexual Renaissance: A Summary and Analysis," *Journal of Social Issues,* Vol. 22, No. 2 (1966), pp. 123-137.

Rice, D. "Employment and Occupations in the Seventies," *Educational Leadership,* Vol. 22 (1964-65), pp. 230-235.

Satir, Vivian. "Why not Marry Five Years at a Time?," digest from paper read at the American Psychological Association, Washington, D.C., Sept. 1967.

"Spotlight on Business," *Newsweek*, Sept. 4, 1967.

Strong, E. K. "Interest Scores While in College and Occupations Engaged in Twenty Years Later," *Educational and Psychological Measurement,* Vol. II, No. 3, pp. 335–348.

————. "Validity of Occupational Choice," *Educational and Psychological Measurement,* Vol. 13, No. 1, pp. 110–121.

Tuddenham, R. D., "The Constancy of Personality Ratings over Two Decades," *Genetic Psychology Monographs,* Vol. 60 (1959), pp. 3-29.

Venn, G., "Vocation Education for All," *Bulletin of the National Association of Secondary School Principals,* 1967, No. 317, pp. 32-46.

Webb, A. P., "Sex-role Preferences and Adjustments in Early Adolescents," *Child Development,* Vol. 34 (1963), pp. 609-618.

Wertz, C. E., "Social Class and Initial Career Choice of College Freshmen," *Sociology of Education,* Vol. 39 (1966), pp. 74-85.

Chapter 14

Socialization and Adjustment During the Middle Adult Years

Since scientific interest in middle age is of recent origin, there has not yet been time to gather data bearing on age changes by the longitudinal method. However, a number of students of human development throughout the life span have provided useful information dealing with personal and social problems arising after age 40. Such information has challenged many traditional beliefs about the middle age period of life.

Personality Characteristics of Middle Adulthood

A working definition of personality with reference to aging is that it is the characteristic way in which an individual responds to the events of adult life. Included in this definition would be the kinds of choices he makes and his characteristic behavior in making choices and in relating to other people. The definition also implies that if we know an individual's present style of responding we can predict what he is likely to do in some future situation. There are two broad categories of responses that the individual makes—an inner, or covert, response and an outer, or overt, response. Inner responses consist of the ways in which we see ourselves, other people, and events; our thoughts and associations about them; and the meanings we read into them. We also respond in terms of moods. Our actions may lead to actions controlled in a way typical of us. Our overt actions involve other people—for example, whether we characteristically move toward or away from others. Among other traits, whether we are friendly and interested in other persons or are suspicious and withdrawing, whether we are disposed to action or passivity, characterize our styles of responding and acting and are elements of our personality.

Physical and Mental Performances. Materials bearing on physical performances at different ages of life were presented in Chapter 4, while materials related to mental performances at different ages were presented in Chapter 8. It was pointed out that continuity in good physical or mental performance through early and middle adulthood depends largely upon one's continued physical and mental performances. One can see evidence of continued superior physical performances in golfers, tennis players, swimmers, dancers, and others. Likewise, there is an abundance of evidence of continued growth in mental performances in the innumerable scholars in various academic areas. A recent interview by one of the writers with a professional dance teacher brought forth the observation that her best students were middle-class people in their 40's or older. She attributed this in part to their superior motivation which brought forth increased effort and an increased desire for practice.

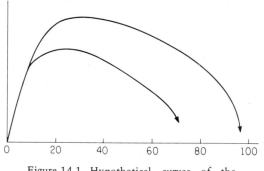

Figure 14-1. Hypothetical curves of the physical performances of man at different ages or stages in life.

The plight of the majority of people in their middle adult years is one of declining physical and mental ability. This is shown in Figures 14-1 and 14-2. The upper line in these figures indicates the potential performances of normal individuals while the lower line indicates the developmental patterns of most individuals. Of course, there are many variations in patterns for different per-

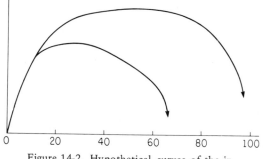

Figure 14-2. Hypothetical curves of the intellectual performances of man at different ages or stages in life.

sons. Surveys show that about 25 million men and women are engaged in work that involves holding down chairs. When not seated the typical worker is standing and seldom exerting much physical or mental energy. The seating problem became apparent to the American Seating Company and other manufacturers of seats some years ago. An investigation of the seats at the famed La Scala in Milan showed that they were as little as 13 inches wide; in America the 18-inch theater seat was discarded by the better theaters many years ago. The trend is toward a 24-inch seat, almost twice that of the seats at La Scala. Perhaps the most important cause of this increase is that Americans are becoming broader largely from spending so much time sitting and doing such a limited amount of bending and other exercises to better distribute the accumulated fat. The problem of overweight and poor distribution of accumulated fat is an acute one for the middle-aged adult. It is not only a health hazard but is partially responsible for poor physical performance on the part of most people during the middle adult years.

Health Care of the Middle-Aged. A new responsibility of the American family, and especially of adult members beyond age 40, is the medical checkup. Anxieties relative to heart conditions and cancer in particular drive adults periodically to the clinic. This also applies to a checkup by an ophthalmologist for glaucoma and cataracts and by a dentist for teeth and gum care. Many adults at this stage are made aware of the seriousness of overweight and lack of exercise. These were not problems for most adults prior to modern technology. Most jobs including homemaking required considerable physical exertion and long hours. Today, with the great amount of mechanical horsepower available there is little need for physical exertion but more need for exercise and dieting. The question arises: Can we find a workable substitute for necessity, which formerly provided the exercise needed by man?

Age can be classified as a determinant of health needs. Each age group has certain minor problems and hazards which are characteristics of that age level. The individual, if he survives childhood, adolescence, and early adulthood reaches the middle years, which have recently been referred to as "middlescence." In these middle years there is an increased incidence of illness that lasts longer periods of time such as arthritis, tuberculosis, diabetes, peripheral-vascular and cardiovascular-renal disorders. An exploration of the major areas of chronic disease of middlescence shows that many problems are related to peripheral-vascular and cardiovascular-renal disorders. Peripheral-vascular disorders refer to all blood-vessel diseases outside the heart such as arteriosclerosis, gangrene, and varicose veins. Heart disease is the leading cause of death of adults in the United States at the present time. There are approximately twenty different kinds of known heart-circulatory diseases. The most common are hypertension and coronary artery disease, which usually occur in people around age 40 or over.

Our modern civilization has not only produced stress that leads to digestive disturbances and circulatory disorders, but it has also influenced mental and emotional problems. Neuropsychiatric disorders (mental illnesses) probably constitute the greatest of the chronic illnesses of all groups. They run the gamut from general malaise or nervousness and drug or alcoholic addiction to frank psychoses. These diseases of psychogenic origin are considered to be the result of faulty individual adaptation. In women of the middle-age group, there is increased stress because of the childbearing and menopausal syndromes. Available statistics indicate that about 25 percent of all Americans have at one time or another experienced psychological difficulties of a considerable magnitude, fewer than 4 percent have seen fit to seek or accept care from mental health sources (Joint Commission on Mental Illness and Health, 1961).

Rigidity of Behavior. "Rigidity" is a descriptive term referring to a tendency to hold to a particular point of view and resist change when the situation suggests that change is called for. Most rigidity in problem solving seems not to lie in attitudes per se, but in changes in abilities. There is evidence from a number of studies that there is an increased susceptibility to the effect of set with advancing age Arnoff, 1959; Canestrari, 1965; Heglin, 1956). In the study by Canestrari two groups of subjects were compared on a task involving spatial-stimulus generalization. The mean ages of the subjects were 59.33 and 41.39 years. The two groups were equated for intelligence as measured by the vocabulary subtest on Form 2 of the Wechsler-Bellevue Intelligence Scale. It was observed that older subjects found it more difficult to inhibit a response once learned when a different response is required.

It was pointed out in the previous chapter that many individuals become quite rigid in behavior with increased age. This may be observed in problem solving during the middle adult period. Problem solving involves many component abilities, each with its own limit, which may change with age. The changes with age in component abilities are both incremental and decremental, and some show no change over the adult years. Generally, the amount of information possessed by an individual rises over the life span. The extent to which a problem has familiar elements determines whether it will be solved more efficiently by the old or young adult. If a problem emphasizes perceptual capacity or memory-held instructions, the young adult will probably perform more effectively. It seems plausible that the adult enlarges his repertory of ready-made solutions over a lifetime and becomes more effective by virtue of them. Because of adaptation, the problem-solving orientation probably declines as a function of years since school. While the disposition to solve problems in terms of known methods is efficient, it can in extreme instances lead to an avoidance of looking at a current problem on its own terms.

Rigidity in behavior can result from disease and changes in ability and brain damage occurring with age, although this is not a factor in every individual. Thus a population of individuals over age 60 is a mixture of those who have limitations of mental abilities because of somatic disease affecting the brain and those who are relatively healthy. In the healthy, up to about age 65, years of education show a greater relationship to mental abilities than does chronological age.

Linton and Haine (1967) note certain personality differences between the rigid and less rigid person. They state (p. 453):

> The more closely a person's behavior is influenced by his environment—that is, the more stimulus-bound he is—the more susceptible he is to change in that environment; and, conversely, the less susceptible a person is to the environment, the less he will respond to environmental changes.

William James (1907) noted, in his classical discussion of the self, that the individual may handle the problem of different social groups evaluating him differently by developing a multiple self-concept. A person with such a self-concept will actually have a number of self-concepts according to the particular group with which he is closely associated. The college professor's self-concept in the classroom, at home, and in a lower-middle-class environment where he spends his vacation will be highly differentiated. The groups with which he is closely associated are widely dissimilar and provide for the college professor's variant evaluations of the self.

Self-Perception and the Sexual Role.   At all stages of development the sex role includes both a social and physical set of expectations. These expectations will vary with cultures and there are indications that important changes are now taking place in our culture regarding sex-role expectations. These are referred to in connection with the sexual revolution, discussed in Chapters 12 and 13. Traditionally the sex role for the woman during the middle adult years emphasizes physical attractiveness, youthful appearance, and a youthful figure; for the male the emphasis is upon strength, physical energy and vigor, and a body build which characterizes a masculine appearance. Many aspects of our culture reinforce the maintenance of these characteristics during the middle adult years. In our affluent middle-class society given to much socializing, such effects as facial wrinkles, gray hair, and the accumulation of fat are sources of concern for the woman; double chins, balding conditions, and the accumulation of a paunch are sources of concern for the man. Concerning the importance of these during the middle years Levine (1963, p. 320) writes as follows:

> The equation of physical attractiveness with femininity and strength with masculinity is the result of certain assumptions about the individual's physical abilities to perform sexually. Such assumptions have little basis in fact, but this does not prevent their having profound psychological significance. . . . The loss of youthful appearance does not necessarily mean that the individual has lost his sex drive or his ability to respond sexually to a member of the opposite sex. Although the amount of drive that persons manifest does decline gradually with age, it is less rapid than is generally assumed and does not terminate for women, as is often believed, with the menopause.

The menopause, which marks the end of menstruation and of ability to conceive and bear children, usually occurs between the forty-fourth and fiftieth birthdays. Along with the cessation of ovulation there is a gradual atrophy of the uterus and mammary glands. Also, at this stage women sometimes experience vasomotor and neuromuscular symptoms. The woman's reactions to the physiological changes are affected by the nature and extent of the physical discomfort and degree to which she responds psychologically to such changes as signifying a "change of life" and the loss of womanhood.

Time Perspective among the Middle-Aged. Kastenbaum and Durkee (1964) noted that in a limited sample of middle-aged people there are relatively few who are inclined to project into the years that lie ahead. This most likely relates in part to the negative social attitudes toward aging which is part of our culture.

This would likely vary with the position on the scale of the large group referred to as the middle-aged people. At the lower end of the scale—the 30's and early 40's—much of the interests will center around family activities, especially the education, social-recreational, and work activities. When the children grow up and move away from home, a new adjustment on the part of husband and wife must be made. At this period of life a crisis in family relations frequently appears. Also, at this age parents' thoughts turn away from problems of child rearing to that of providing for their own immediate needs. It would appear, then, that at this age individuals might project into the future to a greater degree than they did at an earlier age when they were more concerned with immediate problems of child rearing and when the period of retirement from work is still a long way off. One of the writers recalls the case of a college teacher in his late 30's frequently associated with a group of college teachers in their 50's. The latter often talked of retirement and were not particularly interested in further professional advancement, since they had already reached a high professional rank at the institution. One day the young college teacher remarked, "It is hard for me to become highly interested in security and retirement plans, for I really don't know where I will be teaching or what I might be doing twenty-five or thirty years from now." Another college teacher in his mid-40's, who married late and has several children still in public school, remarked, "I can't think of a retirement date, because I have four children still in school who will likely go to college."

Changes in the Family Role

Significant changes appear in the nature and quality of the individual's relationships and responsibilities involving other members of the family. These changes are related to the developmental level of the different members of the family and the developmental as well as interaction patterns formed during the early years of marriage. The roles and responsibilities of the family members will vary in nature and intensity with different families. However, a study of different cultures leads to the general observation that regardless of culture the family serves four basic functions: the sexual, the economic, the reproductive, and the educational. These will vary with cultures, and in many cultures the family serves additional functions, however, these functions are sufficiently identifiable as to be thought of as universal.

The Mother's Changing Role.   When the children are young the mother's role is fairly well defined. Traditionally, earning a living tends to be the husband's responsibility in Western culture, although more than a fourth of American mothers of children under eighteen were employed in 1960 (Nye and Hoffman, 1963). The percentage of American wives who work whole or part-time continues to increase, so that it is estimated that approximately one out of three holds a job outside the home.

Employed wives cause family spending patterns to rise—in some cases almost double, according to figures furnished by the National Consumer Finance Association. The working wife tends to spend more of her money on such nonessential items as cigarettes, alcohol, new clothes, recreational activities, and home furnishings. Manufacturers and merchants are aware of this increased consumption of nonessential items, and pitch their advertisements and promotional campaigns accordingly. This, in turn, causes even more spending on nonessential items.

The wife who remains at home is frequently forced to operate on a light budget, dictated by her husband's salary, or by the husband himself. She is much concerned with buying food on sale, and shopping around for specials that might allow a little extra for recreation and socializing. She more frequently does her own work, takes care of her husband's clothes, and makes her own clothes.

Some Effects of Maternal Employment.   Working wives not only influence the spending habits of the family, they also have a bearing on the cohesion and activities of the family. Social scientists have studied the family life, their children and personal satisfactions of parents where the mother is employed.

> The current consensus is that maternal employment does not necessarily
> have markedly detrimental effects on the children, though under certain circum-
> stances it may be associated with problems; under other circumstances it may
> actually have favorable consequences.   (Hoffman and Hoffman, 1966, p. 39)

It appears that the quality of the relationship of the mother with her children is more important than the quantity of the relationship. Studies reported by Peterson (1961) and Roy (1961) indicate that the employment of the mother does not have an adverse relationship on mother-daughter relationships; neither does it lead to an increase of delinquency. It is not the employment of the mother per se that adversely affects home relationships, but rather the adequacy of maternal behavior which is closely related to her current status. Nonworking mothers who aspire to employment outside the home are more likely to display dissatisfactions in their home relationships than those employed.

It has been noted that husbands tend to take over a greater share of household tasks if their wives work. This has been observed especially among middle-class families. The relative power of the working wife is enhanced so that she shares with her husband major decision making, although her power of decision making tends to be reduced on other areas, such as those having to do with more routine household affairs (Blood, 1963; L. W. Hoffman, 1960). Increasingly the roles of husband and wife are becoming less clearly drawn. Middle-class America in particular has seen the rise of a society in which there is much less sex-role differentiation than formerly, partly from necessity, partly from enlightenment, and partly from the changed vocational status of women.

A study by King (1957) compared the power structure of the Negro family and the white family in the lower class. Power structure was determined by who makes the decisions, as reported by the ninth-grade students in the families. The lower-class category was determined by the father's occupation. The semiskilled included the operative category; the unskilled included service, household, and the unskilled labor occupations.

The overall data indicated that while the sample tended to view decision making more by syncratic power than did the Negro sample, it appears that the Negro family is moving in the direction of white norms involving the equalitarian family. "The Negro adolescent generally tends to perceive the parental differentiation in child rearing more so than does the white adolescent" (p. 73). That is, the Negroes see the same-sex parent as being more involved with problems involving the children.

The Role of the Father. Every family has some division of labor and responsibilities between husband, wife, and children during their growing years. The results of different studies seem to agree that in a large family the father tends to play a relatively greater authority role with the oldest child and the mother tends to be more closely associated with the youngest (Clausen, 1965; Sears et al., 1957). However, Michel (1967) noted that among French as well as American families, "The more often there is an equalitarian repartition in decision-making and in household tasks and the more often the level of education increases among male or female, the more often the score of marital satisfaction of the woman increases" (p. 344).

Nash (1965) has reviewed a large part of the extensive literature on the place of the father in contemporary culture and psychological literature. This summary follows closely his general findings.

1. In the opinion of some sociologists, American society in particular, and probably Western industrial society in general can be epitomized as "mother-centered" in its philosophy of child care.

2. This is in contrast to certain primitive societies with a family cooperative economy, which have typically a way of child rearing which emphasizes father-son and mother-daughter relationships.

3. The difference can be explained by the economic history of our industrial civilization, in which the primitive family cooperative economy has been supplanted by one in which the father is usually the sole support of the family. While engaged in this economic activity, he delegates his place in child rearing to his wife.

4. Psychologists have adopted this cultural philosophy of child care, perhaps uncritically, and many appear to have assumed that it is both the only and the most desirable pattern of child care. In consequence, the majority of psychologists have not perceived the father as important in child rearing, and this is reflected in their writings. Some psychologists have adopted the cul-

tural assumption so thoroughly as to ignore the father entirely or even deny him a position of significance.

5. This culturally determined concept of child care has further removed the father by enhancing the assumption that the rearing of children is specifically a feminine duty.

6. Clinical studies and investigations of delinquents suggest that father-child relationships, and especially those between father and son, may be of considerable etiological importance to both social and psychological abnormality.

7. Psychosexual difficulties, such as homosexuality, apparently result when a child's major identification is with the parent of the opposite sex. If this is the case, a mother-centered system is peculiarly unsuited to the needs of the boy, for although he is under cultural pressure to act as a male he is reared predominantly by women from whom he is likely to acquire a feminine pattern.

8. Identification of child with parent is significant in sex-role and psychosexual development, and can be understood in terms of learning theory: warm, affectionate relationships and prolonged associations are probably among the more vital requirements to successful identifications.

9. Though as yet little understood, critical periods may be found in human development, as they almost certainly are important in the acquisition of some animal behavior traits.

10. There is some evidence from the few available studies of early paternal deprivation that there is a critical period during which the kind of affectional relationship with the father necessary to identification can be built up. This critical period appears to be early, and has tentatively been described as lasting from the time of weaning to entering school.

Size of Family Influences. According to the results of a study by Blood and Wolfe (1960) those parents in the United States who want the largest number of children can least afford them. In general, those higher on the economic and education scale wanted fewer children than those lower on these scales. However, the investigators noted that the desire for children tends to change when a major shift in prestige-level of the husband's occupation occurs. When there is a downward movement, he realizes he cannot provide for the children as he had earlier hoped to do. When there is an upward movement, he figures that having more children will impede him in his career, since it takes time, energy, and money which he now wishes to use to further his career.

According to Blood and Wolfe the educational level of the wife has an important bearing on the number of children wanted. College-trained women have more interests outside the home and assume increased civic responsibilities as well as leadership in community activities. The college-trained woman also has broader social and recreational interests than women with less education. These interests draw her away from her home and children—she doesn't want to be tied down by a large number of children. The college-trained mother is also familiar with some of the imports of child psychology with its emphasis on giving love and attention to each child. The easiest way a mother can give more attention to each child is to have fewer of them.

Middle-class parents manifest interest in their children's progress at school, their activities out of school, and their educational aspirations. Such interest seems to decrease when there are more than four children in the family. However, due to improved living standards, increased educational opportunities for all children, and mass communication through television and radio, class lines are not as clearly drawn today as they were in the early part of this century. However, Douglas (1964) noted that in the middle-class and the working-class English family, infant care and to a lesser degree child management was rated less adequate in the case of children from large families.

Parental Attitudes Toward Child Rearing.   It was pointed out in Chapter 11 that parents have rather definite notions about how children should be raised, and these notions vary considerably even with parents within a similar general culture. Husbands and wives frequently disagree on child-rearing practices, and encounter difficult adjustment problems when they are faced with child-rearing problems.

Parents' attitudes about child rearing are to a marked degree determined by the manner in which they themselves were reared. In many cases the parent feels strongly that the way he was handled by his parents is the best way to bring up a child; such a parent sets about deliberately to treat his children the way he was treated, with little consideration given to changed times and the changed cultural setting today. However, some parents feel they were misunderstood or neglected by their parents and deliberately attempt to correct this condition in their role as parents.

A study by Harris (1959) of school-age children and their mothers furnishes us with three broad groupings of mothers. One group consisted of traditional mothers who tried to rear their children just as they themselves had been reared. A second group of mothers felt they had been cheated, because their mothers had not given them the warmth, love, and affection needed. They generally had unhappy memories of their childhood and were determined to give their children the warmth and love which they missed as children. The third group of mothers were also dissatisfied with their upbringing but felt that they were misunderstood during childhood by their mothers, who had restricted and controlled them too much. These were the rebellious mothers who resolved to be less restrictive and domineering with their children. Some of these mothers were able to carry through their resolution to be less restrictive with their children, while others tended to follow the path of their own mothers, even though they disliked their own mother's child-rearing practices.

The nature of parent-child relationships, like those of husband and wife, have undergone radical changes since the early part of the nineteenth century. This is best noted in court decisions handed down during the past half-century, so that today parents are required to support and educate their children according to the child's needs and aptitude and the financial status of the parents. On the negative side, parents are brought before courts and convicted when child abuse can be proved. Although statistics on child abuse are still alarming, they show that this is a complex problem which is the responsibility of society.

Cullen (1966) noted that the most important variables distinguishing mothers who were positively oriented to a course in child rearing from those who were negatively oriented to such a course were educational status and occupational status. The materials presented in Table 14-1 show that mothers in white-collar occupations emphasize consideration and curiosity as desirable

TABLE 14-1

Working-Class Mothers' Own Occupations and Their
Choice of Characteristics as Most Desirable
in a Ten or Eleven-Year-Old Child
(After Cullen)

Characteristic	Proportion Who Select Each Characteristic		
	White Collar	No Job	Manual Job
Obedience	.26	.35	.53
Neatness, cleanliness	.16	.18	.42
Consideration	.39	.21	.05
Curiosity	.10	.04	.00
Self-control	.13	.14	.11
Happiness	.33	.40	.26

characteristics of ten- and eleven-year-old children, while mothers in manual job occupations emphasize obedience and cleanliness. It seems that differences between siblings and the continuing developmental changes in the various aspects of children's behavior provide a constant source of stimulation to those mothers interested in the forces motivating behavior at different stages of the child's development.

The higher a mother's status the greater the probability that she will choose consideration, curiosity, and self-control; the lower the status, the greater the probability that she will select obedience, neatness and cleanliness. Mothers' values are moreover related to their own occupational positions and educational level. The middle-class emphasis upon internal standards is reflected in their ratings of self-control. Differences in middle- and lower-class parents' values have wide ramifications for the development of moral concepts and behavior of children. Many of these differences can be traced to differences in attitudes and values of parents, which are the roots of the moral concepts and behavior of the children (Kohn, 1959).

Influences of Children Reaching Maturity. An important stage in the life of parents is when their first child is married or when he has left home. The teen years actually prepared the way for this stage, since modern American children tend to spend more and more time with their peers, at school, and in activities outside the home as they progress through the teens. This stage may last for a number of years, usually until the last child is through with his schooling or married or has left home. This change usually makes a greater impact on the mother than on the father, since his job likely occupies a more important place in his life than is the case for the mother. Changes in the role of the wife at this time involve changes in her circle of activity,—not basic changes in the wife or changes in the life activity of the husband, who is still highly involved in his role of worker. Thus a significant gap frequently appears at this time between the importance assigned to the wife's role and that assigned to the husband's role.

Work Adjustments—Middle Adulthood

The vocational problems faced during early adulthood involve vocational selection, transition form school to work, getting ahead on the job, job security, and job satisfaction; those confronting the individual during middle adulthood involve maintaining a high production level, security on the job, job satisfaction, and good physical and mental health.

The rapid pace of technological changes combined with increased educational demands have placed responsibility upon the present-day worker not faced by workers in the past. Many workers are required to learn new skills or adjust

Continuing education in adult years provides opportunities to learn new skills and broaden one's outlook by working with new persons and groups. (Courtesy N.D.E.A. Institute—Tufts University.)

older skills to changed conditions. This is reflected in the large number of women students over age 35 who return to college, after a period of home-making, to refresh and update outworn skills acquired ten or twenty years earlier. A study by the U.S. Department of Labor on "Continuing Programs for Women" pointed out that the number of women age 35 and over in the labor force rose from 10 million in 1950 to 16 million in 1966 (*The Virginian-Pilot*, 1967). Many colleges and universities offer courses designed for the mature woman. Also, many colleges and technical institutions are offering courses to help men upgrade their present vocational abilities and skills or to acquire new skills and understandings to help them maintain their present level of profi-ciency. An important task of middle adulthood is "keeping up," else their services and skills will no longer aid them in their adjustments to demands made by the new or changed jobs.

Employment and Learning. The changes that are continuously operating in present-day employment make it imperative for the person during middle adulthood to be able to learn. The evidence that has been accumulating on both animal and human learning suggests that changes with age in the primary ability to learn are small under most circumstances. When differences do appear, they seem to be more readily attributed to process of perception, set attention, motivation, and the physiological state of the organism (including that of disease states) than to a change in the primary capacity to learn. Since Thorndike's studies in 1928 there has been a general tendency to advance the age at which subjects in learning research are regarded as aged. At the present time there is little evidence to suggest an intrinsic age difference in learning capacity over the employed years, i.e., up to age 60. This is not to say that learning of certain psychomotor skills may not show limitations, or of lifelong habits that elude laboratory study (Birren, 1964, p. 147).

As training and retraining is becoming a commonplace characteristic of adult employment, it is expected that increasing information about adult learn-ing and the conditions that best facilitate it will be provided by industrial studies of learning. Attitudes will change still more as training becomes an accepted feature of a work life in which individuals spend more time in training and less time in direct production. Years of schooling is a more important variable than is age in relation to learning over the work life.

Nicholas Butler (1958) sees adult education as having two objectives; the first is: It must try to reach the individual at a time when his curve of possible growth and accomplishment is still rising and give him new power and ambition. Fifty years from now, if adult education functions as it should, there ought to be a noticeably greater number of persons whose curves of ability will still be rising at age 40. The second objective should be the preservation of open-mindedness, of plastic sympathies, of elastic temper to a much later period than is now customary with the great mass of mankind.

There is no surer way of keeping minds open than to keep them in contact with ideas—ideas of yesterday, if these have shown by their survival that they are probably solid, but better still, ideas of today, and best of all, ideas of tomorrow (Butler, 1958, p. 224).

Men not in the Labor Force.   In the first six months of 1966 about 4½ million men between ages 18 and 64 were not in the current labor market, and were not in most cases looking for employment (Holland, 1967). This figure represents about 9 percent of the male population in this age group. The tabulation by age groups, presented in Figure 14-3 shows that men outside the labor

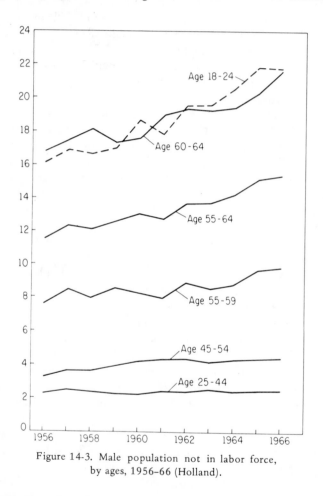

Figure 14-3. Male population not in labor force,
by ages, 1956–66 (Holland).

force are concentrated at the two extremes of the adult male age spectrum: the 18-24 age group and the 55-64 age group. Over the past decade, the proportion of nonparticipants among men 18 to 64 rose from 6 percent of the entire population in 1956 to 8.7 percent in 1966. The sharpest and most persistent rise in nonparticipation occurred among those in the 18-24 age group and in the 60-64 age group.

Of the 2.1 million nonparticipants between the ages of 18 and 24, approximately 1.8 million or 85.7 percent were attending school. Most of the others outside the labor market were waiting to enter the Armed Forces, taking a vacation before returning to school or starting a job, or recovering from illness.

It was pointed out in the previous chapter that the growth in male population not in the labor force has occurred mainly at the two extreme age groups: the 18-24 age group and the 60-64 age group. The proportion of men age 25-54 not in the labor force has traditionally been low (under 4 percent) and stable. From 1956 to 1966, when the rate of employment was high, this held true for the 25-44-year-olds, but there was a slight increase in nonparticipation for the 45-54 age group—from 3.4 percent in 1956 to 4.7 percent in 1966.

A study reported by Rosenfeld and Waldman (1967) indicates that about one-fifth of the 25-64-year-old men not in the labor force have work limitations because of chronic health problems. About half of the nearly 600,000 men age 25-44 who were not working nor looking for work reported some disability; 34 percent were not able to work at all, and 14 percent said they were limited in the amount and kind of work they could perform. In the age group 45-64, a million of the 1.6 million not in the labor force reported they had retired. Among the retired, the proportions who were not able to work or who had some limitations were the same as for the men who had left the labor force but who did not consider themselves retired.

Chronic Illness among Women.   The proportion of women 17 years old and over in the labor force who reported having a chronic condition was about the same as for men, 56 percent and 54 percent respectively. Although a smaller proportion of the 1.6 million unemployed women than of the unemployed men had work limitations, about 10 percent of the women compared with 14 percent of the men. For the unemployed women 45 to 64 years of age, work restrictions were reported by 12 percent, a proportion half that for the men (Rosenfeld and Waldman, 1967, pp. 40-41). Perhaps the older women with work limitations were more likely to have never entered the labor force, or if they entered it were more likely to leave the labor force than men of the same age.

Men average nearly twice as long as women on their current job—5.2 compared to 2.8 years. Job surveys show that women frequently leave the labor force, especially during the central working ages, because of their family responsibilities. Also, a larger percentage of women than men have part-time jobs or jobs of shorter duration. A greater proportion of all employed women than of all employed men are under 25, the age group in which the average job duration is less than one year (Hamel, 1967).

Work Disability and Income.   The lower the family income, the higher the incidence of chronic health conditions. Cause and effect relationships should not be too readily assumed from this finding. Low income may be the consequence of disabling conditions, rather than the cause. It is likely that the educational level of the worker contributes to both the income and the health status. U.S. Public Health surveys show that the proportions of persons with chronic dis-

TABLE 14-2
The Relationship of Family Income and Chronic
Health Conditions for Different Age Groups

Age Group and Family Income	Percent of Total Population with Chronic Conditions which Limit Work Activity
Under 45 years	3.0
Under $3,000	5.6
$7,000 or over	2.0
44 to 64 years	14.4
Under $3,000	30.1
$7,000 or over	7.7
65 years and over	41.5
Under $3,000	47.0
$7,000 or over	32.6

*SOURCE: *Age Patterns in Medical Care, Illness and Disability, U.S. July 1963–June 1965*. U.S. Department of Health, Education, and Welfare, Public Health Service, National Center for Health Statistics, Series 10, No. 32, Table 22.

abilities increase with each age group. This inverse age-income relationship is shown in Table 14-2. It has become apparent to management that low-cost health programs can produce a dramatic lessening of debility and disability among workers. Taylor and Hall state (1967, p. 453): "In these situations major increments in productivity are most readily seen. . . . Whereas lowered morbidity is usually most evident in the increased productivity of working adults, the concomitant lowered mortality effect is more apparent in infants."

The Blue-Collar Worker. The blue-collar worker has frequently been identified as a discrete group with respect to (1) occupational stability, and (2) an orientation toward life and ways of living. A study by Leftorn (1967) dealt with the problem of delineating the blue-collar worker as a discrete group. Interviews were held with 202 auto workers, 110 of whom had been employed at the engine plant less than five years. Of this group 27 percent identified with the middle class, 71 percent with the working class, and 2 percent with the lower class.

The skilled workers and those with more years of seniority registered feelings, attitudes, and judgments concerning themselves which are clearly oriented to what is usually regarded as a middle-class identification. There are also those workers whose attitudinal stance reflected experiences more readily identified in terms of a lower-class frame of reference. Lefton states:

Of special substantive interest in this regard are those findings which show that among blue-collar workers there appear to be modes of experience which prompt and support leanings toward the middle-class orientation. That is, it is not sufficient to argue that the stable working-class person aspires toward the higher social categories of the society—the data presented here suggest that in order for aspirations to become meaningful and relevant to the blue-collar worker, he must first actively experience a series of successes. (p. 169)

The White-Collar Worker. There has been a continuous increase in the percentage of workers classified as white-collar workers, so that by the 50's the percentage of workers so classified surpassed that of those classified as blue-collar workers. In general the white-collar worker has had more years of schooling, finds more satisfaction in his work, and has more of the characteristics of the middle-class person. However, there is no white-collar type, the range is from that of the ordinary clerk to that of the executive.

The white-collar worker is usually subject to more stress than the blue-collar worker. He is in general a conformist, and usually participates in community projects. In general the white-collar worker identifies with the middle class, although he meets frustrations, since his income may not be sufficient to meet his needs and wants. Many present-day white-collar workers at the lower end of the occupational status scale came from lower-class or blue-collar homes. Education was for them a means to improve their social-status position, and they have relatively high educational aspirations for their children.

Man in His Community

Sociologists have given considerable thought to man and his community. Communities have been viewed from different perspectives. Man in his rural surroundings lived in sparsely settled communities where social interactions were infrequent. In contrast to this we see the growth of large urban communities with their many secondary institutional formations. In the cities there is a departure from the small-scale primary relation focus of the small town and rural community. Urban societies diminish primary ties and introduce a range of secondary ones.

Leisure Time and the Middle Aged. In Chapter 1 it was pointed out that one of the fruits of technology was to give man a greater amount of leisure time, or time that he did not have to spend at work. During middle adulthood the individual usually readjusts the tempo of his recreational activities. Those who have spent most of their early adult years at work in an effort to get ahead may have neglected the pursuit of recreational activities. Individuals making up this group will find it difficult adjusting to a life of leisure. Another large group of middle-aged adults have spent their leisure time as spectators, and are not physically fit to engage in even light vigorous physical activity. It was pointed out earlier that the rapid decline in physical fitness during the early and middle adult years will not take place, if the individual continues a reasonable amount of physical activity. The notion that dancing, swimming, hiking, bowling, and similar activities are reserved for the early adult years is not borne out by the experiences of a relatively large percentage of middle-aged adults who continued some physical activities during their early adult years. The pursuance of these activities tends to keep the person physically fit, and should be helpful in the maintenance of mental and physical health during middle and late adulthood.

The middle adult years are a period of warm and intimate family inter-relations and friendship with peers. Many individuals use their leisure time for music, drama, literature, art, and hobbies. Social participation is also important at this stage of life. Informal getting together, dinner engagements, playing cards, and dancing are activities frequently engaged in by middle-aged adults. Thus these years can be rewarding years and a good preparation for late adulthood.

Kinship Interactions.   Despite the disbursements of family and family ties as a result of industrialization, there remain many kinship ties. Firth (1964) points out that extended kinship relationships in modern urban society serves expressive needs for a large percentage of our urban population. They may be used selectively as sources of friendship contacts, and frequently facilitate occupation-based social motility. Furthermore, kinship interactions cater to primary needs, giving families increased security especially in times of emergencies.

A survey by Tomeh (1967) of informal social participation in the greater Detroit area showed that over half the population see their relatives "often" and approximately four out of every ten Detroiters visit their neighbors "quite often." He states: "Although neighbors provide a continuing foundation for primary group relation, relatives are generally much more frequently seen" (p. 88).

Friendship Interactions.   In addition to kinship ties there is a variety of forms of friendship and neighborliness. This is quite noticeable in certain subur-

TABLE 14-3
Total Informal Participation and Population
Characteristics (After Tomeh)

Population Characteristics	Informal Participation		
	High	Low	N
Age			
21–34	59	41	796
35–49	47	53	764
50 or older	33	67	696
Marital Status			
44 or younger			
Not married	53	47	179
Married, no children	58	42	143
Married, children	56	44	1009
45 or older			
Not married	27	73	227
Married, no children	34	66	430
Married, children	38	62	267
Sex			
Males	48	52	1082
Females	45	55	1174
Race			
White	47	53	1942
Negro	45	55	311

ban areas and among different ethnic groups. Through friends contacts are made with clubs, church, and other institutions and organizations. The activities of friends include visiting, which sometimes approximates the traditional conception of primary relationships. The importance of such relations will depend upon the needs of particular individuals and upon the nature of the community.

The results from the Detroit survey, presented in Table 14-3, showing that married adults generally reported more informal participation than single persons particularly at an older age level, suggest that marriage tends to bring with it a more stable life pattern, and consequently, a wider circle of friends. When socioeconomic status is considered, it was noted that higher socioeconomic status tended to bring with it increased social participation. Also, people with more education were involved in more informal participation with others. Unlike other status levels, those with middle status had the highest rate of kinship participation. There is no evidence from this and other studies for the frequently held viewpoint that informal social participation does not occur in the large urban areas.

Social Stratification.   The occupational position of the husband has been used as a basis for determining the social class of the family and for predicting the life style of the family. The occupation of the husband is important in determining a particular life style in part because the income associated with it provides the basis for a particular way of living. It was pointed out in the previous chapter that working wives contribute to the family income and affect considerably the life style of the family. Concerning this Barth and Watson (1967, p. 395) state:

> Since a working wife supplies one-third of the family earnings, her service should be an important asset in attaining or enhancing a given living-style. It does not follow, however, that the wife's income will be allocated in the same way or make the same proportional contribution to life-style as the husband's. . . . A major portion of her income may be saved or invested, perhaps for the future education of the children, and thus be irrelevant, in a certain sense, to the present social standing of the family in the community. On the other hand, in a mass-consumption society there are strong pressures for the allocation of "extra" income for immediate "needs" or desires.

Influence of Size of Community.   A great deal of hypothesizing may be found regarding the relation of the size of the community and the personality of the individual. However, it has already been pointed out that social interactions may be found in communities of all sizes. One aspect of the personality system that is often mentioned as varying with community size is conservatism. Descriptions of city dwellers generally represent urbanites as less conservative in their behavior than their rural counterparts. One of the writers (Garrison) compared the world-mindedness of college students from different backgrounds. Students with a rural background were found to be least world minded, while students from the large urban areas were most world minded.

A study by Photiadis (1967) dealt with community size and aspects of the authoritarian personality among businessmen. Although businessmen do not represent a cross section of a community, their attitudes may give us additional insight about conservatism in communities of different sizes. The investigators found that businessmen in smaller towns are more conservative not only on issues that concern them, but also on general issues, and sometimes on issues contrary to their economic interests. Religion was suggested as a possible intervening variable. Perhaps the conservatism of the small towner is determined by his religion. The speculation seems reasonable because (1) the data indicates that community size is related negatively to orthodox belief, and (2) there is considerable evidence that a positive relationship exists between orthodoxy and the authoritarian personality. This was discussed earlier in Chapter 9.

Summary

Continuity in good physical and mental performance through early and middle adulthood depends largely upon one's continued physical and mental performances. Health care during middle adulthood has become a vital problem.

With age, many individuals become quite rigid in behavior. The individual's self concept continues to be important throughout life. During the middle adult years it is related to a continuation of the sex role, and may be noted in the efforts of the woman to be youthful and physically attractive. The middle-aged person is not inclined to project ahead, partly because of the negative social attitudes toward aging in our culture.

There is a pronounced change in the mother's role during middle adulthood. The percentage of American wives who work outside the home continues to increase and is very high during middle adulthood. There is very little evidence that maternal employment has a detrimental effect upon the children; the quality of the relationship of the mother with her children is more important than the quantity of such relationships. Sex-role differentiation has decreased among middle-class Americans. In the large family the father tends to play a greater authority role with the oldest child, while the mother tends to be more closely associated with the youngest, indicating a "mother-centeredness" in early child care.

Middle-class parents manifest more interest in their children's performances at school as well as their activities outside of school than lower-class parents. Although, due to improved living standards and increased educational opportunities for all children class lines are not as clearly drawn today as they were at an earlier period. The nature of parent-child relationships has undergone radical changes, due in a large measure to the improved educational and occupational status of parents. The time of the youngest child reaching maturity has an important impact upon the home, especially for the mother.

The vocational problems faced by the middle-aged worker is that of maintaining a high production level, security on the job, job satisfaction, and maintaining good physical and mental health. Many workers at this stage may be required to learn new skills or adjust older skills to changed conditions. Thus training and retraining has become a commonplace characteristic of adult employment. The growth of male population not in the labor force has occurred mainly at the two extreme groups: The 18-24 age group and the 60-64 age group. A greater proportion of all employed women than employed men are under 25. Important differences appear in the motivation and problems of the blue-collar and white-collar workers.

Leisure time has increased as a result of technology. This has provided increased opportunities for workers to participate in community activities, recreation, and creative pursuits. The middle adult years are a period of intimate family interrelationships and friendships with peers. This apparent milestone in life is dependent as much on one's attitudes and philosophy as on his arteries—or years.

References

Arnoff, F. N. "Age Differences in Performance on a Visual-Spatial Task of Stimulus Generalization," *Journal of Educational Psychology,* Vol. 50 (1959), pp. 259-265.

Barth, E. A., and W. B. Watson. "Social Stratification and the Family in Mass Society," *Social Forces,* Vol. 45 (1967), pp. 393-402.

Birren, J. E. *The Psychology of Aging.* Englewood Cliffs, N.J.: Prentice-Hall, 1964.

Blood, R. J., "The Husband-Wife Relationship," in F. I. Nye and L. W. Hoffman, (eds.), *The Employed Mother in America,* Chicago: Rand-McNally, 1963, pp. 282-305.

Blood, R. O., and D. M. Wolfe. *Husbands and Wives: The Dynamics of Married Living.* New York: Free Press, 1960.

Butler, N. M. "To Keep Our Minds Open," in W. Donahue, *et al.,* (eds.), *Free Time Challenge to Later Maturity,* Ann Arbor: U. of Michigan Press, 1958.

Canestrari, R. E. "Age Differences in Spatial-Stimulus Organization," *Journal of Genetic Psychology,* Vol. 106 (1965), pp. 129-136.

Clausen, J. A. "Research Note on Family Size, Sib Order and Socialization Influences," unpublished papers, 1965.

Cullen, J. S. "Determinants of Participation in Parent Education Courses," *Journal of Health and Human Behavior,* Vol. 1 (1966), pp. 302-308.

Douglas, J. W. B. *The Home and the School: A Study of Ability and Attainment in the Primary School.* London: MacGibbon and Kee, 1964.

Firth, R. "Family and Kinship in Industrial Society," *Sociological Review Monograph, No. 3,* 1964, pp. 65-87.

Hamel, H. R. "Job Tenure of Workers, January 1966," *Monthly Labor Review,* Vol. 90, No. 1 (1967), pp. 31-37.

Harris, I. D. *Normal Children and Mothers.* New York: Free Press, 1959.

Havighurst, R. J. "The Social Competence of Middle-Age People," *Genetic Psychology Monographs,* 1957.

Heglin, H. J. "Problem Solving Set in Different Age Groups," *Journal of Gerontology,* Vol. 11 (1956), pp. 310-317.

Hoffman, L. W. "Parental Power Relations and the Division of Household Tasks," *Marriage and Family Living,* Vol. 22 (1960), pp. 27-35.

Hoffman, L., and Lois Hoffman (eds.). *Review of Child Development Research,* Vol. 2. New York: Russell, Sage Foundation, 1966.

Holland, Susan S. "Adult Men Not in the Labor Force," *Monthly Labor Review,* Vol. 90, No. 3 (1967), pp. 5-15.

Hurlock, Elizabeth B. *Developmental Psychology,* 2nd ed. New York: McGraw-Hill, 1959.

James, W. *Psychology.* New York: Holt, 1907.

Joint Committee on Mental Illness and Health, *Action for Mental Health.* New York: Basic, 1961, pp. 102-103.

Kastenbaum, R., and N. Durkee. "Young People View Old Age," in R. Kastenbaum, (ed.), *New Thoughts on Old Age.* New York: Springer, 1964, pp. 237-249.

King, K. "A Comparison of the Negro and White Family Power Structure in Low-Income Families," *Child and Family,* Vol. 6, No. 2 (1957), pp. 65-74.

Kohn, M. L. "Social Class and Parental Values," *American Journal of Sociology,* Vol. 64 (1959), pp. 337-351.

Lefton, M. "The Blue-Collar Worker and the Middle-Class Ethic," *Sociology and Social Research,* Vol. 51 (1967), pp. 158-170.

Levine, L. S. *Personal and Social Development.* New York: Holt, 1963.

Linton, P. M., and J. D. Haine. "Relationship of Personality to Reaction under Stress," *Mental Hygiene,* Vol. 51 (1967), pp. 432-457.

Marmor, J. "The Crisis of Middle Age," *American Journal of Orthopsychiatry,* Vol. 37 (1967), pp. 336-337.

Melvin, L. K. "Social Class and Parent-Child Relationships," *The American Journal of Sociology,* Vol. 68 (1963), pp. 471-480.

Michel, A. "Comparative Data Concerning the Interaction in French and American Families," *Journal of Marriage and the Family,* Vol. 29 (1967), pp. 337-344.

Nash, J. "The Father in Contemporary Culture and Current Psychological Literature," *Child Development,* Vol. 36 (1965), p. 261.

Nye, F. I., and Lois W. Hoffman (eds.). *The Employed Mother in America.* Chicago: Rand McNally, 1963.

Peterson, E. T. "The Impact of Maternal Employment on the Mother-Daughter Relationship," *Marriage and Family Living,* Vol. 23 (1961), pp. 355-361.

Photiadis, J. D. "Community Size and Aspects of the Authoritarian Personality," *Rural Sociology,* Vol. 32 (1967), pp. 70-77.

Rosenfeld, C., and Elizabeth Waldman. "Work Limitations and Chronic Health Problems," *Monthly Labor Review,* Vol. 90, No. 1 (1967), pp. 38-31.

Roy, P. "Maternal Employment and Adolescent Roles; Rural-Urban Differentials," *Marriage and Family Living,* Vol. 23 (1961), pp. 340-349.

Sears, R. P., E. E. Maccoby, and H. Levin. *Patterns of Child Rearing.* New York: Harper, 1957.

Taylor, C. E., and Marie Hall. "Health, Population, and Economic Development," *Science,* Vol. 157 (1967), pp. 451-457.

Tomeh, A. K. "Informal Participation in a Metropolitan Community," *Sociological Quarterly,* Vol. 8 (1967), pp. 85-102.

The Virginia Pilot, May 4, 1967, p. 28.

Chapter 15

Personal and Social Adjustments in Later Adulthood

The problem related to aging has come to the forefront as a result of science and technology. What is frequently referred to as old age was very rarely reached prior to the beginning of the twentieth century. Advances in medicine have reduced the mortality rate at each age level, enabling many people to live to what is termed a ripe old age. According to the Bureau of Census (1965), there were about 16 million persons age 65 and over in 1965. It is estimated that this number will increase to over 23 million by 1980 and to more than 28 million by the year 2000, making up at this later date about 13 percent of our total population.

Progress in technology has reduced the need for human labor, and will most likely continue to do so. Thus we can visualize that with increasing automation, not only will work hours be shortened but the working age will be reduced so that by the end of the century a large percentage of our population will not be needed on the labor market. They will pursue activities other than work for profit or production. In our Western society we are able to prolong life and reduce the hours and years of labor; we also have the means available to provide a relatively high standard of living for workers when they retire from productive work. Our modern scientific age has created a new age for men—old age; it faces the challenge of providing the social and psychological needs for the increasing number of individuals living a longer life.

Attitudes toward the aged and treatment of the aged vary among the different cultures. Slater (1964, p. 231) presents the following generalization:

> One crude generalization that emerges from these data is that the prestige of the aged is highest in those societies falling in the middle range of cultural development. It is among the most primitive societies in which the barest subsistence is problematic, that killing or abandonment of the aged is most often found. Yet those societies which approach or achieve a level which we traditionally call "civilized," particularly when characterized by a fairly advanced technology, also show, in many cases, an attitude of disregard for the aged, although tempered by a sense of obligation with respect to their maintenance and care.

A reality that must be faced is that prestige enjoyed by the aged in a given society is largely dependent upon the importance of the functions they perform in that society.

The Biology of Aging: Its Implications

The human life cycle may be divided in many ways, including the ages at which most individuals are presented by society with certain expectations. Development, maturity, and senescence will be divided differently depending upon the use of anatomical, physiological, psychological or social criteria. The aged are affected by the diseases and traumas of a lifetime, and by changes in social, economic, and emotional status which accompany the aging process.

Kallmann and Sanders (1949) state:

> Psychologically it is certain that satisfactory adjustment of aging can be attained only if the biological facts of life are clearly understood, and their acceptance is woven into a plain design of living. In a human world, old age is a comparative classification of vital efficiency and as relative in its definitions as is the faculty of being alive or the quality of being human.

Getting Old.   In most normal individuals getting old starts at about 40. An earlier age decline is noticeable in reaction time and certain other motor abilities. Measurable changes in the speed in which a light stimulus is perceived and in the ability to distinguish different light intensities appears around age 40. Also, there are notable changes in the adaptation of the eyes from light to darkness. This is observable when one enters a movie theater or restaurant with low light intensity; the older person finds it more difficult to find his way for a brief interval while the eyes become adjusted to the darkened condition. Color vision is also affected, especially sensitivity to blue light.

There is also a significant reduction in hearing ability, especially for tones of higher frequency. This reduction is not apparent to the individual during the early stages but becomes apparent to a large percentage of people after age 50.

The differentiation of changes attributable to the aging process from those attributable to acquired diseases is not clear-cut in many instances. Over the years we have found that many of the changes formerly attributed to the aging process are due to disease. Birren (1964) says (p. 22):

> The individual differences in human longevity are determined more by environmental than by hereditary factors. This relationship may be viewed as changing, in the sense that as the environments of modern man tend to become similar and thus restricted in variance, hereditary factors will emerge as larger influence.

A relatively small percentage of people actually die of old age, although this percentage has steadily increased as a result of medical research involving diseases prevalent among the aged. Shock (1962) points out:

> Mortality increases rapidly with age—in precise logarithmic ratio to age in the population as a whole—because the elderly become more susceptible to diseases that kill, such as cancer and cardiovascular disease.   (p. 100)

Geriatrics is the phase of medical services that deals specifically with diseases of old age, while *gerontology* deals with the process of aging. However, this process continues throughout adult life. Although gerontology is a relatively young discipline, studies of the aging process have arrived at some significant findings, among which is that the body dies a little each day.

Decline in Capacity and Function. A significant manifestation of aging is the decline in ability to exercise and do work. Although this is not as important to the vocational life of man today as it was formerly, such a decline correlates directly with a progressive loss of tissue. The loss of tissue is associated with the dissapearance of cells from the muscles, the nervous system, and other vital organs. Laboratory experiments have been set up to study the maximum amount of work a subject can do and have his heart return to normal within two minutes after he stops working (Shock, 1962). The data presented in Figure 15-1 show

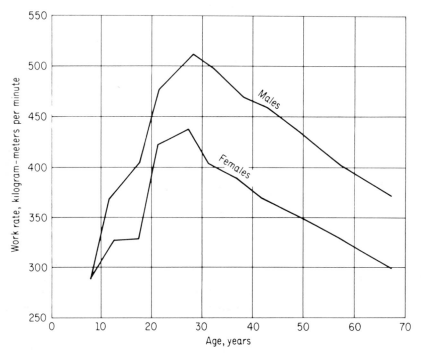

Figure 15-1. Changes in work rate with age are striking. The function reaches a peak at age 28 and declines steadily thereafter. From "The Physiology of Aging" by Nathan W. Shock. Copyright © 1962 by Scientific American, Inc. All rights reserved.

that the changes in work rate with age are striking. The function reaches a peak at age 28 and declines steadily thereafter. According to this chart, at age 70 a man's physical capacity has declined by 30 percent. It should be pointed out, however, that important individual differences may be observed.

Physical performance reflects the combined capacity of the different organ systems of the body working together. Shock (p. 100) states:

> ... The ability to do work depends on the strength of the muscles, the co-ordination of movement by the nervous system, the effectiveness of the heart in propelling blood from the lungs to the working muscles, the rate at which air moves in and out of the lungs, the efficiency of the lung in its gas-exchange function, the response of the kidneys to the task of removing excess waste materials from the blood, the synchronization of metabolic processes by the endocrine glands, and, finally, the constancy with which the buffer systems in the blood maintain the chemical environment of the body.

Since muscles at work require extra oxygen and other nutrients, and produce more waste that must be carried away, the heart is required to work harder so as to move more blood through the system. Although the resting blood pressure in older people is only slightly less than that for younger, a given amount of exercise will increase the blood pressure in the old person significantly more than in the young person. Thus when individuals exert themselves to the maximum, the heart of the older person cannot achieve as great an increase in rate as that of the younger people. During exercise the heart is unable to pump as great an amount of blood per minute in the older person as in the young. This tends to impose a limit on the amount of work the older person can do.

The lungs also play an important role in output. The amount of oxygen that the blood takes up from the lungs and carries to the tissues during exercise is substantially lowered with age. According to Shock, the older individual must move about 50 percent more air in and out of his lungs in order to double the level of oxygen uptake during exercise. It was pointed out in an earlier chapter that there is a decline in vital capacity with age. This impairment is perhaps an expression of a general decline in neuromuscular capacity.

Physiological Changes and Disabilities Associated with Aging. Certain changes and disabilities occur which are associated with the aging process. There is a gradual slowing down of the rate of division, growth, and repair of the cells of the body after injury with a decrease in recuperative ability after damage due to injury or disease. The cells become smaller, and function at a lower, less efficient level. Regarding the aging of cells, Birren states (p. 52):

> It has been quite well established by experimental biologists that cells die with age in many of the critical organs of the body. Thus counts of the number of cells in the brain or kidney will show a reduction in the number by advanced age. In addition to the "spontaneous death" of cells, those remaining may or may not be at peak efficiency. The picture is one of important body organs having a lessened functional capacity because of cell loss. Under critical conditions, the loss in functional capacity may lead to the death of the individual. Cell death is not the same as death of the organism. The organism can tolerate and, with time, adapt to the loss of many cells. In aging, then, the critical cells would seem to be those that are so highly developed or differentiated that they no longer divide.

The basal metabolic rate is slowed down, with a decrease in the caloric intake needed to maintain the same body weight. If the appetite is unchanged, obesity may result. The heart reflects the generalized decrease in muscle cell size and efficiency by a diminished strength of contraction, smaller output, delayed recovery of the ability to contract, and decreased efficiency in converting nutrients, such as glucose and oxygen, into mechanical energy. Concerning the aging of cells, Birren cites (p. 77):

> Cells that do not or cannot divide seem to show aging more than do cells that divide. In the process of dividing, cells seem to discard accumulated damage. In man, several important cells do not divide: neurons of the nervous system and muscle cells. These cells, as old as the individual, thus appear to be critical in the expression of the potential for senescence.

Therefore, the number of cells in the nervous system, and related organs of special sense, such as the eyes, ears, and organs of smell, decrease with advancing age. For instance, there are about half as many brain cells in the frontal, or thinking, portion of the brain at 80 years as there were at 40. Fortunately, the brain has a tremendous reserve capacity and may function very well despite this loss. This is particularly true of those within the upper 5 percent in intellectual ability who show very little change up to advanced ages. However, the decrease in the number of cells and the slowing down of the speed of action and reaction of the nervous system may have harmful effects.

Important individual differences in aging show up in the rate of flow of blood plasma through the kidney. This is shown in Figure 15-2 (Shock, 1962). A complete test of kidney performances involves "measurement of the amount of filtrate formed per minute, the quantity of blood plasma (the liquid portion of the blood) passing through the kidney per minute and the maximum excretory capacity of the nephrons" (Shock, 1962, pp. 104-105). The chart by Shock shows tremendous differences in aging at different age levels by the rate of flow of blood plasma through the kidney. Such differences also appear when studies are made involving other measures of aging.

In seeking an understanding of the fundamentals of the aging process it is difficult to find a unitary mechanism that can account adequately for aging in man. There is a gradual decline in function of many different organ systems most readily explained by a loss of postmitotic cells in nondividing tissues. This is expressed as a decrease in muscle strength, vital capacity, renal function, cardiac activity, and in other areas, but there appears to be no significant decrease in the activity of the bone marrow, of intestinal epithelium, or of liver tissues in which mitosis is a significant feature throughout life.

Shock points out that it would be most convenient if there were some tissue in so orderly a fashion that it could serve as a biological time clock. Such a tissue does exist. It is the mass of lymphatic tissue which shows rapid prepubertal growth, a sharp pubertal fall, and then a steady decline throughout life which is consistent from animal to animal. An assay of the amount of lymphatic tissue in

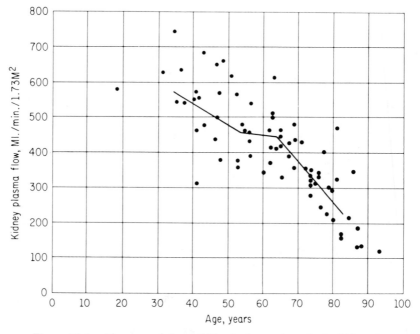

Figure 15-2. The rate of flow of blood plasma through the kidney is plotted against age for some 70 men. The plasma flow is measured in millimeters per minute per 1.73 square meters of body-surface area. From "The Physiology of Aging" by Nathan W. Shock. Copyright © 1962 by Scientific American, Inc. All rights reserved.

a portion of the organism provides a ready assay of the passage of time in that organism. No other tissue appears to behave in so consistent a fashion. The physiological significance of this time clock is rather uncertain, but surprisingly little attention has been paid to it except by scientists interested in the aging process.

Learning, Memory, and Intelligence. Materials bearing on learning, memory, and intelligence were presented in an earlier chapter. The evidence that has been accumulating on both animal and human learning suggests that changes with age in the primary ability to learn are small under most circumstances. When differences do appear they seem to be more readily attributed to processes of perception, set attention, motivation, and physiological state of the organism (including that of disease states) than in a change in the primary capacity to learn. Cowdry (1963, p. 52) noted that:

> Older adults often seem to anticipate difficulties in learning. They appear apprehensive when approaching a learning task, asking detailed questions, seeking meanings, and inviting specific direction. They often appear overcautious and fearful of making mistakes. They seek to avoid new experience and cling to procedures which, if not most efficient, are at least familar. Experience than may deter new efforts and limit new learning.

A high level of intelligence, a good education, and continuous practice in exercising capacity to learn appear to delay onset of any loss of ability to learn. Cowdry contends that learning and memory are two most effective psychologic tools of youth, but that they function less efficiently in the later years, and

> Memory for past events appears to be less impaired than retention of recent experience. Failure in immediate recall, perhaps associated with inability to register what is new, characterizes memory failure in old age. In addition, difficulties in ordering the time sequence of recent events have been noted as an early evidence of confusion. (p. 52)

Longitudinal studies of mental abilities, including memory, generally show a significant decline after age 70. However, we should distinguish between normal healthy aged individuals and those suffering from certain disabilities, such as cerebral arteriosclerosis. In a comprehensive study of cognitive changes with age in a sample of German population, significant differences in test scores were noted for survivors and nonsurvivors; i.e., initial measurements according to subsequent length of life gave significant differences in favor of the longer survivors (Riegel, 1964).

Psychological Adjustments

The psychology of aging touches upon more preconceptions and personal values than do most sciences. This implies an initial slowness in sorting out facts and evolving experiments leading to new discoveries and principles in pursuit of a scientific psychology of aging. Man's behavior over a lifetime both determines and is determined by his environment. It would be highly convenient but overly optimistic to expect that experimental studies will soon indicate that man's aging can be explained by a few simple principles and that by understanding such principles man might control the main events of his life span.

The capacities of the individual are continually involved in adapting. Some problems or tasks face the individual at characteristic phases of the life span. These age-level tasks and the underlying changes in drives and motivations give adult life a characteristic rhythm or tempo. Individual differences, however, are always apparent in aging, just as in development. We have presented the concept of the individual as a complex system moving forward in time to further differentiation. Memory is the likely element that, for behavior, provides an irreversible forward direction to experience. Not all aspects of the organism are regarded as constantly interacting; rather, autonomy exists within subsystems, thus providing for novelty in adaptation. While there are characteristic changes in adults over the life span, aging is a dynamic process with emergent features in both the individual and the species (Birren, p. 22).

Social-Class Differences. The large-scale variables of social class, ethnicity, and income influences how long individuals live and the patterning of their lives. The likelihood of exposure to adverse environmental conditions, such as work hazards and disability due to injury, vary with income. In addition to the social-class variations in exposure to injury and noxious conditions, there are variations in conditions that favor recovery from injury. The individual of low income and low education, lacking a grasp of elementary principles of human physiology, may not understand the significance of an illness or injury or the importance of medical treatment, or of following a diet and adhering to a prescribed regime. Rather, he will hope that he can save the cost of medical care and that the "inconvenience" will pass away with time. He tends to ignore minor and major symptoms of potential danger. The older person with reduced income may avoid medical care because of the costs involved.

Interpersonal relationships also influence the way in which individuals evolve over the life span. Interpersonal relationships of the family are particularly significant in influencing what choices are made at critical points in the life span. The models of interpersonal relationships that have become part of the individual's personal standards will affect his peers and his own children. In general, lower-class behavior is influenced by a struggle for simple subsistence. Behavior tends to be direct and aggressive, but at the same time passive in the sense that the individual does not work toward general or remote goals. Middle-class behavior, not being preoccupied with the struggle for simple subsistence, is more involved in working toward abstract goals and tends to be achievement-oriented.

Class differences influence not only the way in which individuals grow older, but also the types of mental illnesses they develop as adults. Generally, the lowest class is found to have the highest incidence of mental illness. Social mobility is a common feature of life today; perhaps half of the population end their life in a different social class than they were at birth. Upward mobility is associated with more positive features of personal and social adjustment than is the less common downward mobility. Constellations of factors, some unrelated, contribute to the upward or downward mobility of individuals. One characteristic problem for the older person is to adapt to reduced social roles, status, and income associated with retirement. For women, the greatest role change of all is the change to widowhood.

Lifelong Behavior Patterns.   The organization of lifelong behavior patterns determines the way individuals adapt to the characteristic problems that face them over the life span. Over time, a style of adaptation develops that is characteristic of the individual. Young and old adults, upper- and lower-class persons, all live in different contemporary streams of information that influence their perception of the physical and social world and their willingness to seek information and initiate action. While aging and behavior have been viewed as being dependent upon social-cultural influences, nevertheless the individual is also a determining factor in his own evolution and the differentiation of motives and choices of action over the life span.

Man's capacity for complex skills and even his ability to survive depend upon the reception and integration of information from specialized nerve endings, such as those in the eye, ear, skin and muscles. However, there is not necessarily a direct relation between the sensitivity of sensory receptors and the adequacy of behavior. Some amount of reduced acuity can be tolerated without obvious impairment of behavior. For example, reduced taste and smell would usually be less important to an individual than reduced hearing or vision. Generally with advancing age there is reduction in sensory acuity, as a consequence of injury, disease, and changes in the structures and functions of neural tissues that are probably due to primary aging.

The changes in the central nervous system, in the peripheral sensory receptors, and in their specialized structures result in a reduced sensory input with age. The reduction of efficiency found in sensory processes with aging reduces the quality and quantity of the information available to the organism. This reduces the ability of the individual to interact with his environment. Experience may compensate for the decrease in information input, the organism as a whole may respond more efficiently.

Slowing of Behavior. One of the most distinguishing features about aging persons is their tendency to slowness of behavior. Whereas young adults are quick or slow in their behavior in accordance with the demands of the situation, older adults have a general slowness of behavior. Slowness in the young adult can be thought of as nonspecific; a great many factors can lead to slowness of behavior. These factors include stimuli that are unfamiliar, stimuli that are unexpected, stimuli that tend to evoke conflicting responses, and difficult or complex stimuli. Responses that must be made in a sequential manner or responses in which the consequences may be inordinately great may be studiously delayed until the individual feels the conditions are optimum. These factors affect the differential speed of response in older persons as well as in the young, but they represent time in addition to a generalized tendency to slowness with age.

Experiments relating performance to age have shown that, although peripheral organs may set limits in tasks requiring fine sensory discrimination or, at the other end of the chain, strenuous muscular activity, most sensorimotor performance among older people is limited by central mechanisms. These may be conceived as having a finite capacity in the sense that there is a maximum amount that can be done at any one time and in any given period of time. Compensation can to some extent be made for loss of capacity by taking a longer time, and this appears to be a major cause of slowness of performance among older people. If this longer time is not taken, accuracy appears to suffer, and speed and accuracy can be shown to be in principle compensatory.

Striking changes with age are often shown in the method or manner of performance. For example, older people display a rather consistent tendency when possible to shift their emphasis from speed to accuracy. These changes could be viewed, in many cases at least, as being due to an effort to make the best use of the capacities the subject possesses.

The generalized slowness of behavior in older persons is looked upon as being most probably an expression of a primary process of aging in the nervous system, the precise localization or basis of which is not known. The most likely explanations involve the loss of nerve cells with advancing age, reduced neural excitability, physical-chemical changes at the synapse that limit transmission speed, and a lowering of subliminal excitation of the nervous system resulting from changes in subcortical centers.

Although much has been learned about psychomotor speed and aging, not much is known about the modifying conditions that maintain an alert organism with a potential for precise and rapid response. Thus whether continuous high-level stimulation in later life will retard or advance psychomotor slowing is not known, Also, the role of fatigue is unknown in its effect on or relation to psychomotor slowness.

Slowness can be looked upon as a change dependent upon more elementary processes in the nervous system, or it can be examined with regard to its con-sequences for behavior. In the latter view, the slowness of advancing age comes as close as any identifiable process to being an independent aging variable; that is, slowness defined as a minimum operations time in the nervous system can be used to explain other psychological phenomena of aging. One consequence of the slowing is that the individual is limited in the amount of activity or the number of behaviors he can emit in some unit of time. The slowness may also have other consequences or concomitants in mood and energy.

Changes in Concept of Self.   One's concept of self is important throughout life. Major changes in personality during late adulthood reflect the individual's concept of self. Changes in the self-concept in late adulthood result from aware-ness of aging, acceptance of the stereotype of old age, one's feelings about the attitudes of others, and the treatment he receives from others because of his age. According to the role theory postulated by Phillips (1957), those who consider themselves "old" are less well adjusted than those who regard themselves as still "middle-aged." Perhaps the most acute reaction to advancing age is in the area of self-esteem. With increased age, one tends to direct his attitude toward himself, so that he ascribes to himself the characteristics of the stereotype of the aged. Since he thinks younger people reject or look with pity upon the aged, he tends to accept his status as that of a senile person. According to Linden and Courtney (1953), this is the basis for personality deterioration during late adulthood.

What the individual thinks of himself he is likely to become. If he thinks of himself as "old" he is likely to think and behave according to the stereotype of the aged. The time at which a person begins to feel he is getting old varies greatly for different people. Many people use their chronological age as a criterion of their aging; others use such physical symptoms as failing eyesight or hearing, increased tendency to fatigue, decline in strength, lowered sexual potency, or graying hair or baldness; others assess their aging in terms of forgetting, loss of interest in certain everyday activities, or tendency to digress. Once an individual accepts the notion that he is "old," he is likely to adopt most of the stereotype of the aged.

Personality Changes.   Studies based on interviews of social competence and successful aging indicate that normally healthy old people show no systematic change with age and that personality remains remarkably constant throughout later maturity. Most studies of personality changes in the later years indicate that the average older person shows increasing concern with bodily symptoms and decreasing interest in physical activities and that he is less outgoing and less emotionally responsive. As a person ages, his individual characteristics are intensified. It is frequently said that he becomes "more and more like himself" as he grows older. Dependencies and inadequacies, camouflaged in earlier life by supporting social factors, become apparent when the losses of later years take away job, spouse, friends, and an understanding and tolerant milieu.

With advancing age, in the adult organism there are reductions in drive level, including a lowering of spontaneous physical activity and sexual behavior. Studies of many kinds of activities have shown a tendency toward declining social activities and interpersonal relationships. This has given rise to concepts of psychological and social disengagement, since both psychological and social involvement with the environment decline in later life. To some extent, social-role decline is initiated by the environment's placing the individual in a less engaged position—for example, retirement. In addition, there is also a quality of affective detachment from the environment in which older persons have less ego involvement in their roles and activities. Students of personality and aging have described this as in part a consequence of reduced "ego energy."

Significant changes in interests appear with age. This may be observed in the increased interest of some people in nonproductive or service activities and changed attitudes toward work, government, and politics. In a study of aged persons, Ludwig and Eichorn (1967) noted that older farmers, particularly those in poor health, spoke less favorably of farm technology and medical science, appeared less optimistic about the future, and believed less in a benevolent God than young farmers.

The Adult—an Adapting Organism.   The ability to adapt to the period of senescence is part of the equipment and nature of man. However, this ability is displayed in many variations within the limits regarded as normal for this age group. One may conclude that the ability to adjust to aging is dependent upon a combination of etiological components, including genetic differences, health, age-susceptible personality traits, adaptational plasticity, economic security, and emotional and social security.

Studies of personality traits in relation to age and intelligence indicate that age is less important than intelligence in the personality adaptations over adult life. An important qualification must be made, however, in that nonverbal intelligence becomes highly correlated with psychomotor speed in older adults. In the three aspects of the individual-psychomotor speed, nonverbal intelligence, and personality adaptations—there may lie a factor of change in the central nervous system. What the student of personality observes at one level and calls "ego energy" may at another level be measured as reaction time and be called a "change in psychomotor speed."

Evidence in earlier chapters indicates that the human organism at all stages of development is a constantly adapting organism. However, this does not mean that a complete fluidity of behavior patterns, habit patterns, attitudes, ideals, and values are established early in life and affect adjustments throughout life. The adult organism is a more differentiated organism than the child, since he has had a wider range of experiences. Because of the increased differentiation, there is less likelihood of novel adaptations as a function of age. Changes in interests and activities of adults reflect the changing status of the adult in his environment as well as his motivations and established patterns of behavior.

The habit patterns that are built up in the individual over time impose controls over the behavior elicited in response to somatic changes in internal drives and external stimulation. One stable element in the choices of behavior is personal values, although these too may be modified or superseded if the cognitive load placed on the individual becomes excessive, or if the values are in dramatic conflict with the changes and drift in the content of the individual's life. The adaptative person continually modifies his behavior over time, thus aging "successfully." The internal habit systems that promote adaptation are not fully known, and successful adaptation may be brought about by quite a different and almost opposite type of personality organization.

Sociological Adjustments

In primitive cultures each member was part of the tribe; he survived or perished with the family and the tribe; he contributed the best he had according to his ability; he was an individual, and as he grew old, he still deserved and was accorded active participation in the group. In the agricultural period of our life as a nation, the same principles prevailed. However, the vast industrialization of today has robbed many of our older people of a known and desired way of life. Many sit about bewildered and unwanted or shunted between various sons and daughters and, finally, many arrive in an institution for the aged. Thus the aged are frequently required to make social adjustments in their living that are extremely difficult at this stage of their lives. Concerning the expressed desires of the aged as expressed in a poll, Beatty (1962, pp. 106-107) reports as follows:

> The average citizen wants to live his retirement years independent at home, or in a home-hotel or apartment. In case of illness, whether terminal or otherwise, his preference is to go to the community hospital. Yet often, he is thrust into a strange world where, for him, there is no place. Out of fixed income he is also constantly forced to meet rising costs for essentials. He tries to balance his budget by denying himself social contacts or often adequate nutrition. As expenses edge upwards, his plans become out of his control. Then perhaps comes an accident, or a failing heart, or a stroke, and his whole schedule of life and living is reduced to shambles.*

*R. P. Beatty, The Senior Citizen, Charles C. Thomas, publisher.

Change in Roles.   All through life there are changes in roles as a result of changes in the self and changes within one's social world. It is important, how-ever, to recognize that these changes differ from the changes necessitated by age during late adulthood. The changes earlier in life are gradual in nature. The time period involved makes changes from childhood to adolescence, to young adult-hood, to the middle years, and to the late years gradual changes. The older person, whose change of status is precipitated by retirement, sickness, widow-hood, or the like, has not the time for a gradual change of the same kind as enjoyed earlier in life.

Secondly, the changes earlier in life received much support from the home, peers, and various institutions. Society provides for the child entering school by making kindergarten a buffer between the preschool period and the first experi-ence in school. The junior high school has been established to make transition from elementary school to high school less difficult. This is also an important function served by the community college. Very little help has been given to the older citizen forced to retire from a world of work to a world of leisure; al-though considerable attention is now being given to this problem from many agencies, including the federal government. In the third place, the changes earlier in life receive social rewards for a successful transition from one role to another. School brings with it more pressure but also more pleasure than the preschool years. Similarly, the demands of work are accompanied by the reward of money and increased independence. No such rewards are provided for the older adult retiring from his working world; rather, there is a reduction in roles with few compensations that go with such a reduction.

Needs and Drives of the Aged.   Although there are fundamental needs that appear at all age levels, some needs are more important at one particular age level, while other needs are in general more important at another level. Tanen-baum (1967, p. 98) lists the following fundamental needs of the aged person:

> Love; conditions in which social norms are comprehensible to the degree that the transactions in which he participates can be perceived by him against a back-cloth of an intelligible world; the possibility for him to be creative (even though on a very elementary level of activity); and an opportunity to maintain his iden-tity as a person, so that he can feel a sense of *being* in all of its richness and fullness.

A happy and satisfactory sexual life may continue many years after procrea-tion ceases. Sex activity in marriage should continue as long as it meets for the persons concerned a need which is as basic as the need for sleep or for food. Sex activity is only one method of expression of love. Because it decreases with the years is no sign that love is at an.end, provided real love exists and the loved one still lives. Birren states (p. 230): "One of the great limitations of the affects of health, social and biological influences on sex drive is the relative unavailability of an appropriate mate in the older age group."

One of the greatest problems of the aged is social alienation. It leads to suicide or to social withdrawal, to hostility, aggression, and depression. Thus the need for belongingness is important to the older adult. Closely related to needs are values that operate in a particular culture, out of which an individual develops a system of values. According to Kent (1966) there are six main values in terms of which the American culture judges actions and roles. These are: (1) achievement and success, (2) activity and work, (3) efficiency and practicality, (4) progress, (5) external conformity, and (6) science and rationality.

This discontinuity of the role change is personally telling. Earlier in life the role changes were from lesser to greater freedom, from lesser to greater responsibility, from lower to higher status, especially for the male. For the elderly, this rhythm is abruptly halted. In the study, Kent (referred to above) states that the male swiftly changes from increasingly instrumental roles to an integrated one. An instrumental role is geared to active adaptation to the world outside a man; while an integrated or socioemotional role is one of inner integration of the social system and maintenance of value patterns that reforms the goals. Instrumental roles are predominantly masculine while integrated or socioemotional roles are predominantly feminine. Therefore, it can be seen why women adjust to retirement and old age better than men do. Since it hurts the man's ego to be

The Senior Citizens enrich their own lives by working with others and helping collect goods for needy families. (Courtesy of Norfolk Senior Citizens Service Center.)

identified with the woman's role, conflicts between husband and wife in this period of transition into old age are often found.

Employment and Retirement—the Use of Time.   The contemporary adult can expect to live much longer than he would have in previous generations. He thus spends more time in the labor force or in productive activities; however, he also spends more time out of the labor force. Thus while the work life has increased by one third, the period of retirement has increased by approximately one-half. This creates a special problem for the individual, for he must, in most cases, adjust to a life of retirement or leisure for which he is usually poorly prepared. Time is a peculiar thing with us; we strive to reduce hours and years of work, and when we have reduced the years of work, we do not know what to do with the retirement years.

Efforts are being made to find amusements for the aged so they can consume or kill time. He is being molded into a passive individual and kills time in what the experts would call a decent way. If you are a manual worker, you may seek refuge from work as a spectator at different amusements; if you are not a manual worker, you may seek to kill time at reading, listening to lectures, or in some physical activity that does not require too much skill and physical exertion. These are frequent patterns of "killing time" by the aged. Other patterns, not too different from these, are frequently noted. Then there is a smaller percentage of the aged who are beset with the desire to do something worthwhile and engage in various community projects. It is difficult to determine to what extent these are motivated by spiritual values and to what extent they too are efforts used to "kill time" and perhaps enhance the ego in so doing. Boredom is something confronting a large percentage of the retired. Concerning boredom, Fromm (1967, p. 82) states:

> Unconscious boredom in modern culture has tremendous proportions and the success of radio and television and all sorts of similar articles of consumption is only possible because people are bored. In our society we are indoctrinated to believe that to be bored is quite indecent, or at least it's a sign of a failure; if you are bored, you are a failure; the successful man isn't bored.

Interactions with Members of the Family.   It has been customary for aging parents to turn to their children for help in meeting many daily responsibilities. Even when they are not dependent upon their children for help in satisfying their economic needs, they depend upon their children, grandchildren, and close kinspeople of a younger generation for love and belonging. Studies of the family interaction of elderly people in America show that, irrespective of social class, they are more likely to ask their daughters than their sons for help (Shanes, 1962, p. 113). Family-help patterns vary to some degree with social class. The size of the middle-class family is usually smaller, and the elderly are less likely to be dependent upon them for help or to actually live with a member of the family. This does not mean, however, that aged parents within any social class are physically separated from their children. Parke and Glick (1967, p. 265) point out from their review of marriage trends:

> The immediate household of the old person differs by whether he is of white-collar or working-class backgrounds in Britain and the United States and by whether he is of these or of agricultural background in Denmark. However, if an old person has children and there is no child in his household, one of his children is likely to live in the immediate vicinity. White-collar parents are the most likely of all parents to be at some distance from their nearest child, but even the great majority of these persons live close enough to an adult child to call on him for help if it is needed.

Interacting with Friends. A study reported by Rosow (1964) included 1,200 older people, middle and working-class residents of several hundred Cleveland apartment buildings. The apartments varied in the proportion of older tenants. Thus the buildings were classified into the following groups: *normal* (1-15 percent aged households); *concentrated* (33-49 percent); and *dense* (over 50 percent).

The study revealed that

> First, regardless of density, age-grading is even stronger in the working class than in the middle class which has somewhat more flexibility in intergenerational association. Secondly, independent of class, high-density areas concentrate friendships within the age group disproportionally more than low-density areas. (p. 482—see Table 15-1).

TABLE 15-1
Indices of Effective Confinement of Friends to Age
Peers (After Rosow)

	Normal	Concentrated	Dense
Working class	.78		.88
Middle class	.44	.60	.60

The study shows clearly that friendships are formed between people of similar status, notably of age, although similarities of sex, marital status, social class, beliefs, and life style are comparable variables and are selective factors which affect the formation of friendship groups.

Rosow concludes further:

> Our findings do not imply that different age groups should be completely and absolutely separated from one another. But they do indicate the necessary conditions for the social integration of the old through local friendships, especially of people alienated from previous group ties and supports. Such integration clearly requires their embeddedness among others of their own age. Our data are clear and definite: friendship prospects are limited between and viable within generations. (pp. 482-483)

Retirement—Adjustments and Satisfactions

The average working man spends about sixteen years in retirement (Schubat, 1967). These years can be a period of contentment and enjoyment, but too often it is a time of uncertainty, loneliness, and anxiety, marred by increasing separation from society and the world of action and production. Many studies point out the focal nature of the work role in our society in providing self-identification and social interaction. Much of the research dealing with aging and retirement makes use of cross-sectional data in which central tendencies of questionable representative age groups are studied. From these studies many artifacts have been produced and set forth as facts applicable to different age groups. The individual is frequently lost sight of in such studies of retirement—adjustments and satisfactions.

Theoretical Considerations. Cummings and Henry (1961) are among the first investigators to present a general theoretical interpretation of the social and psychological nature of the aging process in American society. Earlier developmental theories had not been explicit about the developmental process in late adulthood. Most of these regarded into the late adult years as an extension of life goals and of social interactions characteristic of the middle adult years. This extrapolation led to the generalization that satisfaction in the late adult years would depend upon a continuity of activities pursued in the middle adult years. "The notion that happy old people would or even could be disengaged has not been a preferred mode in characterizing the aging process." (Maddox, 1964, p. 80)

Cummings and Henry challenged the preferred formulation, in their theory of disengagement, and proposed that the process of social and psychological withdrawal is as much a result of psychological events indigenous to the individual as to societal reactions to the older person's inclusion or exclusion from social activities. The key ideas of the disengagement theory proposed by Cummings and Henry are (pp. 14ff): (1) the process of social and psychological withdrawal is modal for the aging adult population, (2) this process is both intrinsic and inevitable, and (3) the disengagement process is not only a correlate of successful aging but is probably a condition of it. According to Cummings (1963, p. 382) disengagement involves (1) a decrease in new contracts, and (2) interaction in fewer roles involving fewer people among present contacts. Disengagement involves not only a shift away from achievement-orientation, but a shift as well in social relationships in the direction of less intense affectivity in those relationships in which one remains involved.

Studies of retirers show that some persons from similar areas of work adapt to retirement more readily than others. Perhaps the best explanation for these differences lies in personality types. The creative, inventive, and resourceful type of person may be expected to face retirement with greater security than others. He may even look forward to the time of retirement when he can undertake activities or tasks that he has not in the past been able to pursue. The conformist type, who has followed the institutional patterns for meeting problems, may find it more difficult to adapt to retirement; retirement demands of him new or modified patterns of behavior—patterns that are not a part of his past modes of adjustment. This person needs guidelines for his retirement just as he followed guidelines in his working world.

The escapist or withdrawal type who refused to face crises on the job, will not likely find security and satisfaction in retirement. He may take a fatalistic or negative attitude about problems faced in retirement. This is perhaps the opposite of the aggressive and rebellious types, who may also take a negative attitude. If they are healthy they consider themselves too young to retire. Findings from various studies show that a large percentage of individuals do not consider themselves old. Healthy individuals who are physically and mentally active are less likely to consider themselves old than those who are chronically ill or inactive physically and mentally.

There is also the depressed type individuals who are frustrated by the failure of retirement to satisfy their needs. Many individuals in this category have not learned to accept or deal adequately with frustrations. Such a condition frequently leads to loss of appetite, improper diet, illness, and the continued cycle of depression.

Preretirement Attitude Toward Retirement.   Perhaps the single most reliable predictor is the attitude of the worker toward retirement. Theoretically a significantly greater proportion of persons with favorable preretirement attitudes will experience satisfactory retirement than those who have unfavorable attitudes. Although studies disagree about the probable causes of a favorable or unfavorable attitude, the results are in general agreement in showing a strong relationship between orientation toward retirement and outcome of retirement (Simpson and McKinney, 1967).

Each of the three modes of adaptation would seem to be associated with a particular way of perceiving impending periods of uncertainty. Those who have shown creativeness, resourcefulness, and individualism during past crises may be expected to face with greater security the sudden change resulting from retirement. This knowledge should contribute to or produce more favorable attitudes toward retirement. The innovative mode of adaptation, therefore, should be associated with greater prevalence of positive attitudes.

The conformists, who are characterized by their compliance to the institutional means of dealing with crises are likely to be less favorable in their opinions of retirement, due to the relative lack of institutional behavioral guides, unless during the working years retirement has become an institutionalized phase of the life cycle. Presumably, the greater the institutionalization the more likely that the conformists will develop favorable attitudes toward retirement.

The past history of the retreatists is characterized by failure and inactivity in times of stress. It is most likely, then, that impending retirement will be seen within this context, resulting in a negative view. With such an attitude the retreatists will have a generally unfavorable attitude toward retirement.

Retirement—a Time of Adaptability.   Retirement presents a major adjustment problem to most retirees. The picture frequently presented of happy retirees in utopialike settings is not in harmony with scientific studies bearing on the adjustment of the retiree. Rather retirement is frequently a time of uncertainty, loneliness, and anxiety, affected by increasing separation from active participation in social and world affairs.

In a five-year research report by Simpson and McKinney (1967) workers were categorized according to whether they worked primarily with ideas, people, or things. For those concerned with ideas—teachers, writers, composers—retirement seemed to present fewer problems. For those working with people retirement seemed to present more difficulty. High-ranking business executives found retirement the most difficult years of their lives. Manual workers showed little evidence of new interests upon retirement, although many appeared relatively contented. This and other studies indicate that retirement difficulties tend to be greater for those whose work history involves an intense occupational culture, characteristics of college teachers and certain other professional groups. The underlying tone of these studies seems to be one of quiet desperation for the continuity of some sort of meaningful work and/or escapist activity-centeredness. The emphasis is upon activity *as activity*—that is, as an end in itself.

A survey by Aisenberg (1964) of 500 retired people, selected at random from the members of the American Psychological Association who were at least 65 years of age by December 31, 1963, furnished useful information about the influences of retirement. From this number, 174 usable replies were obtained. One question dealt with things about being retired liked most, and another dealt with things about being retired liked least. The replies are presented in Table 15-2.

TABLE 15-2
Things Liked Most and Least by 174 Psychologists About
Being Retired (After Aisenberg)

	Percent of Subjects
Liked Most	
1. More time.	30
2. More freedom	26
3. Not set schedule	16
4. Less pressure	12
5. Independence.	12
6. Varied activity	3
7. Less responsibility	3
8. Can work also	3
Liked Least	
1. Fewer contacts with others, especially students.	20
2. Fewer contacts with professional people.	11
3. Less income or too little money	11
4. Less physical competence or vigor.	8
5. Boring.	5
6. Non-productive or useless.	5

Ballweg (1967) compared the household activities of working husbands over 65 with those of nonworking (retired) husbands representing the same age category. The comparison showed a greater participation on the part of the retired husband, although most of the participation involved the husband taking over certain responsibilities rather than sharing them. Those tasks which the husband carried out were generally of a masculine or marginal nature requiring greater mechanical skill or physical strength. The wife retained responsibility for household dusting, laundry, making beds, and other housekeeping tasks. These findings are in harmony with the availability theory of household tasks—the more available a spouse is to perform a specific task, the more tasks the particular spouse is likely to perform. One may observe the operation of this in reverse in agricultural pursuits in farm communities.

The external motivations of the blue-collar worker seem to make it easier for him to adjust to retirement. Concerning this Maddox (1967) states:

> Longitudinal observations of a panel of white- and blue-collar workers prior to and for five years after retirement indicates that blue-collar workers do adapt more successfully to retirement, especially if retirement income is adequate, than do white-collar workers in the first year of retirement. By the second and third year of retirement, however, the conclusion is just the opposite; white-collar workers report more successful adaptation in the long run.

This reversal can best be explained by the differences in personal and social resources the two groups bring with them into retirement.

Activity and Morale.   There has been general agreement that there is a decrease in the quantity of activity with age. A comprehensive longitudinal study by Maddox and Eisdorfer (1962), involving 250 subjects ranging in age from 70 to 94, showed a continuous decline in mean activity score with increased chronological age. (See Table 15-3.) Objective medical estimates of

TABLE 15-3
Mean Activity Score by Age Category
(After Maddox and Eisdorfer)

Age*	Mean Score
60–64	29.2
65–69	28.1
70–74	27.1
75–79	27.7
80 and over	25.2

*$N = 250$.

health were higher for the high active subjects. The decrease in activity logically follows physical or mental decline as well as a decline in health. Health problems loom large for a sizable percentage of older adults. However, a predisposition to optimism or pessimism about health can be explained, at least in part, by a pattern of social placement and attitudinal factors. Maddox (1964, p. 458) states:

> Optimistic subjects as compared with pessimistic ones tend to be (1) older; (2) relatively active (particularly activity which does not involve contact with other persons); (3) to have modified their work role; (4) to be male; and (5) for the male or head of a household, to have had experience in a nonmanual occupation.

Despite the fact that a positive relationship exists between activity and morale, one should not generalize from this to individual cases. The 250 subjects in the study by Maddox and Eisdorfer were divided into four groups based on activity level and morale level. An analysis of the data from these groups is presented in Table 15-4. Most factors found to be significantly associated with

TABLE 15-4

Proportion of Elderly Persons Classified by a Typology of Activity and
Morale with Selected Social Characteristics (After Maddox and Eisdorfer)

Characteristic	Percentage with Characteristic Among			
	I[†]	II	III	IV
	N = 95	N = 35	N = 33	N = 87
1. Limited modification of usual work role	75	59	42	32*
2. Objective medical estimate of "good" health	86	79	69	58*
3. "Nonmanual" occupational classification	63	60	59	33*
4. Self-estimate of "good" health	82	54	64	42*
5. Self or spouse is head of household	85	100	61	73*
6. Has not changed residence since age 55	64	63	44	46*
7. Reports relatively few disease symptoms	66	44	58	39*
8. Lives with spouse	70	63	52	53
9. Is white	72	73	64	61
10. Is relatively younger (age 60–69)	50	49	40	44
11. Prefers present living situation	61	42	68	42*
12. Is male	44	54	48	54

*The chi-square value of this distribution of the four types in relation to the dichotomized characteristic suggests a reliable association at the .05 level or better (d.f. = 3).
†The typology of subjects:
  I   High activity/high morale
  II   High activity/low morale
  III Low activity/high morale
  IV   Low activity/low morale

"high activity" are also associated with "high morale." However, an unqualified acceptance of the hypothesized association would fail to take into consideration the 33 subjects in Group III. Individual differences appear in that activity is not equally rewarding for all elderly persons. The subjects of Group III seem to have been able to maintain high morale in the absence of activity. It seems likely that a certain amount of withdrawal from hyperactive social participation or other external activity might be satisfying for some people.

Some Patterns of Retirement.   The life styles of three couples pictured as happily retired appeared in the article "When You Retire: Three Ways to Go at It" (1964). The pattern of retirement presented is illustrative of certain retirement trends. One couple chose a shore-front home in Maine; a second couple chose an apartment in a metropolitan retirement development, and the third chose to purchase a home in a Florida retirement village. While the choice of settlement varies, two responses are strikingly similar as to why they feel they made a wise and happy retirement choice. (1) Their retirement choice enabled them to keep busy through such activities (varying from couple to couple) as crafts, hobbies, visiting, church and/or club activity, picnics. (2) As typical of the couple in Maine as with the other two couples who chose communal retirement projects is the report that most of their activities are planned with other retirees.

Two articles by Patton (1961) present an interesting contrast. Like those previously described, these are utopian—but there is not the "tone" of a desperate necessity for busyness and/or productivity. Both couples tend to accept retirement as involving some withdrawal from the larger society, and appear to accept it with a sense of comparative "serenity." The formal working occupations of the husbands were quite different: one was a wage-earner with a limited education, and the other was a college professor. While both couples talk about their hobbies and activities, these do not play the dominating role in giving meaning to their lives. We do find for both couples, however, five common factors not found among many families in our present mobile society.

1. Their settlement pattern is similar. Both couples have lived most of their adult lives in the community in which they retired.
2. Both couples own their homes in these communities, and consider their community as their "home town" after an adult lifetime or near-lifetime of living there.
3. As a result, both couples have close friendship ties within the community in which they live.
4. Both couples have several children, and both have two children living in the same community or nearby.
5. Both couples frequently visit their children and grandchildren, both of which form one of their primary conversation bases in the interviews.

Here are two examples reflecting what research has indicated is in some respects a more typical pattern than was, until recently, thought to exist in an increasingly mobile American society—the prevalence and persistence of the modified extended family unit, and the finding that, with families who have had several children, at least one tends to remain in the vicinity (Shanes and Streib, 1965). We also discover here almost ideal typical instances in the consistency of work history in both the same occupation and the same community. If one's work history has been consistent, research indicates that more strongly developed ties with society tend to emerge and tend to persist after retirement (Simpson and McKinney).

While there is no consistent pattern of influence upon readers, there does appear to be a dominant pattern in most of the articles in the picture of happy and contented retirement they are attempting to convey. With the exception of the *Ladies' Home Journal* articles, there is conscious and intentional support for the popular notion that "happy old people are busy old people." The emphasis, in fact, tends to be "proactivity" to an extent that becomes "antidisengagement." The two couples who appear most contented with their situation, however, are those who have accepted some degree of disengagement—buffered, in these instances, by supportive environmental reinforcements. These are the two couples, we may recall, with a continuous work history in the same community and with children living nearby. Perhaps in the absence of such reinforcements the activity syndrome may be a necessary or at least the most viable alternative for many retirees.

Planning—the Use of Leisure.   There was a time when older people were supposed to work, that is, to continue productive activity until they were physically unable to do so. This is still the pattern in many societies, even though certain old people may be freed from the standard. In our society and in most occidental countries, the concept of retirement has become so pervasive that we expect people to cease productive work at 60, 65, or 70. This means a transition from the work and money-oriented value system of an older society to a free-time program with living costs met (Anderson, 1958, p. 43). James A. Garfield put the question succinctly: "We may divide the whole struggle of the human race into two chapters: First, the fight to get leisure; Second, what shall we do with our leisure when we get it?"

If the Aristotelian concept is correct that leisure is that which work has earned, then we must look upon all leisure time as the reward of labor. Since we already know that, to many individuals, enforced leisure is neither sought after nor desired, we are confronted with the interesting philosophical paradox that the reward of leisure is indeed often unrewarding.

Linden (1950, pp. 96-98) has set forth a decalog of recommendations to individuals preparing for the appropriate use of leisure in advanced maturity:

1. Continue to develop your resources—popular thought maintains that the mental and emotional supplies of the human mind undergo a decline at or near the middle years. Recent studies strongly suggest that the reverse is more likely to be true. Psychologists have found that the human mind continues to develop its capacity for comprehending conceptual processes well into the seventh and eighth decades of life. The capacity for judgmental functioning and the integration of the human faculties that combine to create wisdom are

still on the upgrade late in life. To be sure, certain physical and some emotional abilities, which were present in abundance early in life, tend to be on the downgrade in aging, but other qualities have not yet reached their highest developmental goal even in later maturity. In this respect, you can think of the arrival at later maturity as the attainment of a broader outlook on life.

2. Increase your social effectiveness—channel the potential for greater concentration and focusing of effort, with the end result of increased social effectiveness in almost every sphere of activity.

3. Enjoy your wisdom—one of the never-ending sources of deep satisfaction in the human mentality is the pleasure that is to be obtained from logical and reasonable behavior. The increase in sagacity and the values of the senior mind which are more in keeping with the realities of human life than at any other time in the life cycle can become the source of gratification formerly denied the youthful mind.

4. Advance the tenets of human progress—there is evidence that suggests that the conservatism of older minds is of great value in conserving the indispensable ethical system and mores that make civilization possible.

5. Externalize your interest.

6. Place your values in quality.

7. Don't be a spendthrift of time.

8. Make your human relationships durable.

9. Don't capitalize on dependency.

10. Exercise judicious independence.

A New Look at Retirement. In this age of expanding medical knowledge, it has become apparent that reaching old age, if not a certainty, is a probability; however, we seldom prepare for such an eventuality. Most of us realize that we are getting old; yet we blunder into old age as if it were the most unexpected happening in our existence. We expect to live a long life; but the moment we retire we seem shocked that we are still alive. But the fact is that if one is to live an old age of significance, one must prepare for that old age. There is a creative art of growing old which most people either do not understand or refuse to accept.

Education for aging must become a new feature of our society. If habits learned in working life are continued into retirement, then preparation for retirement should begin in the fifth if not the fourth decade of people's lives.

The retiree (or in case of women, when the last child leaves home) should keep in mind that the unfortunate reputation of old age arises from the misconception that aging means only decline. This is untrue. For losses in certain physical and mental capacities, there are gains in others. With waning powers of speed in adaptation come compensating increases in skill. A certain amount of decline in memory for petty details is often offset by better judgment. Broader vision and great consciousness of social responsibility are other gains of later maturity. Often the gains exceed the losses and the mature years provide a rich potential for growth of character and wisdom.

If the older person begins to turn in upon himself, to feel useless and unwanted and decrepit, he may find himself moving in an unhappy circle. Frustration frequently leads to depression, depression to loss of appetite, loss of appetite to improper diet, improper diet to illness, and illness to further depression, whereupon the individual starts around the circle again. It should be emphasized that senility from emotional causes can be prevented by efforts on the part of the individual himself.

Summary

Our modern scientific and technological age has created a large population of people over 65 years of age who are no longer needed on the labor market. Thus the problem of adjusting to retirement has come to the front.

Aging has its biological, psychological, and social problems and implications. Until recently little consideration was given to problems related to social and psychological adjustments. Biologically, it may be noted that decline starts at a relatively early age. Significant physiological changes and disabilities are associated with aging. Individual differences are apparent in aging. There are also significant social-class differences; although lifelong behavior patterns determine the way individuals adapt to problems they face over the life span.

Major changes in personality during late adulthood reflect the individual's concept of self. Individuals who regard themselves as "old" are less well adjusted than those who regard themselves as still in the middle years. This, too, varies considerably with individuals. As a person ages, his individual characteristics are usually intensified. He displays less ego involvement in his roles and activities. However, the ability to adapt to the period of senescence is part of the equipment of man. One relatively stable element in choices of behavior is personal values.

Interaction with members of the family and friends continue throughout the period of life. Age-grading of friendships is stronger in the working class than in the middle class. Technological changes have produced important problems related to retirement, with the notion that disengagement from work leads to unhappiness. Some retirees adapt to retirement more readily than others. This can best be accounted for by the nature of the work from which they retire and the personality of the retiree. The attitude of the worker toward retirement is an important indicator of his adjustment to retirement.

There is no single pattern of retirement suitable to all workers. Perhaps education for aging must become a new feature of our society, with some preparation for retirement beginning in the fifth if not the fourth decade of life.

References

Aisenberg, Ruth. "What Happens to Old Psychologists? A Preliminary Report," in A. Kastenbaum, (ed.), *New Thoughts of Old Age.* New York: Springer, 1964.

Anderson, J. "Psychological Aspects of the Use of Free Time," in W. Donahue et al. (eds.), *Time-Challenge to Later Maturity.* Ann Arbor, Mich.: U. of Michigan Press, 1958.

Ballweg, J. A. "Resolution of Conjugal Role Adjustment After Retirement," *Journal of Marriage and Family Living,* Vol. 29 (1967), pp. 277-281.

Beatty, R. P. *The Senior Citizen.* Springfield, Ill.: Charles C Thomas, 1962.

Birren, J. E. *The Psychology of Aging.* Englewood Cliffs, N. J.: Prentice-Hall, 1964.

Bureau of the Census, United States Department of Commerce, *The U.S. Book of Facts, Statistics, and Information,* 86th ed. New York: Pocket Books, 1965, pp. 6-7.

Cowdry, E. V. *The Care of the Geriatric Patient.* St. Louis: Mosby, 1963.

Cummings, Elaine. "Further Thoughts on the Theory of Disengagement," *UNESCO International Social Studies Journal,* Vol. 15, No. 3 (1963).

Cummings, Elaine, and W. Henry. *Growing Old: The Process of Disengagement.* New York: Basic, 1961.

Eisdorfer, C., and Cornelia Service. "Verbal Rote Learning and Superior Intelligence in the Aged," *Journal of Gerontology,* Vol. 22 (1967), pp. 158-161.

Fromm, E. "Psychological Problems of Aging," *Child and Family,* Vol. 6, No. 2 (1967), pp. 78-88.

Guillerman, Jacques. *Longevity.* New York: Walker, 1963.

Hansen, P. F. (ed.). *Age With a Future.* Proceedings of the Sixth International Congress of Gerontology, Copenhagen, 1963. Philadelphia: Davis, 1964.

Issacs, B. *An Introduction to Geriatrics.* Baltimore: Williams and Wilkins, 1965.

Kallmann, F. J., and G. Sanders. "Twin Studies on Senescence," *American Journal of Psychiatry,* Vol. 106 (1949), pp. 29-36.

Kathovsky, W., Anne Preston, and V. J. Crandall. "Parents' Attitudes toward their Personal Achievements and toward the Achievement Behaviors of Their Children," *Journal of Genetic Psychology,* Vol. 104 (1964), pp. 67-82.

Kent, D. P. "Influencing the Mental Health of the Aged," *American Journal of Orthopsychiatry,* Vol. 36 (1966), pp. 680-685.

Linden, M. E. "Preparation of the Leisure of Later Maturity," in Wilma Donahue et al. (eds.), *Free Time—Challenge to later Maturity.* Ann Arbor, Mich.: U. of Michigan Press, 1950.

Linden, M. E., and D. Courtney, "The Human Life Cycle and Its Interruptions: A Psychologic Hypothesis; Studies in Gerontologic Human Relations," *American Journal of Psychiatry,* Vol. 109 (1953), pp. 906-915.

Ludwig, E. G., and R. L. Eichorn. "Age and Disillusionment: A Study of Value Changes Associated with Aging," *Journal of Gerontology,* Vol. 29 (1967), pp. 59-65.

Maddox, G. L. "Disengagement Theory: A Critical Evaluation," *Gerontologist,* Vol. 4 (1964), pp. 80-83.

————. "Human Aging as a Social Process," paper presented at the 123rd annual meeting of the American Psychiatric Association, Detroit, Mich., May 1967.

————. "Self-Assessment of Health Status: A Longitudinal Study of Selected Elderly Subjects," *Journal of Chronic Diseases,* Vol. 17 (1964), pp. 449-460.

Maddox, G. L., and C. Eisdorfer. "Some Correlates of Activity and Morale among the Elderly," *Social Forces,* Vol. 40 (1962), pp. 254-260.

Parke, R., and P. C. Glick. "Prospective Changes in Marriage and the Family," *Journal of Marriage and Family Living,* Vol. 29 (1967), pp. 249-256.

Patton, Margaret. "Our Lives Were Good, Our Lives Are Good," *Ladies' Home Journal,* Vol. 78 (June 1961), pp. 118-119.

Phillips, B. S. "A Role Theory Approach to Adjustment in Old Age," *American Sociological Review,* Vol. 22 (1957), pp. 212-217.

Riegel, K. F., and Ruth Riezel. "Changes in Associative Behavior During Later Years of Life; A Cross-Section Analysis," *Vita Humana,* Vol. 7 (1964), pp. 1-32.

Rosow, I. "Long Concentrations of Aged and Intergenerational Friendships," in P. F. Hansen (ed.), *Age With a Future.* Proceedings of the Sixth International Congress of Gerontology, Copenhagen, 1963. Philadelphia: Davis, 1964.

Schubat, T. "Retirement Reaction Varies," *Virginian Pilot* (Jan. 8, 1967), pp. 8-11.

Shanes, Ethel. *The Health of Older People: A Social Survey.* Cambridge, Massachusetts: Harvard U. P., 1962.

Shanes, Ethel, and G. F. Streib. *Social Structure and the Family: Generational Relations.* Englewood Cliffs, N.J.: Prentice-Hall, 1965.

Shock, N. W. *Aging . . . Some Social and Biological Aspects.* Baltimore: Horn-Shafer, 1960.

Shock, N. W. "The Physiology of Aging," *Scientific American,* Vol. 206 (Jan. 1962), pp. 100-110.

Simpson, Ida H., and J. C. McKinney. *The Social Aspects of Aging.* Durham, N.C.: Duke U. P., 1967.

Slater, P. E. "Cross-Cultural View of the Aged," in A. Kastenbaum (ed.), *New Thoughts on Old Age.* New York: Springer, 1964.

Slavick, F. *Compulsory and Flexible Retirement in the American Economy.* New York: School of Industrial and Labor Relations, Cornell University, 1966.

Tannebaum, D. E. "Loneliness in the Aged," *Mental Hygiene,* Vol. 51 (1967), pp. 91-99.

"When you Retire: Three Ways To Go at It," *Changing Times,* Vol. 18 (June 1964), pp. 7-11.

Zimmerman, G. "The Secrets of Successful Retirement," *Look,* Vol. 25 (March 14, 1961), pp. 26-35.

Appendix

Glossary of Terms

Ability. Actual power, physical or mental, whether inherited or acquired, to perform.

Academic aptitude. Combination of abilities needed to do school work.

Adjustment mechanism. A technique used in resolving anxiety and tension.

Adolescence. Period beginning with puberty, between childhood and adulthood.

Ambivalence. Tendency to be pulled in psychologically opposite directions, e.g., acceptance-rejection, love-hate.

Androgen. Hormone produced by the gonads of the male influencing the development of maleness.

Anoxia. Interruption of the flow of oxygen to the brain frequently resulting in brain damage.

Antibody. The opponent of antigen, manufactured by the body or inserted into the body to defeat the antigen.

Antigen. A foreign invader of the body including a wide variety of proteins, harmful or harmless, and viruses.

Anxiety. An emotional state in which a present and persistent strong drive or desire seems likely to miss a goal.

Aptitude. A capacity or potentiality for special achievement, if the person is trained and applies himself in certain directions.

Arteriosclerosis. Degenerative thickening and hardening of the arteries.

Articulatory defects. Indistinct or confusing speech, resulting from failure or inability to pronounce the commonly accepted speech sounds.

Attitude. An enduring, learned predisposition to react or behave in a consistent way toward a given class of objects and situations.

Audiogenic. A genetic condition involving hearing produced by sound.

Automation. Instances where machines perform humanlike activities.

Bilingualism. Utilization of two languages with equal or near equal ability.

Capacity. A potential ability, or one largely inherited but not necessarily fully developed; seen in the power to absorb.

Carrier.   An individual heterozygous for a recessive gene that is not expressed; it is indistinguishable in appearance from the homozygous dominant.

Catalyst.   (metaphysical) An agency that markedly influences the social process without being an integral part thereof.

Centromere.   Small body that holds together at its middle the double strands forming each chromosome.

Character.   A property of an organism in regard to which observation of similarities or differences are noted.

Chromosome.   One of a number of thread-shaped bodies in the nucleus of cells, visible at cell division; contains the genes, the bearers of hereditary traits.

Classical conditioning.   A second stimulus which did not originally elicit a response when presented simultaneously with or slightly before the unconditioned or original stimulus will come to elicit the response.

Cognition theory.   An interpretation of the facts of learning postulating central brain processes as intermediary, i.e., what is learned is a cognitive structure rather than a response, and that learning involves the structuring of an individual's way of life.

Concept.   A classification of stimuli having certain common characteristics; it requires both abstraction and generalization.

Conditioned.   A response tendency resulting from training or experiences where reward or punishment was part of the total situation.

Conflict.   A condition that arises when an individual is faced with incompatible and/or conflicting motives, needs, or goals.

Correlated.   Closely connected, systematically or reciprocally related.

Culture.   That part of the environment that is learned; the way of life of a group of people.

Cytoplasm.   The protoplasm of the cell surrounding the nucleus; the substance of the organic cell.

Defense mechanism.   Stereotyped response pattern spontaneously and unconsciously used to protect one's ego from threats and anxieties.

Delinquency.   Violation of the behavior code of the larger group; a minor violation of the legal code.

Dementia praecox.   See *schizophrenia.*

Demography.   Study of human populations, including vital statistics, geographical distributions, and causes of increase or decrease.

Dependency.   Lack of self-reliance; tendency to seek help from others in making decisions or in carrying out difficult action.

Development.   Increase in complexity of structure or function.

Developmental psychology.   The branch of psychology that studies how individuals develop psychologically.

Developmental tasks.   Levels of achievement in a given society, and at a given age which are considered appropriate or necessary for socially acceptable functioning.

Disengagement.   Moving away from, e.g., in case of the aged, retiring from their work and less involvement in decision-making activities.

DNA.   Abbreviation for deoxyribonucleic acid, considered to be the primary substance of the gene.

Dominance.   Complete suppression of the expression of one allele by another at the same locus in the chromosome.

Drive.   Resultant tension pertaining to an unmet need and directed toward a goal or valence.

Ductless glands.   See *endocrine glands.*

Dysfunction.   Abnormal or incomplete function of some structure or structures.

Eclectic.   One who attempts to find valid elements in all doctrines or theories and to combine them into a harmonious whole. The resultant system is open to constant revision.

Egg.   The female germ cell; in animals, an ovum.

Ego.   The self; in psychoanalytic usage, the conscious part of the mind which acts as the mediator and the barriers to its satisfactions.

Egocentric.   Self-centered; describing a state in which all things and happenings seem to center around the self.

Embryo.   A young organism in the first stage of development; the early stage of development.

Endocrine gland.   Glands of internal secretion that secrete directly into the blood stream and not through ducts—also called ductless glands.

Endogeneous.   Growing from or on the outside.

Estrogen.   Any of the female sex hormones, so called because they are capable of inducing estrus in the female, thus contributing to the development of female characters.

Ethnic group.   An arbitrarily recognized population having more or less distinct cultural characteristics.

Eugenics.   The science of improving human abilities and fitness through the control of heredity.

Existentialism.   A modern philosophy that claims basically that existence cannot be conceived, but may be experienced and lived; man here is presumed to be both free and responsible.

Extrovert.   A personality whose feelings and thoughts are directed chiefly outwardly, and toward others and external affairs.

Fertilization.   The union of a male gamete (sperm) with an egg (female gamete) to form an embryo.

Fetus.   The prenatal stage of mammals, from the embyonic stage to birth.

Fixation.   The persistence of infantile, childish, or adolescent response patterns, thoughts, and modes of adjustment.

Free association. The spontaneous response of an individual to a stimulus; in psychotherapy, the patient's act of saying what feelings occur to him as he talks about himself and his problems.

Gamete. A mature reproductive male or female germ cell; the ovum of the female, the spermatozoid of the male.

Gene. The discrete hereditary determiner located in the chromosome. The gene is compounded primarily of DNA molecules.

Genotype. The genetic constitution as determined by the number type, and arrangement of the genes.

Germ cell. A mature reproductive cell; a gamete capable of uniting with another gamete in reproduction.

Germ plasm. A special kind of protoplasm transmitted unchanged from generation to generation.

Gerontology. Study of the effects of aging and the problems of the aged.

Gonad. A gland, such as an ovary or testis, in which gametes are produced.

Growth. Increase in size, quantity, or quality.

Heredity. All developmental influences biologically transmitted from parents to offspring at the time of conception.

Heterosexual. Referring to both sexes; preference for members of the opposite sex as sex objects.

Heterozygous. A hybrid for any gene pair, with different alleles for the gene.

Homosexual. Centered on the same sex; a person who finds sexual satisfaction with others of the same sex.

Hormone. A chemical substance produced in small quantity in an organ from which it is carried to other parts of the body and exerts a specific influence.

Hybrid. A cross of unlike organisms, or parents of different genotypes.

Hypothesis. A tentative interpretation of a complex set of phenomena on the basis of some supporting data or findings.

Id. In psychoanalytic usage, the unconscious dynamic part of the self, involving drives which continuously demand satisfaction.

Identical twins. Twins derived from a single egg, which following fertilization divides to produce two zygotes; both of the zygotes have identical genotypes.

Identification. Accepting as one's own the purposes and values of another person.

Immunity. The ability to resist, or freedom from susceptibility to, disease-producing organisms or poisons.

Incidence. Range of occurrence or influences of a condition or disease.

Individuality. That which differentiates one person from another.

Induction. The product inferred from a variety of observations.

Inhibition.   Prevention of certain behavior processes from beginning by inner control, although the eliciting stimulus is present.

Instrumental learning.   Orderly change in response as a function of reinforced stimulus.

Introvert.   A personality type, the opposite of extrovert, characterized by a tendency to withdraw from social interaction.

Level of aspiration.   A person's expectation of his success on a task, or the goal he expects to attain.

Linkage.   The association of two or more characters in inheritance resulting from two genes associated in the same chromosome.

Maladjustment.   Inability to cope with one's environment; the absence of responses necessary for normal activities and relations with others.

Malfunction.   See *dysfunction*.

Maturation.   Developmental changes that take place more or less inevitably in all normal members of a species; growth and development resulting from inner forces.

Menarche.   The first menstruation; beginning of puberty for girls.

Mental age.   Level of intelligence expressed as the numerical equivalent of the chronological age of the average child having the same level of intellectual development.

Mental conflict.   See *conflict*.

Mental hygiene.   The application of the principles and practices necessary for the preservation of mental health.

Metabolism.   Building up or breaking down of protoplasm within an organism; sum of chemical changes whereby nutrition is affected.

Monoglot.   A single language.

Monozygotic.   Derived from one fertilized egg.

Morals.   An individual's personal standards of right and wrong, usually influenced by the group with which one identifies.

Mores.   Those customs of a social group that are regarded as having qualities of right and wrong.

Mutant.   A variant from the normal or wild type inherited in a Mendelian manner.

Mutation.   Failure of precision in the basic property of self-copying gene activity resulting in transmission of hereditary modifications in the expression of a trait.

Need.   A complex system of motives, or a second-order inference about tendencies to see certain goals.

Negativism.   A method of expressing one's will by continuously refusing to respond to ideas or suggestions of others.

Neonate.   A newborn infant.

Neuromuscular.   Pertaining to the structure and functions of both nerve and muscle.

Neurotic.   Mentally and emotionally disturbed, characterized by recurrent symptoms.

Normative need.   A statement of the needs required by a person to adapt successfully to the society in which he lives.

Obesity.   The accumulation of excess fat.

Ontogenetic.   Development from the ovum to the adult form.

Operant.   A response that an individual can and does make.

Ossification.   Formation of bone; state or process of being converted into bone.

Ovary.   Female reproductive organ in which eggs are produced.

Ovum.   The female germ cell.

Pathology.   Condition produced by disease or injury.

Personality profile.   A graphic representation of the personality characteristics or traits of an individual.

Phenotype.   That which actually makes its appearance into a living being; a manifested structure, condition, or function.

Phenylketonuria (PKU).   An inborn error of metabolism.

PKU.   See *phenylketonuria.*

Population.   A defined group or collection of people, characteristics, behaviors, and the like.

Potential.   A possibility; not an actuality. The highest level at which a person can develop or perform.

Precocious.   Early or rapid development.

Primipare.   A woman who is pregnant for the first time, or who has borne just one child.

Projective technique.   A testing method in which the subject is required to ascribe his own thoughts and feelings either to a stimulus or situation.

Psychological need.   A stable tendency to be motivated in certain ways such as seeking certain kinds of goals.

Puberty.   The period of physiological development signaling sexual ripening, begins with the menarche in girls.

Quartile.   Division into four equal parts in terms of the population involved.

Quintile.   One of the four points that divide a serial ranked distribution into five parts each of which contains one-fifth of the population or scores.

Rationalization.   Justification of one's behavior through plausible and acceptable but irrelevant motives.

Recessive.   A term used by Mendel to describe characters which are suppressed by the dominant allele in the F_1 generation.

Regression.   An unconscious defense mechanism by which a person attempts to deal with frustrating obstacles or disagreeable situations by reverting to childhood or earlier behavior.

Reinforcement.   Any facilitating stimulus or condition for strengthening special behavior patterns.

RNA.   Ribonucleic acids of different composition that occur everywhere in the cell.

Role.   The part played by an individual in a situation, especially social situation.

Role playing.   A procedure whereby an individual enacts or imitates the role behavior of another person.

Sample.   A selected group of persons, characters, or events chosen to represent a larger group, called the population.

Scattergram.   A diagram for plotting the scores of subjects on two measures. A scattergram graphically shows the correlation between two variables.

Self-concept.   An individual's beliefs about and evaluations of himself as a person.

Self-realization.   The lifelong process of development marked by self-direction along the lines of one's interests and abilities.

Senescence.   Pertaining to the behavior of the aged.

Senile dementia.   Mental deterioration closely associated with aging.

Senility.   Marked by loss of physical and mental functions in old age.

Sex chromosome.   A chromosome usually designated X or Y, concerned with sex determination.

Sex linkage.   An unusual type of inheritance caused by genes located in the X chromosome; of a heritable character.

Socialization.   A progressive development of relating to others, especially family, peers, and groups.

Sociometric device.   A technique for gathering data on preferences of individuals among members of a particular group.

Somatic cell.   A cell in the body of the organism, with two N chromosomes in contrast to the germ cell with n chromosomes.

Sperm.   The mature male germ cell or spermatozoon.

Stereotype.   A concept formed about a group, objects, or situations on the basis of false analogy or without accurate or adequate information.

Symbol.   In its broadest sense, anything that stands for something else.

Syndrome.   An aggregate of symptoms that occur together and characterize a disease or disorder.

Therapy.   Any method used to treat a disease or condition.

Trait.   A distinctive and enduring characteristic. See also *character.*

Unconscious. A psychoanalytic concept referring to that part of the mind that influences one's thinking and actions, of which the individual is not consciously aware.

Value. The importance one attaches to an object, situation, or condition. Relates to standards.

Variation. Differences in typical characters, characteristic of all living organisms of a species.

Vital capacity. Relates to lung capacity.

Withdrawal mechanism. A technique by which the individual withdraws rather than face an annoying or unpleasant situation.

Youth. A postpubertal person; continues into the early 20's.

Zygote. The result of the fusion of male and female gametes; a fertilized egg cell.

Index

Author Index

Subject Index